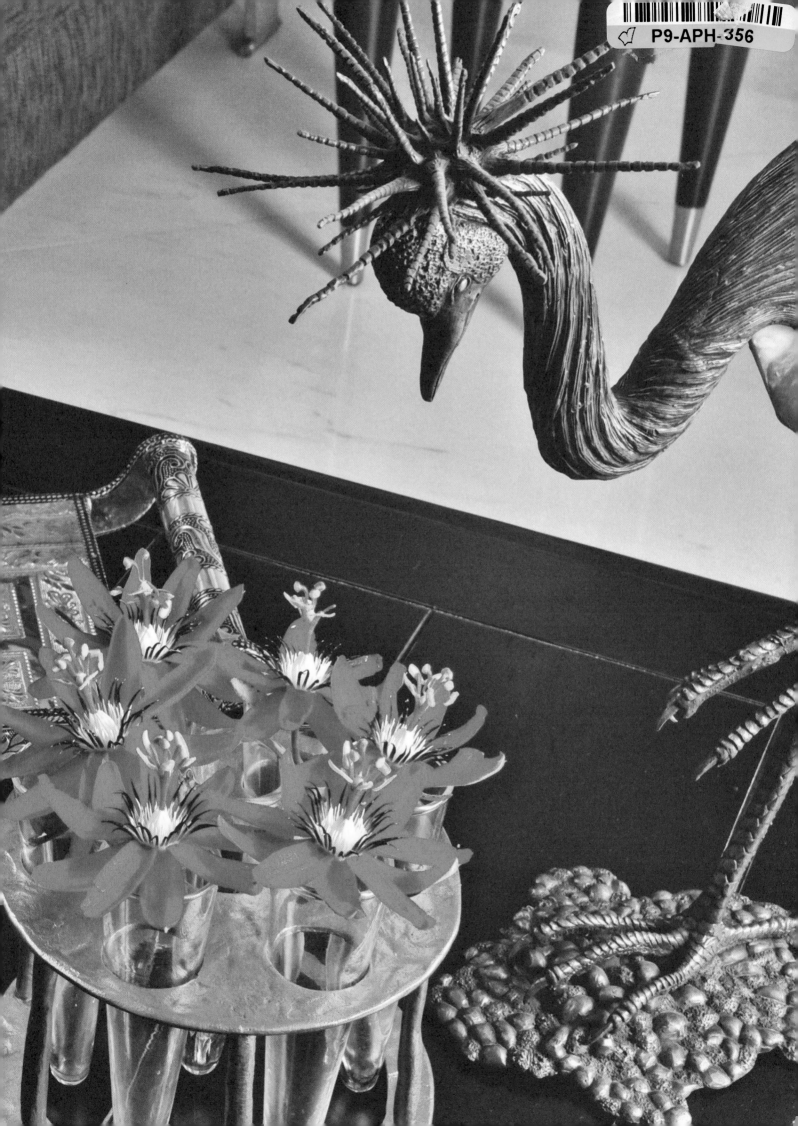

Decorating with
Flowers

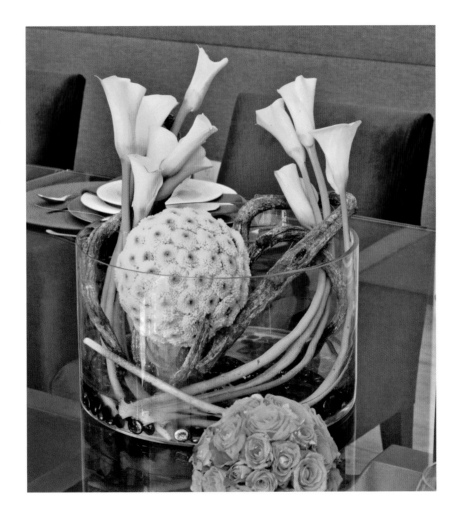

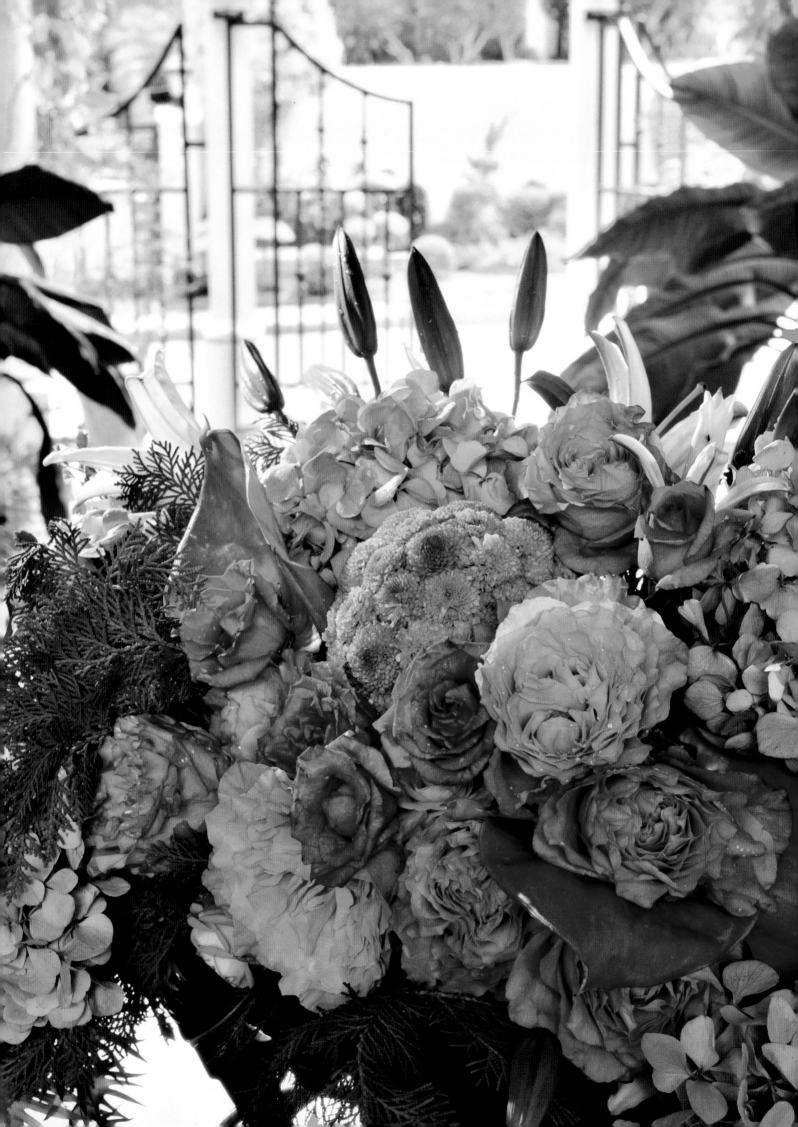

Decorating with Flowers

BY ROBERTO CABALLERO AND ELIZABETH V. REYES

PHOTOGRAPHY BY LUCA INVERNIZZI TETTONI

TUTTLE Publishing

Tokyo | Rutland, Vermont | Singapore

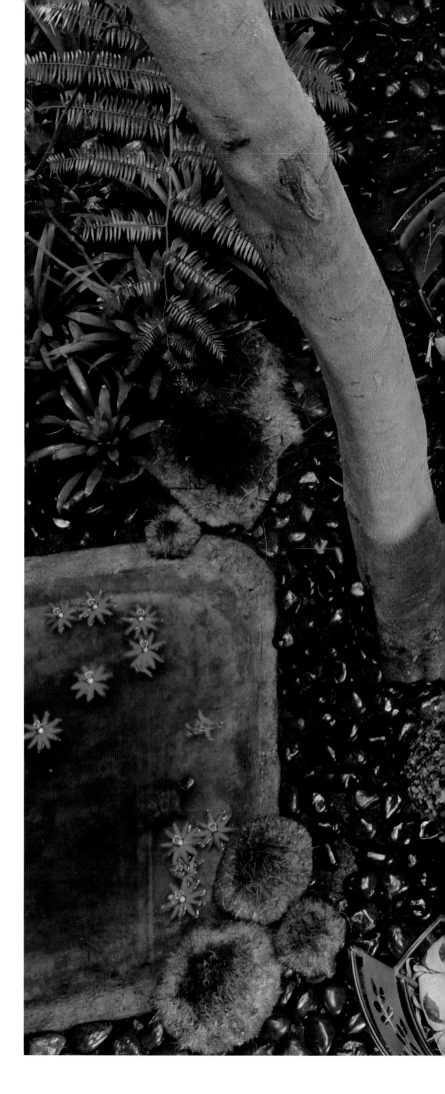

Published by Tuttle Publishing, an imprint of Periplus Editions (HK) Ltd

www.tuttlepublishing.com

ISBN 978-0-8048-4232-7

Distributed by
North America, Latin America & Europe
Tuttle Publishing
364 Innovation Drive, North Clarendon, VT 05759-9436 U.S.A.
Tel: 1 (802) 773-8930; Fax: 1 (802) 773-6993
info@tuttlepublishing.com
www.tuttlepublishing.com

Japan
Tuttle Publishing
Yaekari Building, 3rd Floor, 5-4-12 Osaki,
Shinagawa-ku, Tokyo 141-0032
Tel: (81) 3 5437-0171; Fax: (81) 3 5437-0755
sales@tuttle.co.jp
www.tuttle.co.jp

Asia Pacific
Berkeley Books Pte. Ltd
61 Tai Seng Avenue, #02-12, Singapore 534167
Tel: (65) 6280-1330; Fax: (65) 6280-6290
inquiries@periplus.com.sg
www.periplus.com

16 15 14 13 12   10 9 8 7 6 5 4 3 2 1

Printed in Singapore   1110CP

FRONT ENDPAPERS Under watchful eyes, passion flowers arranged by
Jim Tan gleam in shot glasses near a champagne service (page 143).
BACK ENDPAPERS Cynthia Almario's outdoor dining table, placed on
a platform surrounded by water, and lit from below at night, is a dramatic
setting for equally bold green and white floral statements set amidst a
collection of green tableware (page 37).
PAGE 1 An "out of the vase" ball of orange roses adds more novelty to
Pico Soriano's waterless composition of yellow pom-pom balls and yellow
calla lilies and stems (page 110).
PAGE 2 Bountiful massing by Pico Soriano of roses, dendrobium orchids,
Casablanca lilies, lime pom-poms, anthuriums, ferns and cypress greens
heralds the range of global flora available for the new wave of creative
floristry in the Philippines (page 109).
PAGES 4–5 Ponce Veridiano's quirky table setting comprises a "tablecloth"
of jungly vines set with red-rimmed handmade plates (page 89).
PAGE 6 A two-level arrangement of hydrangeas, snap dragons and wild
berries in the home of Chito Vijandre and Ricky Toledo (page 163).

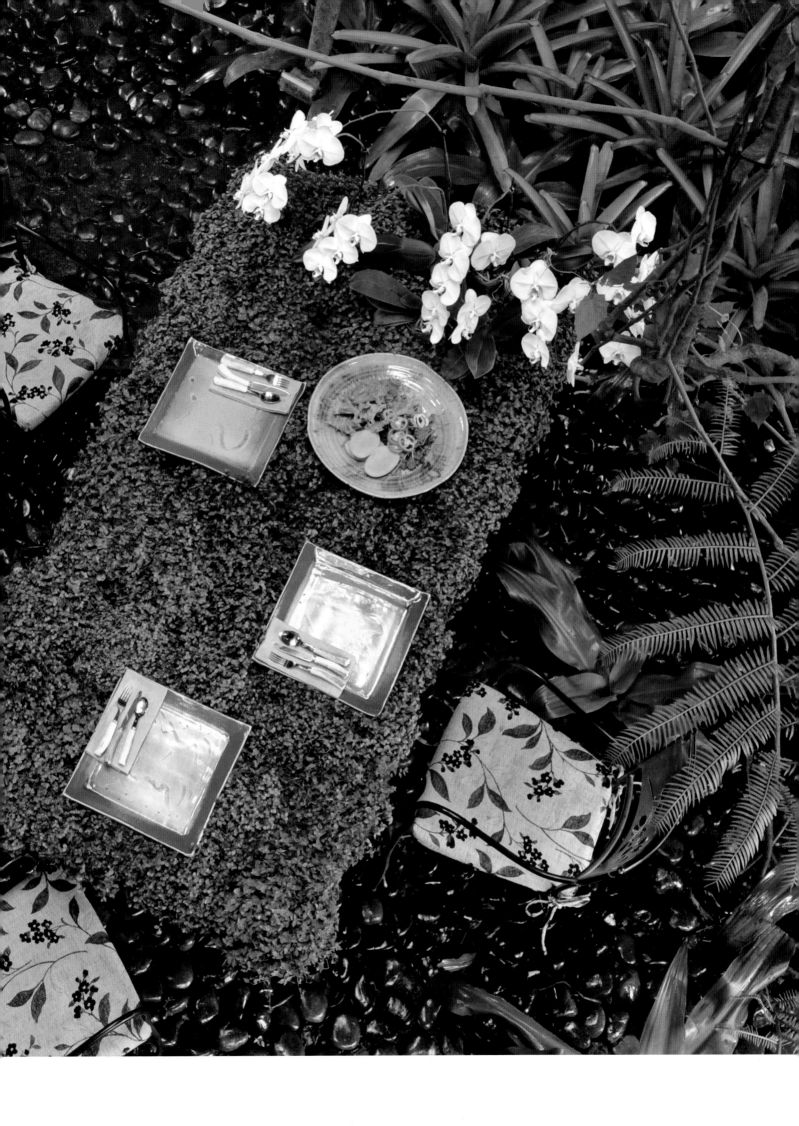

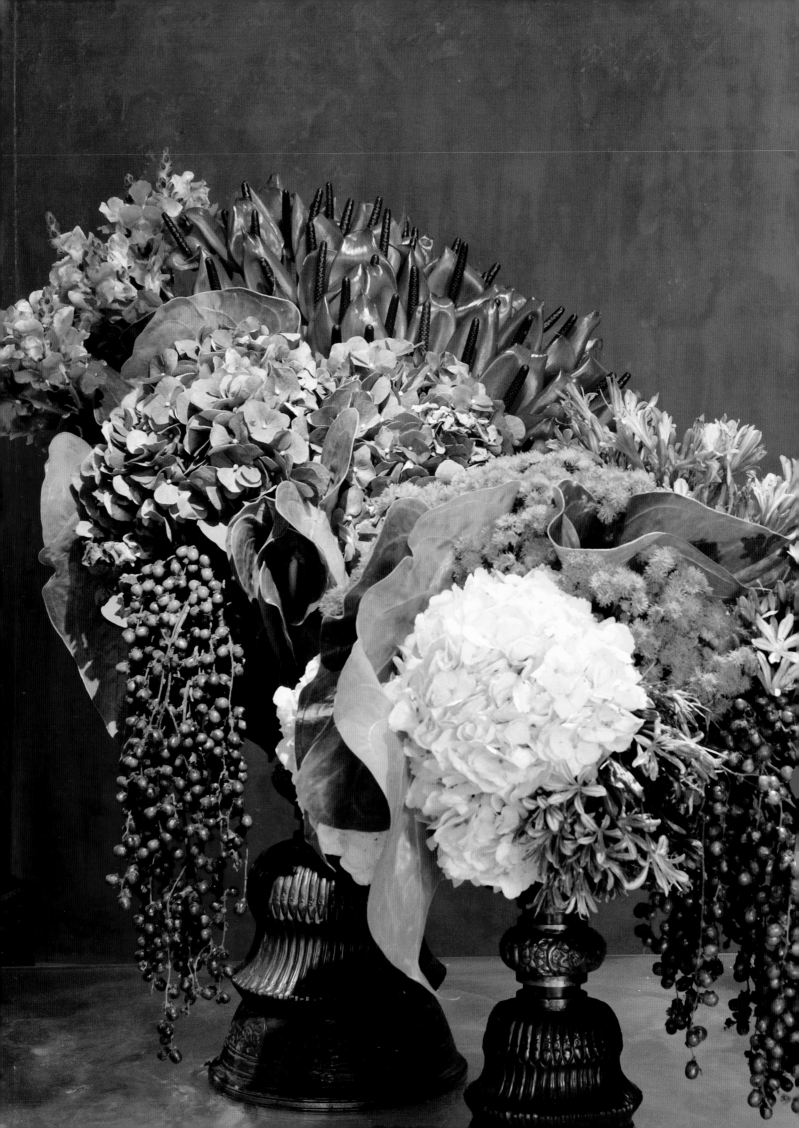

contents

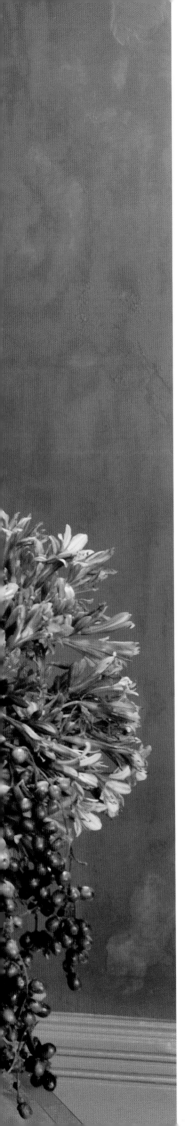

Fabulous Floral Arrangements for Every Occasion

Fresh flowers are a delight to the senses. They are also an integral part of the cultural fabric of most countries. In the Philippines, flowers are woven into the daily lives of people and play an important role in festivals and celebrations. They are also a constant reminder of the wealth and diversity of the country's tropical environment, its abundant sun and rainfall and changing seasons that contribute to a plethora of lush, moisture-loving plants, both native and imported, and spectacular flowering trees.

This book demonstrates how the vast palette of flowers and foliage and organic materials available in the Philippines can be used to create fabulous floral arrangements that elevate flowers beyond simple and mundane displays to sensational and memorable works of art that cannot fail to impress. At the same time, the book shows that these works of art are not impossible to achieve, that they are within the reach of those interested in replicating them. All that is needed is access to a good flower market that supplies blooms and foliage, or to one's own garden, and a variety of interesting containers, not necessarily purpose-made vases, of all shapes and sizes. A fondness for flowers, a little creativity and imagination, and the desire to fashion arrangements that complement a particular look in the home or elsewhere are other necessary ingredients. The determination to be an outstanding and caring homemaker and host also helps.

Most people prefer to entertain at home. To complement the food and the drinks they serve and the background music they choose for the occasion, they are happy to make an effort to create the right ambience. There is no easier way to do this than with flowers. A spectacular floral centerpiece can set the tone for a gathering, capture its spirit and enhance the festive mood. Indeed, beautiful arrangements of flowers and foliage on dinner tables and other surfaces are every bit as important as elegant tables set with gorgeous plateware, flatware and glassware, or luxurious home furnishings.

Simple floral arrangements in very simple containers, however stunning they may be, are best suited to modern, uncluttered interiors. Lavish, upmarket homes, on the other hand, lend themselves to exuberant, inspirational arrangements of the type shown in this book. In these homes, flower arrangements for special occasions are no longer simply table arrangements. They have become grand and creative works of art with big nature themes and visual glamour. Original choices of flowers, foliage and raw materials are combined in unusual shapes and colors with innovative, sometimes unexpected, containers. The flowers themselves become the stars of the show, enlivening an interior, a table, a sideboard, or turning a special container into a living statement.

Not surprisingly, this focus on inventive, cutting-edge floral arrangements has given rise to a new field of expertise—the art of floristry—in demand at high-profile events and for very special occasions. It is a global phenomenon that has spawned some outstanding "lifestyle designers." Foremost among them are a number of American and Japanese stylists, who have been the main inspiration for Filipino florists based either in America or in their home country. Currently, the best-known names in floral design in the USA are designers such as Preston Bailey, Daniel Ost, Jeff Leatham and Italian-American

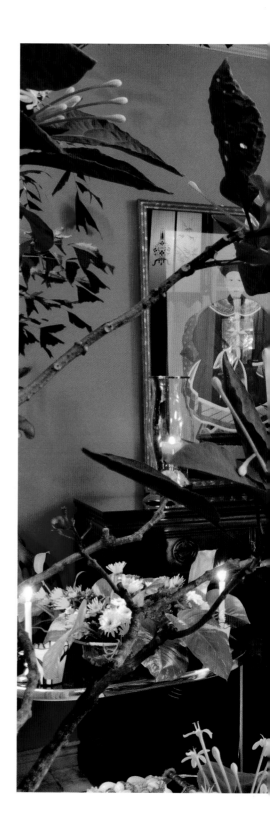

Mandarin red walls, black lacquered consoles and soaring vegetal canopies make a perfect setting in this dining room for a lavish multi-vase table "runway" of red and white carnations, cockscomb, stargazers, statice and white asters (page 164).

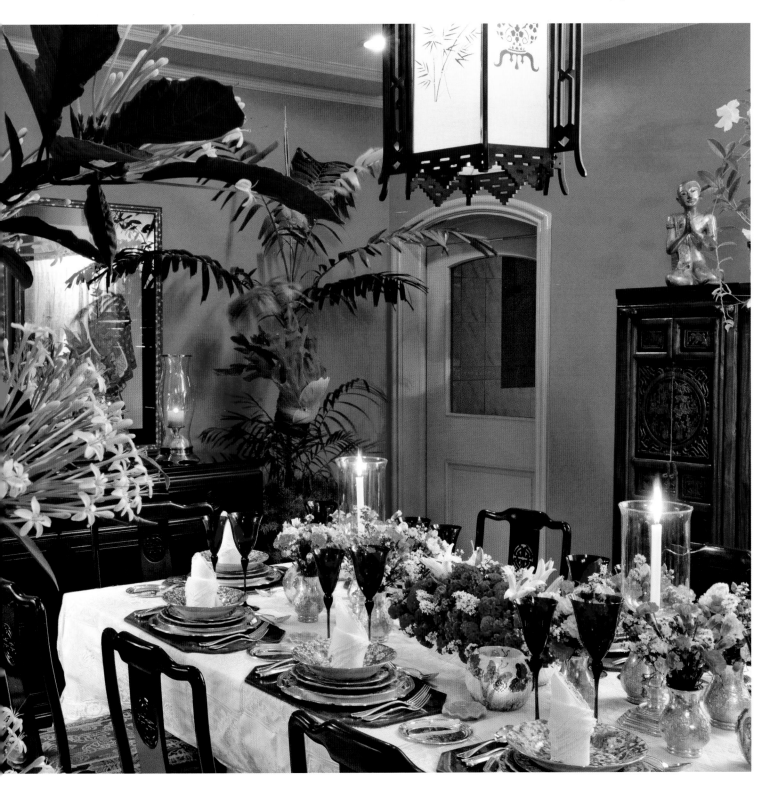

fabulous floral arrangements for every occasion

Alberto Pinto. Preston Bailey is a high-profile events planner and floral artist who creates extravagant theatrical settings for American weddings and big corporate affairs. Daniel Ost is a gifted artist and floral engineer doing plant mechanics that Filipino creatives call "simply genius." Jeff Leatham showcases the beauty of flowers by clustering and magnifying blooms in unusual and unexpected ways, while Alberto Pinto, a classic-romantic designer based in New York City, conjures up glamorous table settings with fantasy and period themes. From Asia, the Japanese art of cut flower arrangement or ikebana, particularly the Modern School originated by Sogetsu masters in Tokyo, Japan, has been particularly influential on Filipino floral design. The Sogetsu brand of cut flower arrangement is a very intuitive and nature-sensitive form of floristry. Several Filipino florists featured in this book actively practice Sogetsu, including Connie Gonzalez, Leo Almeria and Pico Soriano.

While Filipino floristry is influenced by Western design trends and Japanese Sogetsu, the exotic flowers and foliage and earthy, organic materials available on tropical soils offer a rich source of inspiration with which to create memorable floral arrangements. The innate artistic talents of the Filipino people, combined with their well-known passion for song and dance, have also caused floristry to flourish, to move in new and exciting directions and to reach new heights. The floral talent that abounds in the Philippines is obvious from the creations of the ten professional floral stylists profiled in this book, and a further nine talented designers who lent a stylish hand. Their work is showcased in thirty-two homes built in a variety of spectacular architectural styles, and all furnished in an equally spectacular way.

The dazzling designs that these floral stylists have fashioned are all the more remarkable when you consider that the Philippines does not as yet enjoy a major flower trade. Floral designers have thus learned to make the most of a comparatively limited supply of cultivated flowers on the commercial market. The country's traditional floral varieties, which are primarily sourced from the Baguio and Davao highlands, comprise chrysanthemums, starchy statice or sea lavender, asparagus ferns, roses, gerberas, delicate fennel and asters. Over the years, more varieties of orchids have emerged—vandas, phalaenopsis, butterfly orchids, dendrobiums, cattleyas—mostly from the far-flung cities of Mindanao. Closer to Manila, the provinces of Laguna and Quezon supply Birds of Paradise, bromeliads, anthuriums, heliconias, wild gingers, torch gingers, wild ferns such as the giant bird's nest fern, and the fan maidenhair fern. Fortunately, commercial production of flowers is on the increase.

The flower supplier closest to Manila is The Flower Farm, located on a seven-hectare site in Tagaytay City, and owned by Ging de los Reyes, who started her business of cut flowers out of a personal passion for fresh long-stemmed roses in her home. Today, her shop supplies Manila's florists with gerberas, heliconias, gingers and chrysanthemums. Recently, The Flower Farm has started to cultivate and promote such exotics as green lanterns (hairy balls) and an assortment of tropical gingers.

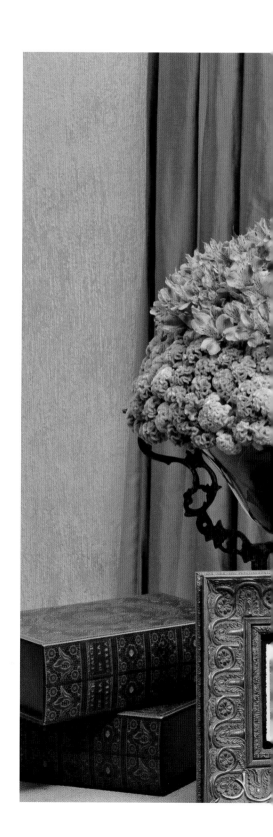

In the foyer of the Villa Michelangelo, Cynthia Almario's massed arrangements of varying heights amidst carefully chosen artifacts from the Pietro Collection make a cheerful, harmonious and welcoming display (page 75).

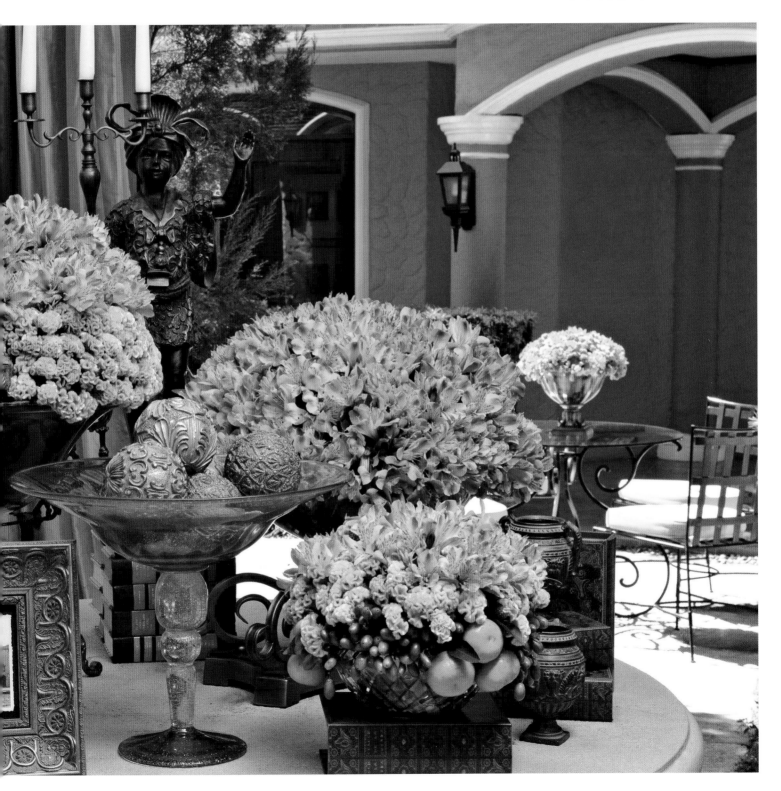

fabulous floral arrangements for every occasion

The leading flower importer and supplier of flowers to the élite is star florist Antonio Garcia of Mabolo Inc. who sources flowers from suppliers and auction houses abroad. He imports a number of species from Thailand, Holland and South America. For one of our photography sessions, he brought in flowers from three countries—Sweden, Japan and Holland. This very popular florist has a list of demanding and discriminating clients who constantly challenge him to deliver more flower varieties.

Perhaps in response to the comparatively limited supply of fresh cut flowers, florists have become expert at utilizing discarded organic materials in their arrangements. It has, in fact, become trendy to use exotic tropical fruits or fruit-like blooms such as sugar palm, known locally as *kaong* or *kabo negro*, pomegranate, sea grapes, edible passion flowers, green peppers, lantern-like heart peas or *parol-parolan*, and even Arabica coffee beans, known as *bunga de jolo*. Other innovative florists use furry achuete pods, whose red coloring is used for certain foods, dark-stained nipa palm nuts or the dried pods of the golden shower tree. The bulbous "Mickey Mouse" (nipple fruit) shrub made its debut years ago. Some creative florists also employ ordinary garden vegetables, such as broccoli and cabbage flowers, for earthy, tactile effects. Mountain cacti and succulent herbs are other popular materials. The echeveria cabbage rose and related succulent hybrids were recently introduced in the Philippines and have attained great popularity among floral artists.

While the flamboyant Scottish florist Ronnie Laing was the true pioneer of Philippine floristry in the 1950s, the most elegant wedding arrangements came from the iconic florist Toni Serrano Parsons, creative owner of Manila's top flower shop, 517 Remedios. It was she who gently steered upper-class Manilenos away from conventional wedding bouquets down a long design aisle toward innovative and exquisite flower creations never seen or imagined before. It is said that one of her fabulous church settings comprised hundreds of silvery tillandsia or air plants combined with other silver-sparkling accessories. Toni also triggered the "organic" wave in floral design that swept through Manila in the 1990s. Her organic compositions featured giant succulents mixed with long vines or wiry stems, like the rare lycopodium clubmoss, peat and tree bark, long-stemmed "burros tails" with terminal pale pink flowers, and spectacular cymbidium orchids. These outstanding arrangements continue to be emulated.

Restaurateur-cum-florist Margarita Fores, one of the most creative stylists featured in this book, has fashioned her own floral name on the most rustic-organic installations in town. For her catering events, she adds berries, rattan clusters (locally known as *binting dalaga*), lotus blooms and fruits to achieve a memorable look. Her unusual eco-assemblages have pushed the boundaries further with fresh or dried pods from common trees, wild vines and lacquered fruits of pandanus or screwpine juxtaposed with multiple flower-like succulents and cacti. Margarita styled a lovely Filipiniana table in Gianna Montinola's home using fragrant white sampaguita, magnolias, rosal and tuberoses to go alongside traditional *pina* (pineapple fiber) table linens.

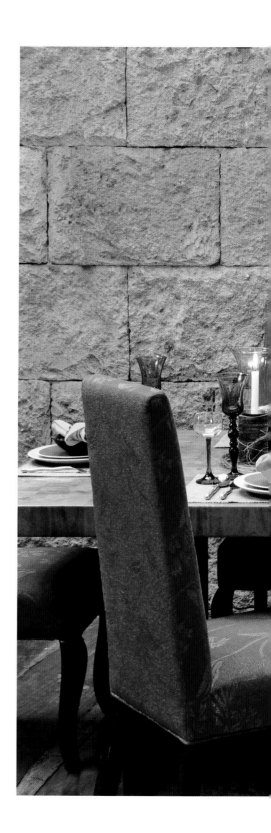

Tall sea anemone-shaped vessels filled with berries from the five finger plant tower over cosy "nests" of brilliant fuschia gloriosa blossoms and San Francisco leaves in this table arrangement by Estien Quijano (page 23).

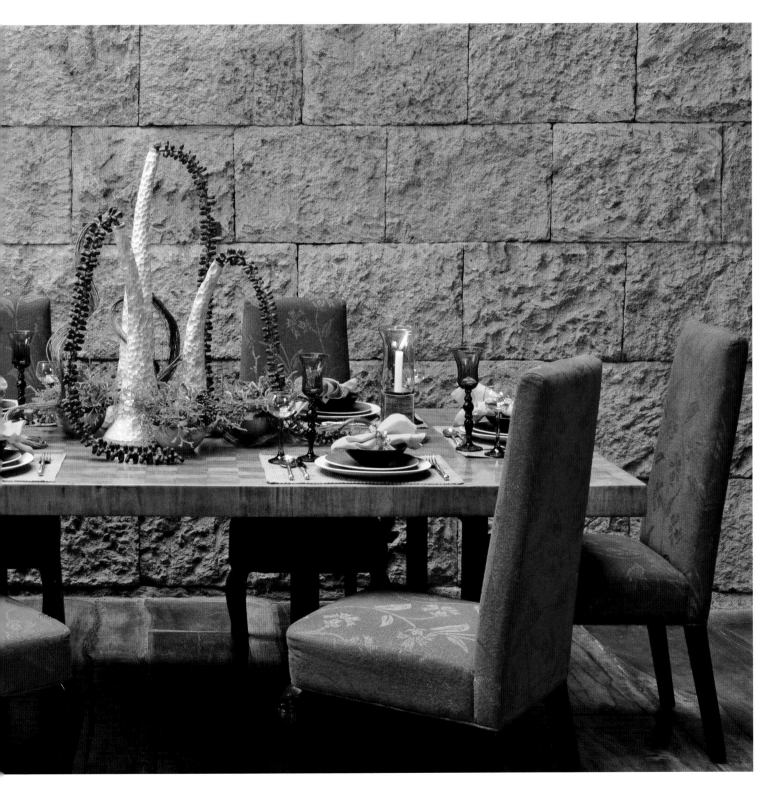

fabulous floral arrangements for every occasion

Another well-known name in local floristry, Pico Soriano, a Filipino-American florist, flew into Manila to "dress" a few homes for this book. Pico combines a background of floristry education in California with a love of Philippine flora. He was delighted to find the inflated yellow green pods of the balloon plant (*Asclepias physocarpa*) native to South Africa, grown in Sagada, as well as his favorite hydrangeas. He also brought with him some new techniques. For the modern Tantoco home, he created "waterless" installations and "out-of-the-vase" floral settings, put together patiently with glue guns. For the Tuscany-style Rojas home, he structured an opulently romantic setting for every room. Fantasy came through the use of balls of flowers alongside hanging beads, sequins, feathers, glittery fabrics and transparent Lucite cylinders. He also provided tips on doing Flemish classical arrangements for vintage period interiors—grand floral installations that do not compete with the period furniture and classic art gracing the walls of a home.

New discovery Nathaniel Aranda has emerged as a floral master of the romantic kind. On seeing beauty queen Margarita Moran Floreindo's glamorous condo and homeware, he was inspired to create an opulent carousel of flowers towering over her dining table. Later, on viewing the fine art collections of Lizette Banzon Cojuangco, he fashioned a spectacular floral chandelier and a modern Valentine's tablescape of "big bold roses," each made from 50–100 deep violet cordyline leaves (called ti) which took him over three days to assemble. He also styled the old-fashioned flowers in the homestead of the Santos-Andres heritage mansion in Antipolo, using only common flowers and native foliage of the countryside. These included cadena de amor and gloriosa climbers; azucenas and sanggumay orchids, plus many unnamed grass pods and field grasses.

A versatile and passionate floral artist featured in this book is Rosabella Ongpin, who trained in floristry in Sydney, San Francisco and Manila. In her rambling home and garden, Belle assembled a delightful floral show of stylish centerpieces, water-glass and pool installations, and a floral chandelier. The high priestess of contemporary chic interiors, Cynthia Almario produced amazing black and white compositions. In one illuminated installation, dark green leaves with purple undersides create crisp and modern images with the blue evening lighting from the swimming pool. Ace florist Antonio Garcia, a major floral importer, used blooms from Spain, Japan and Venezuela to enhance a classic upmarket home. His use of curious ivory spikes of lily of the valley radiating from green velvety mounds of boule de mousse was particularly outstanding. Interior designer Leo Almeria summoned ikebana techniques to dramatize an edgy white "windowless" home. Anton Barretto created a magical Moroccan theme with a palette of fiery sunsets contrasting with cool blue hydrangeas. Eric Paras, a consummate design catalyst, articulated the passions of various home owners and worked seamlessly as eclectic stylist and florist for three vastly varied locations. Finally, Roberto Gopiao, an award-winning bonsai stylist, landscape designer and art collector, displayed how ultra-creative floral compositions can blend dynamically with contemporary modern art.

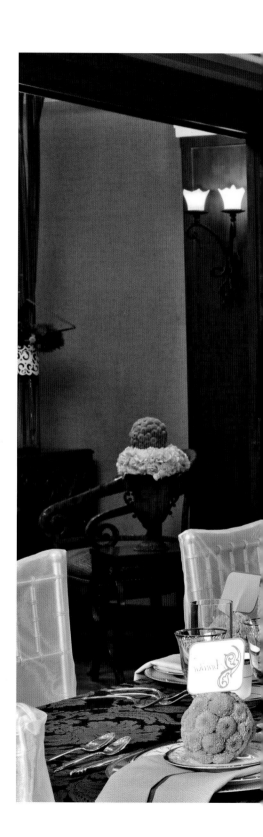

BELOW Pico Soriano's ethereal floating "clouds" of white Casablanca lilies, white roses, chrysanthemums and crystal dangles set on upturned long-stemmed goblets, and his place name holders formed of balls of lime button mums, illustrate his novel waterless approach to floral creations (page 104).
NEXT SPREAD Nathaniel Aranda's floral carousel, anchored on a pedestal, and his centerpiece arrangement comprise an unusual mix of romantic blooms and fleshy succulents, pale colors and bright ones (page 63).

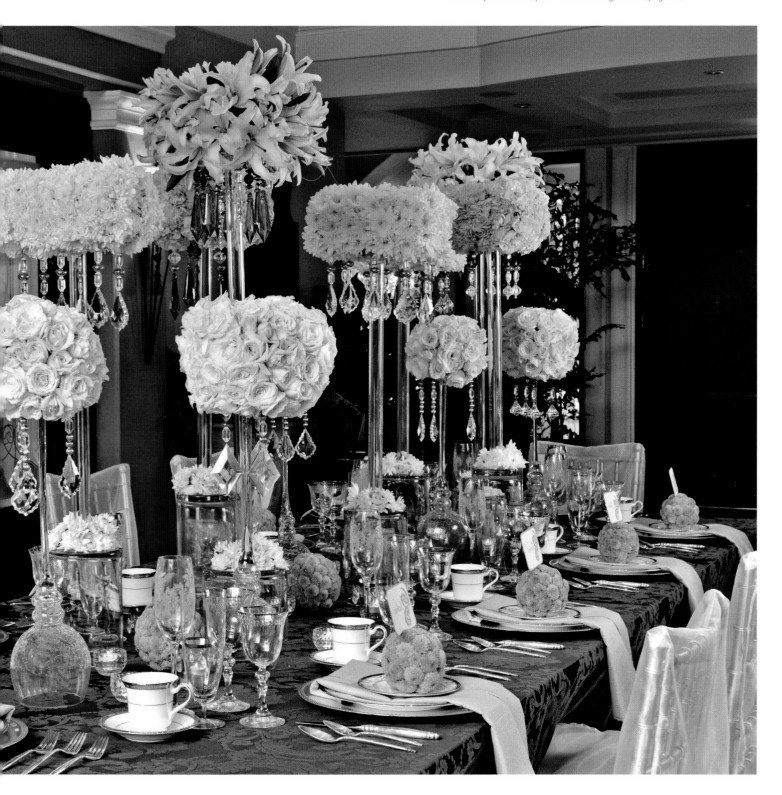

fabulous floral arrangements for every occasion

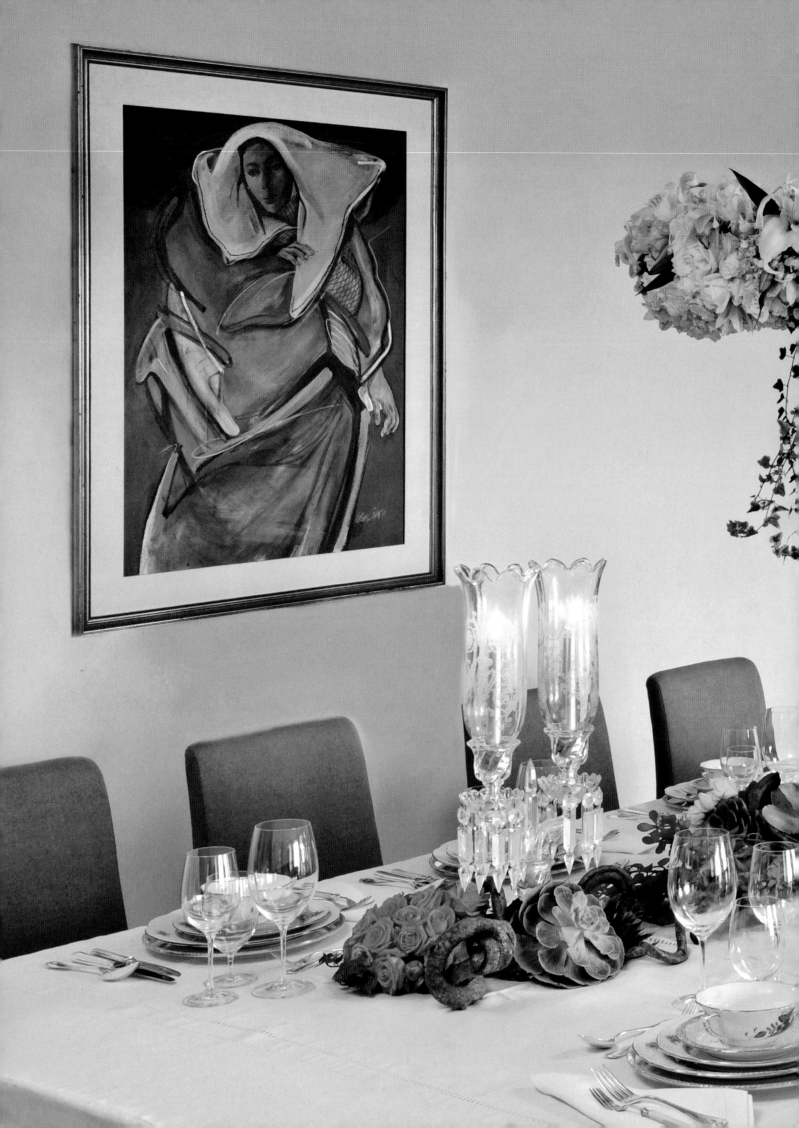

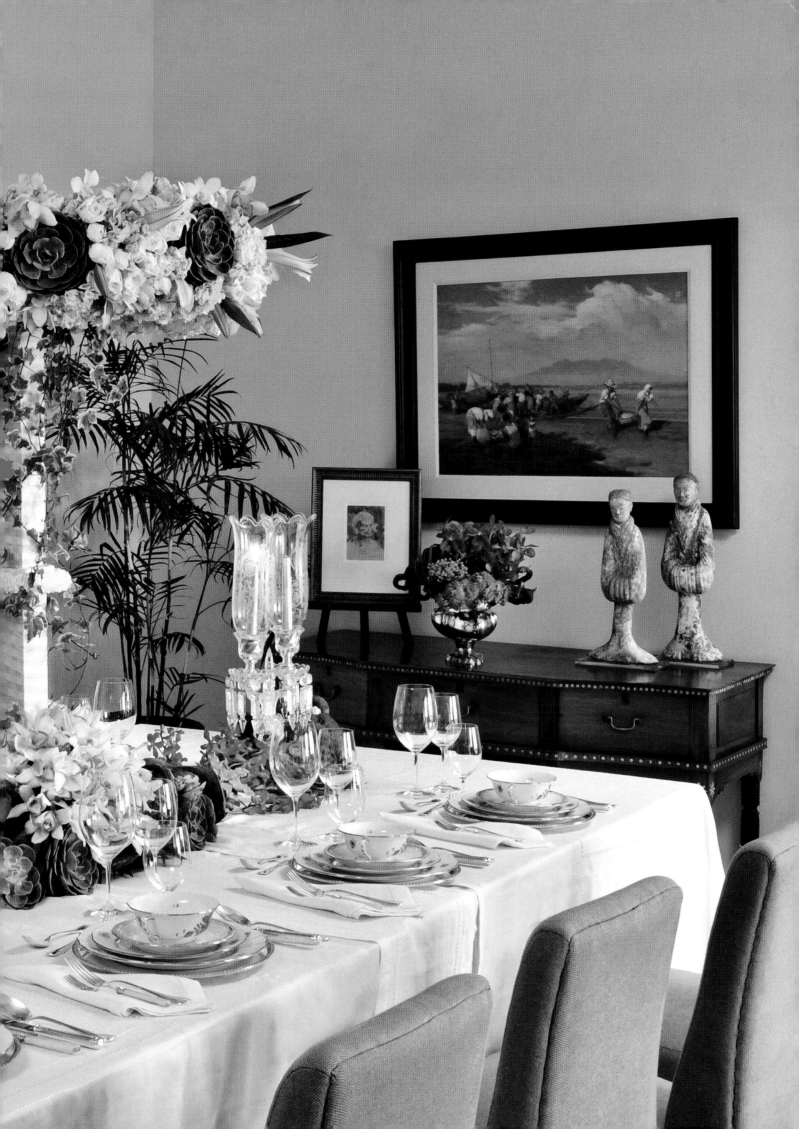

exotic floral forms mirror art

FLORIST ROBERTO GOPIAO took one look at this pavilion mansion, then chose the path of harmony. "I could see immediately that the owners loved Philippine art, more especially tribal art, with its bright colors and curled carving details. So I took off on this."

The elevated three-level home, sprawling over 3000 sq m of land in Dasmarinas Village, Makati City, has a built-up area of around 2000 sq m. The lady of the house had her ideas for the house interpreted by G. A. Formoso architects. "I wanted it to be like a second home, the feeling of all of us gathering in a beautiful retreat environment."

There are no visible fences, save for glass security panels hidden by shrubs that shield the property from the street level.

Towering wooden columns support the high-pitched roof of the house. Both the formal living room and the grand drawing room open into the garden. "The flowers pull the garden into the house. The gardens draw the residents and visitors out to explore the multilevel spaces."

All the bedrooms look out over the garden and the free-form pool. The hewn stone walls support huge bas-relief murals by the late Filipino master, Carlos "Botong" Francisco. Giant Muslim drums and gongs stand out against the purple, greens and yellows of the *malong* or tubular Muslim ladies skirts used as couch throws.

In the open-air *sala*, built entirely of traditional hardwoods, florist Bobby Gopiao created three luxuriant arrangements. His favorite rests on a low *dulang* coffee table. "I'm particularly proud of this ikebana study of red gingers and contrasting yellow calla lilies with circular patterns of dried palm fronds," he says. By the entrance, his other favorite is the suspended trio of boat-shaped carvings filled with yellow and red bromeliads and berries."

"The arrangement by the terrace spa is inspired by the Sarimanok, the mythical plumed bird of Filipino Muslim legend. I used yellow 'rattlesnake' calatheas, and wired some dried palm frond spines onto a native gaming *sungka*. The whole effect is very contemporary," Bobby concludes.

The next day, florist Estien Quijano took the same Muslim color cues from the house for the dining room. "I used green and gold woven placemats to bring out the beautifully crafted golden *gmelina* wood table by Albert Avellana.

"In the center, I used a triad of tall sea anemone-shaped vessels to hold exotic palm nuts called *buko-buko*, with vine roots cascading down. Yellow-orange berries from a plant called five fingers blend with the red high-backed chairs. Vera Wang plates topped with fine Japanese stone bowls bring polished contrast to the rustic feel. I added slender bottle green wine flutes for a final flourish," Estien sums up.

RIGHT This tropical pavilion home in Makati City is a rich repository of Philippine arts and crafts. A trio of Muslim boat-shaped vessels are filled with three types of bromeliads and a flowing green vine called *manaog-ka-irog*, meaning "descend my beloved."

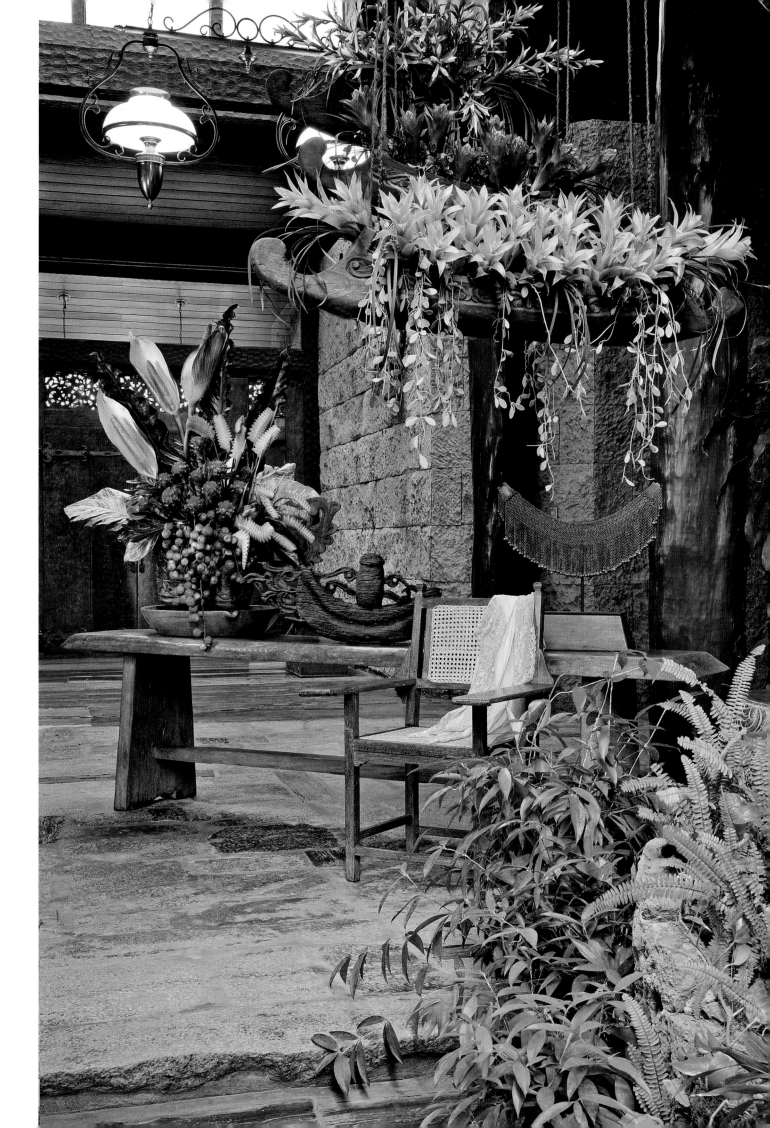

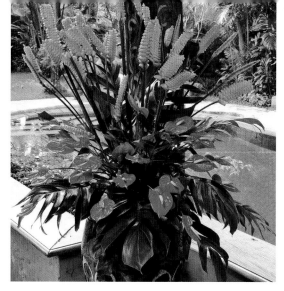

BELOW The neutral palette of the stoneware plates by Joey de Castro on the rustic wood table is complemented by a subdued but stylish centerpiece of clustered berries. Tropical foliage lines the pathway to the pool.

BOTTOM The stylized modern *butaka*, once a "birthing" chair, has evolved into a chair for siestas, ideal for slinging one's legs over the extended armrests. The *baul* or wooden chest nearby holds a tropical feast of Philippine fruits.

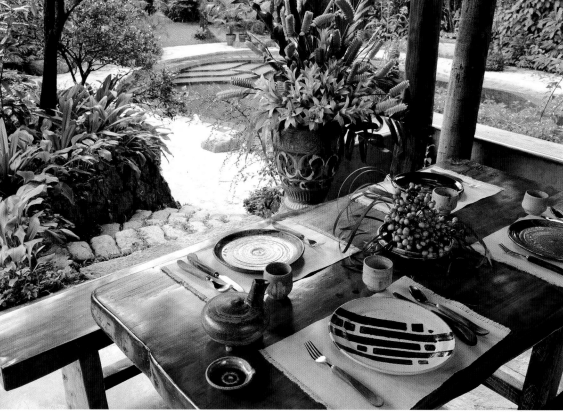

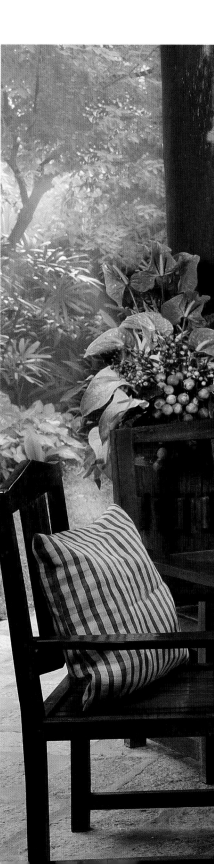

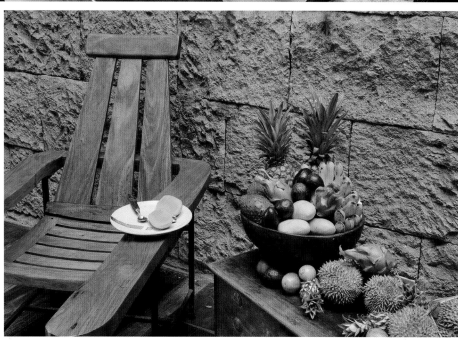

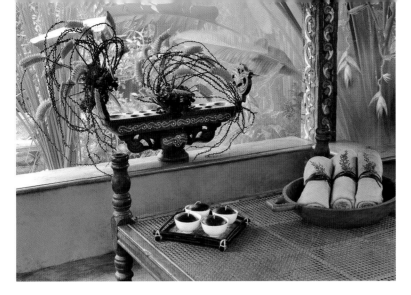

OPPOSITE TOP A polychrome musical drum from Mindanao serves as a base for a flamboyant arrangement of red anthuriums and yellow calatheas from a giant mother plant.

LEFT The floral arrangement on the ledge, depicting a stylized Sarimanok, the mythical bird of Muslim legend, is artistically executed in a swirl of palm frond spines and yellow calatheas on a Philippine gaming board called *sungka*.

BELOW A duet of heart-shaped anthuriums and red berries tower over a table arrangement of torch gingers and palm frond spines in this stunning tropical *lanai* setting of lustrous Philippine ebony and molave hardwood furniture.

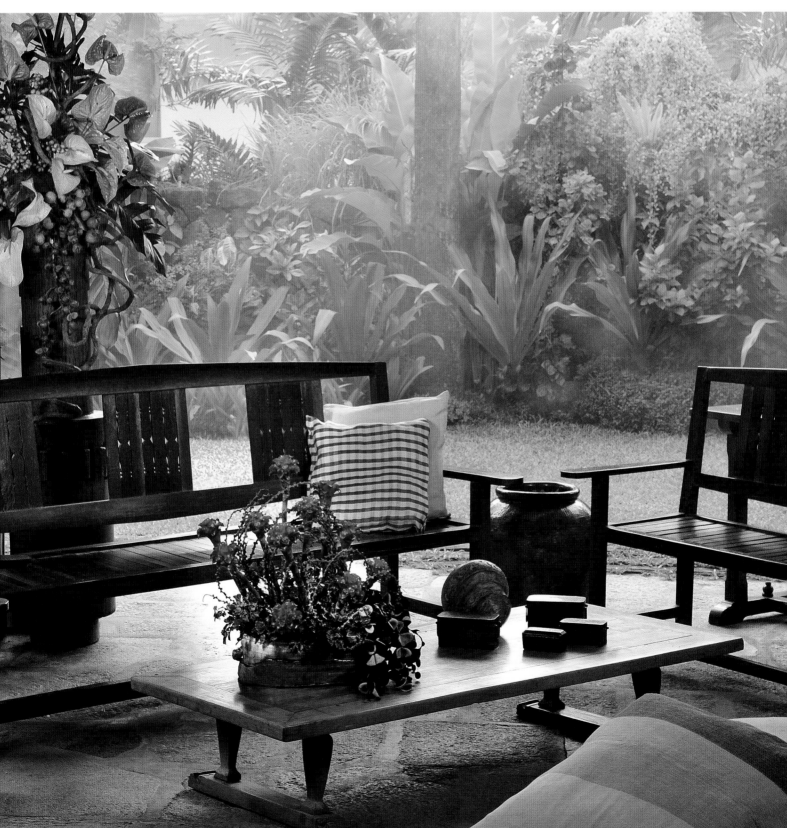

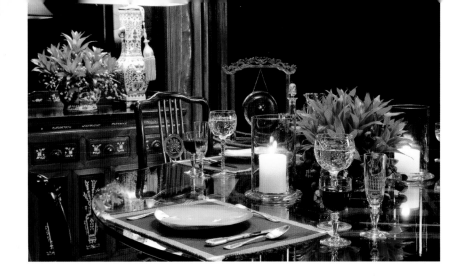

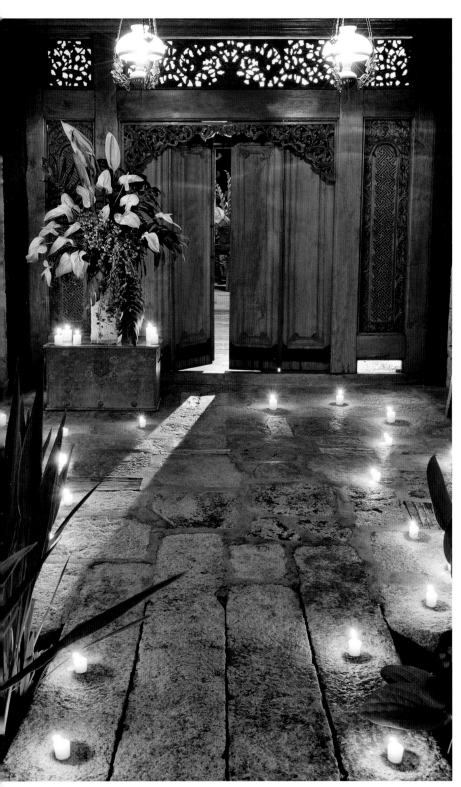

LEFT Clusters of red bromeliads in porcelain vases make a cheerful and harmonious display in the octagonal-shaped, glass-paneled dining room, and provide a relaxed contrast to the formal Chinese furniture and Muslim gong used to summon each course.

BELOW LEFT Flickering votive lights on Piedra china slabs lead visitors to the front entry. An imposing floral "sentry" composed of heart-shaped anthuriums harmonizes with the intricate detail of the Balinese carved wooden doorway.

BELOW Two berry compositions. Above, broad lilac anthuriums, torch gingers, cockscombs and red berries stand atop a bronze-studded wooden chest. Below, framed by a brass-hinged wooden door, a Muslim vessel holds cascading *buko-buko* palm nuts. The white tiger lilies in front blend beautifully with the white candlesticks.

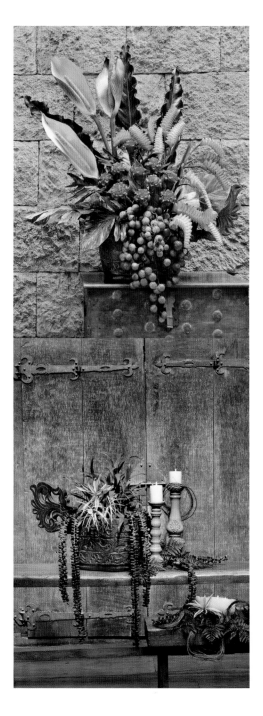

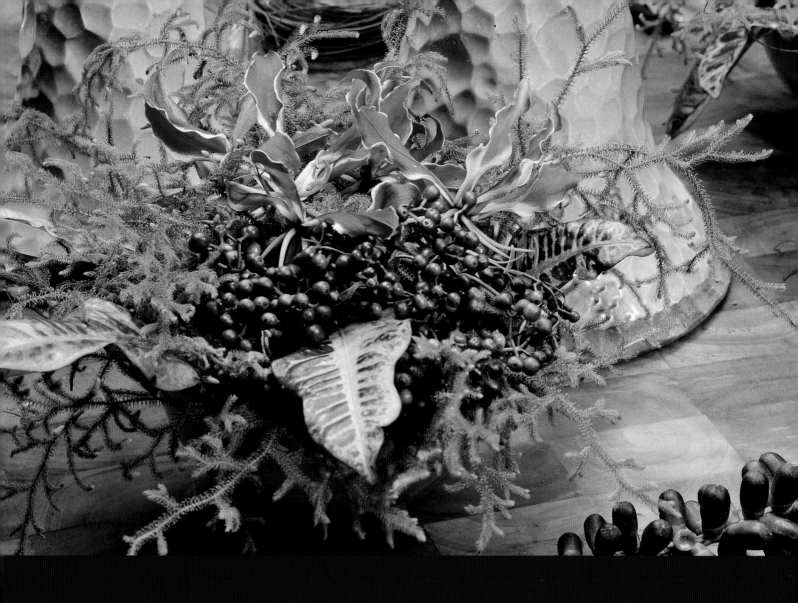

ABOVE Berries from the
five finger plant, together
with San Francisco leaves,
form a cosy nest for
brilliant fuschia gloriosa
blossoms.
RIGHT Albert Avellana's
golden table of laminated
gmelina ("white teak")
cubes enrich the table setting. Handmade Japanese
stoneware bowls are set on
Vera Wang china, flanked
by bottle green stemware
from Rustan's.

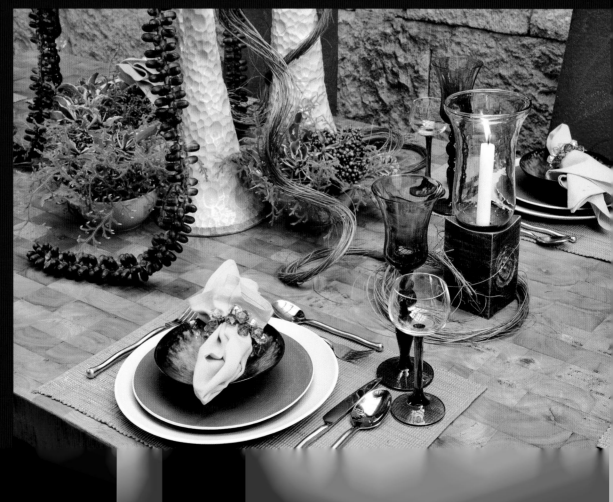

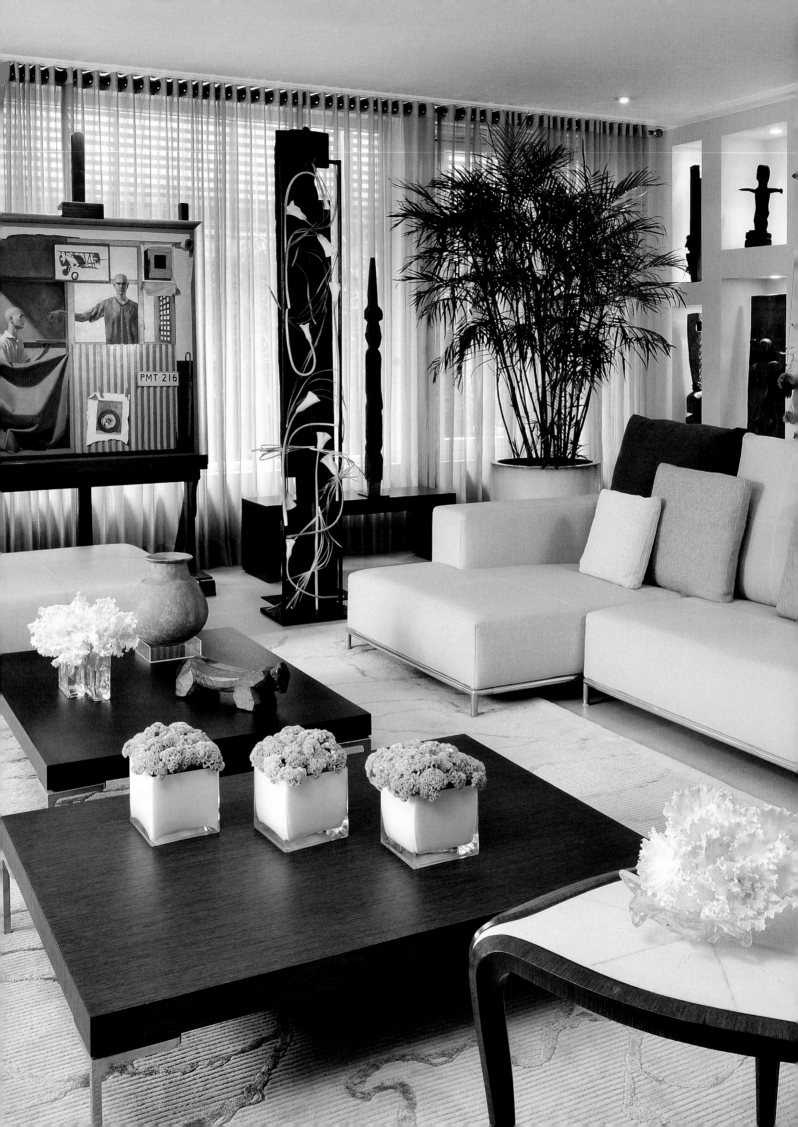

floral fantasies
for a collector's home

ARTFUL SETTINGS

Stylist Jonathan Matti with Robert Blancaflor

THIS UNDERSTATED HOME in Dasmariñas Village, Manila, is a contemplative setting for a businessman who collects Philippine modern art in the family tradition, along with tribal sculptures from the Philippine Cordillera following his own heart. An entire wall in an otherwise minimalist interior comprises a well-lit display unit for his collection of ethnic Ifugao *bulol* or rice gods. The rest of the house is likewise low-key and orderly, an ideal backdrop for a fine collection of Filipino modern paintings.

The residence was designed and styled by architect Jonathan Matti, who is better known for his "classic opulent period-specific" interiors for vintage art collectors. In mounting this modern art collection, Jonathan kept a controlling hand on the minimalist space and trod softly on the use of flowers. "We don't want to have the home look like a flower shop!" he quips, while directing his florist friend Robert Blancaflor to provide restrained, minimalist flower arrangements.

The dominant floral tone of the arrangements is yellow—from the trio of small white vases filled with yellow cockscomb blossoms on the living room coffee table to the stunning "floral canvas"—a freestanding installation of yellow calla lilies—displayed among the dark rice god *bulol*. The lilies, seemingly dancing in the air, are wired to a metal frame and nurtured by tiny vials of water tied to their stalks.

The dining room, in a completely different color palette, is a memorable setting for art. Here, the spirit of the classical tableau is driven by a vibrant European modern work displayed on an easel. This arresting portrait of an Old World prince, costumed and collared with realistic fruits and a surreal frog, is complemented by a large celadon bowl of roses and hydrangeas and tall silver candelabra on the dining table.

The overall effect is one of edgy period elegance, much like a set from "Phantom of the Opera"—a subtle undertext that well pleases the art collector's architect.

OPPOSITE Rich tufts of yellow cockscombs in matching containers on the *sala*'s coffee table and the striking yellow calla lilies on the "living sculpture" provide a bold injection of color amidst the owner's dark-hued Ifugao treasures and quiet furnishings.

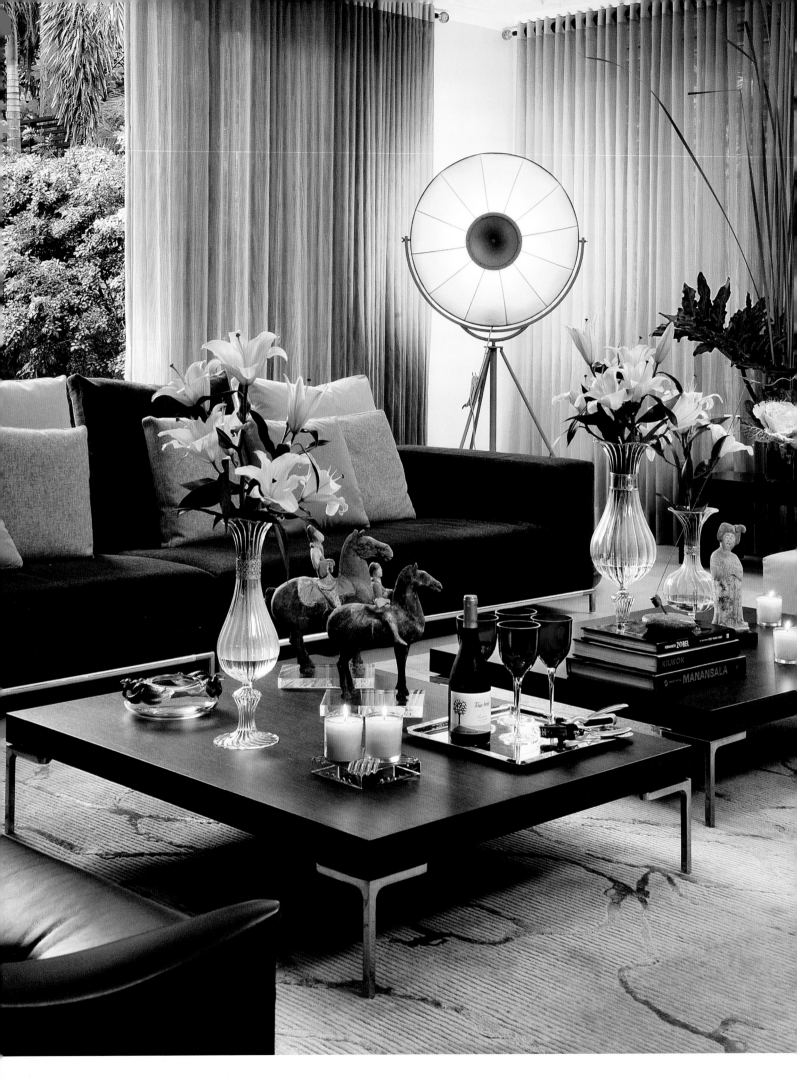

The house is quietly modern with understatement; floral arrangements are used as low-key accents amid the settings.

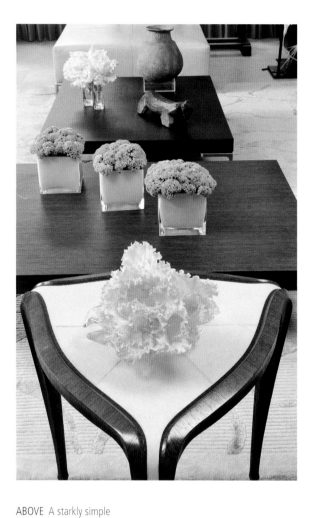

ABOVE A starkly simple bouquet of white cabbage roses is spotlighted on a remarkable pedestal—a modern Art Deco-inspired three-legged table.

LEFT The timeless elegance of lilies in classic crystal vases is a perfect counterpoint to the modern Klieg light, used as a décor accent in a corner.

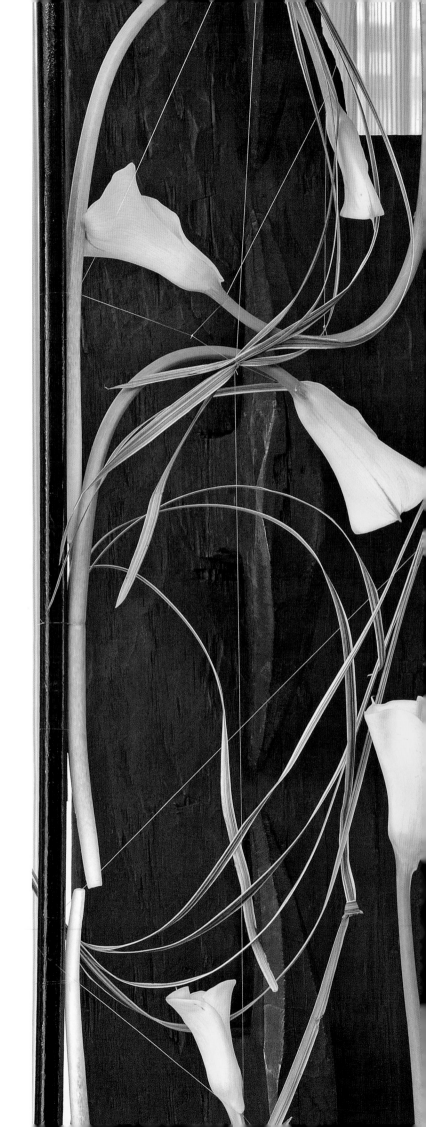

RIGHT Florist Robert Blancaflor's fascinating sculptural installation highlights the inherent form and line of the yellow calla lily. Appearing to dance in the air, the lilies are wired to a freestanding iron panel and fed by tiny vials of water tied to their stalks.

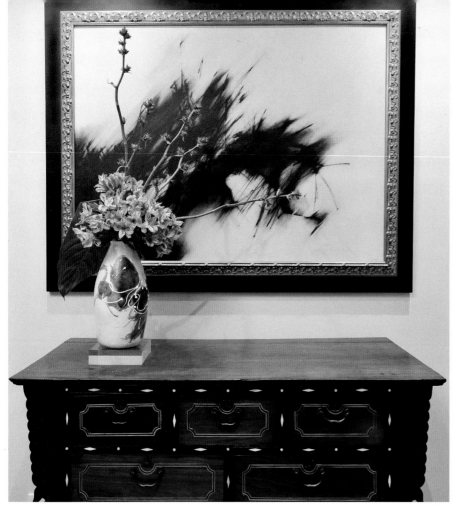

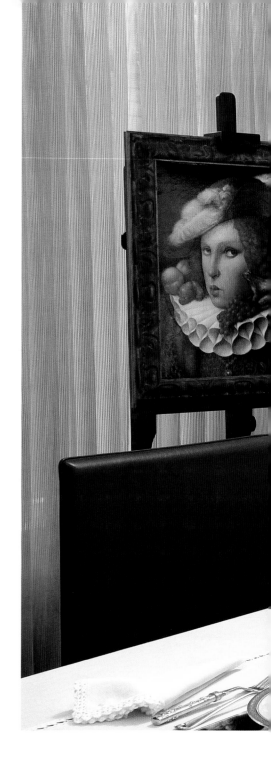

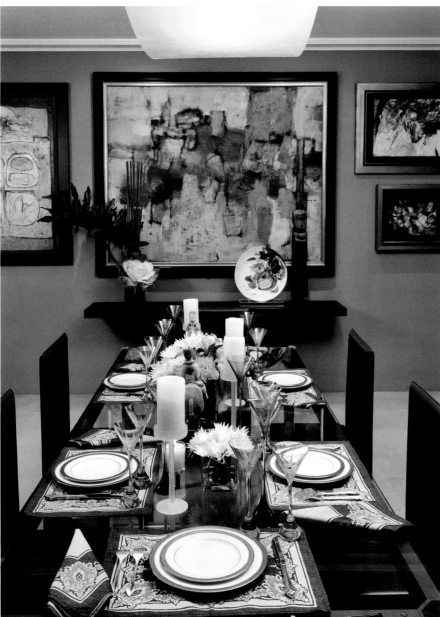

ABOVE LEFT At the entrance, a sculptural monochromatic arrangement of rose-colored alstroemerias mimics the movement of Fernando Zobel's zen masterpiece hung above a bone-inlaid altar table from Batangas.

LEFT The collector's dining table displays gold-rimmed plateware and English linens in a room lined with vintage Filipino paintings by Joya, Manansala and HR Ocampo. The flower arrangements are kept deliberately low-key.

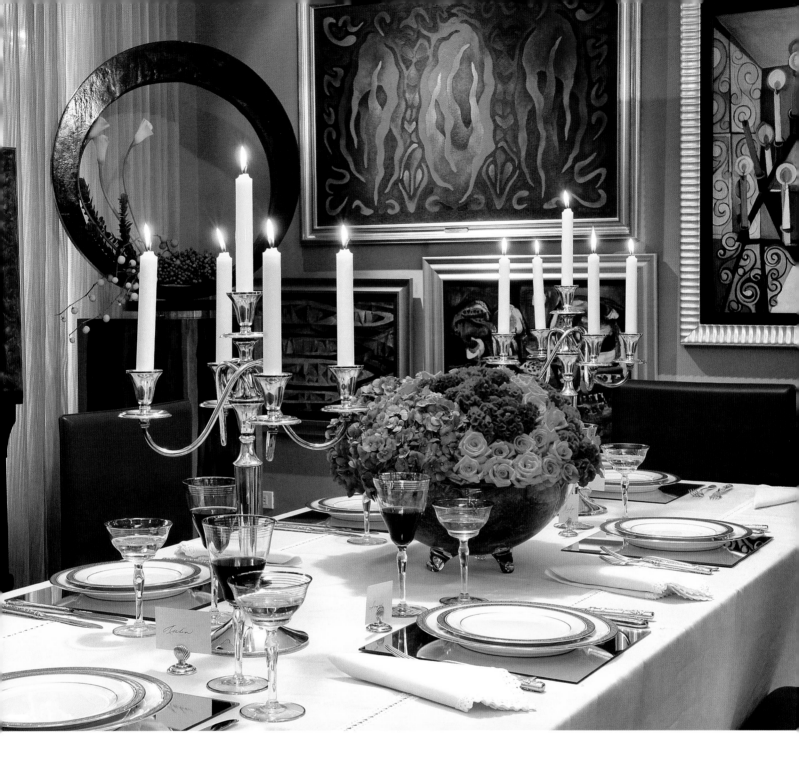

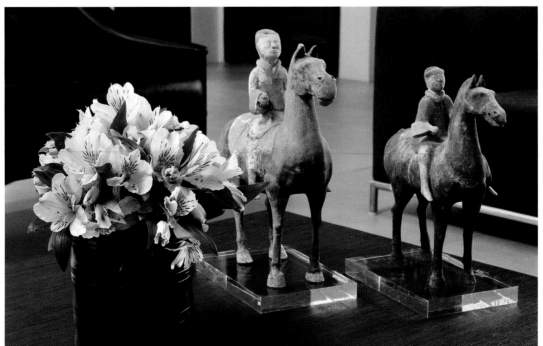

ABOVE A majestic combination of red roses and purple hydrangeas in an elegant silver urn is the perfect choice for a room filled with colorful modern art and a table set with classical dinnerware and fine silver candelabra.

LEFT A simple bunch of white alstroemerias peeping out from a bamboo vase makes a superb contrast to a display of antique clay figures of Chinese Tang horsemen.

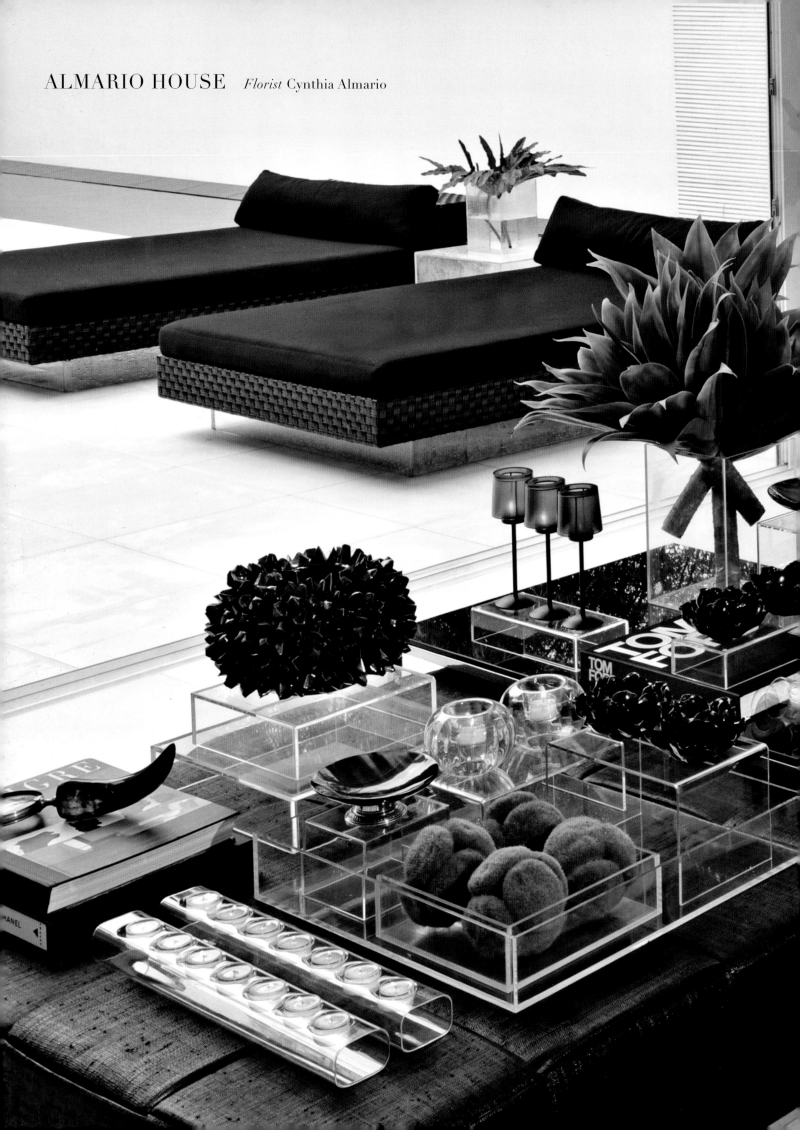

ALMARIO HOUSE *Florist* Cynthia Almario

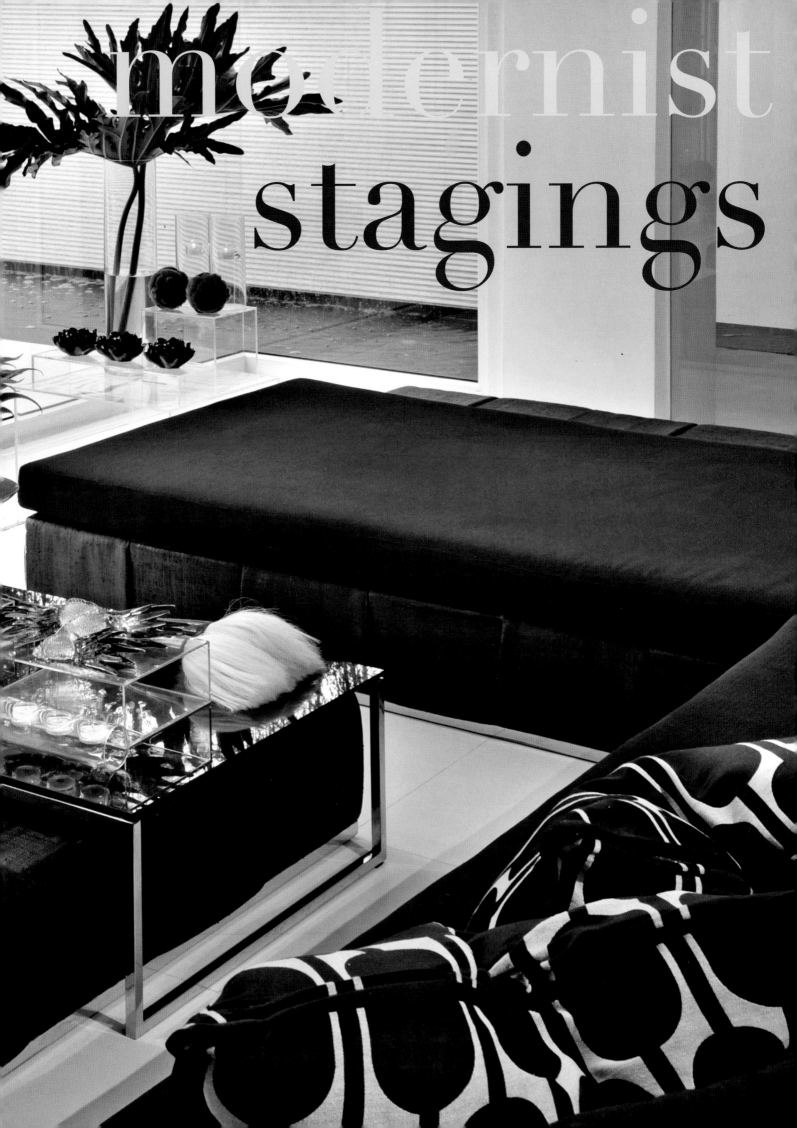

modernist stagings

INTERIOR DESIGNER and stylist Cynthia Almario lives in a bright white showplace built by Filipino modern "star-chitect" Ed Ledesma in a breezy subdivision in Paranaque. It took a three-year collaboration to configure three levels of modernist walls and endless picture windows into a 650 sq m chic lifestyle space.

The stylist's home makes strong architectural statements from the front gate inwards. From here, the building presents itself standing majestically white over a dark, surrounding dipping pool. The long white platform protruding into the pool is where Cynthia and friends often dine — a windy stage over designer waters! In all corners the modernist house is planned for designer eyes and modern points of view. It has been carefully plotted for an awesome "floating" experience amid a vast composite of mirrors and glass and water features.

As the ever-stylish designer of chic residences, boutique hotels and Asian-themed restaurants, Cynthia has realized her own dream home. Here she enjoys making her creative tablescapes to express and enhance an upscale East–West lifestyle influenced by long years spent in California. Always balancing and adjusting elements for color, shape and height, she loves composing themes for settings. "Creating thematic table settings is really my favorite thing! Sometimes I style parties for good friends and clients."

Her floral installations are decidedly geometric, graphic and modern minimalist, and are often made to coordinate with her personal collection of plates and figurines on the large uplighted presentation table.

For the first photography session, Cynthia used a large cubic module composed of rustic tree branches as a natural platform for suspending rows of apple green spider chrysanthemums. Set between two contemporary loungers by the dipping pool, the installation concentrated the dominant color of the bamboo grove and garden palms.

Elsewhere in the white house, the stylist orchestrates vegetal decorating materials into loose or sculptural installations to suit the architectural surroundings. Among her favorite mixed media materials are white calla lilies, tall pandan grasses and fuzzy green moss balls (from Pottery Barn USA). Standing tall, the graphic flowers take stunning center stage in the modernist house.

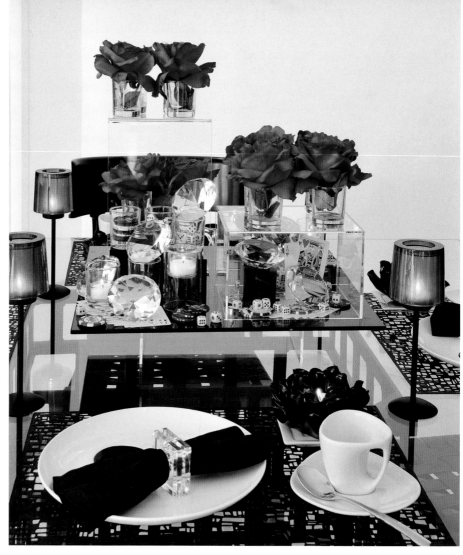

ABOVE A playful table setting on a casino theme, complete with chips, cards and dice, would not be complete without the drama of voluptuous red Ecuardorian roses, black placemats, white tableware and sparkling glass.

RIGHT Deep red cockscombs on tiered metallic tree trunks make a brilliant statement against a photo-backdrop of trees, all washed in amber light on this lavishly laid dining table.

PREVIOUS SPREAD Cynthia's world is a black and white stage. The modern *sala* is dominated by a grouping of Plexiglas boxes enhanced with foliage and tealights.

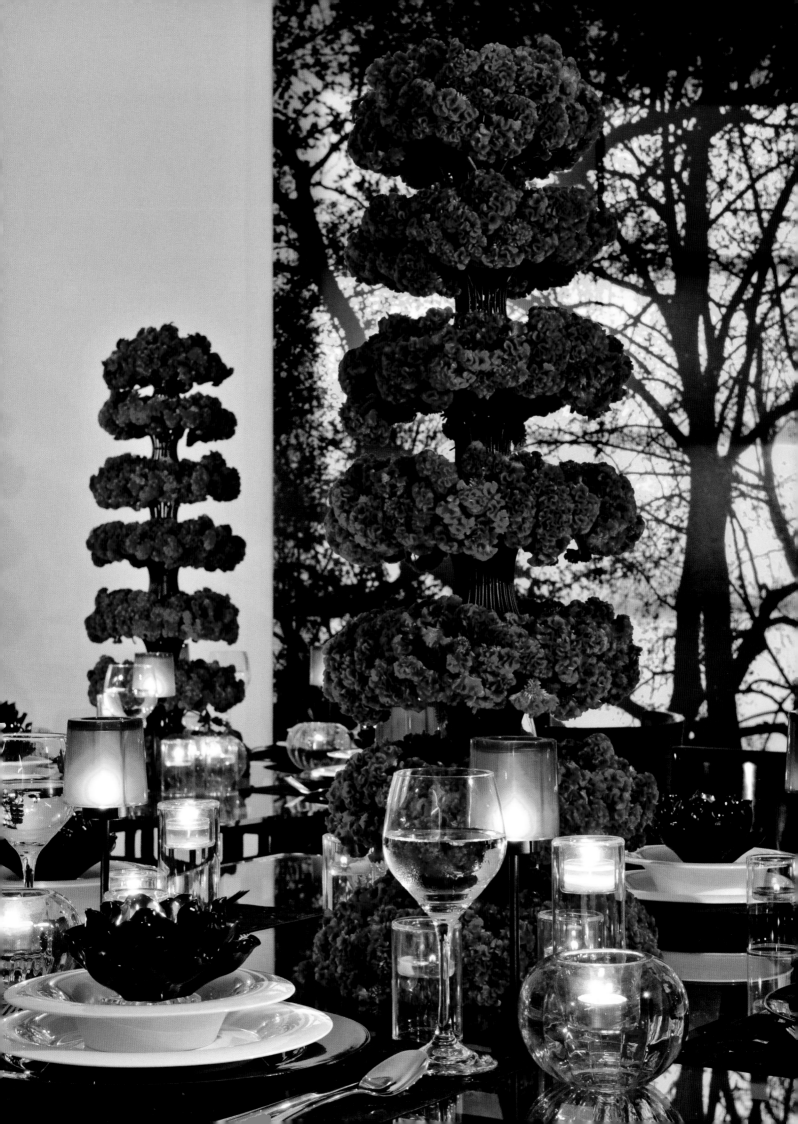

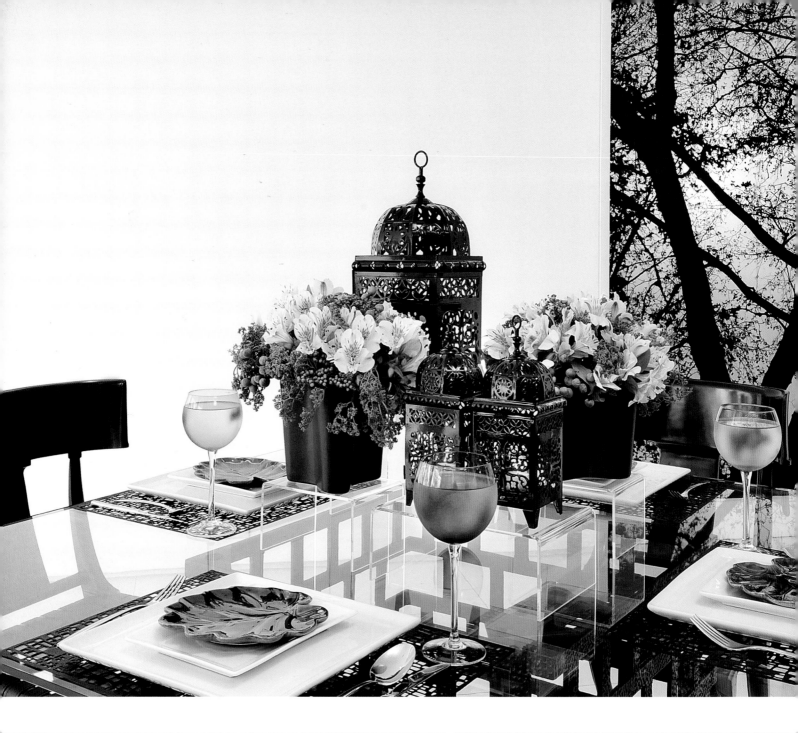

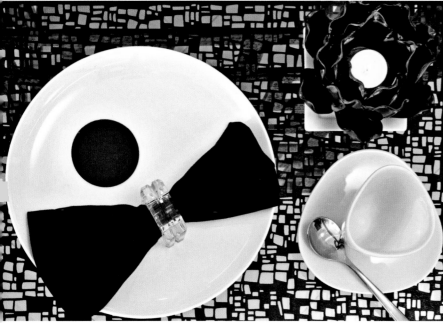

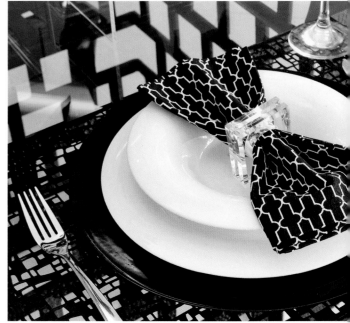

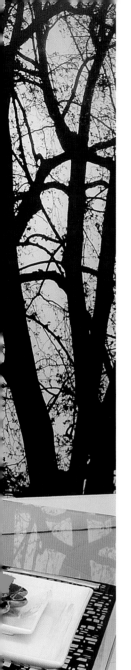

LEFT Leaf-shaped green ceramic dessert plates encircling pierced metal lamps on Plexiglas stands are coordinated with small green and white floral bouquets.

RIGHT Budji Layug's asymmetrical console table is accessorized with fine branches and tealights in this artistic installation.

BOTTOM LEFT AND CENTER Cynthia adds variety to her dramatic table settings by mixing and matching ebony and ivory accessories.

BOTTOM RIGHT Large spiked foliage raised on Plexiglas stands gives this table setting a stylish modernity.

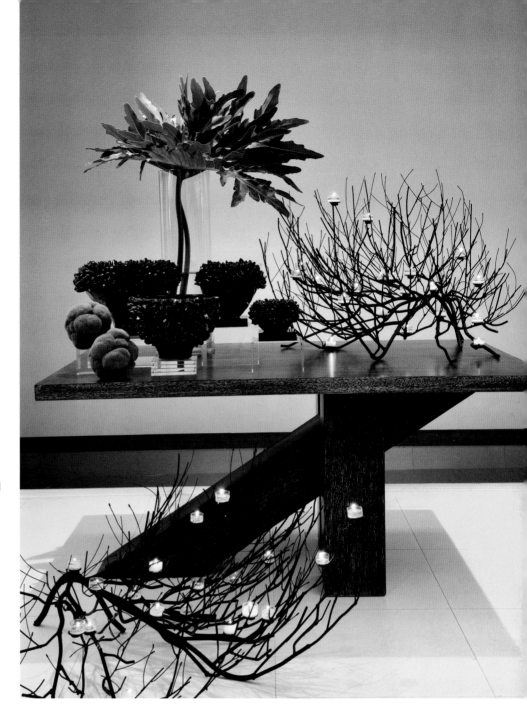

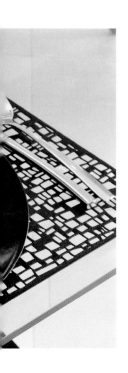

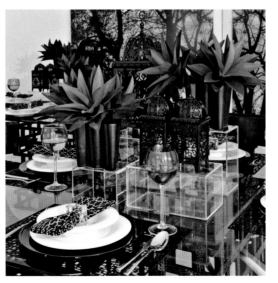

Interior designer Cynthia Almario does flowers and styles events for good friends and clients. "Creating thematic table settings is really my favorite thing," she says.

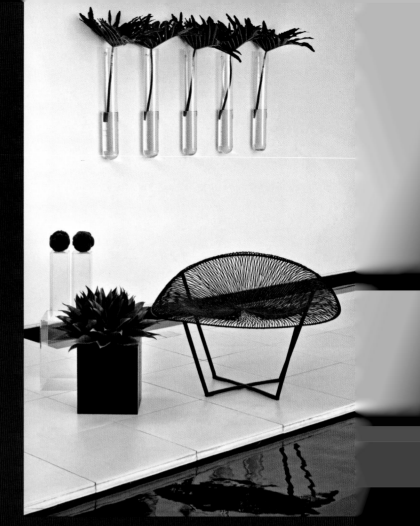

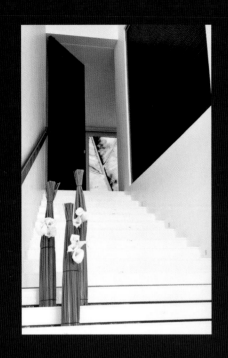

LEFT Freestanding installations of pandan leaves and calla lilies stand sentinel at the entrance to the starkly modern white house.

RIGHT The green and white theme continues near this water feature: five leaf-bearing tubes suspended on a wall complement a fused wire leaf chair by Ann Pamintuan.

BELOW LEFT Fuzzy green moss balls, natural foliage and accents of calla lilies provide textural contrast to pierced metal vessels.

BELOW RIGHT The pure sculptural forms of calla lilies resting in Plexiglas harmonize beautifully with the modernist architecture.

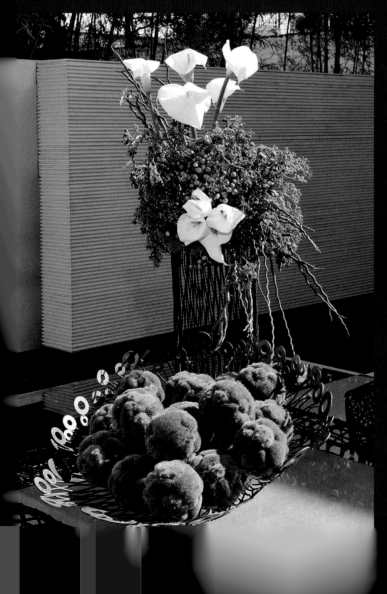

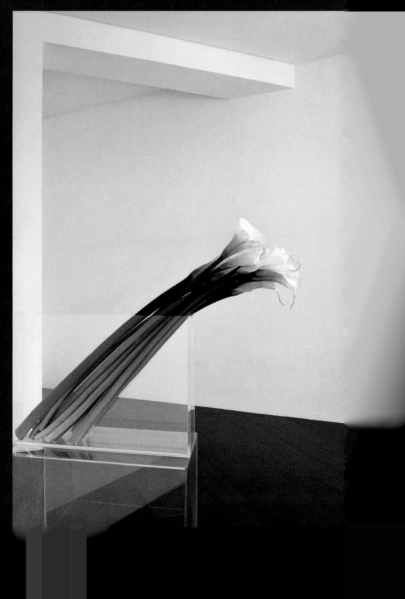

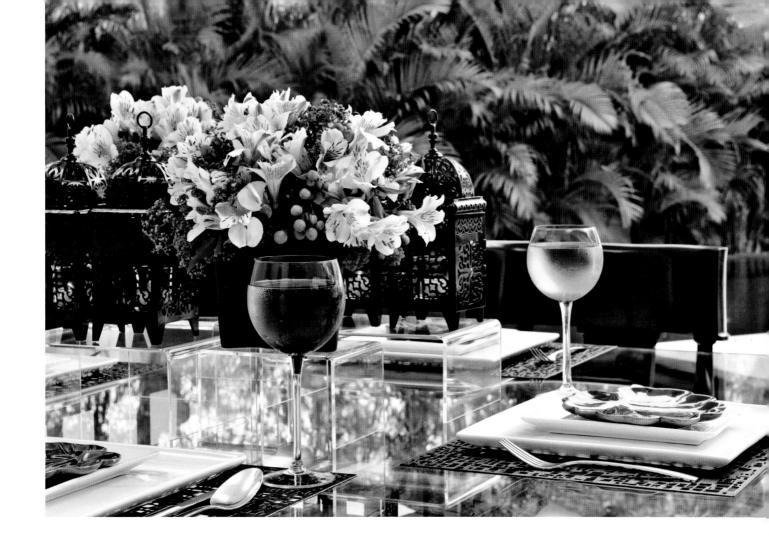

ABOVE Framed against a backdrop of palm garden greens, Cynthia's contemporary alfresco floral arrangement features a bouquet of white alstroemeria and green berries.
RIGHT The outdoor dining table, placed on a platform surrounded by water, and lit from below at night, is a dramatic setting for her equally bold green and white floral statements set amidst a collection of green tableware.

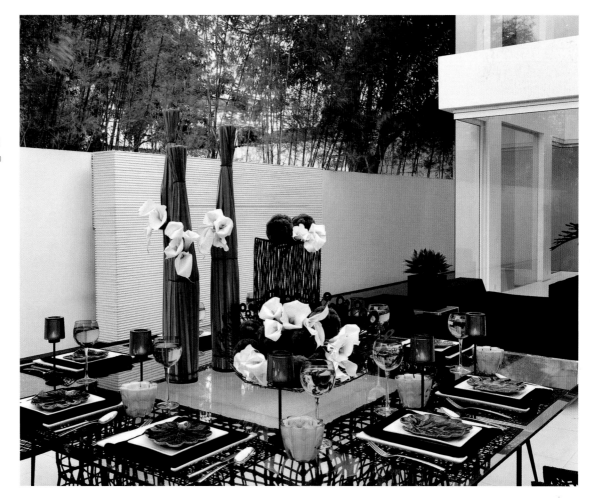

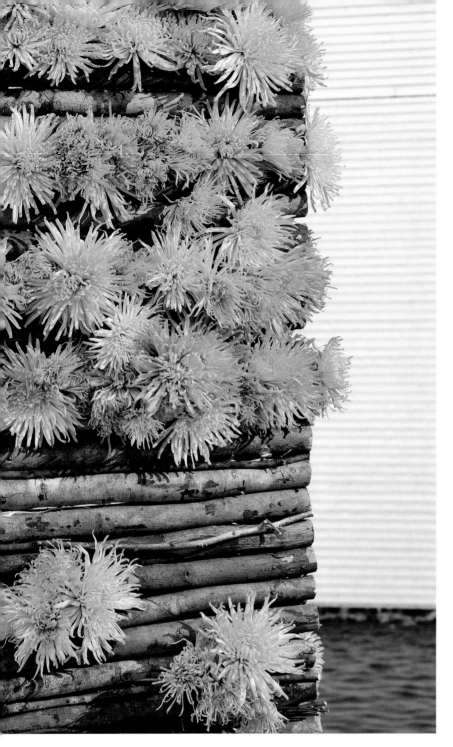

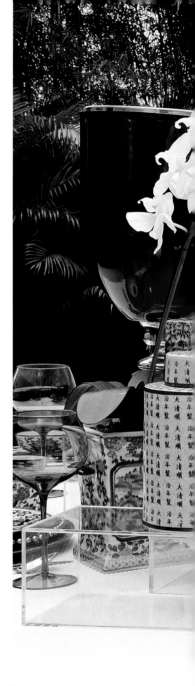

LEFT Brown wood and apple green spider chrysanthemums combine to infuse warm tropical color into a restrained setting.
RIGHT Cynthia's favorite table setting comprises Chinese blue and white artifacts collected during her Asian travels. Here she gathers them under an umbrella of pristine white phalaenopsis orchids.

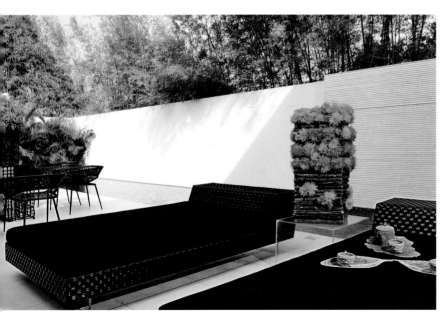

LEFT Matching lounge beds flank the floral installation. The green theme, perhaps inspired by the leafy green bamboo backdrop, is carried through to the leaf-inspired ceramic teaset.
OPPOSITE BELOW The perfect stage for chic dining—a platform projecting into the pool—framed by the canopy of Ed Ledesma's modernist architecture.

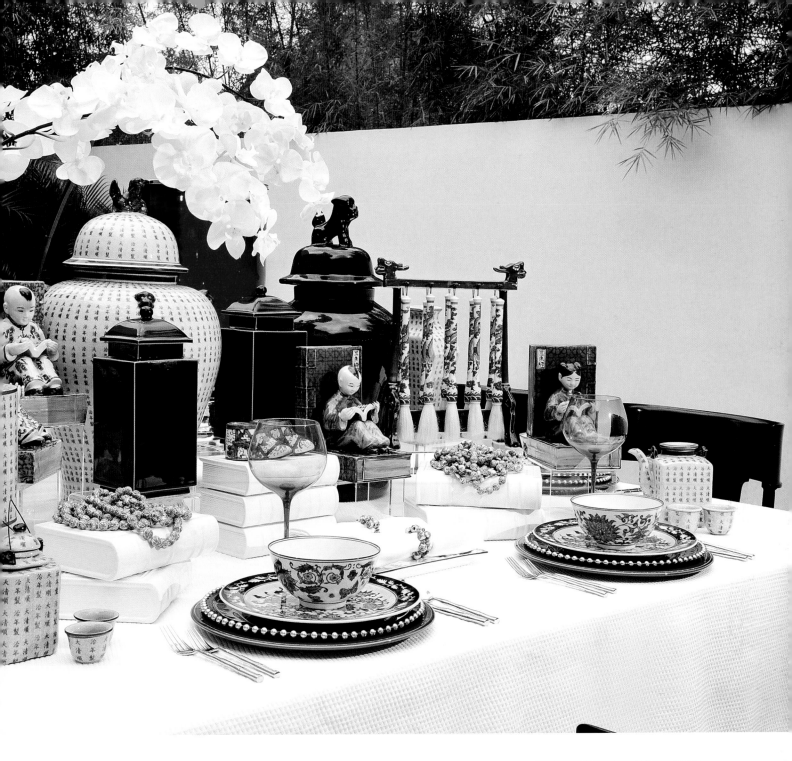

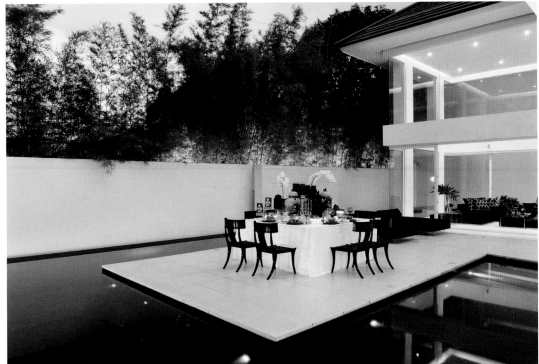

MOROCCAN MEMORIES
REKINDLED BY ROMANTIC BLOOMS

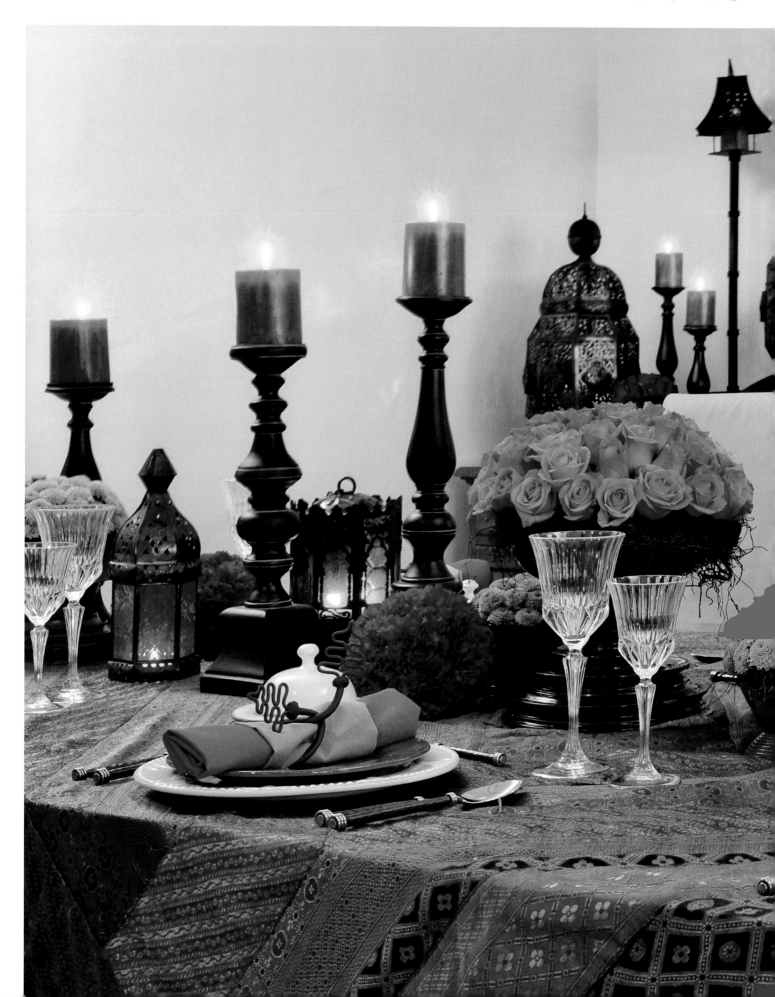

ARANETA-MALIK HOUSE   *Stylist* Leo Almeria   *Florist* Anton Barretto

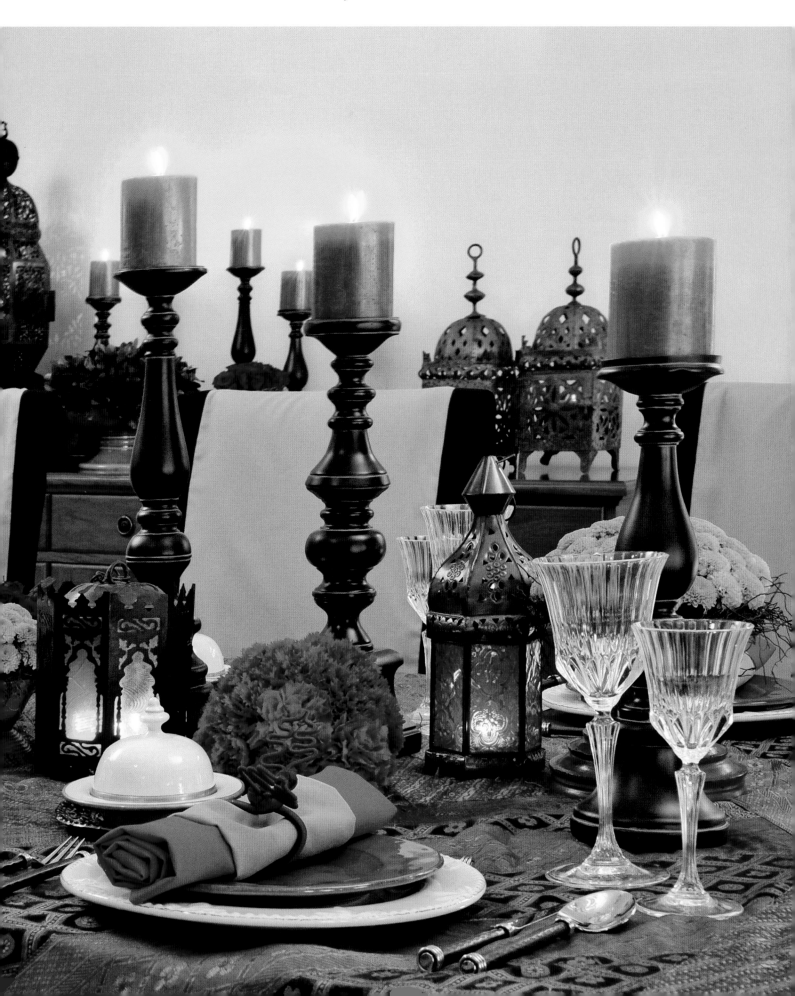

THE SPRAWLING two and a half story mansion of Sylvia Araneta-Malik stands on a prominent incline in a tree-filled gated community in Quezon City. The lot is around 800 sq m, with a floor area of 1000 sq m.

As interior decorator-stylist Leo Almeria observed, "Sylvia's home is perfect for year-round tropical entertaining. The high ceilings allow all-day cross-ventilation. Ground floor rooms open to the garden."

The home gleams with terracotta. Intricate patterned doorways from Morocco of blue and green spiced with contrasting reds and oranges gave instant clues to florist Anton Barretto and stylist Leo Almeria.

During an initial meeting, the subject of Morocco inspired fond recollect-ions from Sylvia and Anton of visits to the country. It was agreed to stage a Moroccan theme for an early afternoon to evening soiree, known in Manila as *merienda cena*.

The lady of the house enjoys these soirees. "My guests have the choice of dropping by early in the afternoon and leaving before dinner, while others who have had a long day come for an early dinner. It means we all get to retire fairly early in the evening."

For the reception area, Anton used a huge ball of red carnations floating in a waterless cylinder capped by a long-stemmed philodendron. "I like to contrast red with lime green mums for daytime arrangements," Anton said, "They give a bright, daytime welcome." Leo flanked Anton's florals with graphic circles of jade and tall spindle candleholders.

Leo decked out the playful swinging divan by the terrace with gold-flecked pillows and a smoking pipe for a decadent look. Anton completed the setting with an arrangement of cool blue and purple hydrangeas resting on a cloud of lime green mums.

RIGHT An octagonal wood-framed watercolor on a gold-hued wall suffuses the table setting with a rich, intimate glow.
BOTTOM LEFT Heirloom silver adds a regal air to a luncheon setting. A low bowl of purple vanda flanks patterned mint tea glasses.
PREVIOUS SPREAD Treasured memories of Moroccan mystique inspire an arrangement of metal lamps, red roses, red cockscomb, red-mounted candles and red table linen. Lime Malaysian mums provide a soothing contrast to the red.

"To enhance the Moroccan mood, I brought along my family's antique silver tea service from London and matched it with Moroccan tea glasses," said Anton "I also perched hurricane lamps on Moroccan tambourines to throw light on Sylvia's exquisite plates and flatware." Blue cups and deep celadon plates pick up the tones of the hydrangeas. Anton's antique rug from the Beluch tribe in Afghanistan, placed under the teaset, made the composition perfect," Leo adds.

As the sun set, the red candles were lit and the dining room became fiery with mystique. An Indian patchwork throw served as a tablecloth accented with Moroccan pierced metal lan-terns. "I used lacquered Burmese food containers to hold the flowers, and again red carnation balls, orange roses and green button mums. With a theme, it's all right to repeat flower colors as you can always play with lighting," summed up Anton.

Leo concluded, "Pre-production is key. Look around your or your host's home first, and most likely you'll find enough artifacts and ideas to build up a theme successfully."

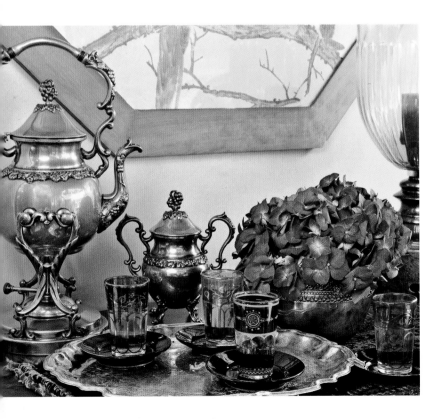

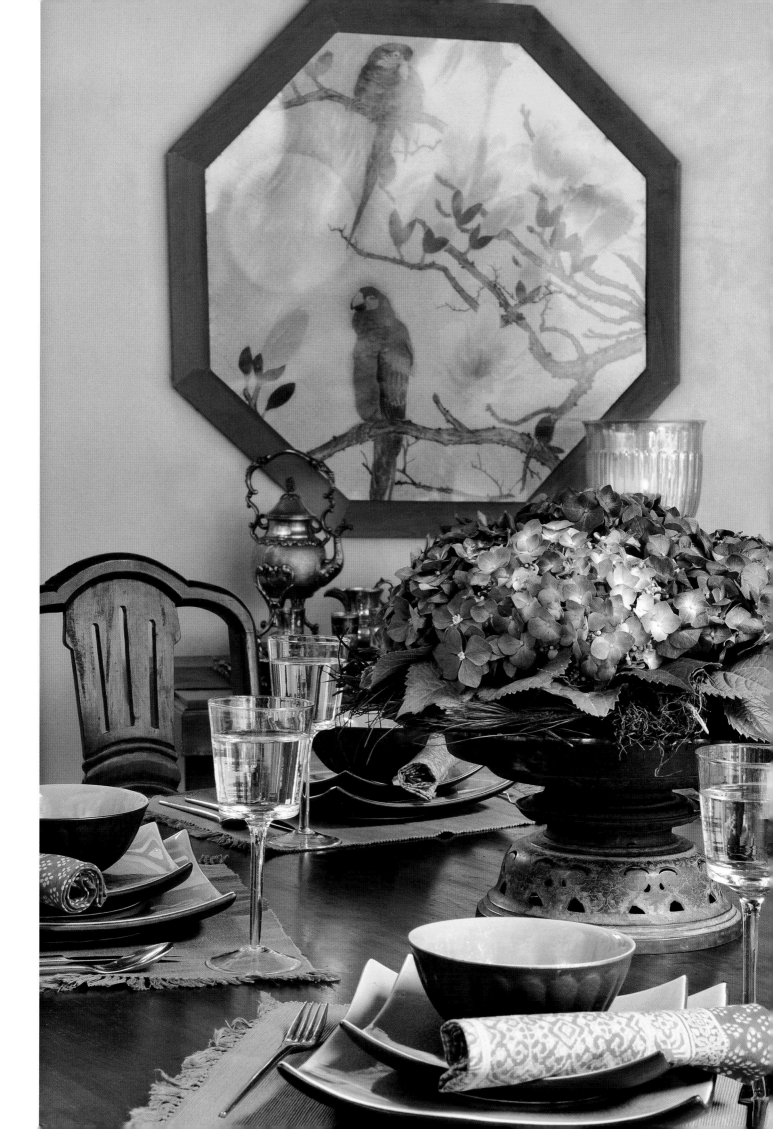

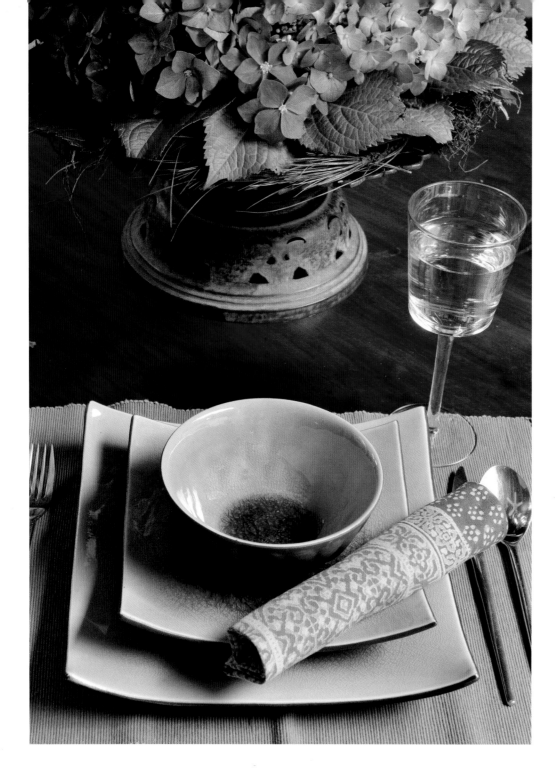

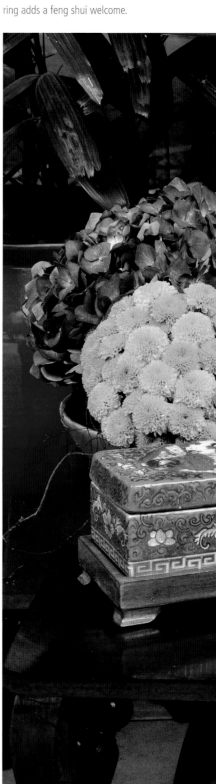

LEFT A lush crown of blue and purple hydrangeas emerging from an old brass pedestal tray catches the colors of the owner's stacked celadon ombré plates and mauve tablemats.

RIGHT A glass-topped neo-Chinese table holds balls of lime and red mums. Leo Almeria's mounted jade prosperity ring adds a feng shui welcome.

RIGHT A Moroccan lamp casts a warm glow on clusters of lime button mums and red roses, their colors echoed in the Indian patchwork tablecloth, the napkins and unusual Moroccan rings, and the Burmese lacquer food stands.

FAR RIGHT A swinging daybed facing the garden, strewn with gold-stamped cushions, and a side table bearing a cloisonné casket, bone pipe and mug of mint tea, invite a lazy lounge or nap.

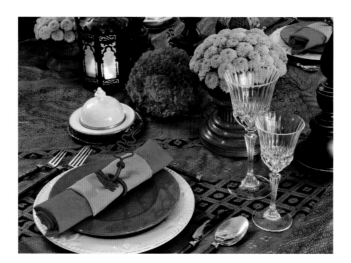

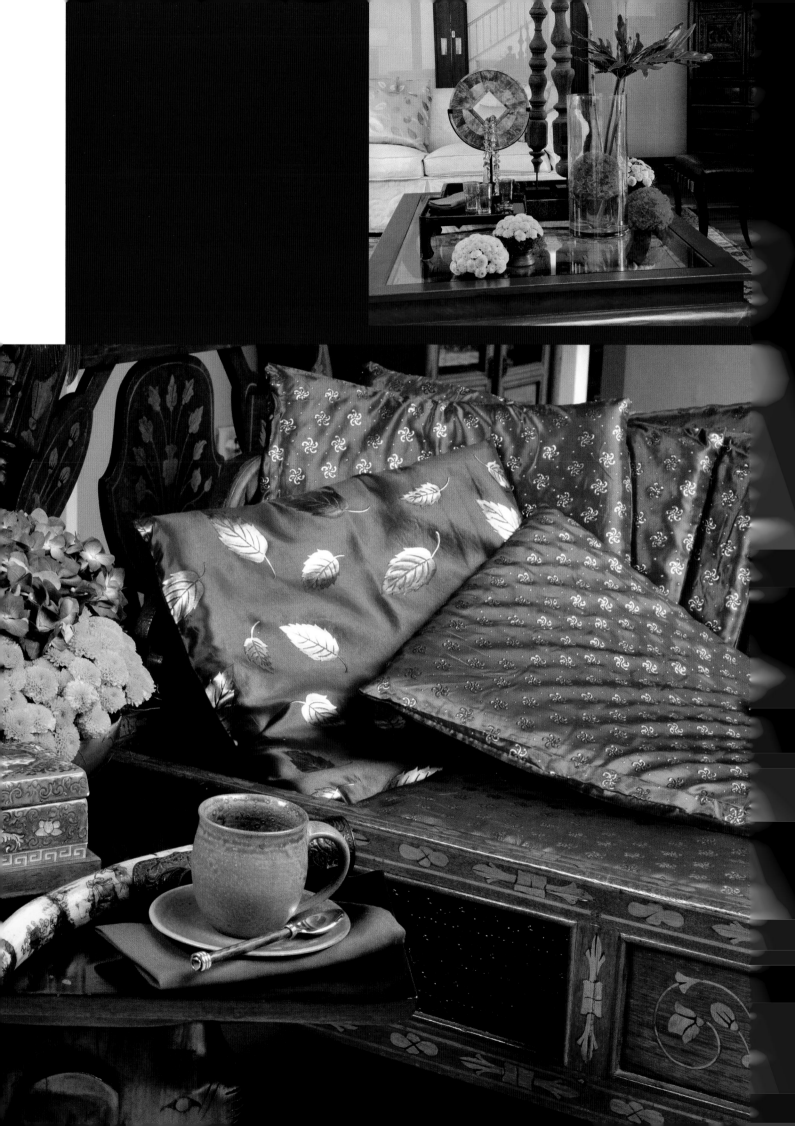

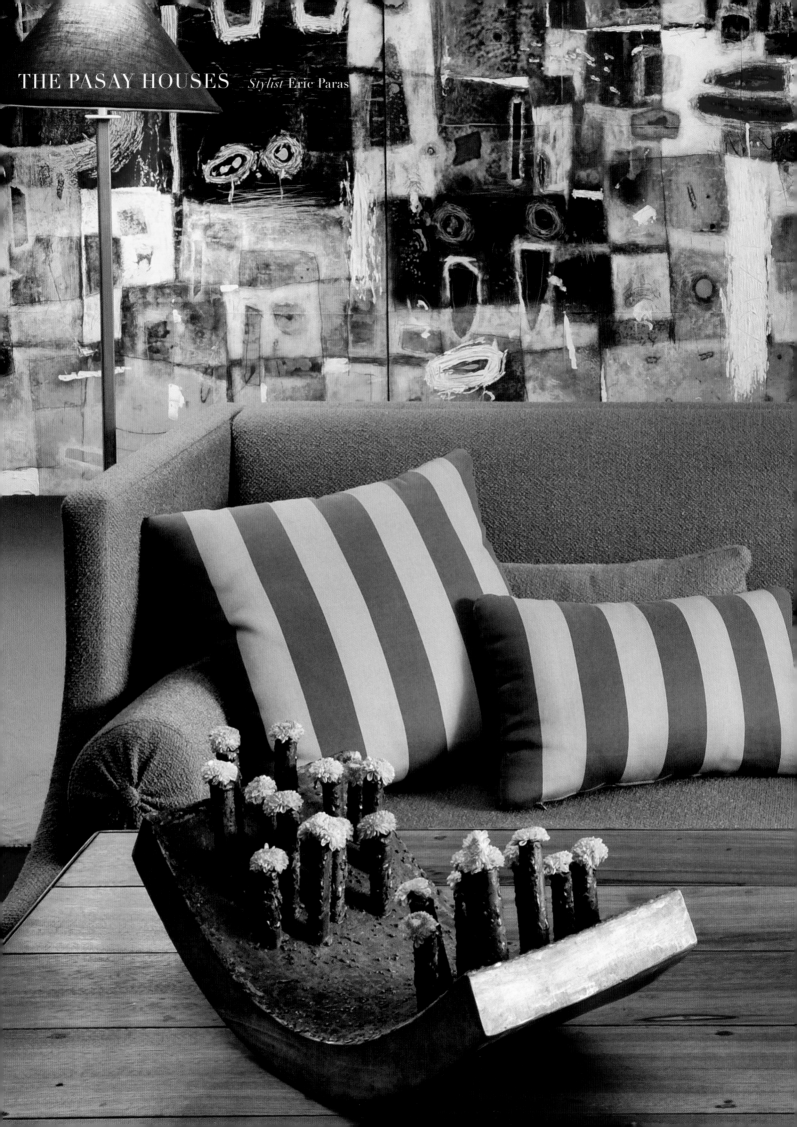

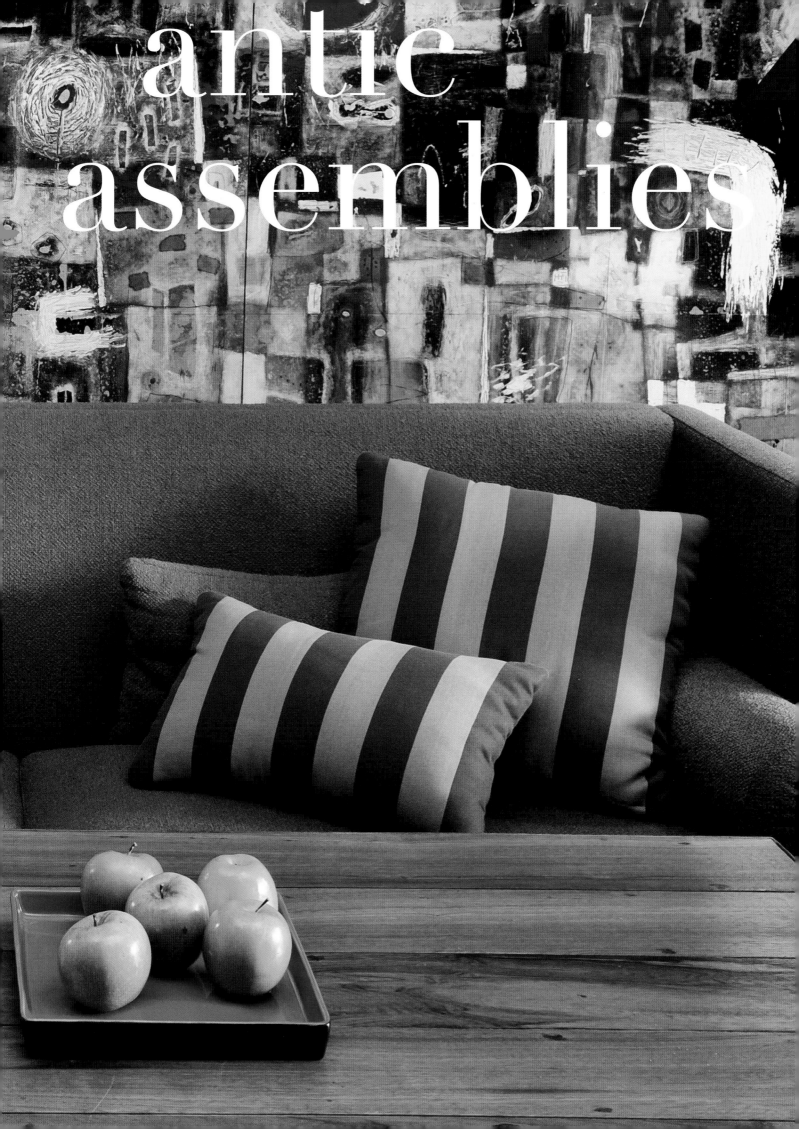

antic
assemblies

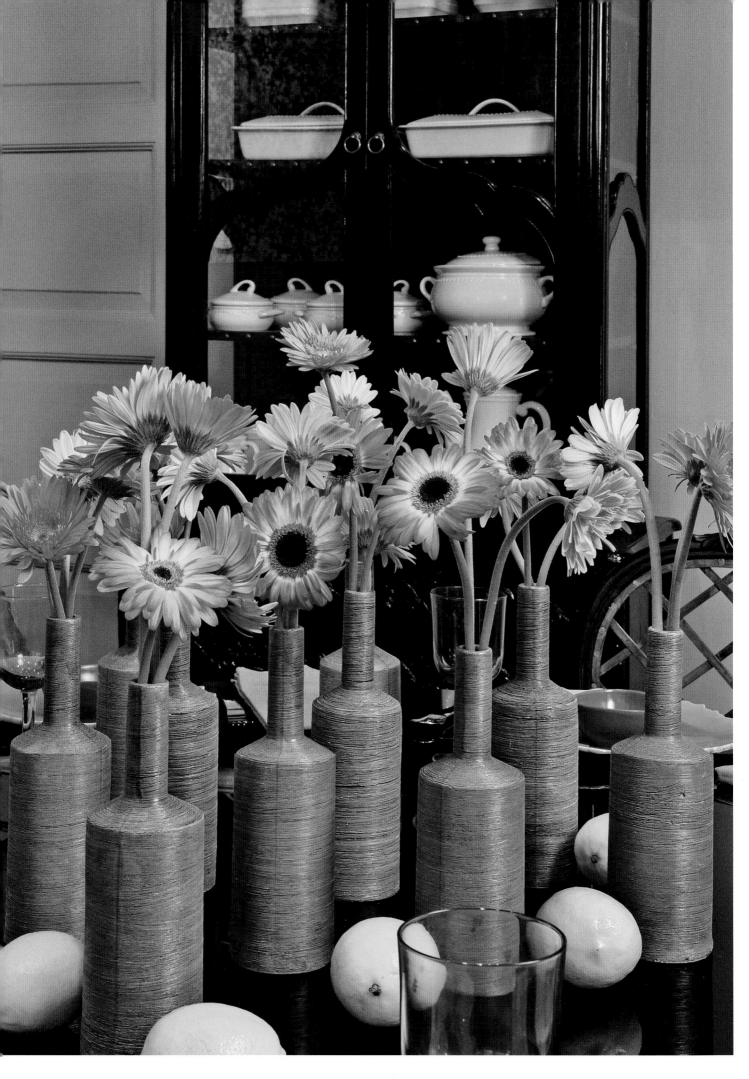

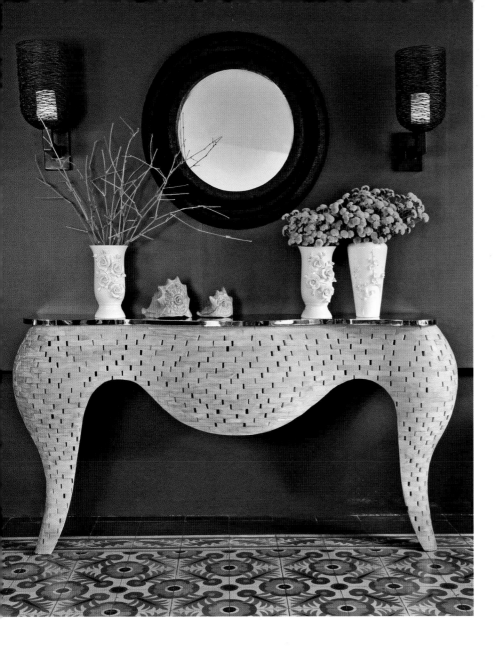

proclaims. Other like-minded artists have snapped up long leases for the old Pasay houses. They hold joint exhibitions of furniture and accessories. They also party a lot together!

Eric Paras's mantra is: "The shell of a house doesn't have to lock you into an interior theme or style. How you mix or assemble your stuff is what counts most. Effect is the name of the game!"

He sometimes travels with his clients, bringing back a trove of accessories, from pots and plates and modern dining implements to funky old chandeliers and exotic lamps.

For this book, Eric set up character scenes in his showrooms. Imagine dining off a tablecloth made from acrylic carpet grass accompanied by steel herons perched in between long-necked vases styled with sunflowers. Or lounging on a steel blue couch beside a table displaying pink blossoms sprouting out of ceramic funnels next to a tableau of green apples on a red lacquer tray.

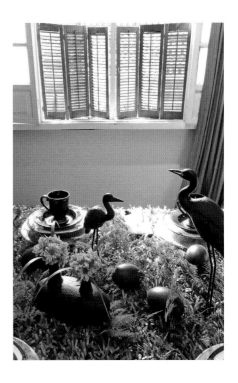

LEFT Hot-colored gerberas sprout from a cluster of ceramic bud vases from China. Eric did this creative table setting in one of the dining areas in his three A11 showrooms. Scattered lemons add citrus accents.
ABOVE The dramatic contrast of Eric's design of Passad Inc.'s curvy console in recycled, bleached gmelina wood against a buffed dark wall and black wall mountings is given a further injection of contrast with tufted green Malaysian mums and spindly twigs in white vases with high-relief roses.
RIGHT Herons perched on a unique table cover of fake carpet grass scattered with real green ferns, smooth stones and golden gerbera accents make a stimulating lunch setting.
PREVIOUS SPREAD A dazzling mural by Lexygius Calip is muted by a cool steel blue couch with striped cushions. On the table, a rocking sculpture, another of Eric's ceramic creations, holds white-dotted pink mums, locally known as *puto-puto*.

ALONG MANILA BAY is a city called Pasay where there is a one-hectare enclave known since the 1950s as the "Chinese compound." Today, it has become an art and craft lair and design community. Here maverick designer Eric Paras holds court in four of the fourteen look-alike two-story houses he has leased.

Eric uses one of the 1950s houses as his home and the other three as his showrooms, installing within mock-ups of settings that are brimming with style, character and unusual ideas. "I am a design consultant for several furniture export companies in Southeast Asia and Europe. This gives me a head start on what's hot for the next season and year, both in America and Europe," he

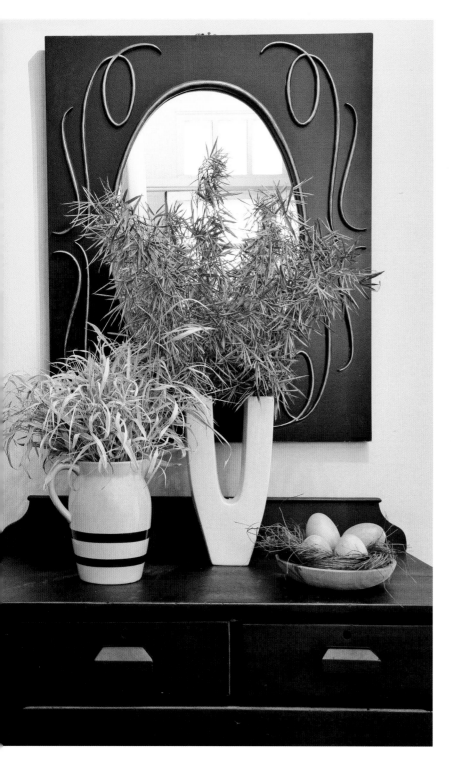

Applying the same philosophy to floral arrangements as to interior decoration, Eric shows us that one can be playful, surreal, cool and hip with flowers.

Demonstrating clever ideas for floral styling, he explains, "Flower accents start with the choice of unusual vessels—which can be repeated in nice rows or in groupings or can be massed together for optimum effect…. Flowers can be inserted in common bottles or in interesting sculptural pieces. They can also be submerged in water or used in waterless submersibles. The sky is the limit when it comes to containers."

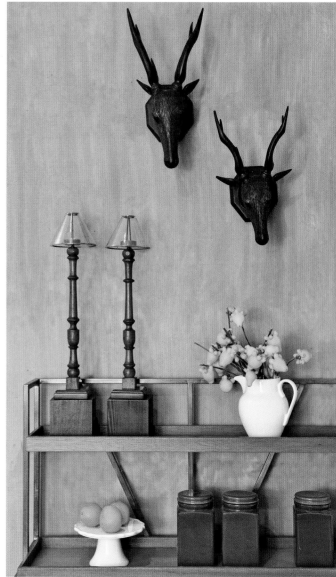

ABOVE Dry arrangements can break the monotony of having fresh flowers, especially when none are available. A basket of golden pears and mangos on a nest of twirled fine vines brings out the deep chocolate tones of the mirror frame and console.

RIGHT Mickey Mouse fruits, an inedible variety of eggplant, arranged in a simple jug, bring comic relief to a display of house-hold accessories in one of Eric's showrooms.

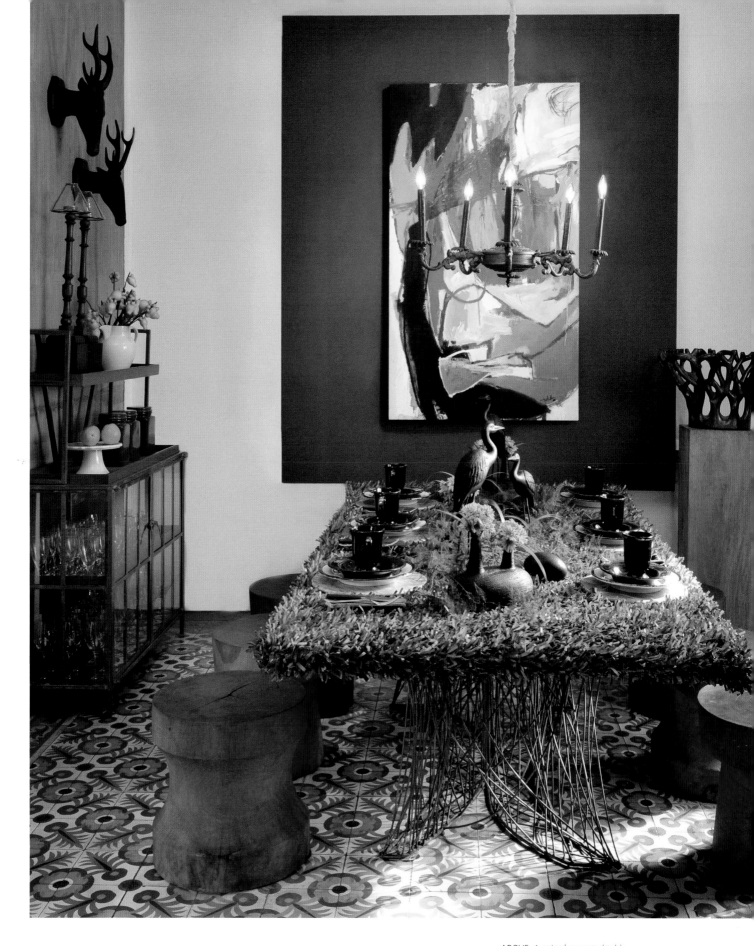

ABOVE A spired mounted table
of fake grass, metal herons and
rounded wood stump stools from
Eric's workshop spell high drama.
The painting by Tosha Albor is
lit by a reincarnated chandelier
spotted in a junk shop.

antic assemblies

"How you mix or assemble your stuff is what counts most. Effect is the name of the game!" beams Eric Paras.

BELOW Twin vases of alstroemeria hold center court in a receiving room filled with period-style seating. The Machuca floor tile pattern is the only indication that this home was built in the 1950s.

RIGHT An Alan Cosio canvas of blossom-like splatters adds to the hip and cool luxury feel, signaled by a caramel banquette and updated cane dining chairs with metal trellised backing.

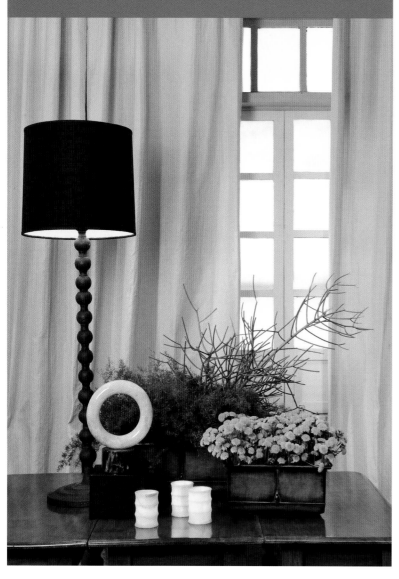

ABOVE A mounted ring by sculptor Impy Pilapil glows against a mass of greens and spicky twigs behind green Malaysian mums. Hollowed Romblon marble candleholders add more glow.

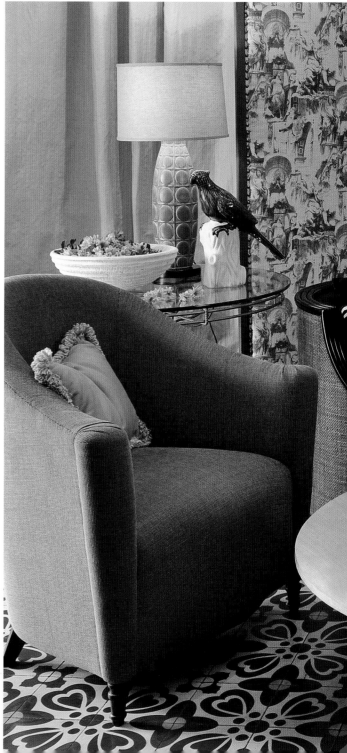

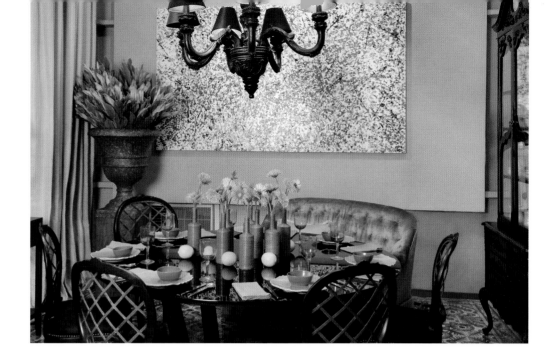

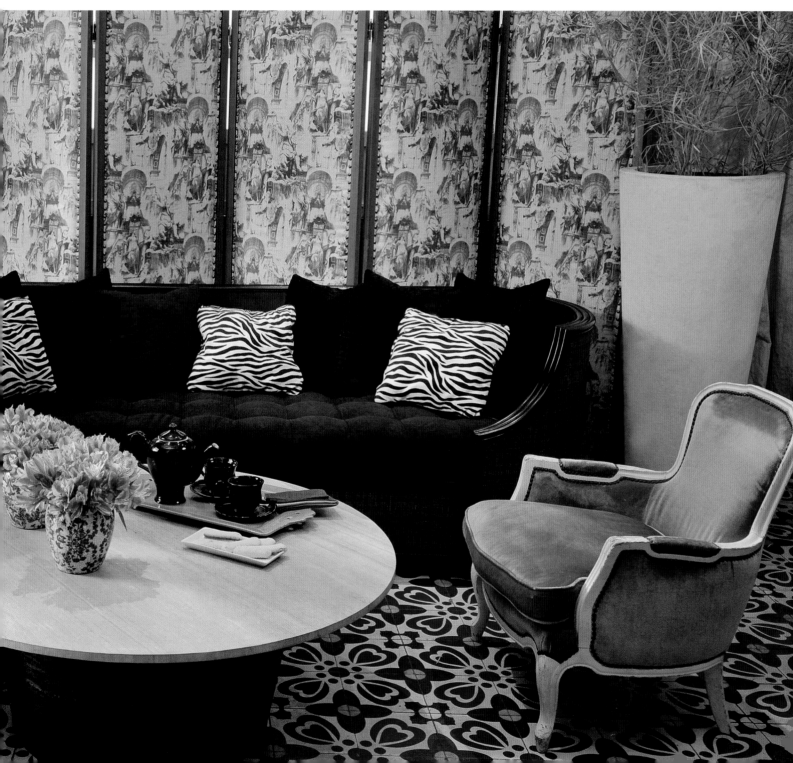

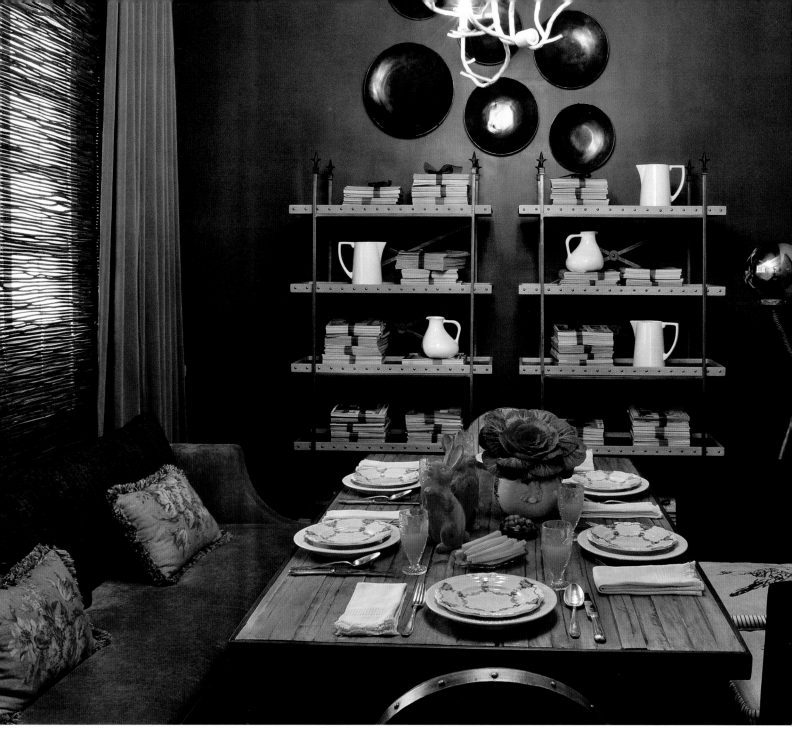

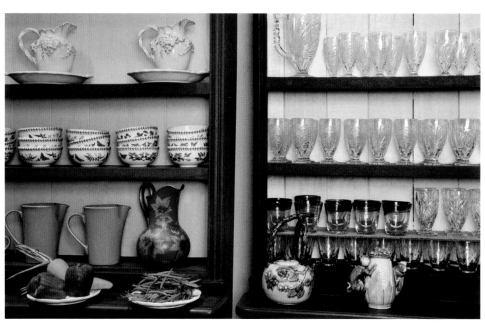

ABOVE Eric's three showrooms double up as contemporary dining rooms. A stunning pink cabbage rose in the midst of carved wood rabbits and carrot slices playfully underscores the Year of the Rabbit theme. Most of the tableware comes from China.

RIGHT Star attractions in Eric's kitchenware display are two teapots with high-relief florals and playful green monkeys. His displays are his stock rooms.

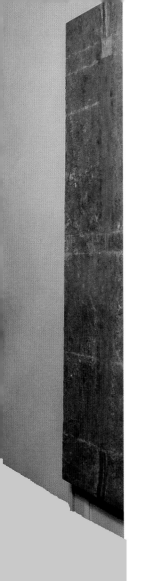

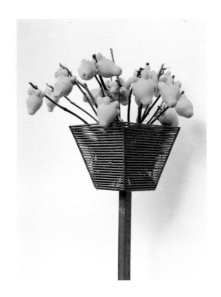

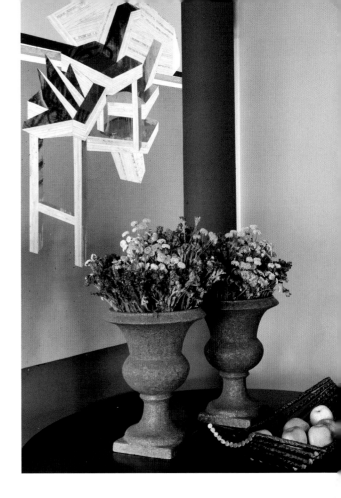

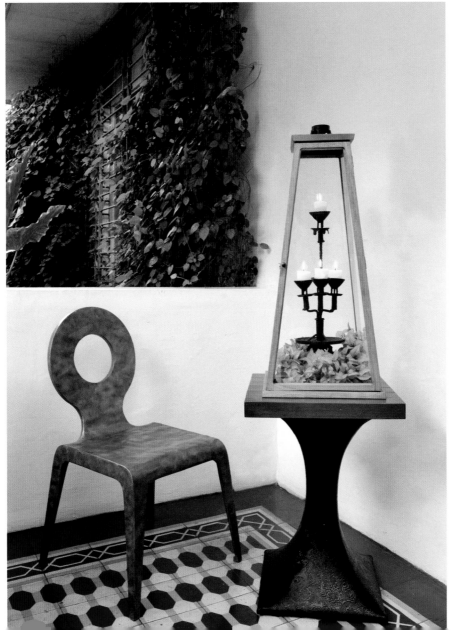

ABOVE Molded rice husk vessels hold masses of purple statice and pink and white centered mums or *puto-puto*.

ABOVE LEFT Comical Mickey Mouse fruits perch up high in a standing metal plant box.

LEFT An opened-framed obelisk foyer lamp housing a two-tiered candleholder with charming pink bougainvillea blossoms clustered at the base is paired with a donut-backed chair of cut sheet metal designed by Eric Paras.

antic assemblies

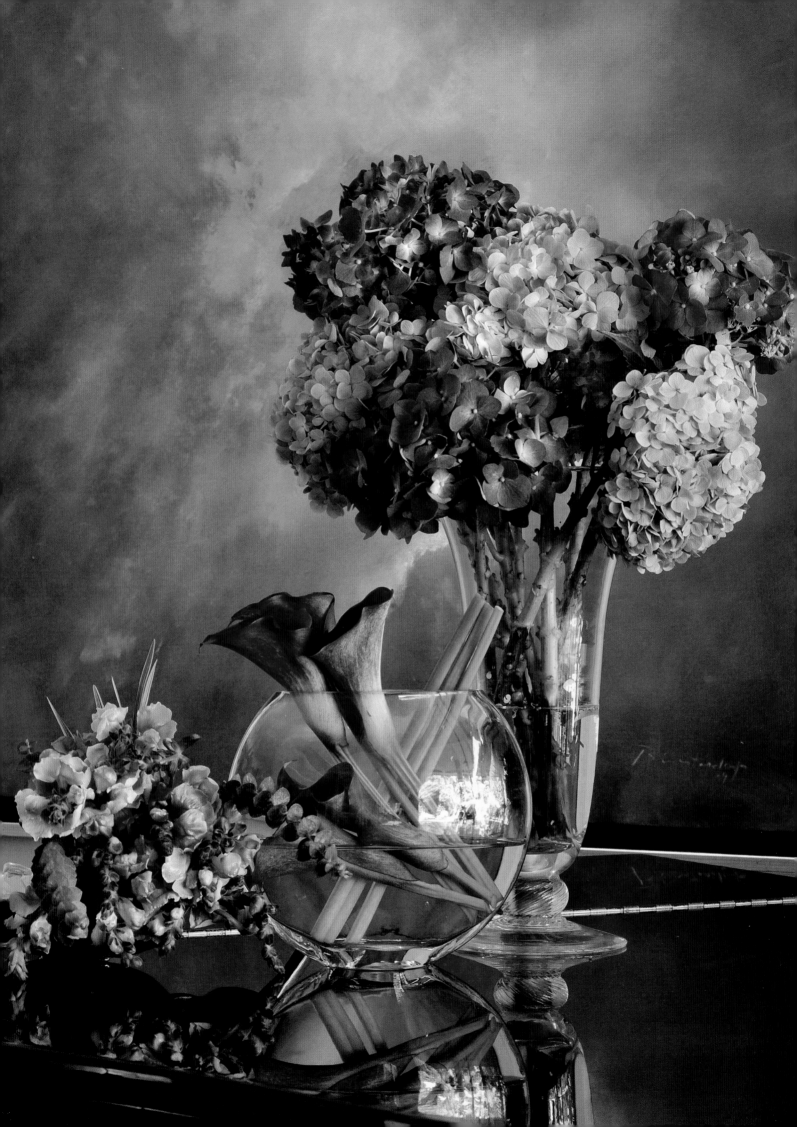

a gentle way with *flowers*

FINE ART PHOTOGRAPHER Denise Weldon is a natural artist playing with natural light, who constantly seeks out nuance and translucence with her inner eye. Intuitively, she responds to light, playing upon her favorite subjects—flora, fauna and landscapes. The photographer extends her artistry to floral design and creative table settings. She is famous among friends for styling beautifully fresh tablescapes.

"I just love going to the flower markets to see what blooms are available," she says, as she nudges a calla lily into an Art Deco crystal glass. "Inspiration starts from an initial walk through the market and the anticipation of what's to come. In the late of night, the culling begins. I get excited at the sight of things odd but beautiful, as well as the commonplace. The silhouettes and colors of the flowers dictate the design direction. I ask myself, 'How can I do something different? What complements what? What creates contrasts?' The whole process is very intuitive and fun. It's like painting with flowers!"

Her residence is a simple low-slung bungalow in Makati, with expansive white couches accented with bright colored soft furnishings, inlaid wooden cabinets and cane-woven chairs. An intriguing mix of contemporary art on the walls is matched by an eclectic display of floral arrangements.

For a formal dinner beneath a large graphic black painting by artist Arturo Luz, Denise sets a white-linened table with fine china and silverware. Along the center of the table is an eye-catching arrangement of exotic pink and green anthuriums, green chrysanthemums and azucena amid tussled layers of foliage.

A masterful selection of vases and other unusual containers complement Denise's choice of flowers. The simplicity of stems in water and glass is shown in the trio of arrangements—hydrangeas, calla lilies, snap dragons and eucalyptus leaves—poised artfully on the piano in front of a fiery cloudscape by Besty Westendorp. Massive purple cabbage roses and Casablanca lilies stand regally in front of a quiet photograph by Denise. In a corner, white roses, alstroemeria, green lantern blossoms and green spider chrysanthemums make a fanciful still life before a paper screen by artist friend Paola Dindo.

Where did she learn her gentle way with flowers? Denise reveals that her mother, Ditas Calero, had worked with the late great Filipino florist Ronnie Laing in the 1950s. Her mother's floral experience has clearly entered Denise's artistic soul.

LEFT Three shades of hydrangea, burgundy calla lilies, pink snap dragons and eucalyptus leaves—the stems and leaves visible in versatile glass containers—make a charming display on the piano in front of a fiery painting by Betsy Westendorp.

RIGHT Denise Weldon's comfortable home *sala* is a picture of
modern chic—with a hint of a
Mandarin accent.

BELOW Flowers can be casually
romantic, as in this corner "still
life" composed of pale alstroemerias, white roses, green lantern
pods and green spider chrysanthemums set against a paper
screen by artist friend Paola Dindo.

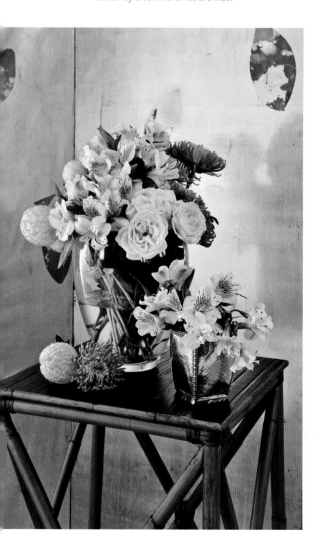

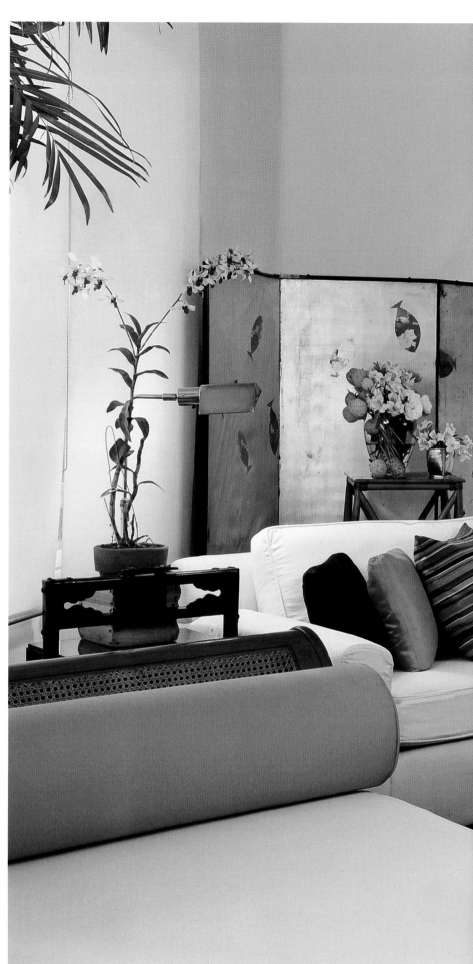

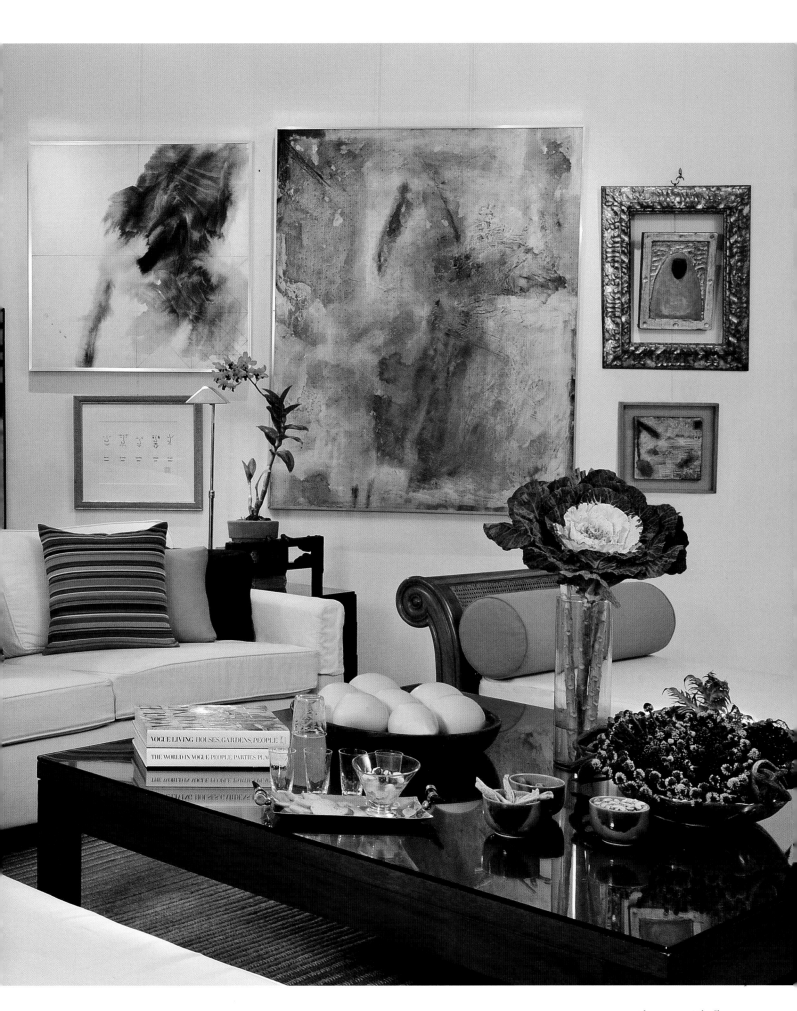

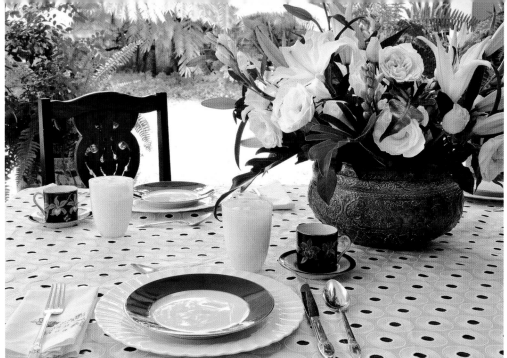

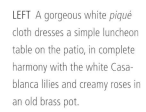

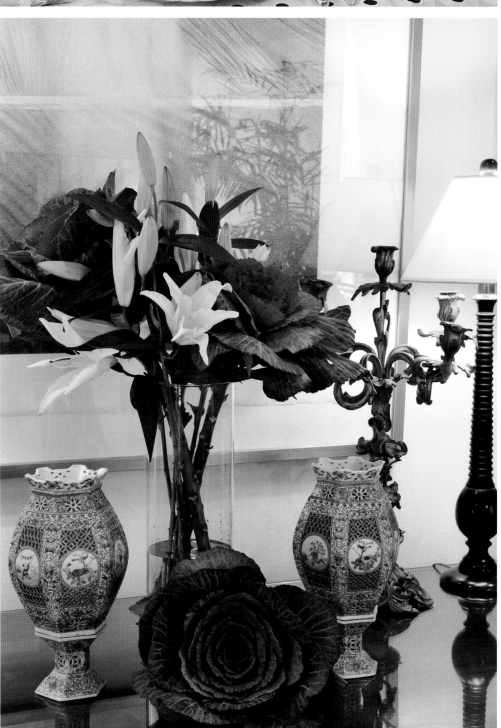

LEFT A gorgeous white *piqué* cloth dresses a simple luncheon table on the patio, in complete harmony with the white Casablanca lilies and creamy roses in an old brass pot.

RIGHT Pink anthuriums are loveliest dancing among the ferns and green spider chrysanthemums of the centerpiece, and echoed on the dinner plates.

LEFT The dynamic form and violet centers of giant cabbage roses, juxtaposed with pure white Casablanca lilies, provide an exotic frame to matching Oriental cloisonné jarlets.

FAR RIGHT Bright-hued clusters of roses from the Baguio highlands light up a trio of water vessels.

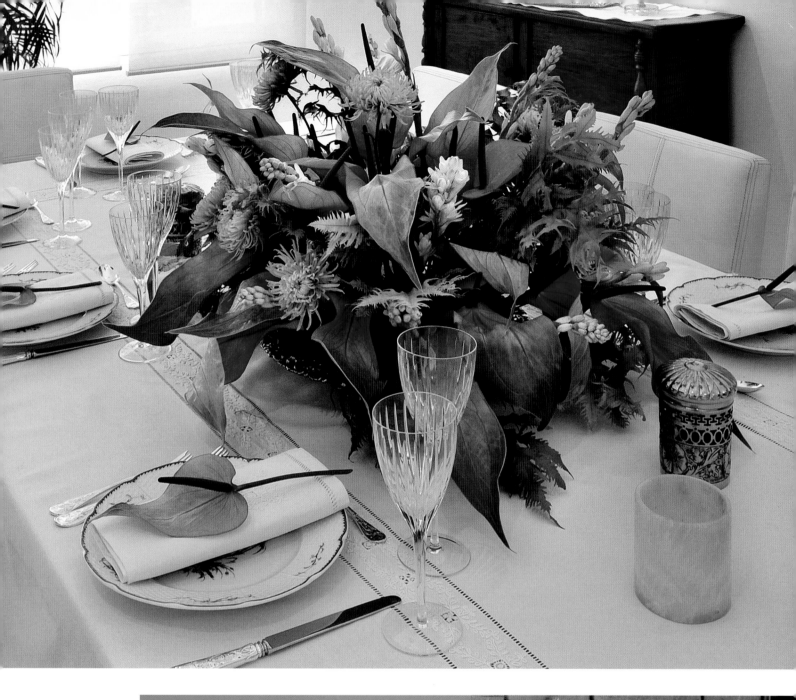

Photographer Denise Weldon extends her artistry to floral design and creative table settings. "The whole process is very intuitive and fun. It's like painting with flowers!"

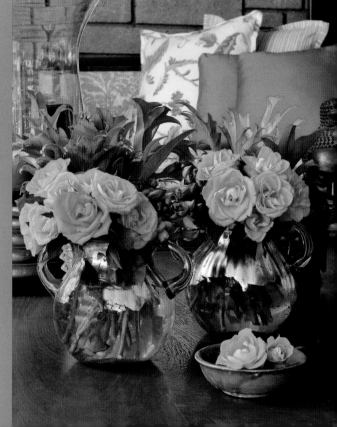

homecoming
dinner party

FLOIRENDO CONDO HOUSE *Florist* Nathaniel Aranda

"YOUR TIMING IS PERFECT! We'll do a welcome dinner setting for my daughter who's arriving from London," exclaims hostess Margarita Moran Floirendo, a radiant former Miss Universe, who lives in the Essensa condo designed by I. M. Pei, in the Global City, Fort Bonifacio.

Measuring some 290 sq m, the apartment curves graciously into the living room facing the dining room. "I manage to fit in eight people comfortably. Otherwise, I entertain elsewhere," says Margarita.

Florist Nathaniel Aranda, tasked with the floral arrangements for the dinner party, is a relative newcomer to the business, but not to the intuitive art of styling flowers. Until recently, his "aesthetic" role in the three ultra-chic restaurants he co-manages has been to style the ambience of each venue with tasteful floral arrangements and subtle lighting.

He says, "For the centerpiece, I opted for a romantic tower below the modern glass chandelier by Ramon Orlina." The carousel-like floral installation contains traditional white roses, Casablanca lilies, white cymbidium and dendrobium orchids, along with pale green succulents as an accent. This is anchored with a tabletop installation of pink cymbidium orchids, burnt orange roses, blood red cockscomb and succulents."

Margarita happily brought out her exquisite collection of china and flatware, mostly purchased in England, saying, "It's a great occasion, what with my daughter graduating from university in London! So I worked with Nathaniel on the fine details of my Welcome Home table setting. We used Riedel wine glasses and Sheffield bone china plates, Baccarat candleholders, my favorite chargers and these amazing fish knives. They are actually English antiques with ivory handles. The fish sets go very well with my Christofle cutlery. It took me years to acquire them, set by set. The center wall painting is by Ben Cab, the National Artist. Over the console is a pastoral scene by Fernando Amorsolo, the Filipino classicist."

The living room area features a curvaceous modern sofa upholstered in white Jim Thompson silk with a center table for coffee or champagne service. "I like to mix and match my champagne flutes among the guests. The modern Bohemian blown glass flutes that I've collected provide great contrast to the classic Limoges."

Floral stylist Nathaniel Aranda closes with a tip: "Beyond asking for the client's preferences, you can mix colorful flowers and add native berries, vines and twine. The effect is relaxing, yet dramatic, which is what most hostesses aim for."

RIGHT A floral carousel anchored on a pedestal, with English ivy swirling down to meet a spread of fiery roses, Philippine fire orchids, rose cactus and jungle vines, forms a highly unusual counterpoint to the refined tableware by Limoges, ivory-handled silverware and Baccarat lamps.

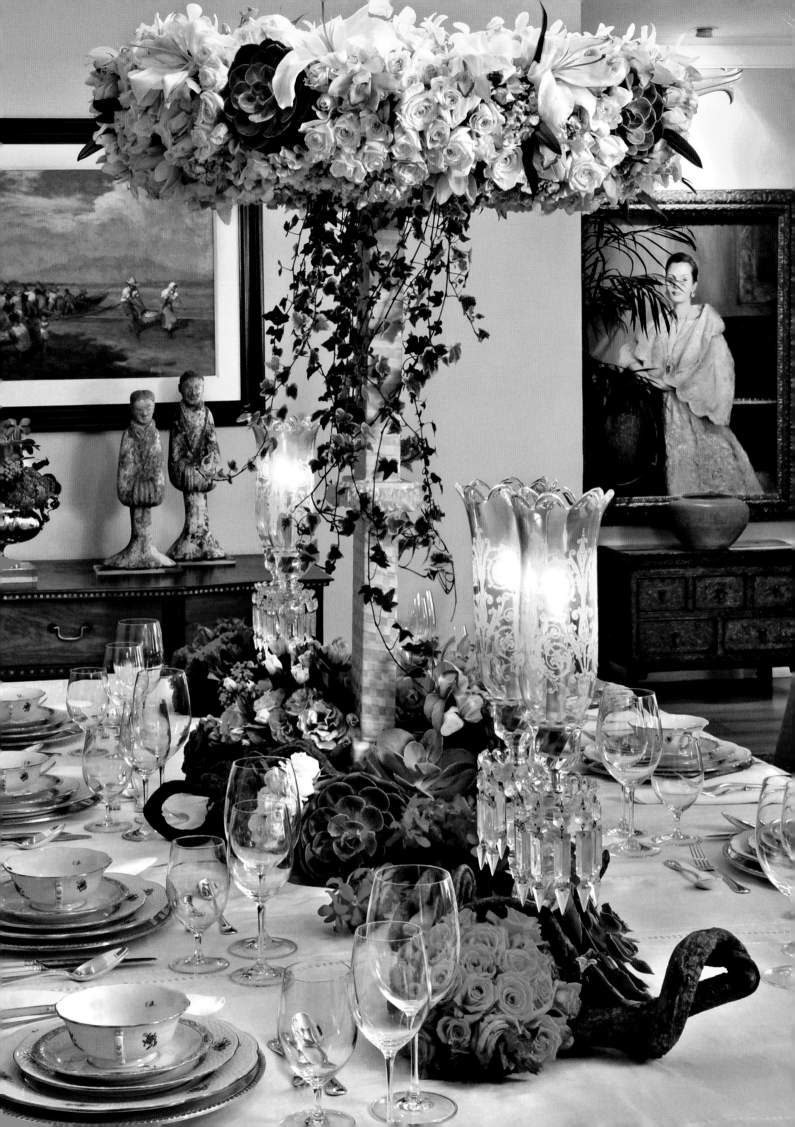

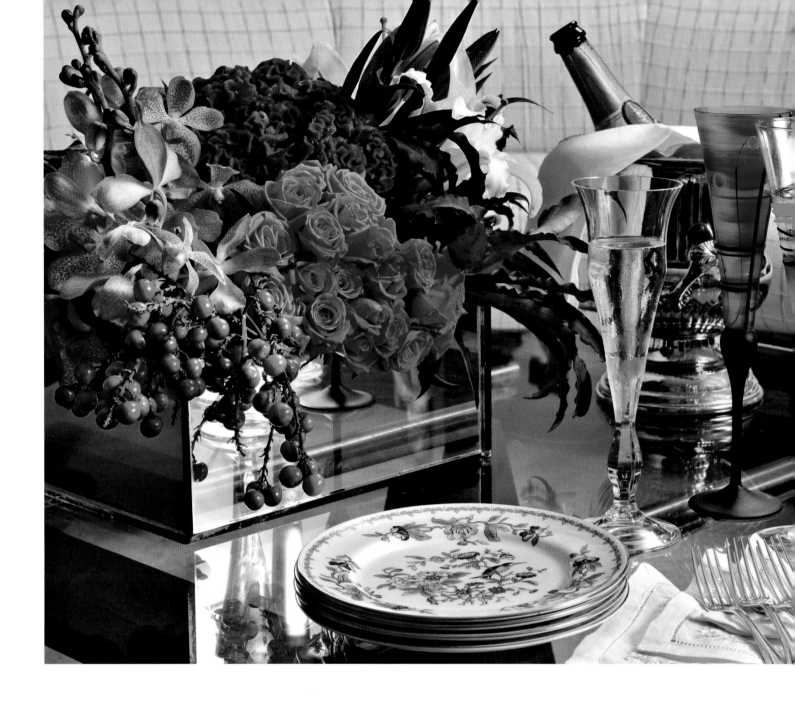
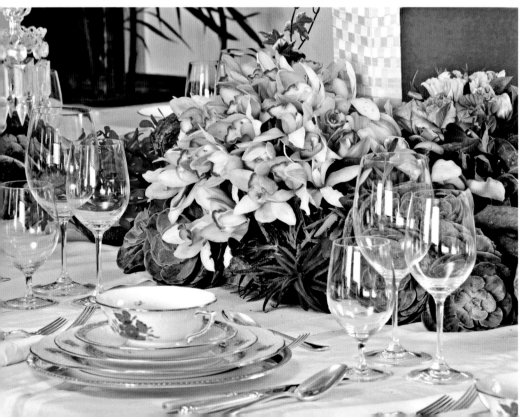
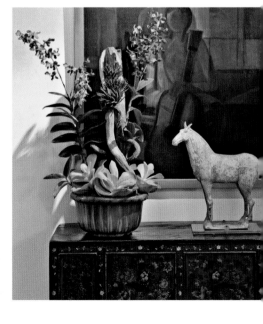

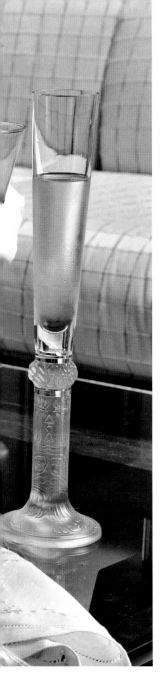

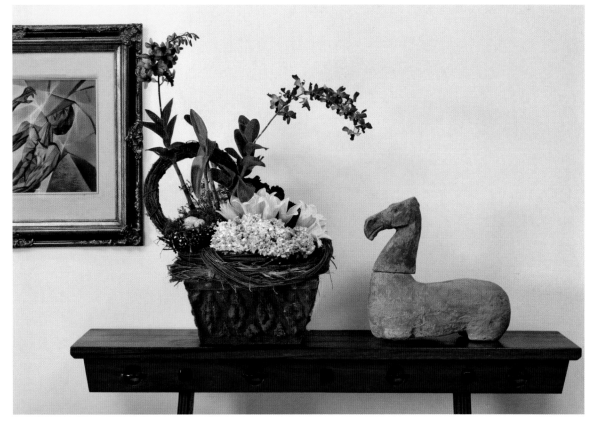

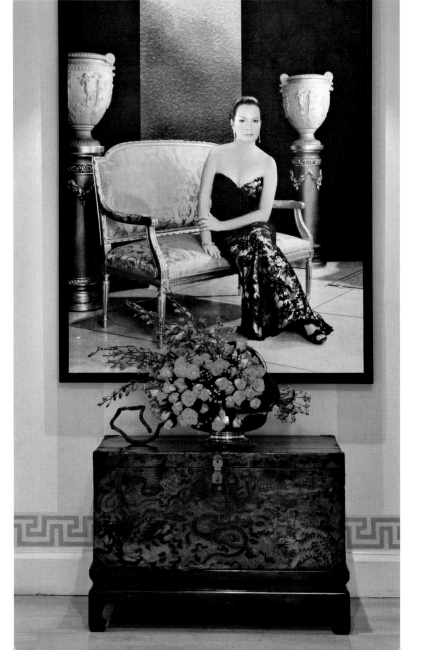

ABOVE A swirl of jungle vines supporting an egg-filled mossy bird's nest, soaring dendrobiums and a bed of alstroemerias and white mums echoes the shape of the watchful terracotta horse on the fine hardwood console.
LEFT Placed on an exquisite Chinese lacquered chest, a voluptuous arrangement of red roses and blue dendrobiums in a silver bowl, with a vine accent below, draws the eye straight to Margarita's stylish portrait.

OPPOSITE ABOVE Pink vandas, red berries, red cockscombs and white Casablanca lilies for color relief, held by cordyline leaves, blend beautifully with colorful Bohemian flutes and classic Limoges floral plates.
OPPOSITE BELOW LEFT Pink cymbidiums spill over rose cactus while pink roses and yellow statice add richness to the lush centerpiece composition.
OPPOSITE BELOW RIGHT A foyer greeting of dendrobiums interlaced with driftwood and cool succulents at the base.

alfresco garden party

SET HIGH ON TAGAYTAY RIDGE, just south of Manila, Moon Garden is a rustic, romantic hideaway filled with flowers, lotus ponds, dining "islands," flowered garden rooms and open-sided thatched-roof Ifugao-style dwellings. It is a unique venue from which to view the majestic Taal volcanic island surrounded by a freshwater lake. When decorated for dreamy moonlight weddings and other events, Moon Garden more than lives up to its evocative name.

Moon Garden was the perfect venue for a trio of plant lovers to converge and create rustic table settings under the moon. Among them was Emily Campos, a crafts designer and exporter who created ultra-organic tables with bamboo, banana trunks and vegetables; Belgian chemist Peter Geertz, avid gardener and inspired creator of the Moon Garden; and Ely Bautista, a gardener-trader who traveled from his flowered hillside home in Laguna. All three plant lovers did installations to demonstrate how fresh flowers plucked from the garden can be easily fashioned into stunning alfresco table settings.

In the entry courtyard, a long pergola built from tree trunks and draped with a dazzling cascade of orange-yellow thunbergia provided a cosy setting for an evening dinner party. Balancing the intense colors of the thunbergia, Ely combined deep purple table linens with blossoms of yellow, orange and pink and bunches of green berries. Elevated bowls of white blossoms provided color relief.

Emily used a section of a banana tree trunk to start her installation for a luncheon on a rustic table surrounded by billowing white muslin curtains to reduce the midday glare. "Vegetables are just as colorful as flowers," she says. "Their shapes are intriguing, humorous and sensual. I like to use banana leaves as placemats."

Peter suggests, "Take a long look at the garden. The colors will emerge and you can make your design plan easily. For table- and glassware, our malls have amazing reproductions of designer goods. Combined with beautiful fresh flowers, everything can look grand."

RIGHT Moon Garden's low-hanging lamps match Emily's rustic bamboo vases filled with clusters of charming China hat flowers. A pedestal vase filled with orange bromeliads against an ochre wall continues the color theme.

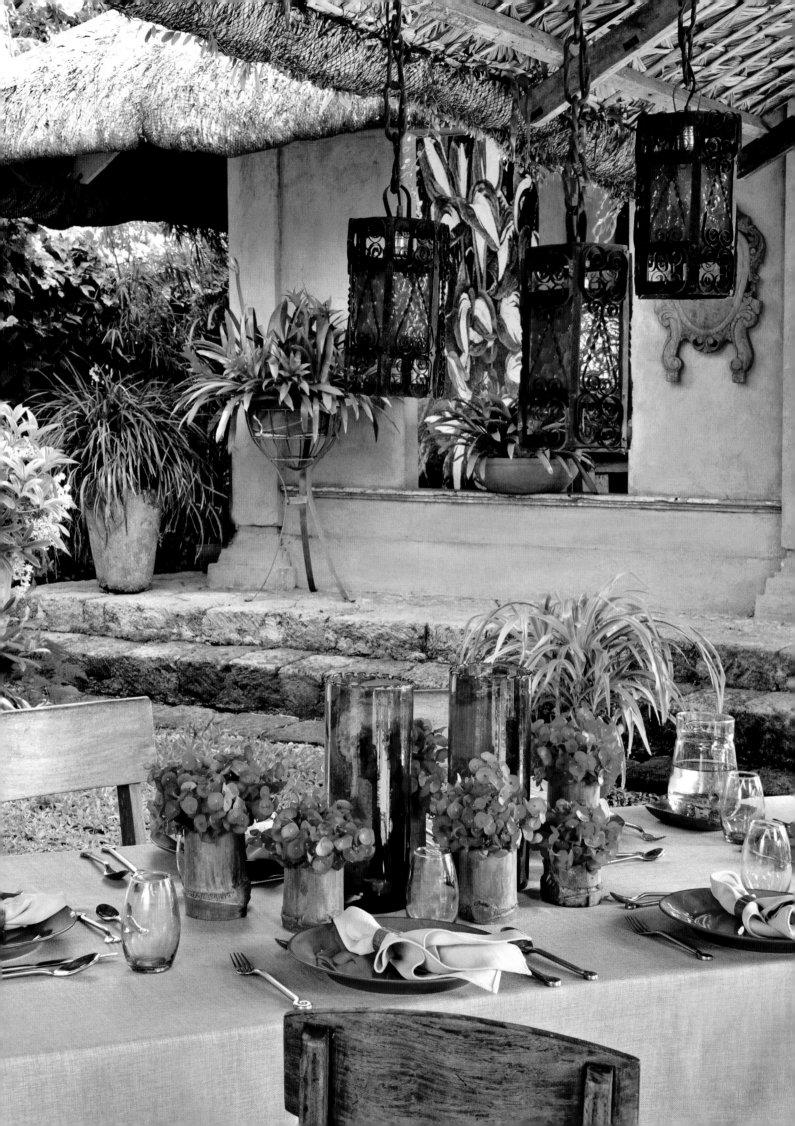

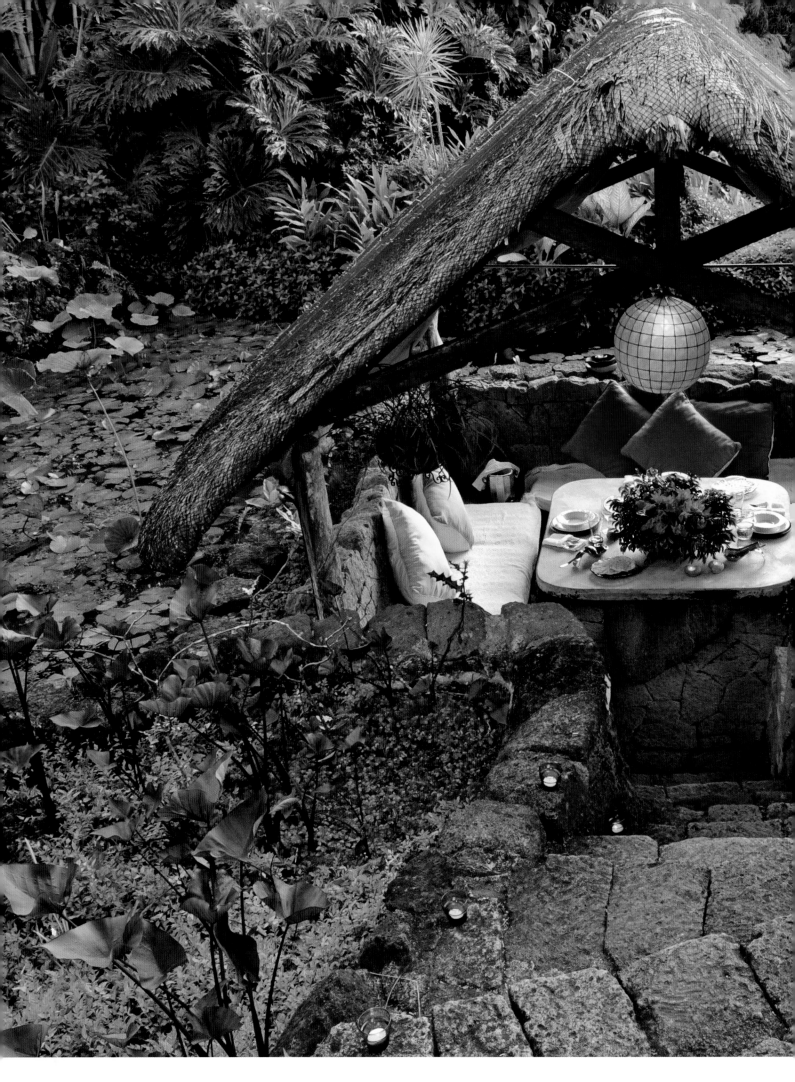

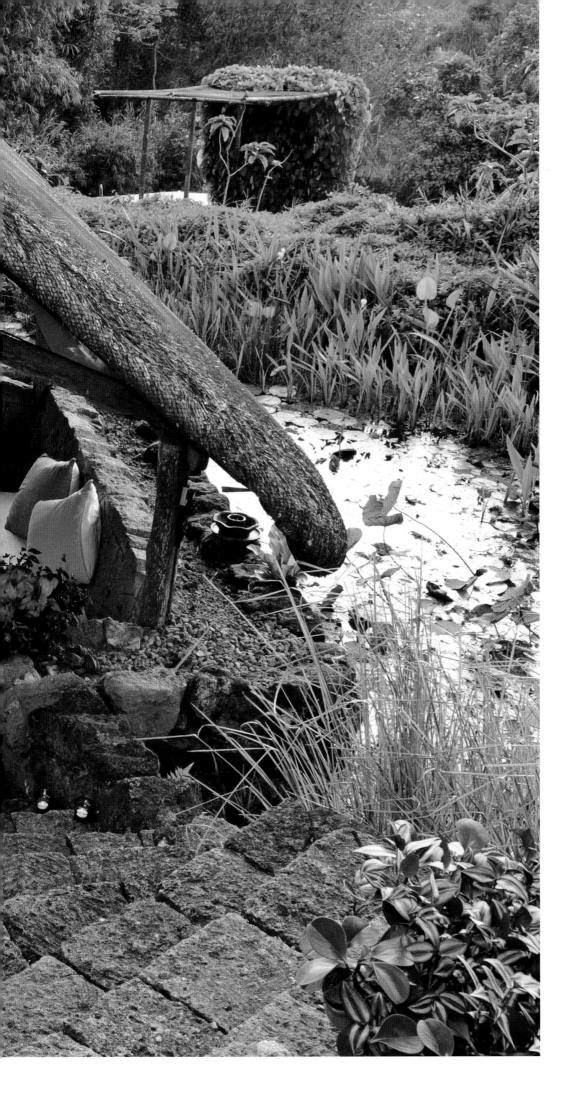

"Take a long look at the garden. The colors will emerge and you can make your design plan easily," intones owner Peter Geertz.

Hewn stone steps lit by candles lead down to a sunken dining island edged in stone set into Moon Garden's pond, filled with lotuses, water lilies and irises. Bowls of red African tulips add bold color in the rustic thatched roof Ifugao dining hut.

alfresco garden party

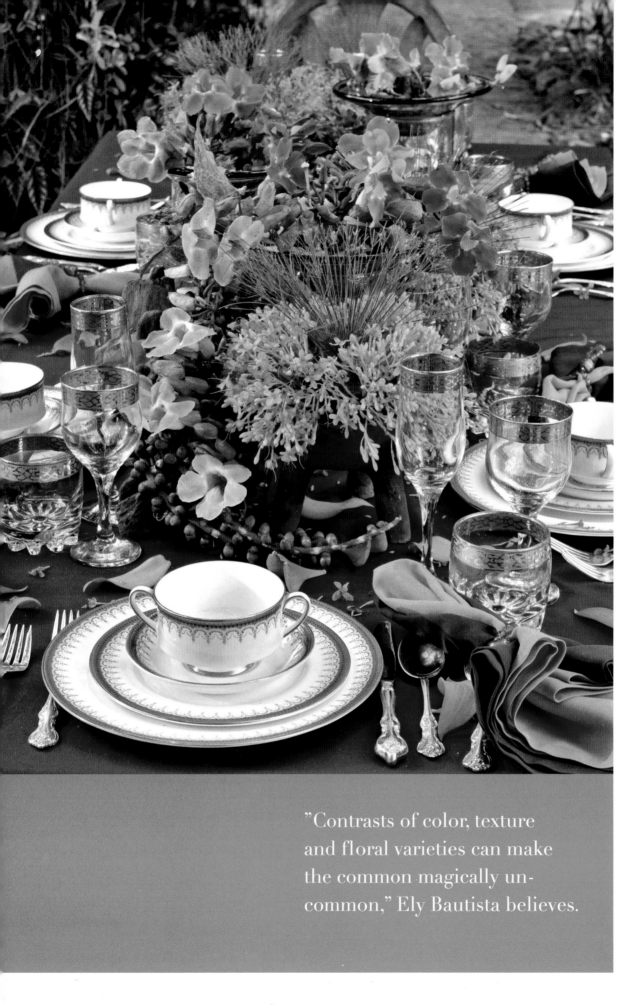

LEFT Masses of purple thunbergia, orange saraca tree flowers crowned by spiky papyrus grass and *nata de coco* berries are a celebration of the abundance of color and fecundity at Moon Garden. Brilliant gilt-edged plateware and stemware add to the vibrance of Ely Bautista's table setting.
RIGHT Draped with cascading orange-yellow thunbergia, the long wooden pergola is an unforgettable setting for a sumptuously decorated table and an alfresco dining experience.

"Contrasts of color, texture and floral varieties can make the common magically un-common," Ely Bautista believes.

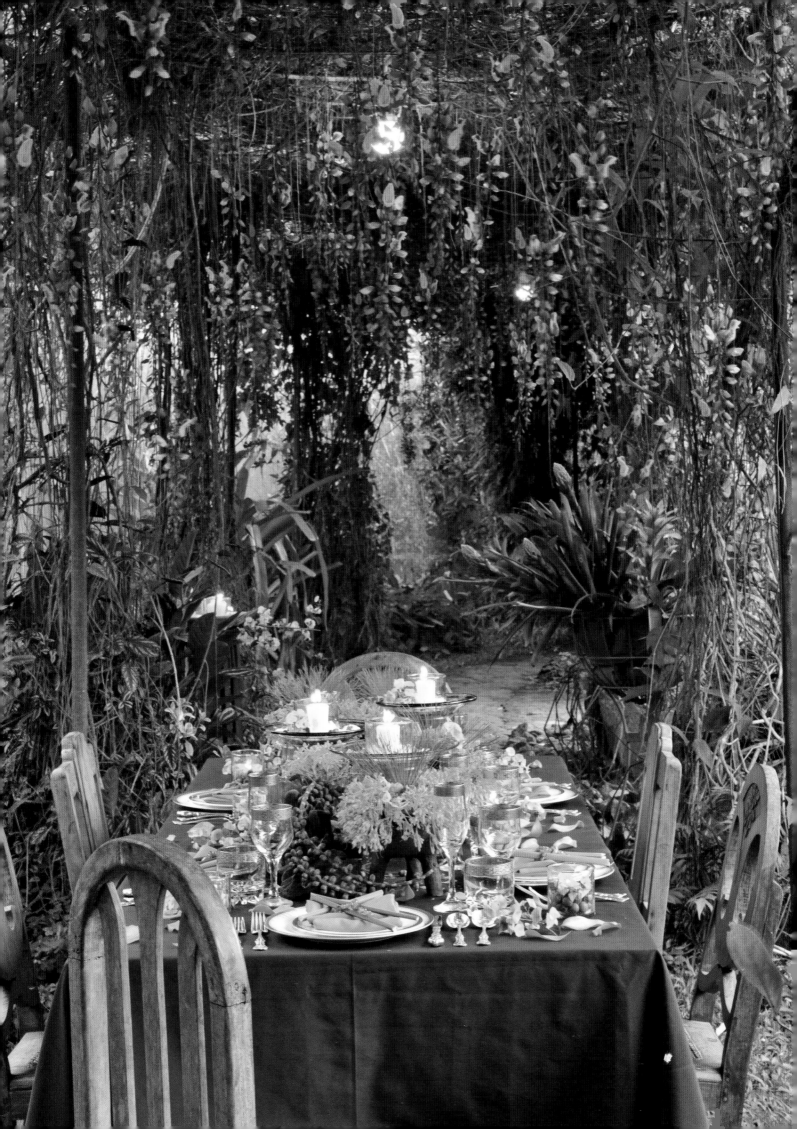

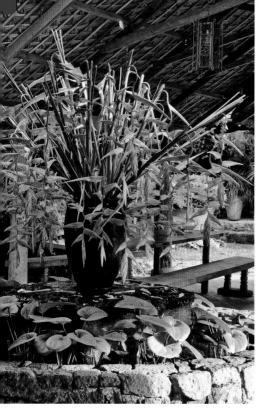

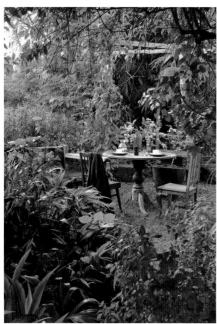

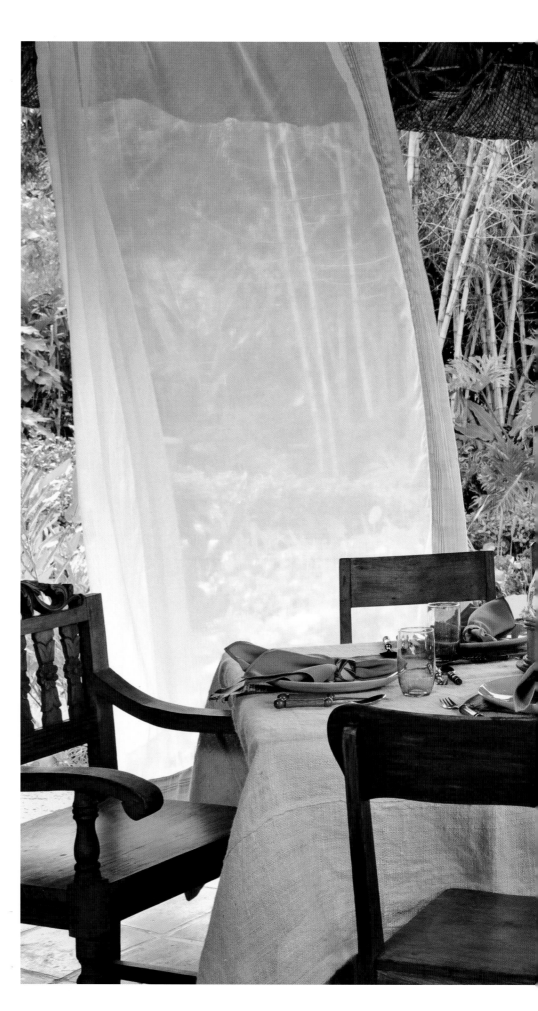

TOP Sexy pink heliconias in a large earthen water jar standing tall on a circular water fountain, form a vivid focal point at the entrance to the main restaurant pavilion.
ABOVE The atmosphere of the meandering gardens is understated but undeniably romantic.
RIGHT Emily Campos's forte is styling creative centerpieces: fresh vegetables anchored on a banana trunk perk up a breezy lunch setting. Banana leaves form novel placemats.

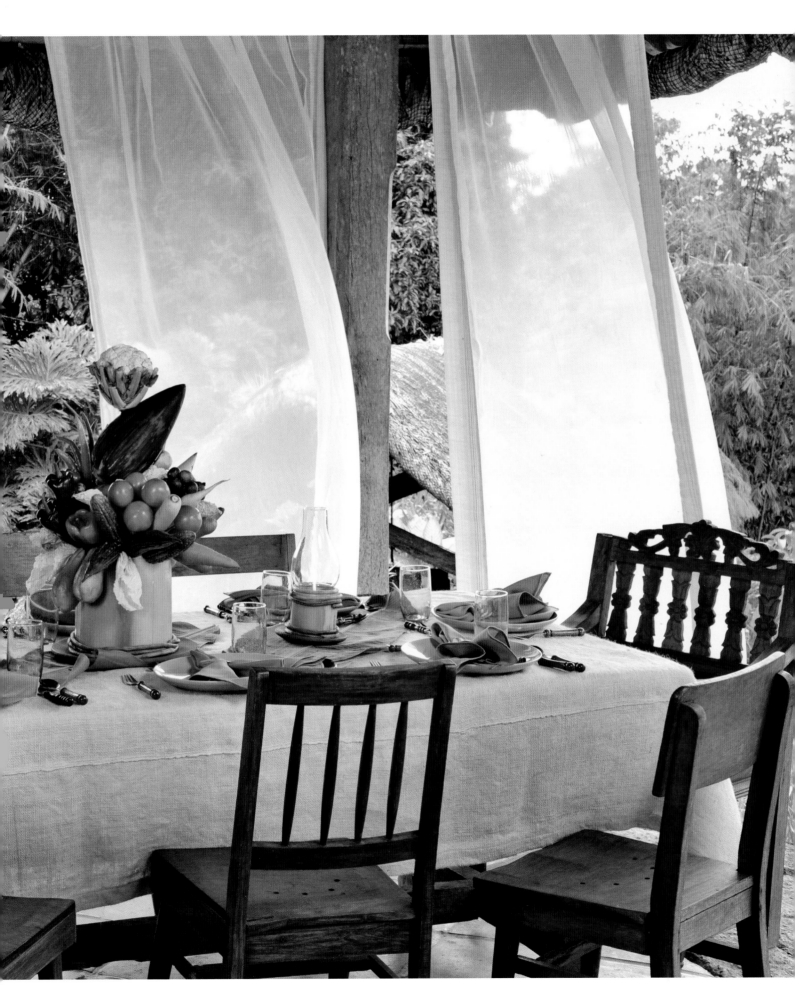

alfresco garden party

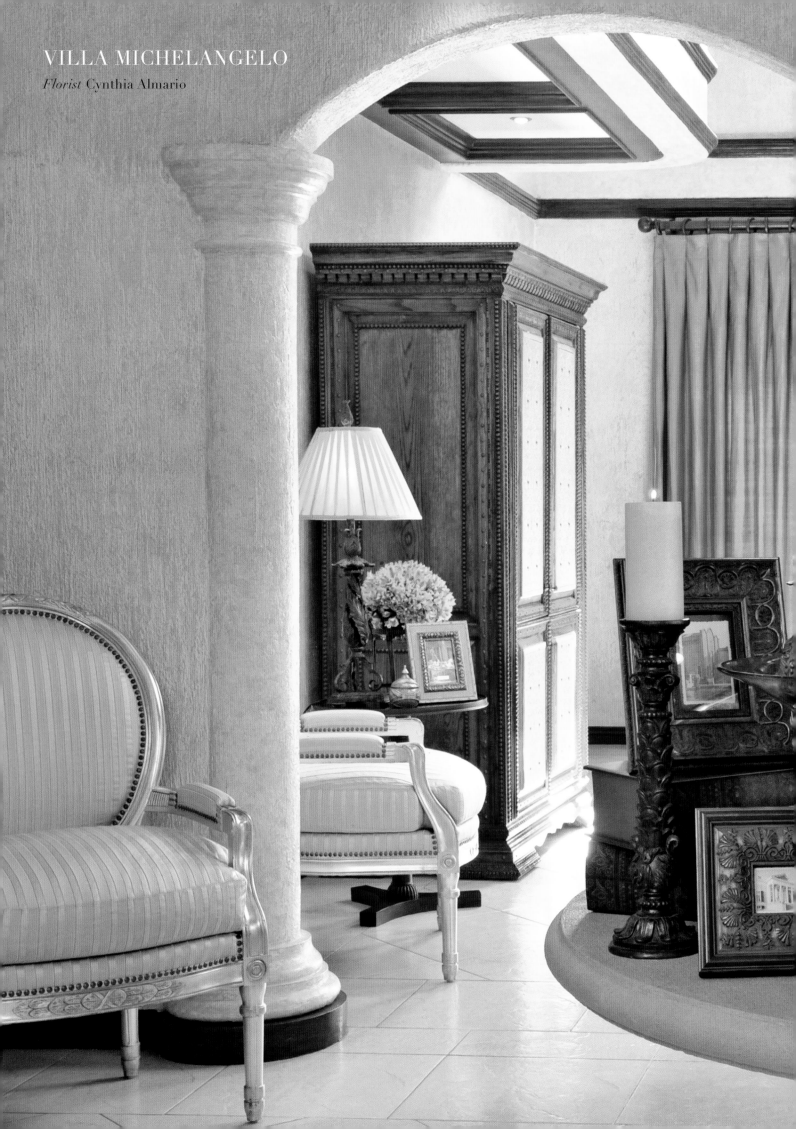

VILLA MICHELANGELO

Florist Cynthia Almario

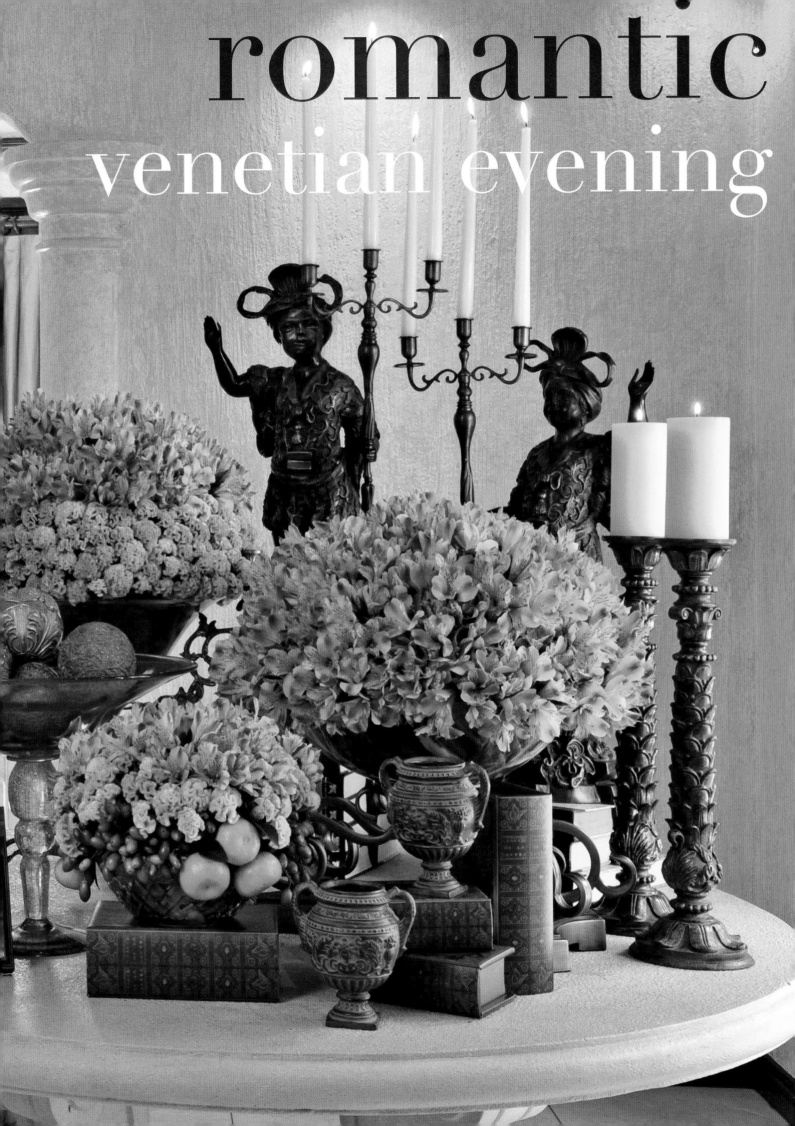

romantic
venetian evening

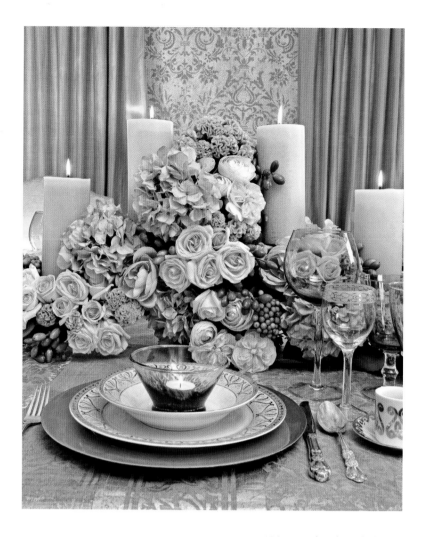

VILLA MICHELANGELO is a house of Italian flavor inspired by classical Renaissance architecture, the golden shades of Tuscany and the decorative notion of Venice. The villa is a show-place of Portofino Development in Evia, south of Alabang, built in the chic villa style favored by many urban Filipinos. The 640 sq m house features a garden courtyard and a modern waterfall within a C-shaped structure. Indoors and out, the high mezzanine and the five bedrooms, each with their own balconied terrace, look inward to the central courtyard and ornate *sala*.

The interiors were designed in a Venetian palazzo style by Atelier Almario, the top local designers of "contemporary chic," who specialize in picturesque themes. The grand living room, with its double-height ceiling, features a crystal-drop chandelier, Fortuny-inspired silk wall panels, throw pillows and an Aubusson rug. All décor elements are harmonious and posh, champagne and gold, ornate and ornamental.

Photo-styled by Cynthia Almario, the passionate florist in the company, Villa Michelangelo comes alive with flowers that are in complete harmony with the finely furbished space. Cynthia orchestrates a patently feminine floral suite in the show villa. She chooses a monochromatic color palette comprising three main flowers: golden to burnt orange alstroemerias, yellow to sage cockscombs and green and grape-colored berries with fresh oranges. Overnight, she weaves the flowers

into glass vases; by morning, she has installed the sumptuous accents in the beautifully coordinated space.

In both the foyer and the grand salon, the floral bouquets are displayed in Cynthia's signature style—symmetrically balanced at all levels and ever-harmonious with the surroundings. Flower sets are arranged among bronzed décor artifacts from her favorite Pietro Collection—bookends and Blackamoor sculptures, ornate picture frames, carved vases and candleholders. All exude an air of Venetian classic chic!

The villa's dining room is a symphony of powdery pink and gold, from the gold-lacquered chargers, gold-edged plates and shimmering sari tablecloth to the delectable floral tablescape set under another chandelier. A seamless combination

ABOVE Cynthia Almario's choice of blush roses, light-toned cockscombs, hydrangeas and berries, gathered around four giant candles, forms an alluring centerpiece on the dining table. PREVIOUS SPREAD In the foyer of the Villa Michelangelo, massed arrangements at varying heights amidst carefully chosen artifacts from the Pietro Collection make a cheerful, harmonious and welcoming display.

of blush roses, light-toned green and yellow cockscombs, hydrangeas, ivory ranunculus and grape-colored berries are gathered round four giant candles, forming an undeniably romantic centerpiece for the table.

Says Cynthia on her role as florist: "When the style and colors of your interiors are matched and expressed in a monochromatic palette in flowers, the home will sing in harmony."

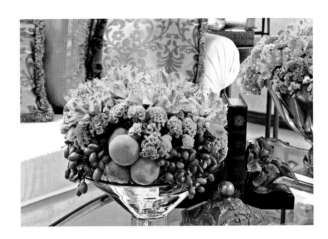

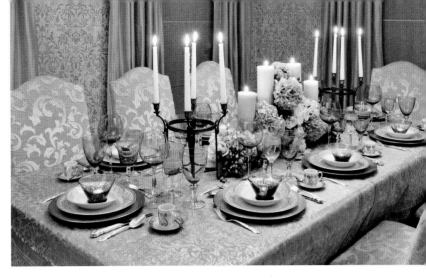

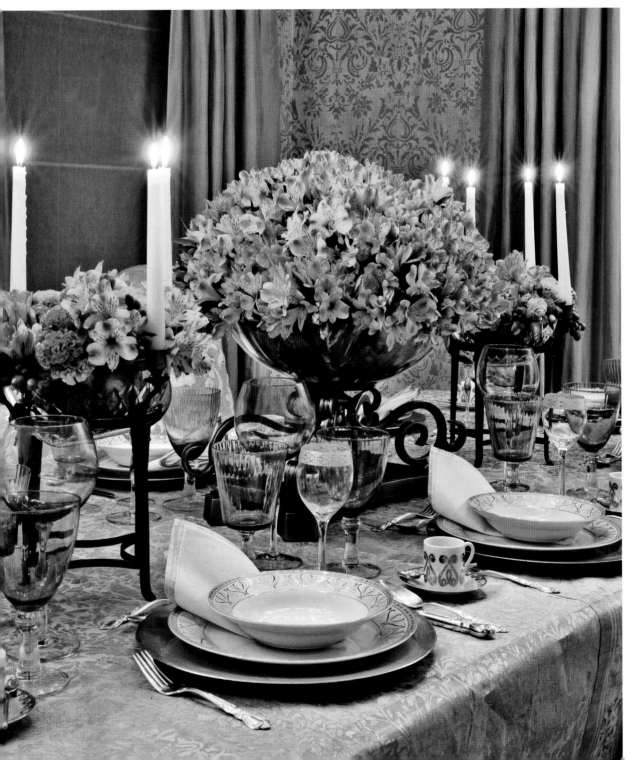

ABOVE LEFT In the Venetian *sala*, this lush flower and fruit ensemble, with its golden alstroemerias, yellow and sage cockscombs, green and grape-colored berries and small oranges, conveys a sense of abundance and celebration.

ABOVE AND LEFT The two different centerpieces created for the dining room capture the powdery pink and gold colors of the surroundings, from the luxurious silk-covered walls and fine sari tablecloth to the exquisite gilt-edged tableware.

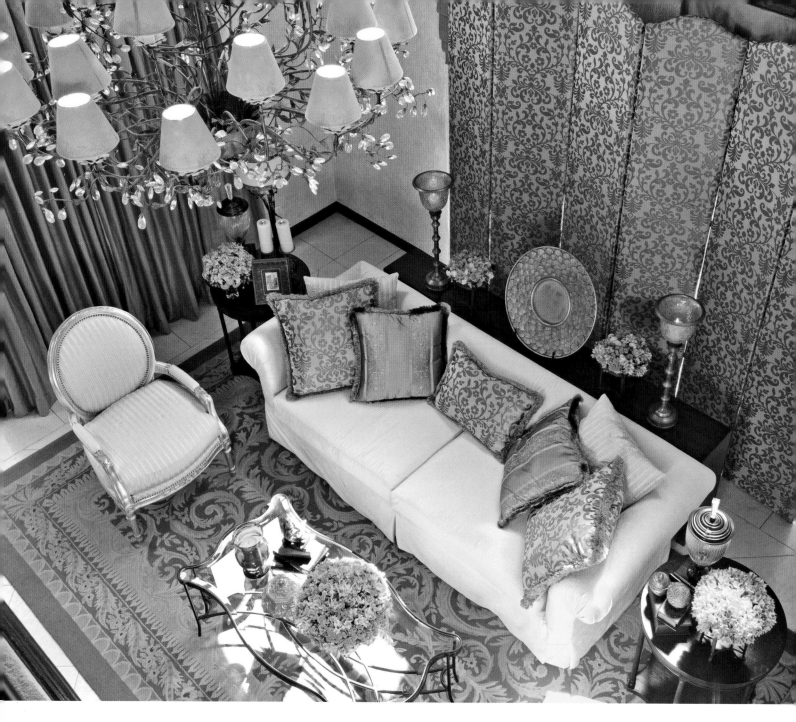

ABOVE The Venetian palazzo style of the Villa Michelangelo is apparent in the crystal-drop chandelier suspended from the double-height ceiling in the grand salon, the Fortuny-inspired silk wall panels and cushions and the ornate Aubusson rug. Luxuriant massed floral arrangements complement the rich décor.
RIGHT In the terracotta-hued entrance hall, a floral bouquet of golden alstroemerias flanked by Blackamoor figures bearing candelabra exude a warm welcome.

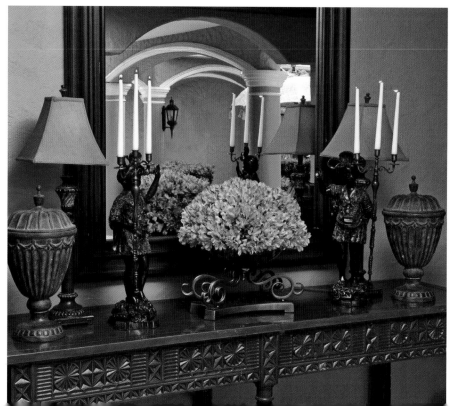

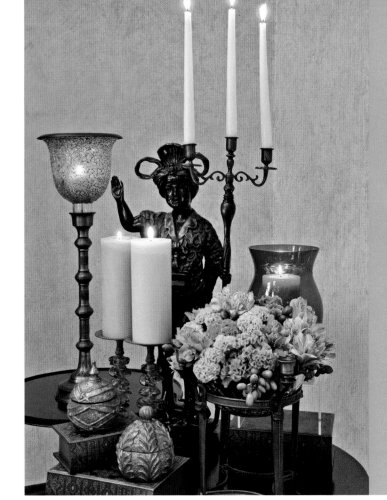

RIGHT Photo-styled by its original interior designer, Cynthia Almario, Villa Michelangelo comes alive with skillfully chosen flowers, candles and accessories that fit perfectly with the villa's architecture and décor.
BELOW The monochromatic color palette evinced by golden to burnt orange alstroemerias, yellow to sage cockscombs and green and grape-colored berries is one of Cynthia's favorites.

"When the style and colors of your interiors are matched and expressed in a monochromatic palette in flowers, the home will sing in harmony," says Cynthia Almario.

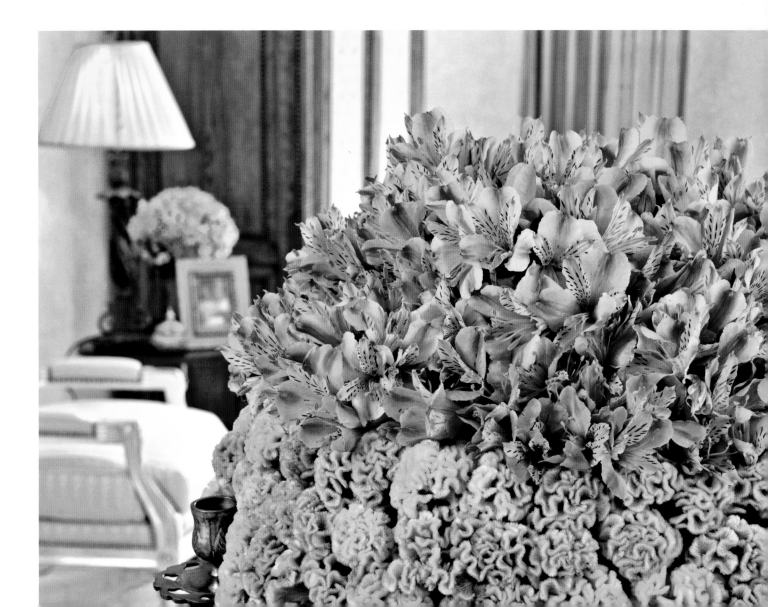

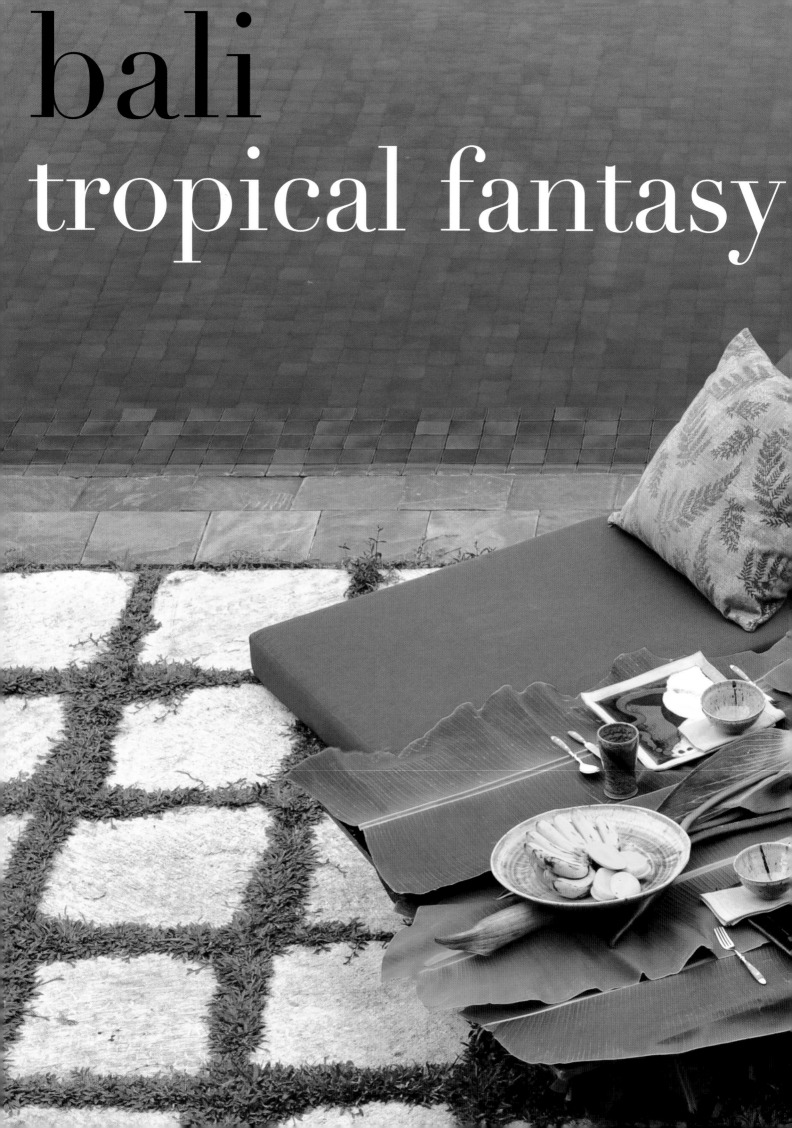

bali
tropical fantasy

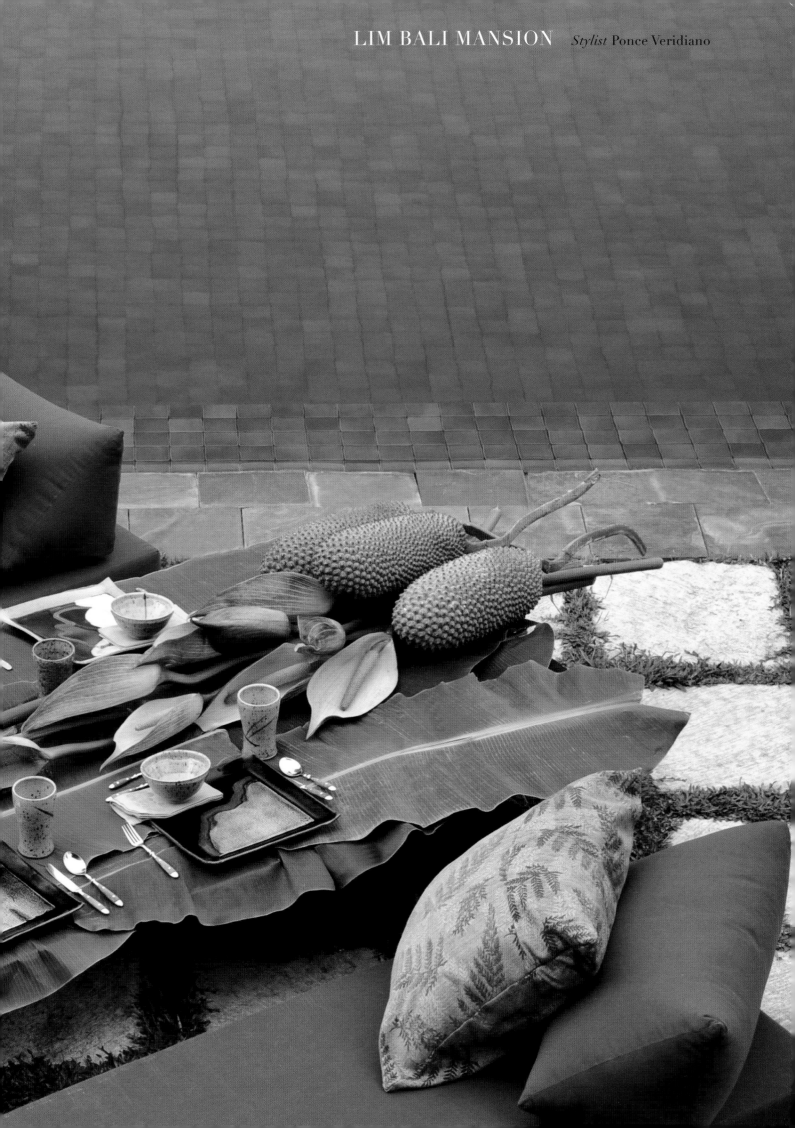

VIOLETA LIM IS ONE Bali lover who has realized her dream of owning a Bali-inspired mansion. When not busy with the family construction business, she would venture to Bali, the Island of the Gods, to collect carved doors, wooden items—and misty inspiration—to create her own "Wanakasa" (House in the Forest) in the hinterlands of Silang, Cavite.

The rustic wood and stone structure feels like a giant tree house. Set below multiple thatched roofs, the three-level assemblage of decks, terraces and open staircases includes six bedrooms in separate pavilions built near tiered lotus ponds and waterfalls. The front entry welcomes guests with wispy curtains of hanging vines; the back garden ends at a blue infinity pool looking out to the forests of Cavite.

Violeta's creative retreat house was built by environmental architects Edward Tan and Agnes Lambuson. Tan says of its open-air, all-plane structure, "The function makes the form." While it took four "innovative" years to realize the unique family retreat, the owner had collected the contents during visits to neighboring Asian countries long before construction of the house began.

Violeta engaged landscape designer and old friend Ponce Veridiano, who shares her love of plants, fern gardens and rustic fantasy settings, to style the violet-and-white themed floral arrangements for her daughter's wedding, held at various spots in and outside the mansion, and other arrangements specially for this book.

The modern Chinese-style dining room on the upper level, where some guests were seated, displayed a ménage of violet and lavender hydrangeas, white roses and Ponce's signature dark-stained nipa pods—flowers that were echoed on the guest tables below.

On another day, Ponce created his more personal "organic" tables using giant wild plants gathered in the forests of Laguna, including huge anthurium-like flowers from the wild alocasia plant and the common nipa palm fruit. Most astonishing was his thick grass-covered table set with square stoneware plates by potter Hadrian Mendoza and hand-blown glass goblets, offset by white phalaenopsis orchids. Ponce advises homemakers to go natural. "You don't have to spend money on imported flowers. Just look to the jungle and create your own fantasy."

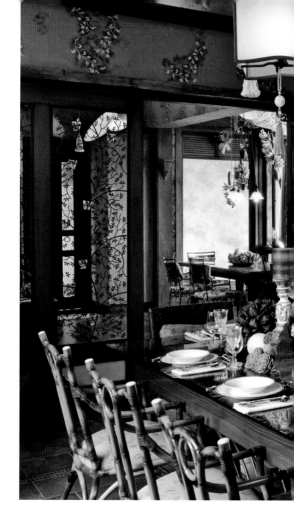

ABOVE AND RIGHT Oriental lamps, découpage red walls and a red painting in Violeta Lim's stunning modern-day Chinese dining room create the perfect atmosphere for Ponce's celebratory table centerpiece of violet and lavender hydrangeas, white roses, green succulents, dark-stained nipa palm fruit pods and white ostrich eggs.
ABOVE RIGHT At the front entry, a bold display of nipa palm seeds, red gingers and vines welcomes guests to the rustic open-air tropical mansion.
LEFT A pale powder blue stoneware platter by artist Hadrian Mendoza receives an artful snap dragon and vine twist.
PREVIOUS SPREAD What better setting for a picnic by the pool than earth-toned lounging cushions and square stoneware plates by Hadrian Mendoza laid on banana leaf plates? Ponce's novel centerpiece comprises jungle flowers and giant jackfruit.

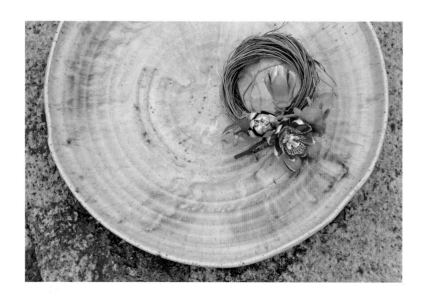

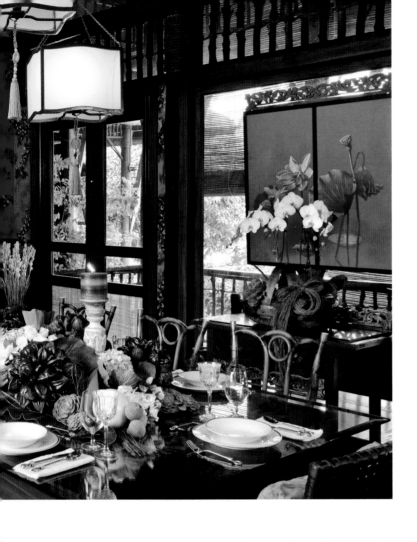

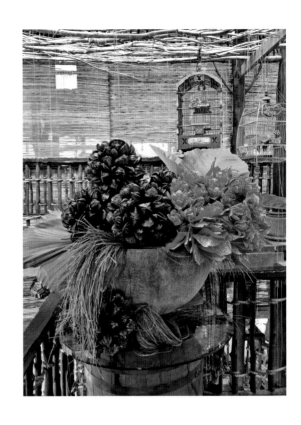

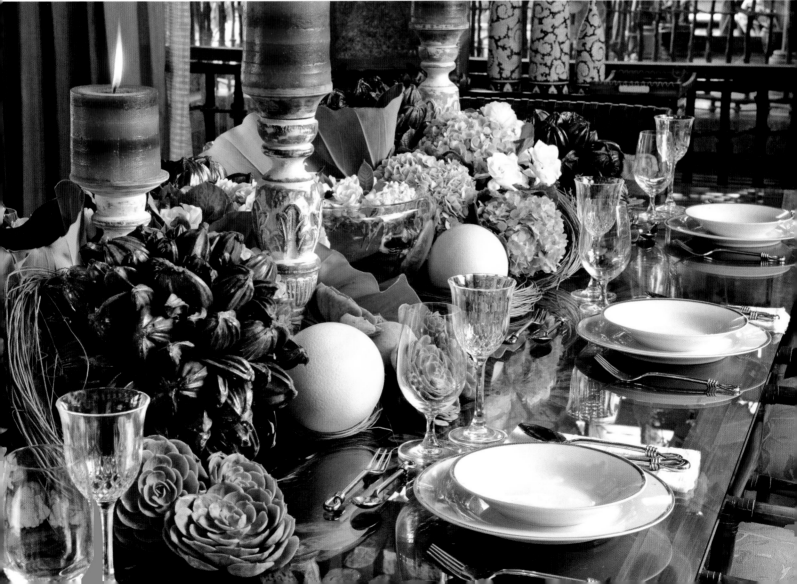

Ponce Veridiano advises homemakers to go natural. "You don't have to spend money on imported flowers. Just look to the jungle and create your own fantasy."

BELOW The luscious arrangement on the bridal table in the temporary chapel—the car shed dressed up for the day—comprised white roses, white lilies and tuberoses encircling a fleshy green succulent nestled on vines.

OPPOSITE ABOVE Violeta's daughter had a picturesque Bali-style reception at "Wanakasa." The "presidential" bridal table took center stage on a platform constructed over the blue infinity pool at the back of the house.

OPPOSITE BELOW An ultra-romantic centerpiece of roses, hydrangeas, succulents and finely intertwined vines graced the all-white gala table setting by Bizu Catering at the white-and-violet color-themed wedding.

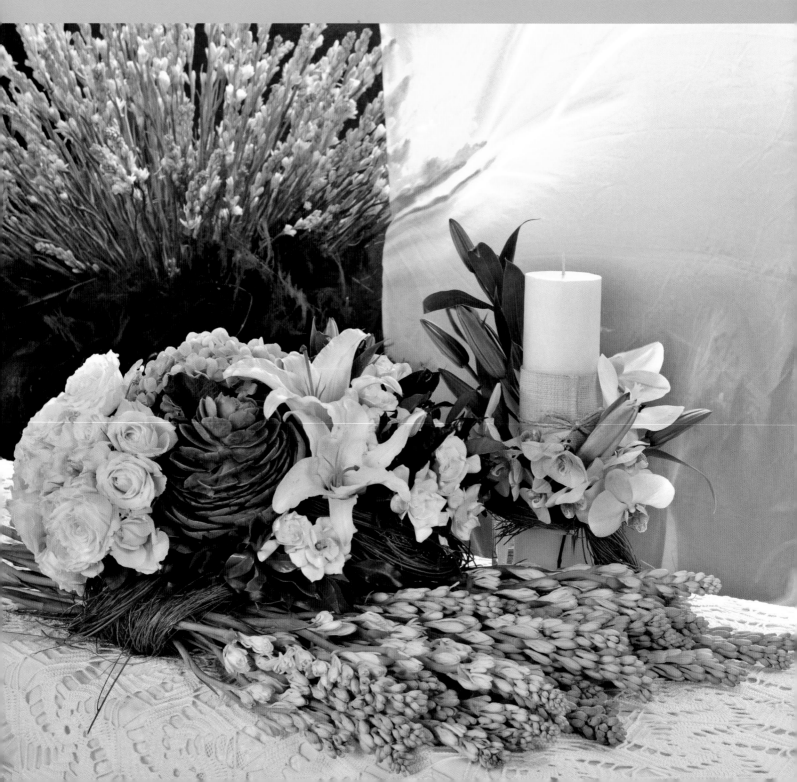

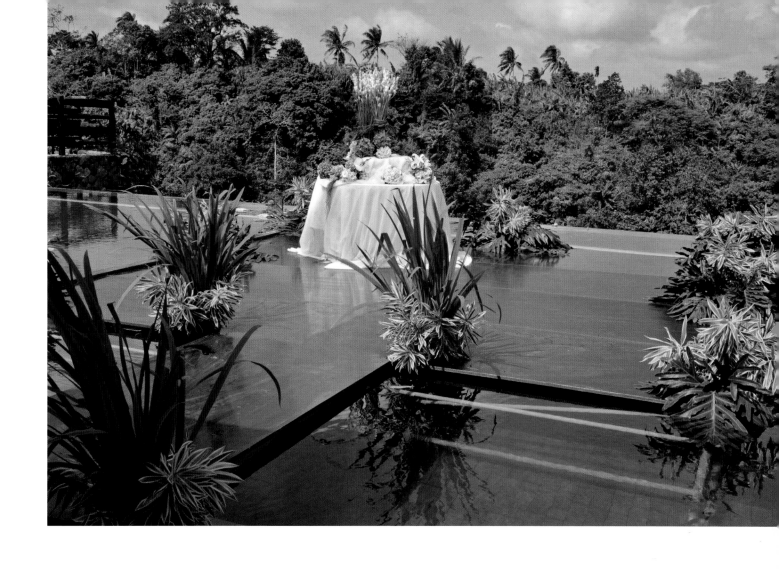

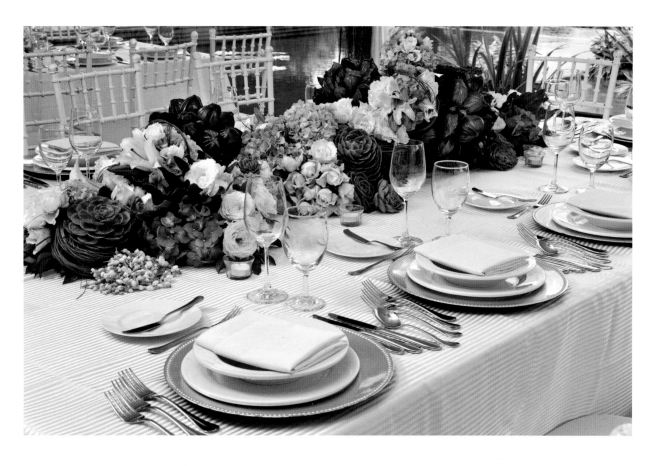

bali tropical fantasy

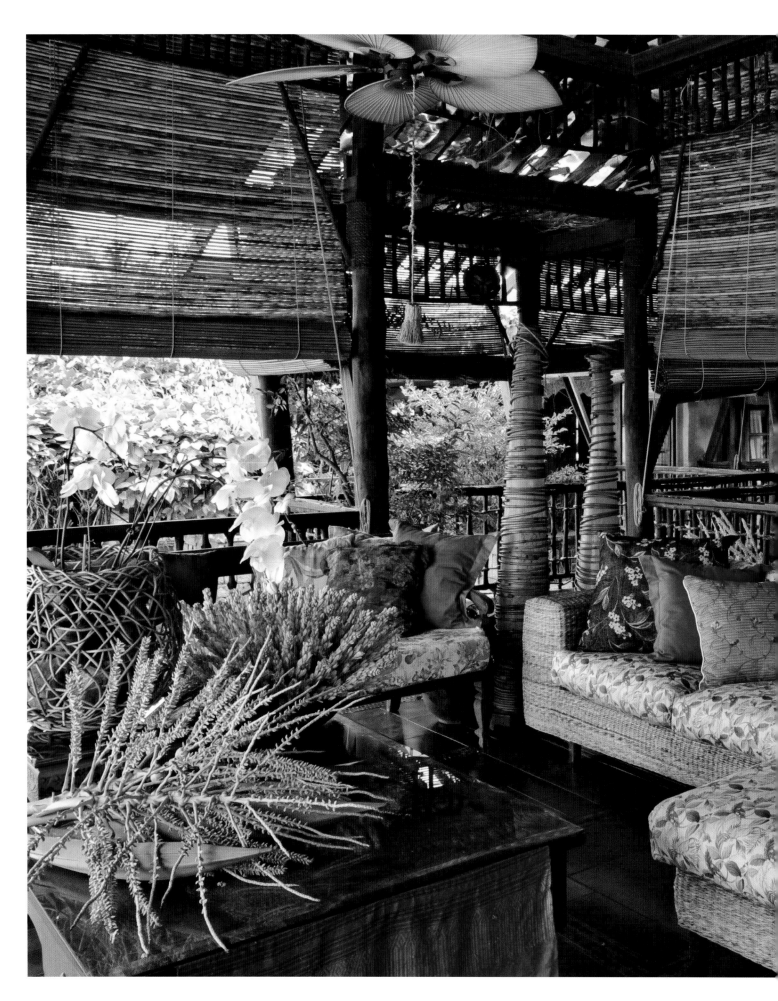

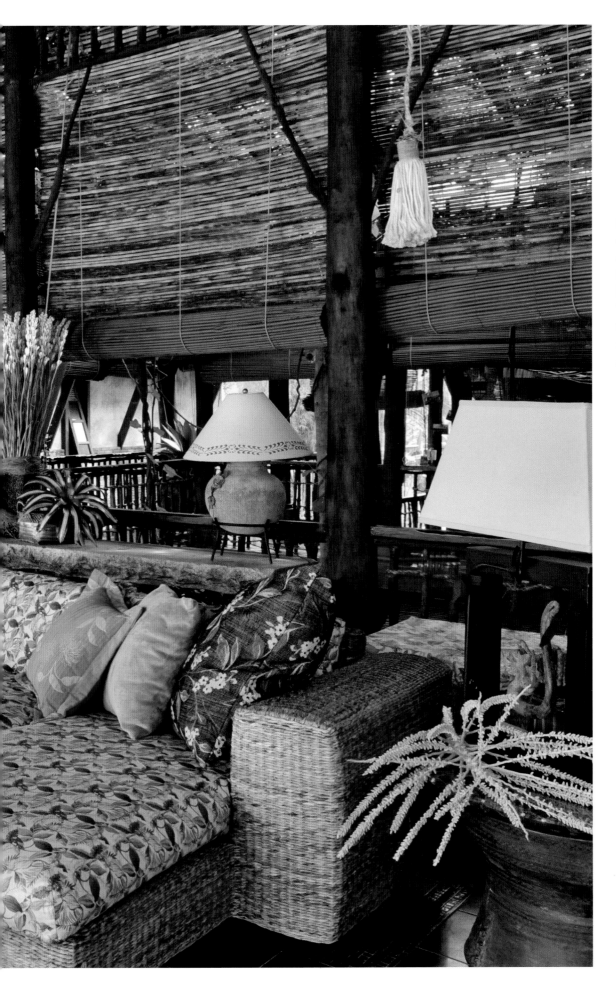

Realtor Violeta Lim's tropical dream house was realized by architects Edward Tan and Angela Lambusan and accessorized by her own creative hand. Ponce Veridiano's floral arrangements, styled with giant pods and coconut flowers, make suitably bold statements in the large space.

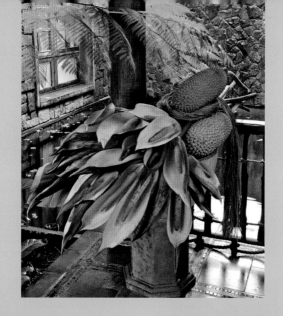

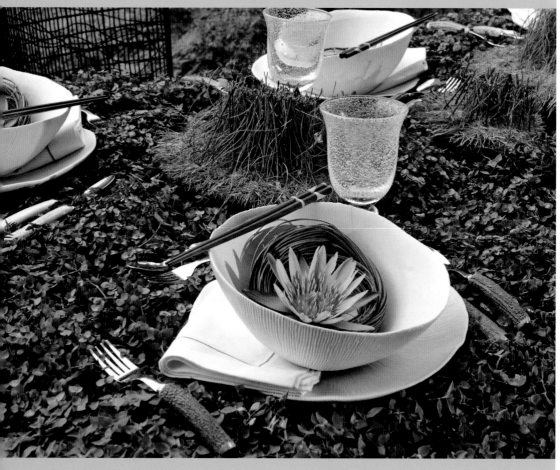

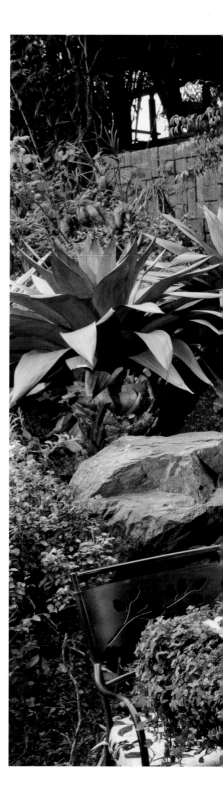

TOP Ponce loves fashioning
dramatic arrangements in every
convenient corner. His current
floral passion—wild anthuriums—are here combined with
a nest of jackfruit to take on
the function of a sculpture.

ABOVE AND RIGHT A quirky,
eco-friendly table setting comprises a "tablecloth" of thick
blocks of jungly vines on the
edge of a tropical fern garden
that Ponce designed for Violeta
four years ago. The white stoneware bowls, hand-blown glass
goblets and deerhorn-handled
cutlery are accented by hairy
root bases from Violeta's hanging vines and the pink water lily
blooms nestling in the bowls.

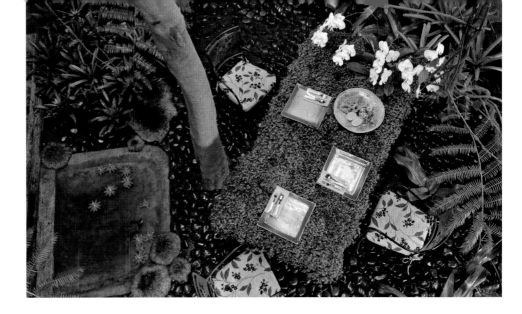

RIGHT A bird's eye view of Ponce's wild grassy table surrounded by a "carpet" of dark gray Laguna river stones. The red-edged stoneware plates by Hadrian Mendoza and the vivid red floating passion flowers provide color contrast.

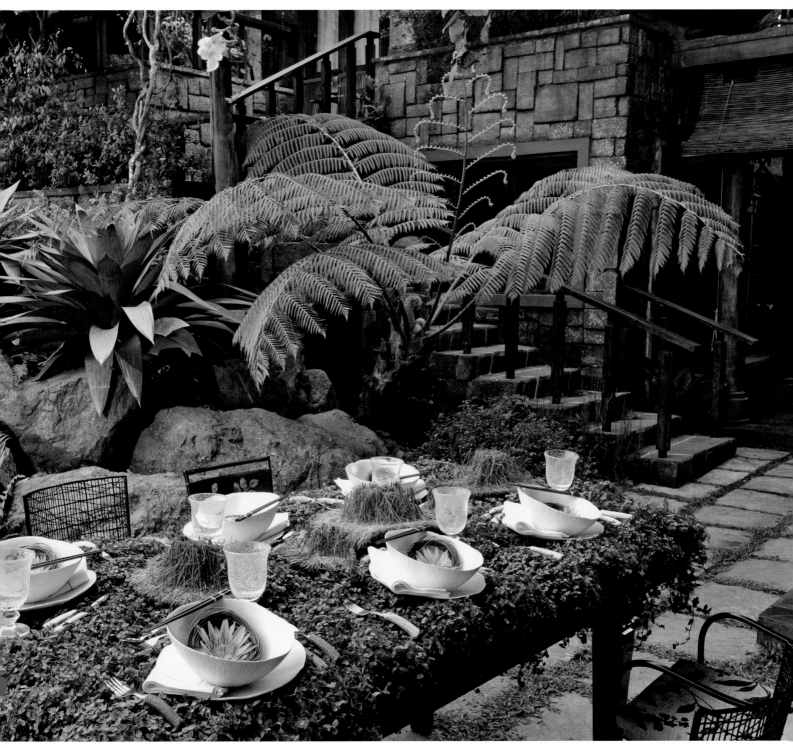

bali tropical fantasy

a passion for
highland art

TAGAYTAY RESTHOUSE *Stylist* Jonathan Matti

THE TAGAYTAY RESTHOUSE, perched on a hill in scenic Tagaytay, one of the Philippine's cool summer capitals, is owned by a passionate and private art collector. Most of the year, the resthouse is a safe and stylish repository, a private home-cum-museum for the owner's collection of sacred and profane arti-facts—tribal Cordillera rice gods or *bulol* and antique ivory heads from old carved religious statuettes called *santos*, with a sprinkling of small earthenware pots. Ensconced in the highland house along with the dark ethnic figures is the owner's collection of modern expressionist paintings, primarily the tormented Christ paintings of the late Filipino National Artist Ang Kiukok, and an array of modern European furnishings.

A double-height great room with a grand view of Tagaytay's rolling highlands is divided into quadrants, with each area featuring an eclectic mix of traditional and modern furnishings. At the center of the main living room set is a pair of modern Knoll sofas covered in natural cowhide, made by George Smith of the UK, accompanied by six wood and cane-woven plantation chairs called *butaka*. All the seating is arranged around a massive square table made of kamagong wood or mabolo, a dense fruit wood found

only in the Philippines. On the coffee table, silver *objets d'art* and Chinese ceramics vie for attention with an arrangement of fresh giant cabbage roses.

The formal dining area features ceiling-to-floor display shelves filled with Cordillera wooden rice god *bulol*, rural home implements and earthen pots, alternated with cubist paintings by Ang Kiukok. Architect-designer Jonathan Matti says of the house: "It's a juxtaposition of tribal and modernist art. I love that the dichotomy of the old and the new can exist beautifully in a given space!"

While he downplays flower décor—the arrangements shown here are by florist Loreto Sasi—Jonathan says: "In the upland setting of the Tagaytay, there grows an abundance of tropical flora in the cool climate all year round. Homes can open into the gardens with their private views…. And fresh flowers, vines and leaves collected from one's own garden can be the simplest and most cost-efficient way to bring a home to life." To complement the home owner's private art collection, Loreto used bright but common flowers plucked from the public gardens—red salvia, cordyline leaves, pandan grass and the brilliant carmine flowers of the African tulip tree.

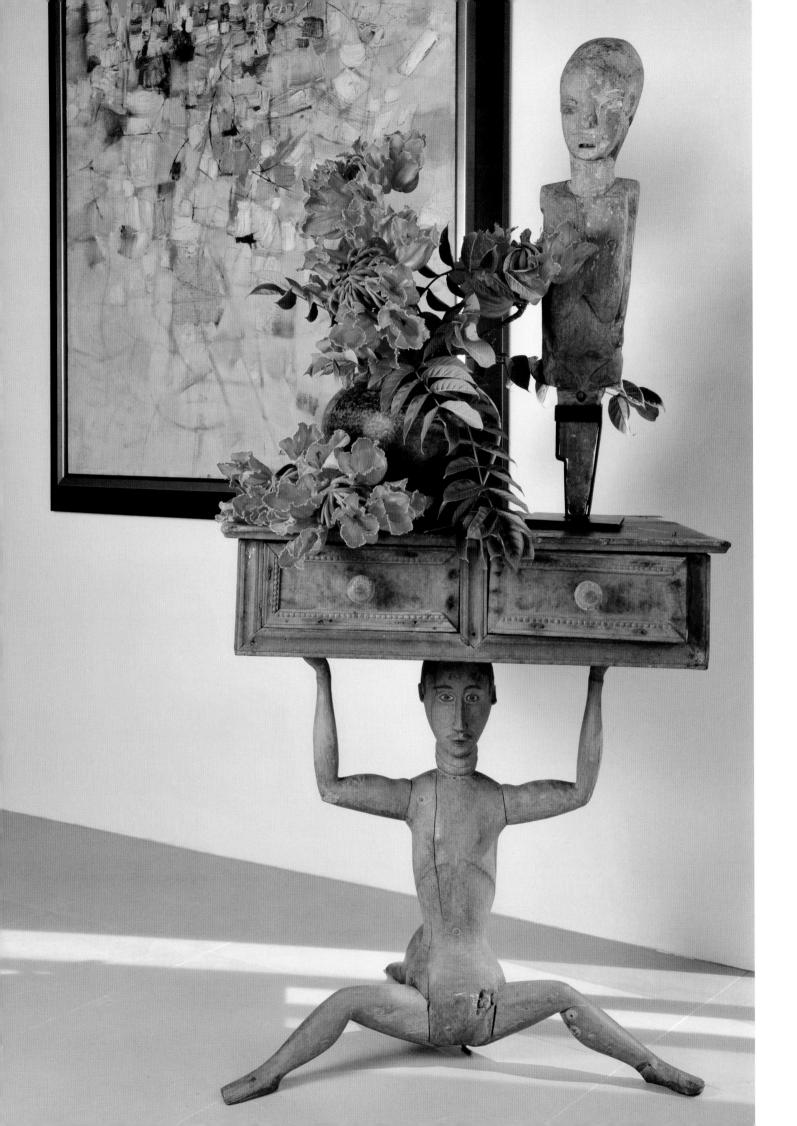

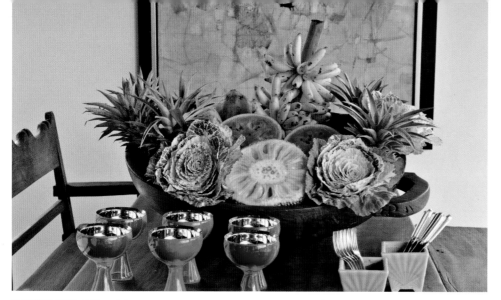

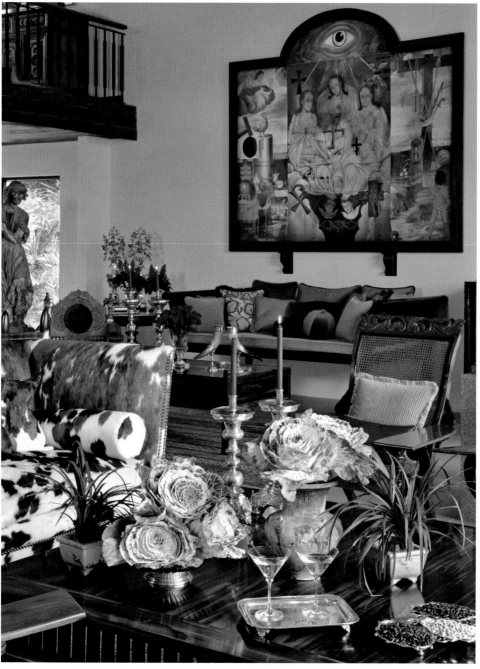

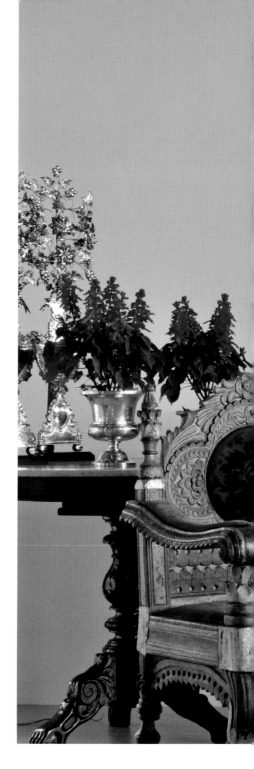

ABOVE LEFT A wooden washbasin from the Cordillera packed with photogenic tropical fruit—bananas, pineapples, papayas, watermelon and jackfruit—and giant leafy cabbages is a pleasing alternative to a conventional floral arrangement.
LEFT The giant kamagong coffee table in the living room, adorned with giant cabbage roses, is surrounded by two English cowhide sofas by George Smith, and four *butaka* plantation chairs.
PREVIOUS SPREAD A brave warrior carries his own wooden drawers. The folksy table, made by an Ifugao carver, holds an old ritual figure and a floral offering of African tulips. On the wall is a modern abstract by the late National Artist Jose Joya.

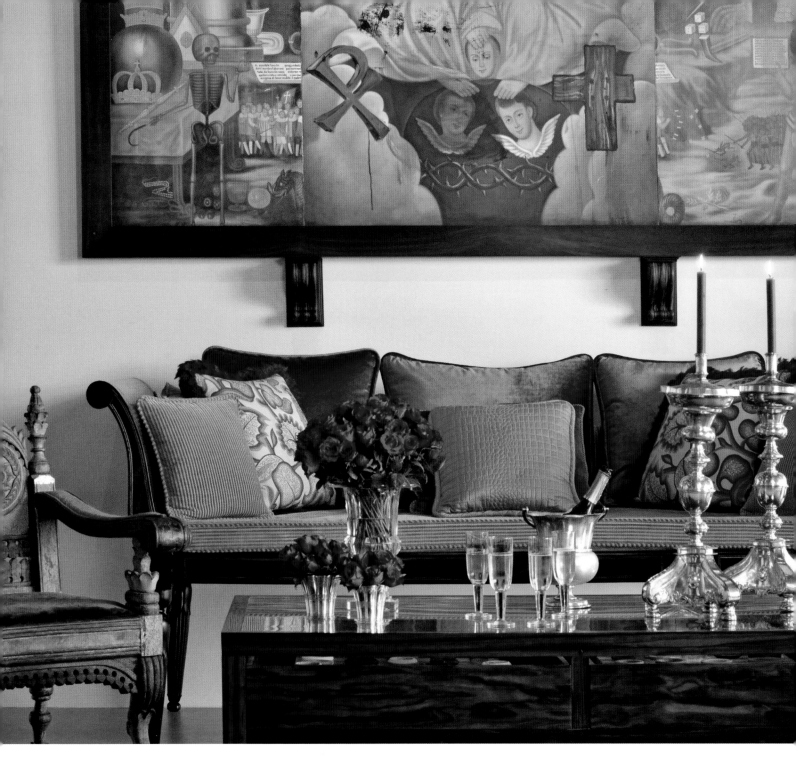

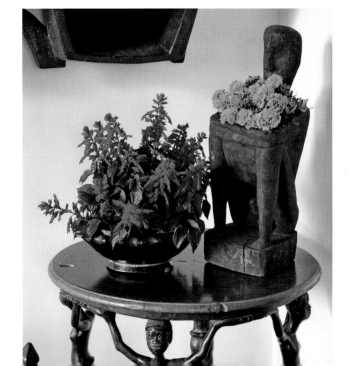

ABOVE The "Christianity corner" features such classic furnishings as a carved wood and velvet Archbishop's Chair, silver altar pieces and candelabra and a religious painting by Manuel Ocampo. Tightly packed vases of red roses and a side table arrangement of salvia make elegant accompaniments.

LEFT In this modern Ifugao vignette, a traditional seated *bulol* or rice god carries an armful of orange marigolds from the garden. On his own holding table, borne by four more *bulol* figures, is a bowl of vivid salvia.

a passion for highland art

RIGHT The front door is set within finely carved wooden parts from a church altar, forming a magnificent gateway to the collector's highland haven. On the left, red salvia flowers trim the bases of tall river reeds.
BELOW Bright orange marigolds arranged in an Ifugao ritual box shine among the rice gods. Stylist Jonathan Matti says, "Just pick ordinary flowers from the garden for the dining table!"

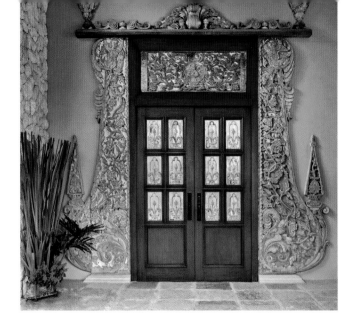

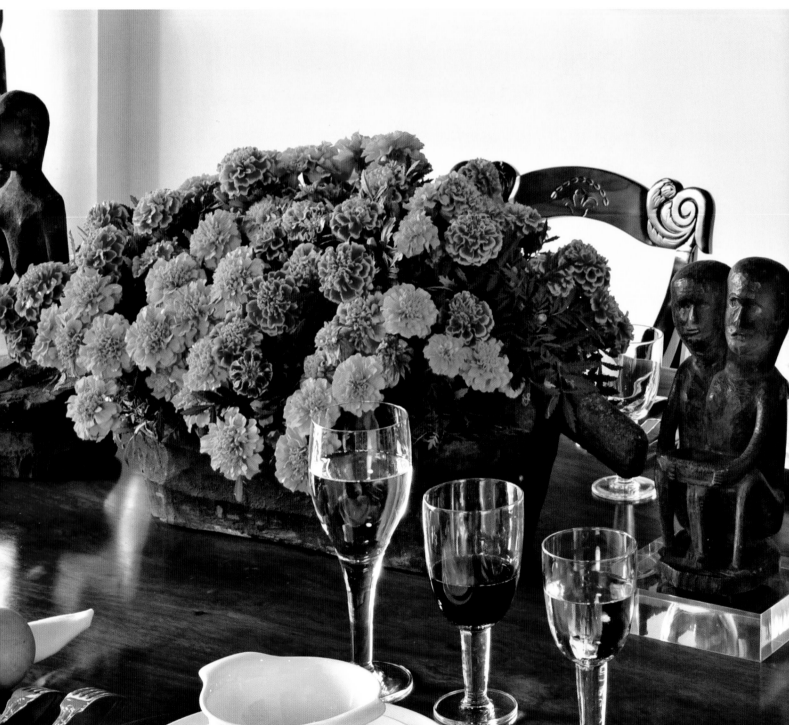

Says home stylist Jonathan Matti, "Fresh flowers, vines and leaves collected from one's own garden can be the simplest and most cost-efficient way to bring a home to life."

BELOW RIGHT Splashes of marigold orange and salvia red offset the somber tones of the Ifugao artifacts and modern cubist paintings by Ang Kiukok that adorn the dining room display wall.

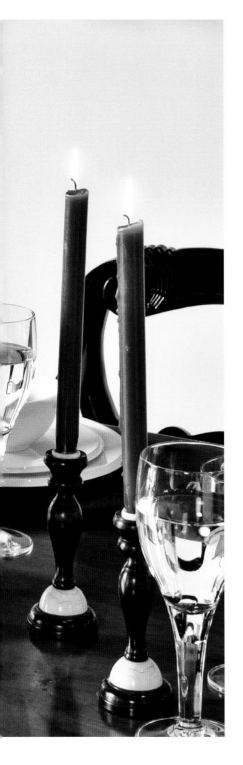

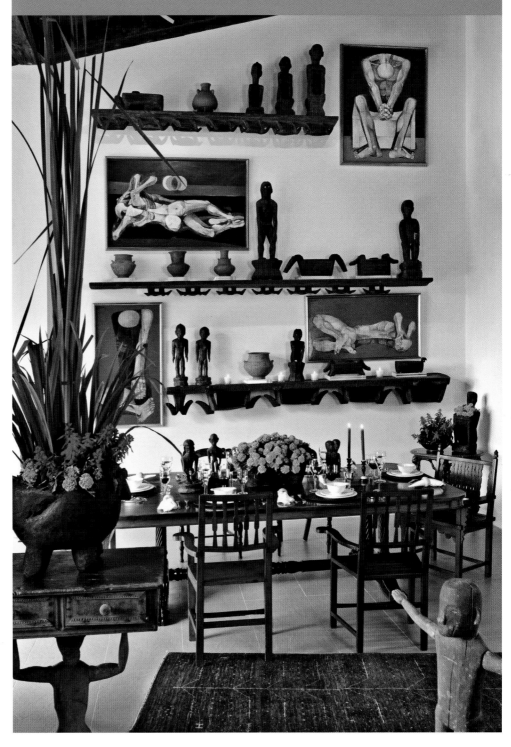

vintage *chic* updated

CONTEMPORARY FLORALSCAPES can bridge and elevate the iconic look of vintage mansions. Sprawling, split-level bungalows—like this Madrigal mansion built in the 1950s—can be brought into the present by a combination of well-edited decor, Asia-modern food and vintage-chic fashion.

The old Madrigal house straddles half a hectare in "New Manila," Quezon City. This gracious residential area is where postwar Filipinos built big ranch homes like those in urban America.

Lisa Tinio Bayot is the well-traveled doyenne now managing the Madrigal manor and several family homes abroad. She appreciates designs in both traditional and modernist genres—and found a kindred spirit in interior designer Eric Paras. An eclectic stylist, Paras has a flair for merging the old or dated with the new or contemporary.

The furniture, tableware and décor objects at Lisa's disposal included heirlooms from her husband's family and her own, unique "trophy buys" from foreign flea markets, and antique bone china and vintage silverware from both the family houses. For our task of "contemporizing" a dated mansion, Lisa and stylist Eric Paras chose Lisa's love of India as the unifying design focus.

The exotic dining room is the major scenario. Decorative spreads of Indian embroidery and appliqué underlay French plateware and English silverware. An Empire-style chandelier and alabaster pieces evoke a regal and colonial feel within the room. The shimmering central table setting gives way to Indian silver phoenix figures, acrylic décor items and ivory eggs in playful disarray. The side console tables hold tall vases of orange and mauve gladioli.

The grand *sala*'s cathedral ceiling dictates the height and volume of flowers in silver trophy urns set beside towering royal palms and giant ferns. On the 1950s open-air *lanai*, with its low ceiling covered in flat-woven bamboo, the vintage-chic stylists lay out Limoges cups and antique crystals to contain Indian sweets. Bright colors clash and patterns splurge in a joyous cross-fertilization of objects and ideas.

RIGHT An alabaster Empire-style Parisian urn, a Phoenix palm and a soaring column of Renaissance leaves loom over heirloom furniture draped and cushioned with prized bazaar fabric finds. A silver vase of lavender and violet paper roses and a capacious glass bowl of wild orange lilies pick out the dominant tones of the fabrics and pull the color scheme together.

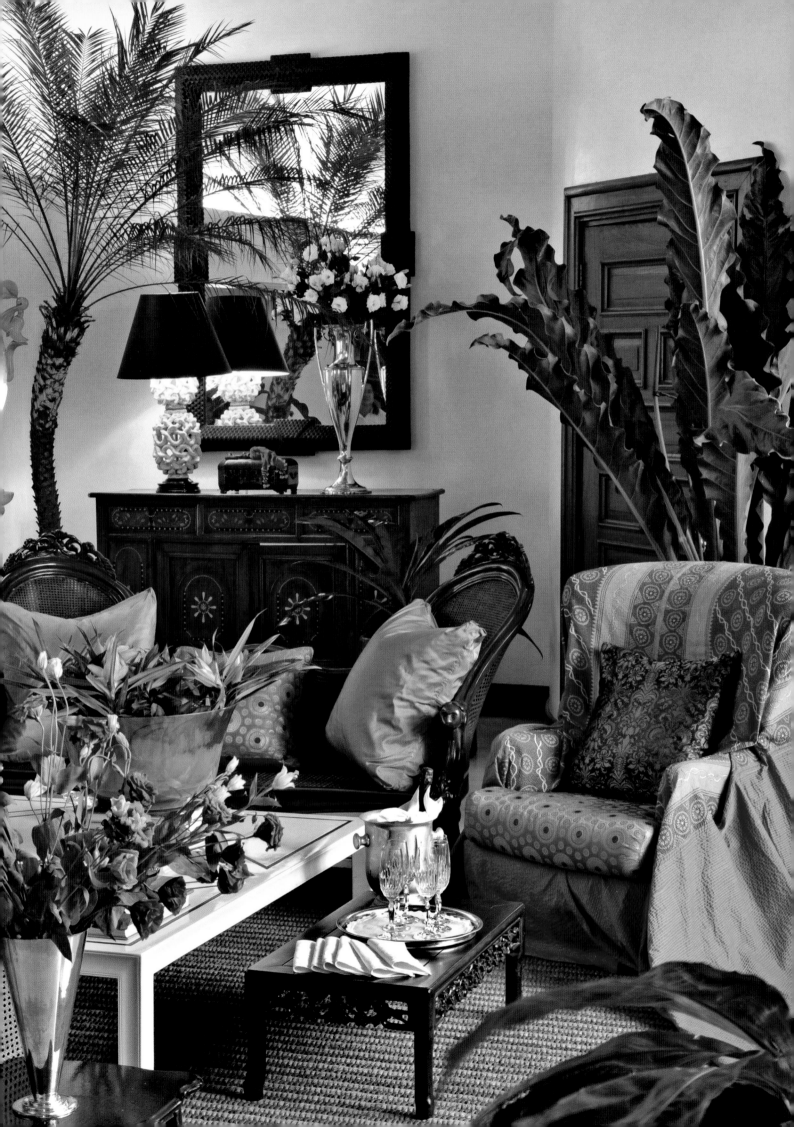

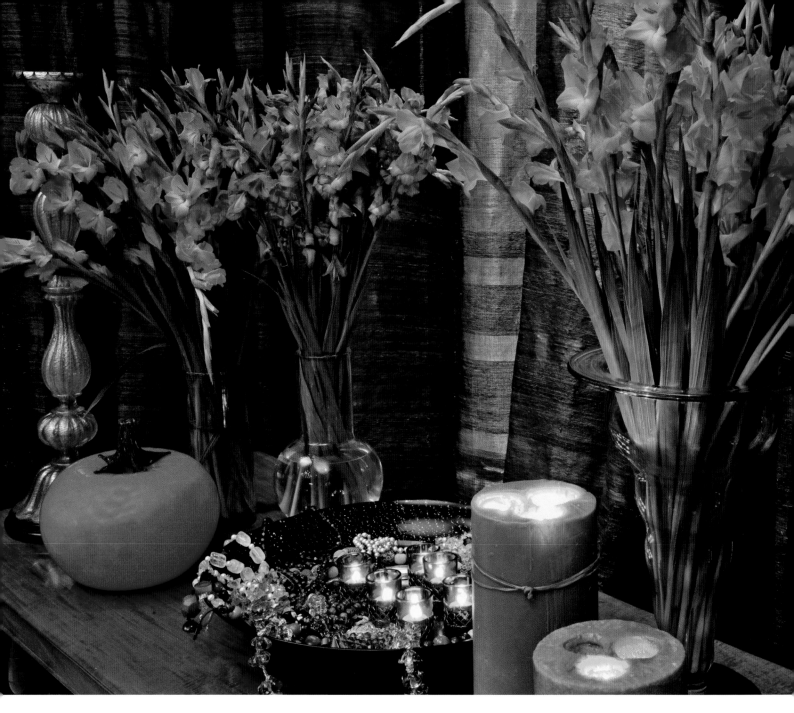

"Pre-production
with the owner is
key. I consider my
task a success once
a client like Lisa
showers me with
encouragement
in the first hours
of planning," says
stylist Eric Paras.

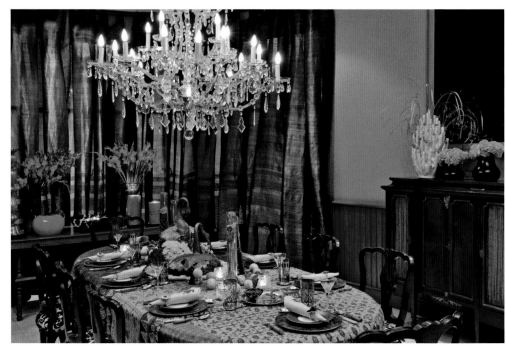

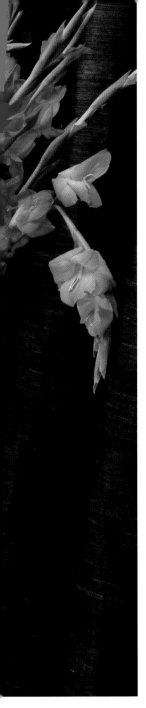

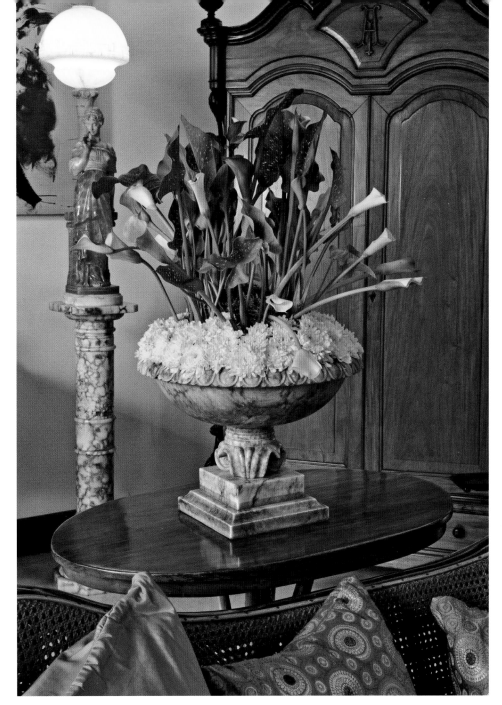

LEFT Lush vases of red and mauve gladioli, bold candles, a bowl of beads and other *objets d'art* add color accents to the dining room scheme.

RIGHT A stunning French Empire-style alabaster figure and pedestal vase draw attention to a fine narra cabinet with kamagong trim. The scale, height and volume of the lily and chrysanthemum arrangement are perfect for a high-ceilinged room.

LEFT The dining room departs from its 1950s look with silk russet drapes. A vintage Baccarat chandelier adds glamor to a colorful and eclectic table setting.

RIGHT A pair of beaten silver phoenix gaze at a tilted centerpiece of yellow chrysanthemums and pink mums, which echo the colors of the Indian table fabrics. Glass columns of amber and rare egg-shaped ivory balls make great conversation pieces.

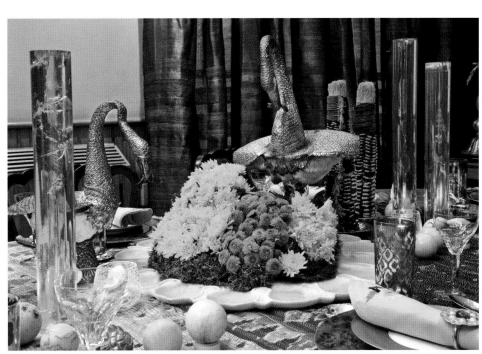

vintage chic updated

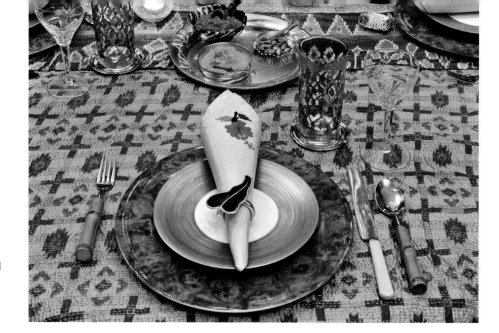

RIGHT A pastiche of curry colors accented with yellow embroidered napkins held by green-lacquered leaf rings, hint of a long dinner of Indian delights.

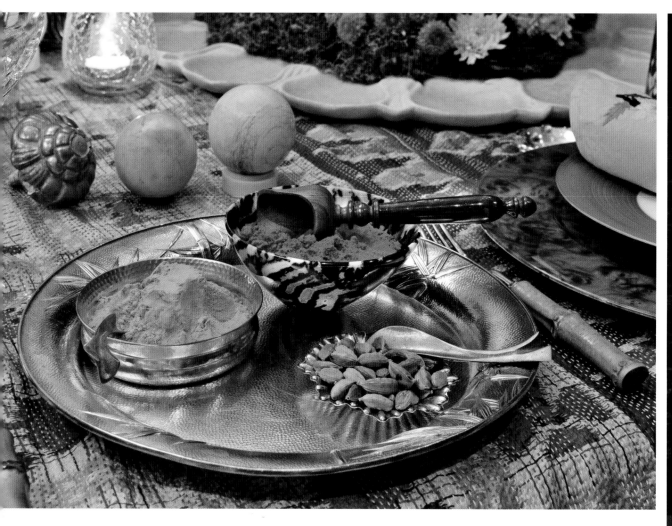

ABOVE An Art Deco-patterned tray on the dining table holds bowls of red chilli powder, golden turmeric and green cardamom seeds, adding to the color fantasy of this stylish setting.

RIGHT Surrounded by a sensual arrangement of pink carnations, scattered mums, floating impatiens and red candles, a curious alabaster shell opens up to reveal a mischievous winged Eros waking up Dawn with a kiss.

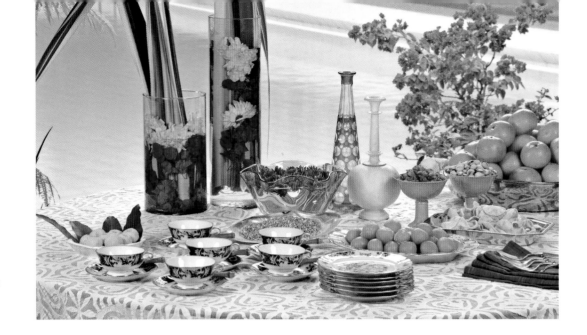

RIGHT Submerged red rose and yellow chrysanthemum heads clinging to long pandan leaves add a dramatic touch to a pool-side coffee table set with English bone china, Indian sweetmeats, nuts and oranges.

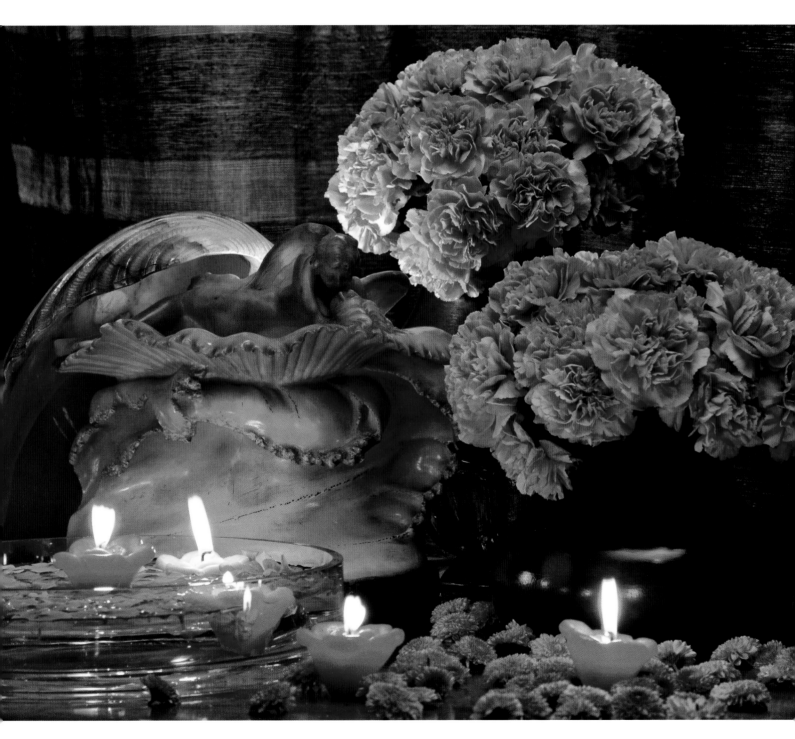

vintage chic updated

silver anniversary celebration

ROJAS HOUSE *Florist* Pico Soriano

CARMEN AND ROMEO ROJAS are a rare example of a couple who are as successful in their business union as they are in their marriage of nearly forty years. Their resplendent Tuscan-style home in Alabang, south of Metro Manila, was largely inspired by their association with their former Italian business partners and the many business trips they made to Italy. A deep interest in things Italian influenced both the architecture and décor of their house as well as the landscape design and planting in their extensive garden.

"The countryside of Italy has such strong floral colors," says Carmen. I don't know the plants by name, but when I see something I like, I get my gardener to look for it here and plant it where it will flourish.... I particularly love thunbergia. It's so versatile and it will grow everywhere. In fact, it's all over the garden here."

Carmen and her brother Pico Soriano, who is currently making waves on the west coast of the USA with his floral installations,

share a deep interest in plants, flowers and entertaining. "My husband and I entertain a lot. I simply cannot imagine a dinner party without floralscapes," says Carmen. "Nor my home without fresh flowers, whether I'm entertaining or not. The house needs flowers every day. My garden is my pride and joy and it's the main source of flowers for the house. In fact, my garden flows seamlessly into some parts of the house."

For this book, Pico flew to Manila for a two-week working vacation, during which time he did floralscapes in five styles for five different houses. For his sister, he created a silver anniversary celebration of her and her husband's business union. Says Carmen, "Our silver wedding anniversary was held in a hotel. It was lovely, but not as grand as we would have liked it to be. But with our fortieth or Ruby anniversary coming up, I'm already thinking up schemes and themes!" Florist brother Pico Soriano is almost certain to be in charge of the floralscapes.

RIGHT Balls of lime button mums serve as novel name place holders, while ribbed table napkins are uniquely folded under small silver chargers. An exquisite ink blue brocade tablecloth subtly brightens the array of gleaming silver and crystal stemware.

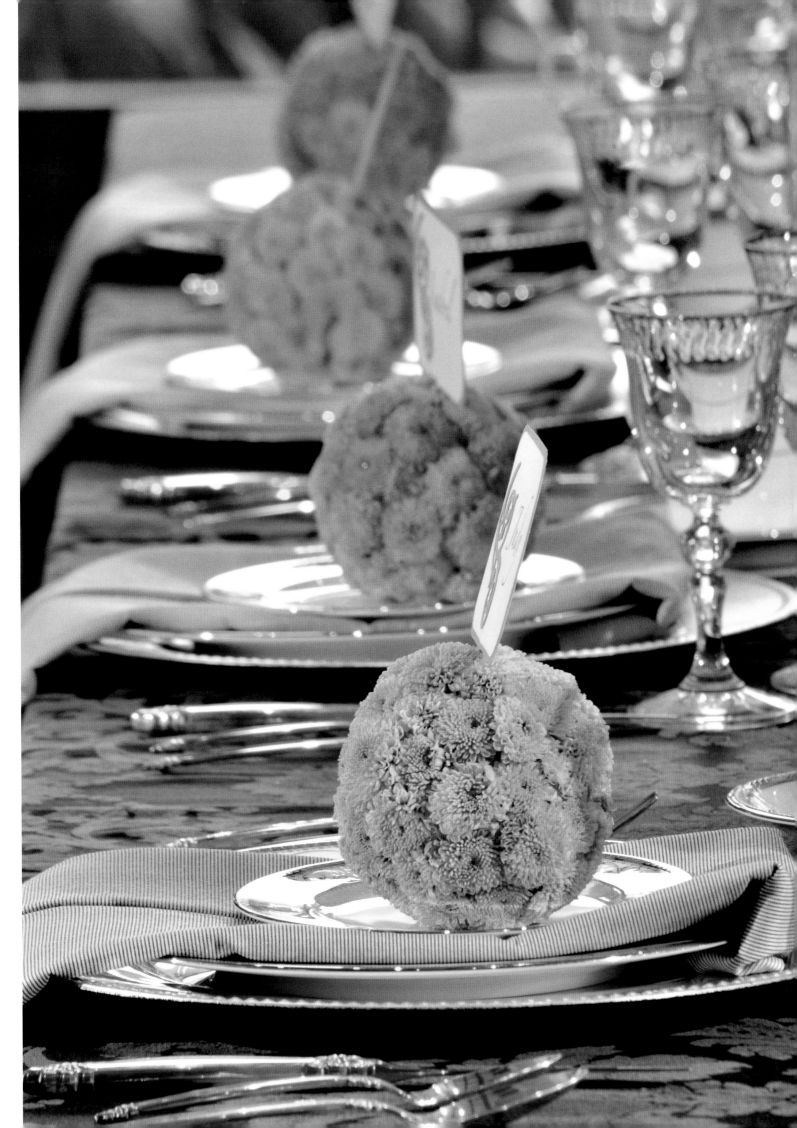

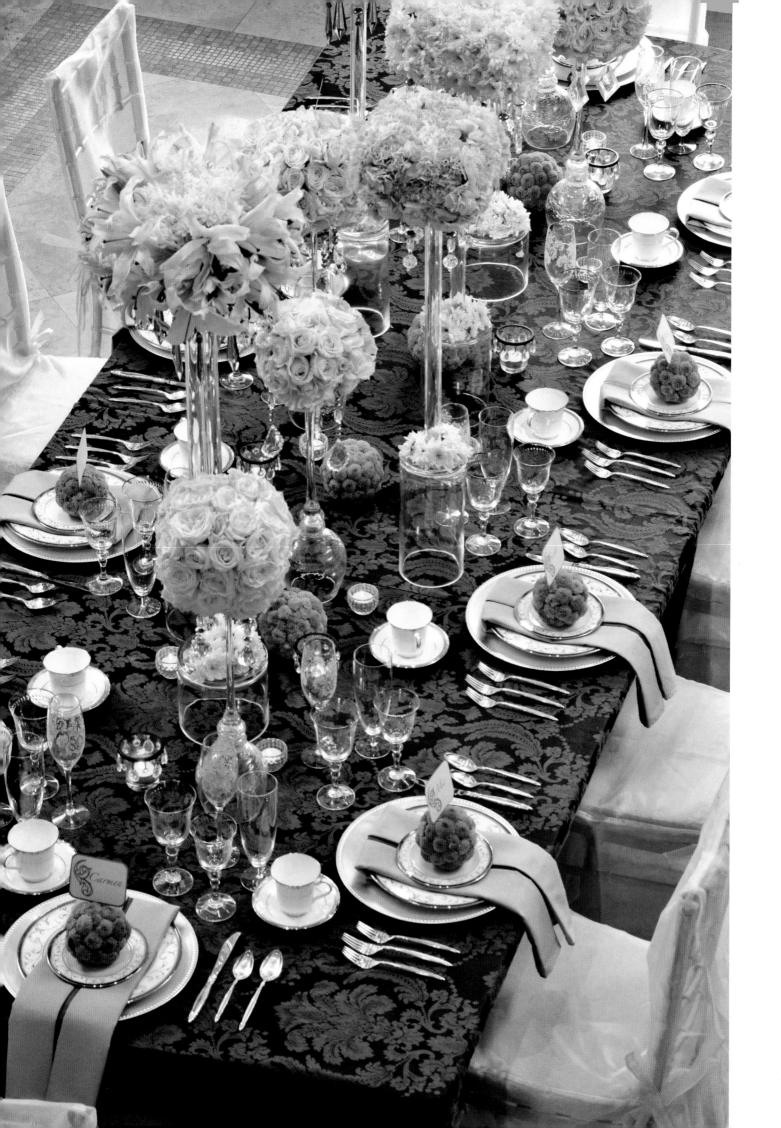

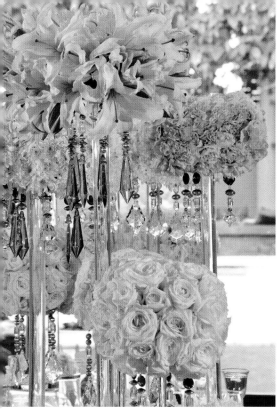

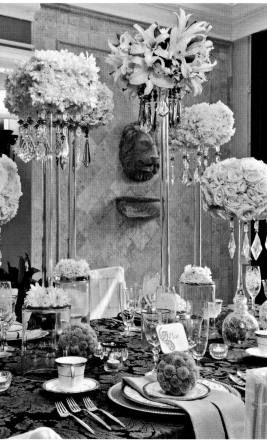

LEFT The floating "clouds" of blooms, with their crystal dangles, appear weightless. Pico and his support team of Nelia and Ricardo purchased them from the garment market in Manila.

ABOVE AND LEFT Pico upturned long-stemmed goblets from Rustan's and glued them onto glass vases to create ethereal floating "clouds" of white Casablanca lilies, white roses and chrysanthemum blooms. Blue and white chandelier crystals suspended from the "clouds" united the flowers with the dark blue brocade tablecloth and opulent tableware. "My vintage silverware is by Rogers and was my first major purchase in my early years of marriage," explains Carmen. Gossamer-sheathed French iron chairs by Nelia Silverio complete the elegant scene.

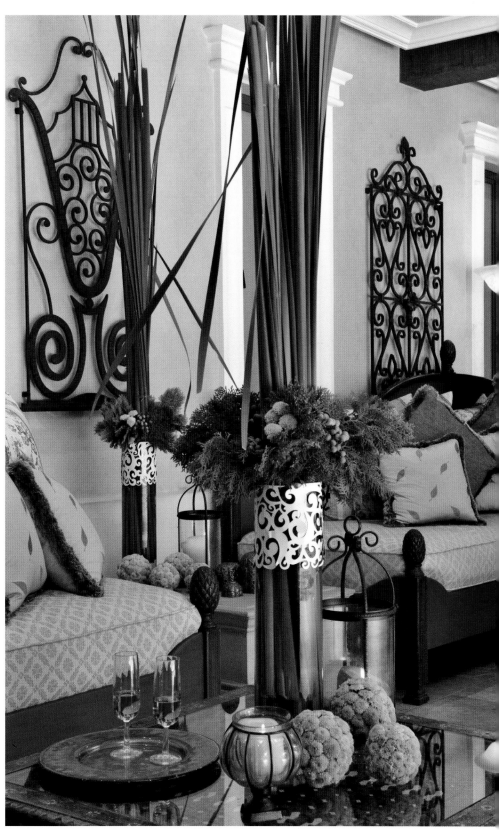

BELOW Facing the pool, sumptuous lounge seating is flanked by cooling towers of river reeds in tall vases with cypress leaf "skirts." The paper cutouts around the rims harmonize with the patterns on the iron wall hangings.

silver anniversary celebration

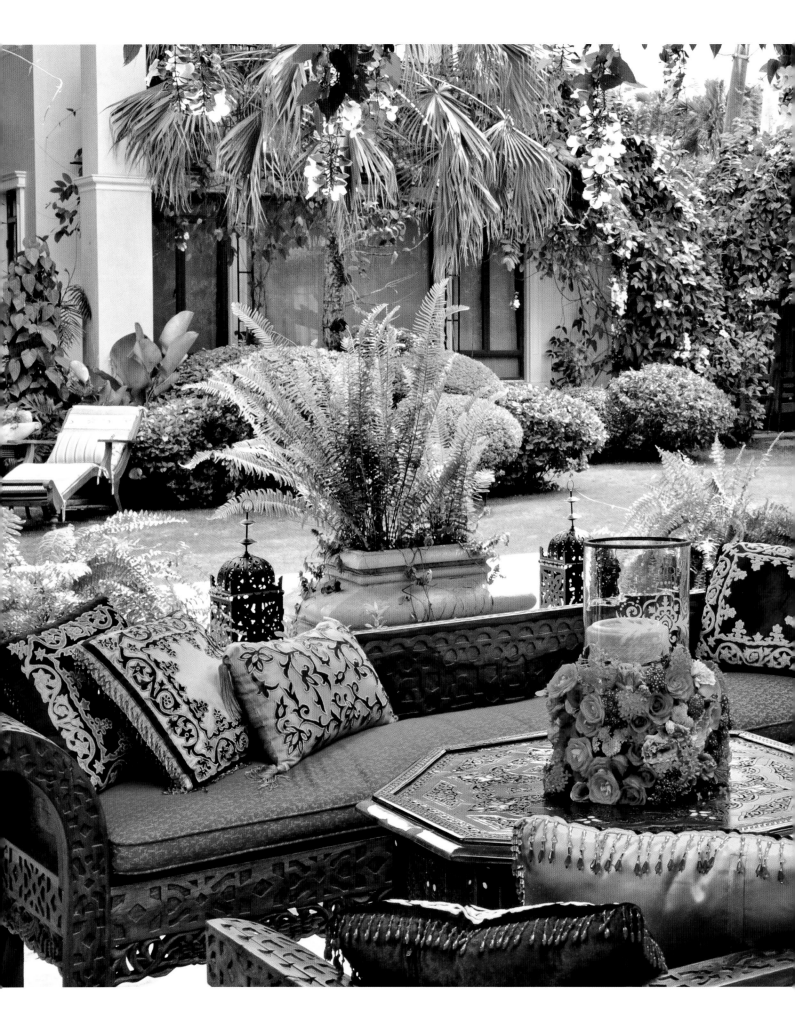

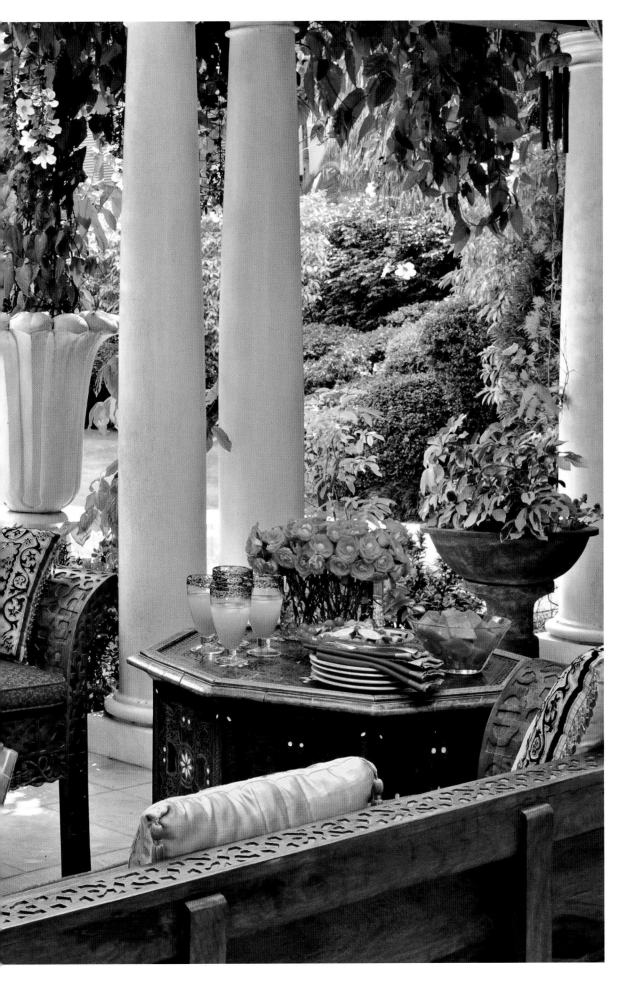

Rich, warm-toned Italian fabrics fashioned into plump cushions set the color key for Pico's flamboyant installations of red and orange roses, red santan flowers (ixora) and lime mums plucked from the garden. Purple and white thunbergias create natural sunscreens for the Moroccan-styled patio nook.

silver anniversary celebration

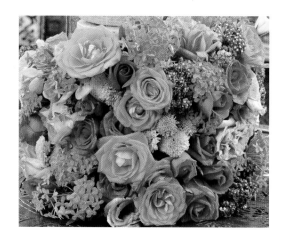

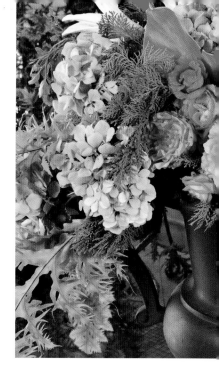

"When planning for a milestone event at home," says Pico Soriano, "use fresh flowers to spark the fireworks. Forget monochromatic flowers and single-look themes. Go for different colors in each room setting."

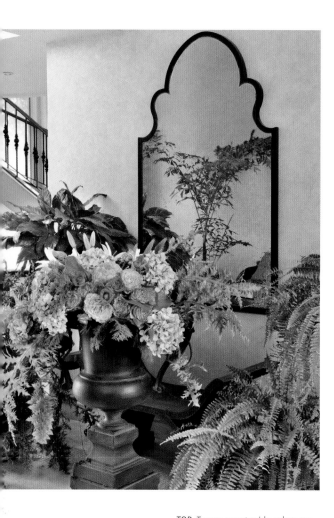

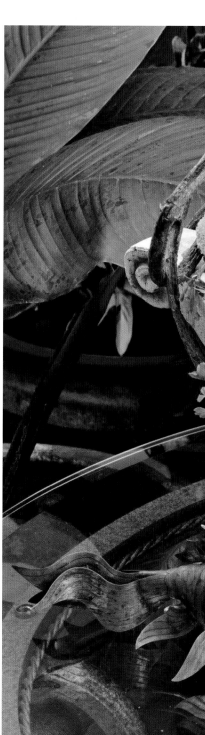

TOP CENTER Pico's passion for hydrangeas cools the fiery tones of red and orange roses.

TOP RIGHT Hot blooms in a cool white vessel add a spot of sunshine in a predominantly green-toned garden.

RIGHT Simple jungle twine, tube stalks and variegated crotons lend a casual air to a bountiful blossom palette of red, orange, lime and purple set on a glass-topped water jar next to bronze open-mouthed goldfish.

TOP Tuscan countryside colors are captured in a spectacular grouping of red and orange roses, lime mums and santan flowers (ixora).

ABOVE Pots of ferns and mounted urns make it easy to bring Carmen's garden inside.

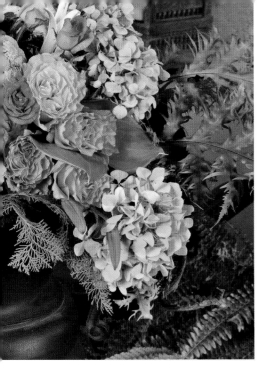

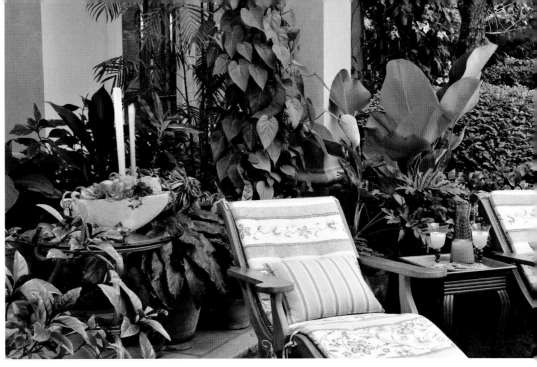

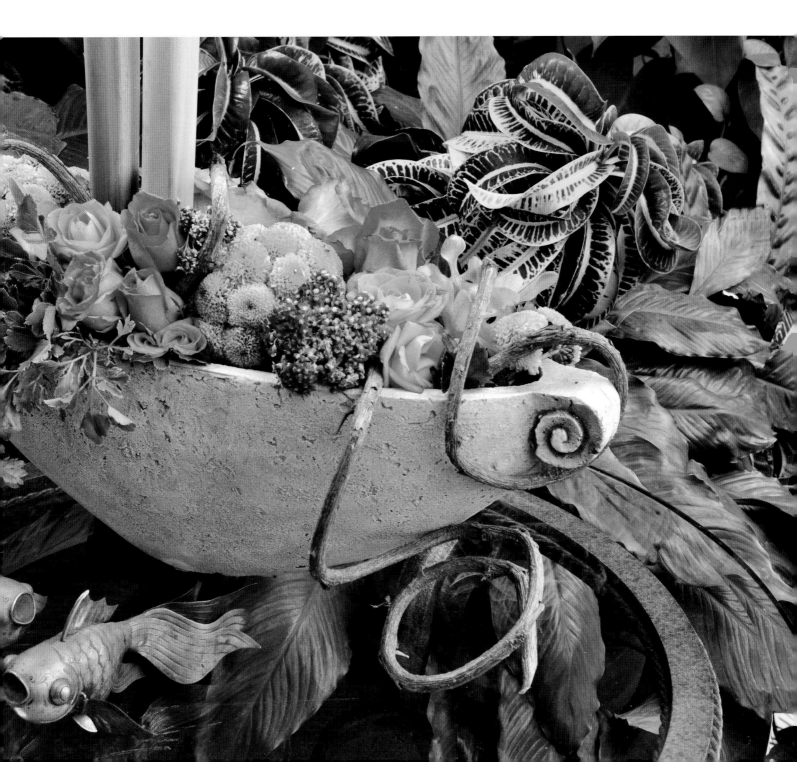

TANTOCO HOME

Florist Pico Soriano   *Flowers* Rustan's Flower Shop

sogetsu style

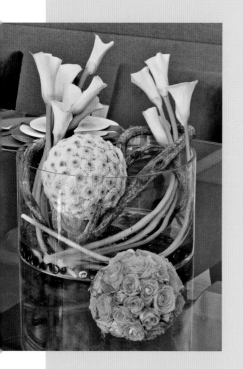

ABOVE In this modern waterless installation, a ball of yellow mums nestles among a swirl of yellow calla lily stems, their trumpets blazing in the face of guests. Orange rose balls scattered on the table add color contrast. OPPOSITE Pico debuts "out-of-the-vase" installations with yellow button mums glued on the outside of a tube vase, visually linked by a twirling jungle vine. On the left are button mum balls resting on a twisted vine inside a vase.

VISITING FILIPINO FLORIST from the US west coast, Pico Soriano took one look and dived straight into the assignment for Marilen Tantoco's Dasmarinas home. Equipped with artifacts from Rustan's and outlets such as Firma and Townes, Pico dazzled with the "waterless" installations he created.

Marilen's house, set on 800 sq m, makes an unusual entry statement. All is long and high. The front door leads through a serpentine-like maze before a huge, cubistic living room is revealed. The towering ceiling is paired with picture-perfect glass windows. The dining room is likewise long and cathedral-high. A garden *lanai*, again with towering posts, and a gargantuan open space look out over a linear swimming pool.

The dining room can accommodate up to twelve guests. "With all the red hues around and the Moroccan-patterned Limoges, I opted instead for a contrast of yellow lilies paired with balls of yellow mums, lying curled and low, with mounted bursts of orange carnations and red anthuriums. Tall funnel vases hold sylloum leaves topped with lipstick plant flowers and red roses. Guests don't feel that they are too far away from each other," Pico declares with satisfaction.

"These high ceilings really work well with big crowds," Marilen explains. "We have a big family on my parents' side. Also, as a buyer for our store, Rustan's, I entertain with frequent dinners. I can't imagine a party without fresh flowers."

Pico surprised everyone with his "out-of-the-vase" installations. Yellow mums were gun-glued on the outer face of tubular vases in descending belts, from large to small. A single twisted vine broke the symmetry. Very ikebana.

"I like drawing inspiration from the Sogetsu ikebana style. It's timeless and modern," Pico states. He was intrigued by the shadows and towering posts in the house. So, for the *lanai*, he installed playful yellow lilies that sprout out of "cakes" of white daisies that match a white chocolate cake. "With a glue-gun, good vases and tall funnels, you can start to explore new territory and create your own Sogetsu-style floral installations!"

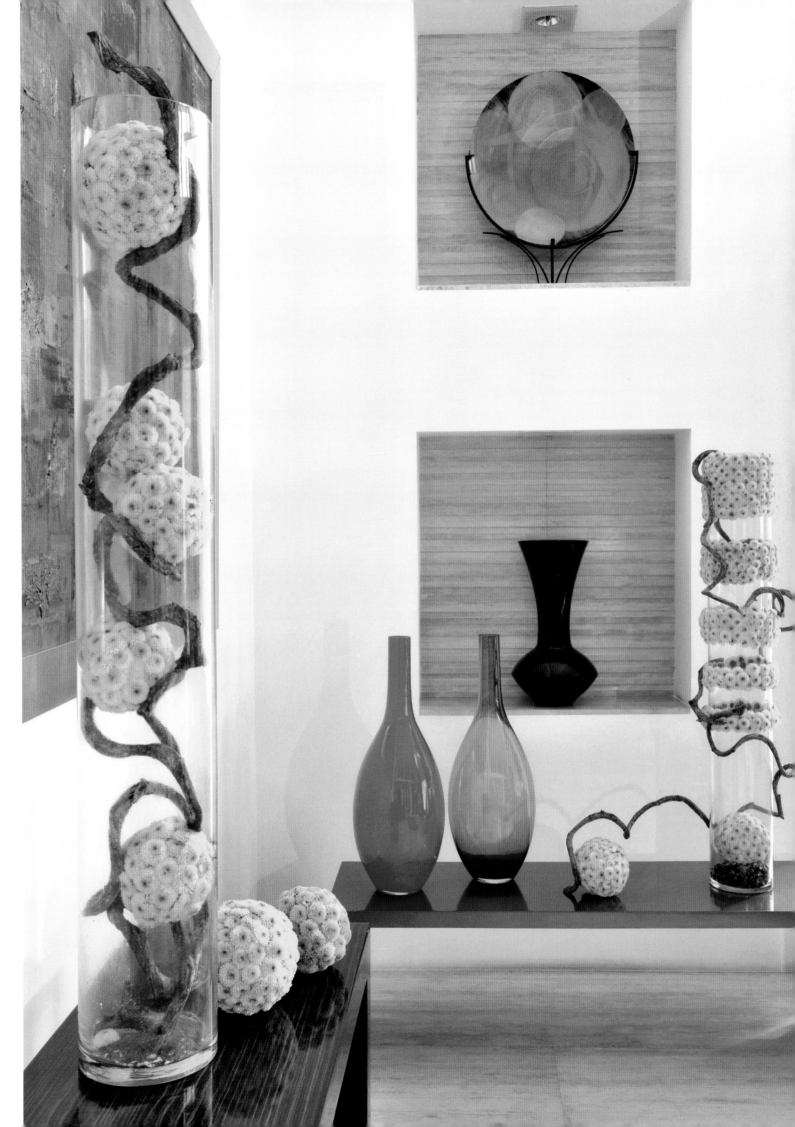

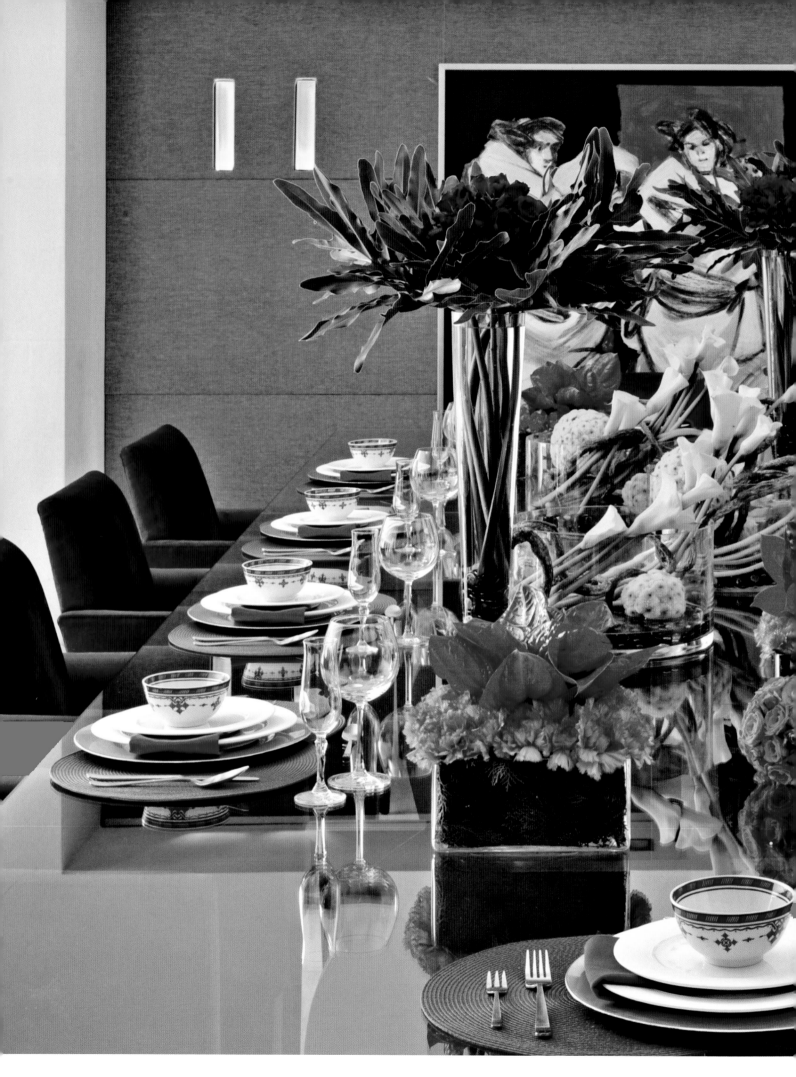

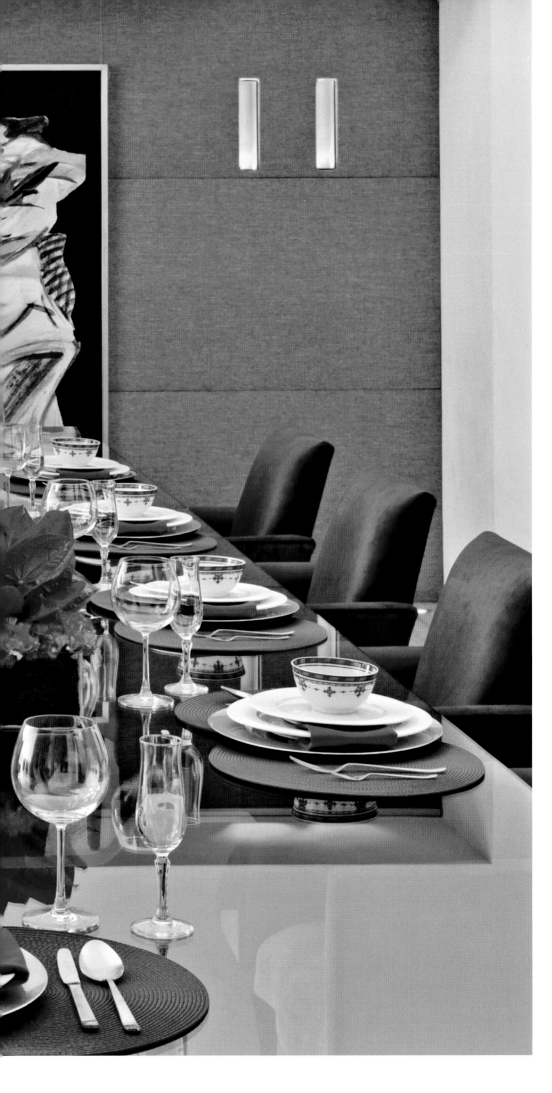

"We have a big family on my parents' side," explains Marilen Tantoco. "Also, as a buyer for our store, Rustan's, I entertain frequently. I can't imagine a party without fresh flowers."

Magnificent deep red lipstick flowers and red roses braced in tall, slim vases by long-stemmed sylloum leaves tower over glorious yellow calla lilies reclining amidst yellow mum balls in circular glass bowls. Bouquets of pink carnations topped by anthuriums peep out of foliage-filled containers, complementing the orange scattered rose balls. Red and white Moroccan-patterned plates resting on red mats, golden chargers and gold Herdmar cutlery emphasize the rich red and gold theme.

sogetsu style

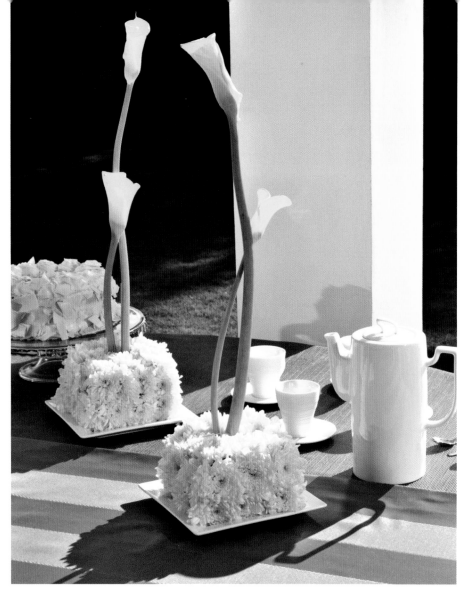

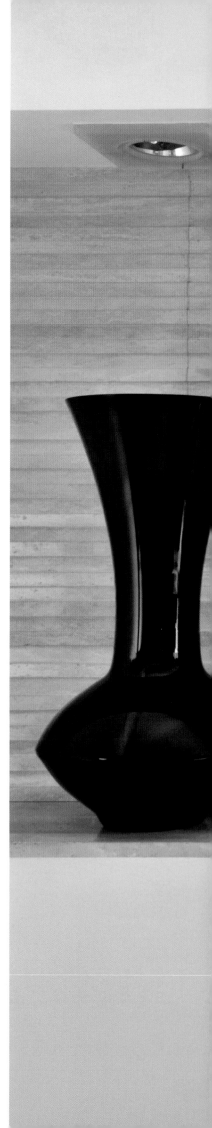

ABOVE Yellow calla lilies form tapers on square "cakes" cleverly formed of white mums, next to a real white chocolate cake. A pure white coffee service laid on striped fabrics by Townes creates pillar shadows on the *lanai* table.

RIGHT The high hung drapes and raindrop crystal lights in the cathedral-height room add casual drama to the grand dining table setting below.

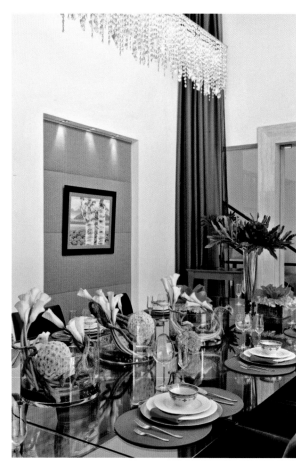

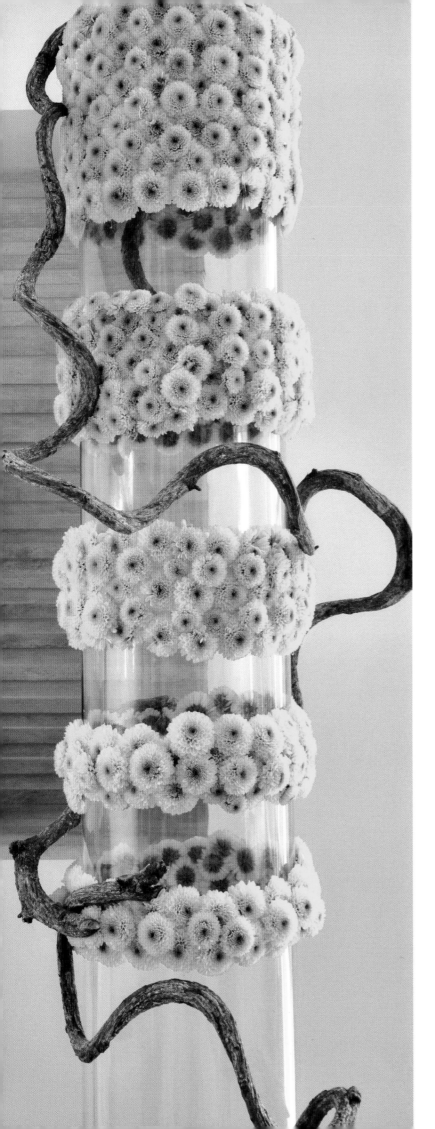

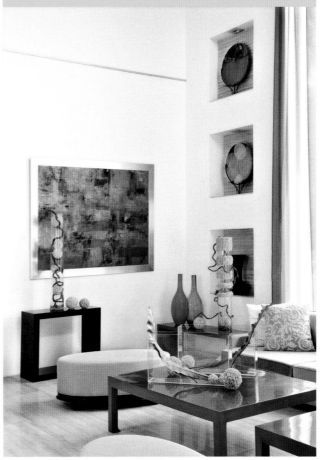

"I like drawing inspiration from the Sogetsu ikebana style. It's timeless and modern," Pico Soriano declares.

LEFT "Out-of-the vase" floral magic created with a simple glue gun and yellow button mums. Jungle vines provide a rustic contrast.

ABOVE The living room is bathed with light from towering glass windows. Recessed shelves show-case prized ceramic art. On the low coffee table, leaves from the bird's nest fern or *pakpak lawin* are paired with large lime green and small yellow mum balls.

sogetsu style

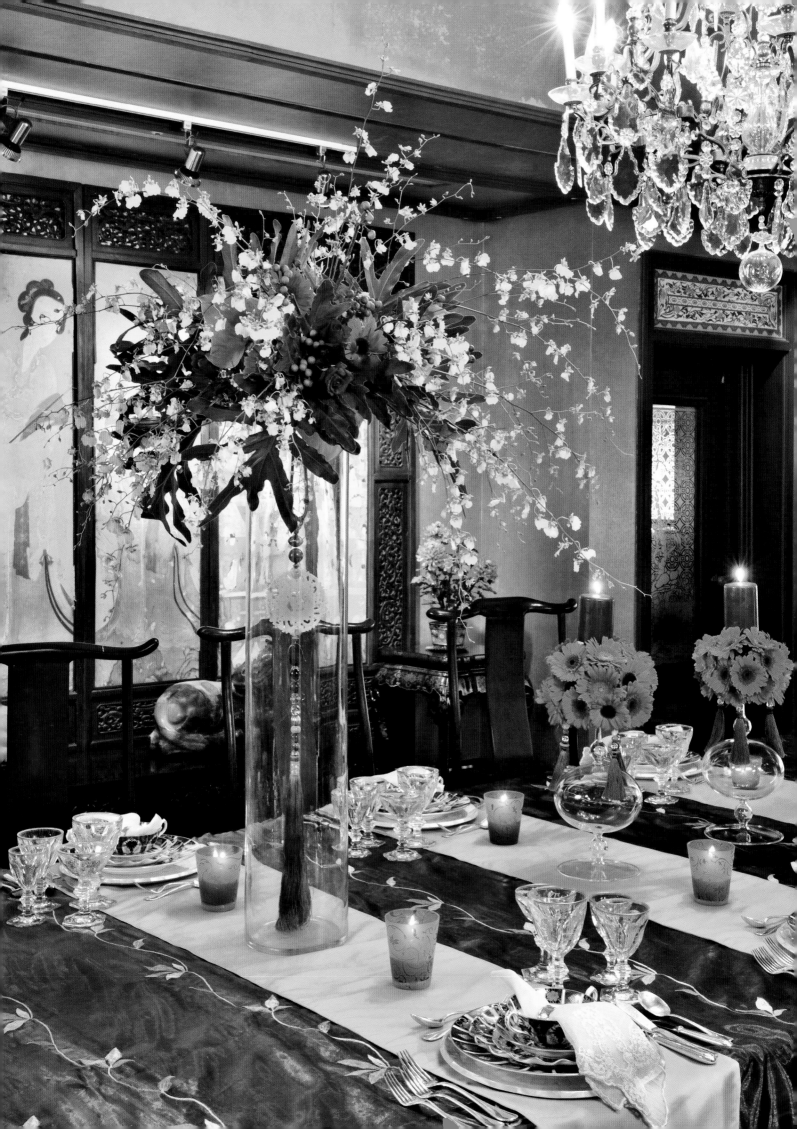

ambassadorial
artistry

TANTOCO MANSION   *Florist* Pico Soriano   *Flowers* Rustan's Flower Shop

RETIRED AMBASSADOR Bienvenido Tantoco may be a diplomatic "empty nester," but his luxurious home in Manila is still a much-used and admired venue for receiving important guests and extended family. Grand floral arrangements are an important accessory in the house when he is entertaining.

For this book, the challenge facing Filipino-American florist Pico Soriano was to "contemporize" a dated mansion filled with old treasures—Philippine turn-of-the-century oil paintings, Czarist malachite tables, Louis IV furniture, gem-studded Moroccan tapestries and much more.

Pico's décor strategy was simple. "Use fresh flowers on a grandiose scale and express exuberant ideas with simple flowers and modern color schemes. Don't let fresh florals compete with period furniture and art. Complement them instead in color and scale. Use bold volume and height to reflect the grandiose detailed period art and furniture collection. By repeating a color in a room, you can pull all the elements together."

Pico's 2010 award-winning entry in a floral competition in San Francisco, which reflected his design philosophy, was re-enacted in the Tantoco mansion. For the ambassador's chinoiserie dining room, regally set for a dinner party for twenty, Pico re-created his signature waterless floral installations in two dominant colors—red and yellow—to harmonize with the décor of the room. Two towering glass cylinders crowned with yellow oncidium orchids, popularly known as "dancing ladies," red roses, red gerberas and red carnations tucked within philodendron leaves and suspended at the glass rims by bamboo sticks, reach up to meet the room's vaulted gold-leafed ceiling and grand Baccarat chandelier. To complement the chinoiserie theme, each towering tube contains a jade plate suspended on a beaded silk tassel, created by Chito Vijandre of Firma. Globular glass vases filled with masses of red gerberas, with more beaded tassels, and red glass candleholders complete the grand table setting.

In other parts of the mansion, Pico employed his other floral love—hydrangeas—here pale green blooms clustered with orchids, roses and mums in toning shades. A huge bouquet of tiny white baby's breath, another award-winning arrangement, graces the grand piano in the drawing room. Vivid red anthuriums at the base spell modernity.

OPPOSITE A regal dining table for twenty under a Baccarat chandelier displays Pico's amazing waterless installations. A jade plate on a beaded tassel hangs inside a towering vase. Glass globes magically balance clusters of red gerberas topped by russet candles.

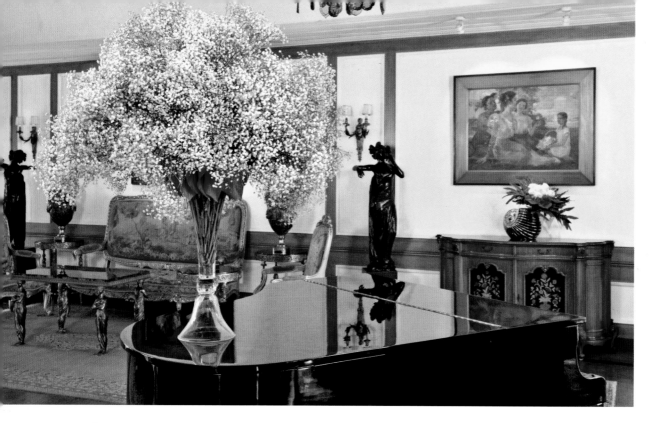

ABOVE Pico Soriano's award-winning arrangement, a giant burst of white baby's breath braced at the rim by a circle of vivid red anthuriums, injects a contemporary feel in the formal drawing room.

RIGHT A bold mass of pale green hydrangeas and green button mums topped with white roses brings lightness and ease to a room full of stately royal European furniture and deep green malachite decorative items.

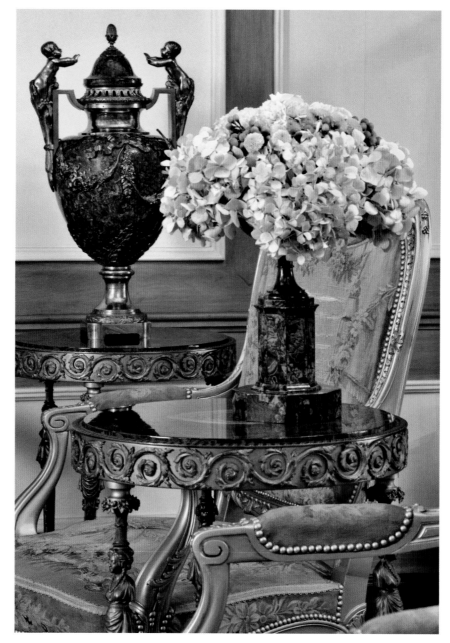

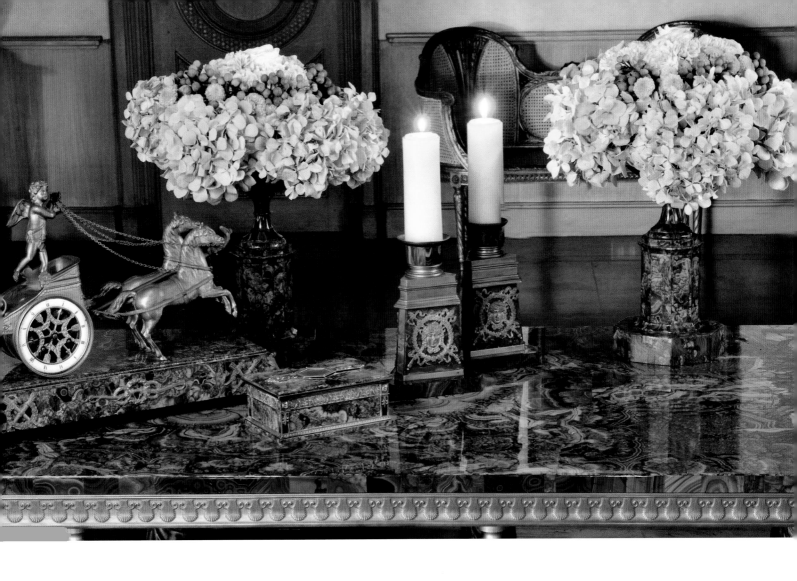

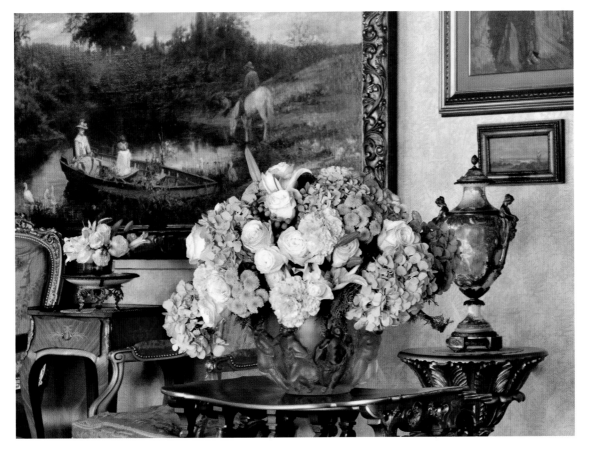

ABOVE Clusters of pale green hydrangeas topped with berries and white roses soften the hard-edged Czarist malachite desk accessories.

LEFT The foyer, replete with fine art and exquisite period furniture, gleams with a fresh color palette of pale green hydrangeas, pink and white roses and white stargazers.

ambassadorial artistry

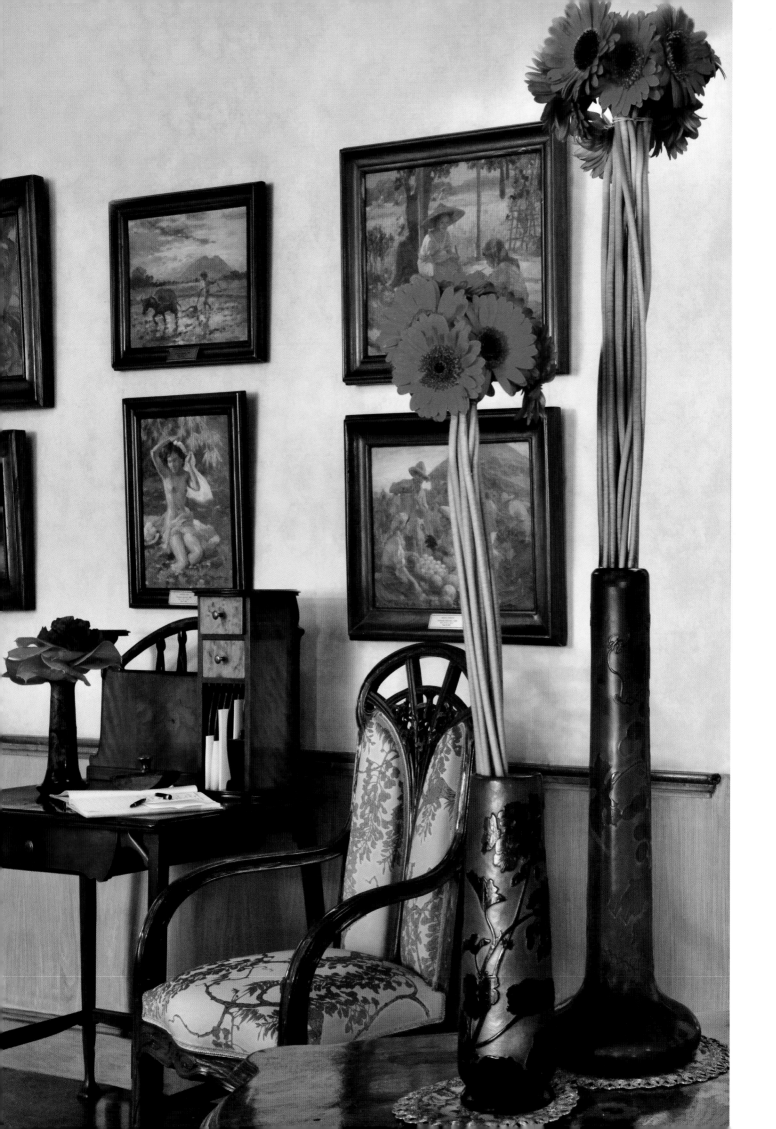

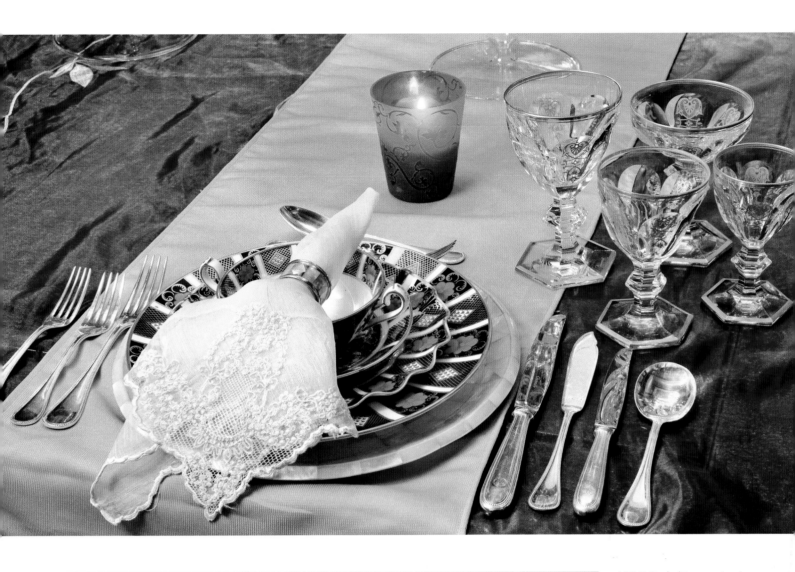

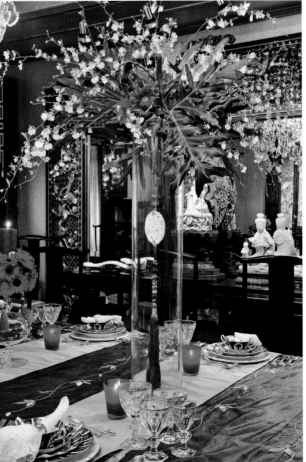

Pico Soriano suggests, "Don't let fresh florals compete with period furniture and art. Complement them instead with color and scale."

ABOVE Stacked Japanese Imari-patterned porcelain and delicate embroidered pineapple fiber napkins are flanked by Christofle cutlery. A votive candle glows on the elegant gold and russet silk table covers.

LEFT This contemporary display of oncidium orchids or "dancing ladies," brilliant gerberas and philodendron leaves holds its own against magnificent chinoiserie treasures. Waterless floral installations allow guests to see and converse across a dining table.

OPPOSITE Two Bohemian glass vases hold towering bunches of gerberas tied below their heads, a modern contrast to the wall of Amorsolo oils in the retired ambassador's study.

ambassadorial artistry

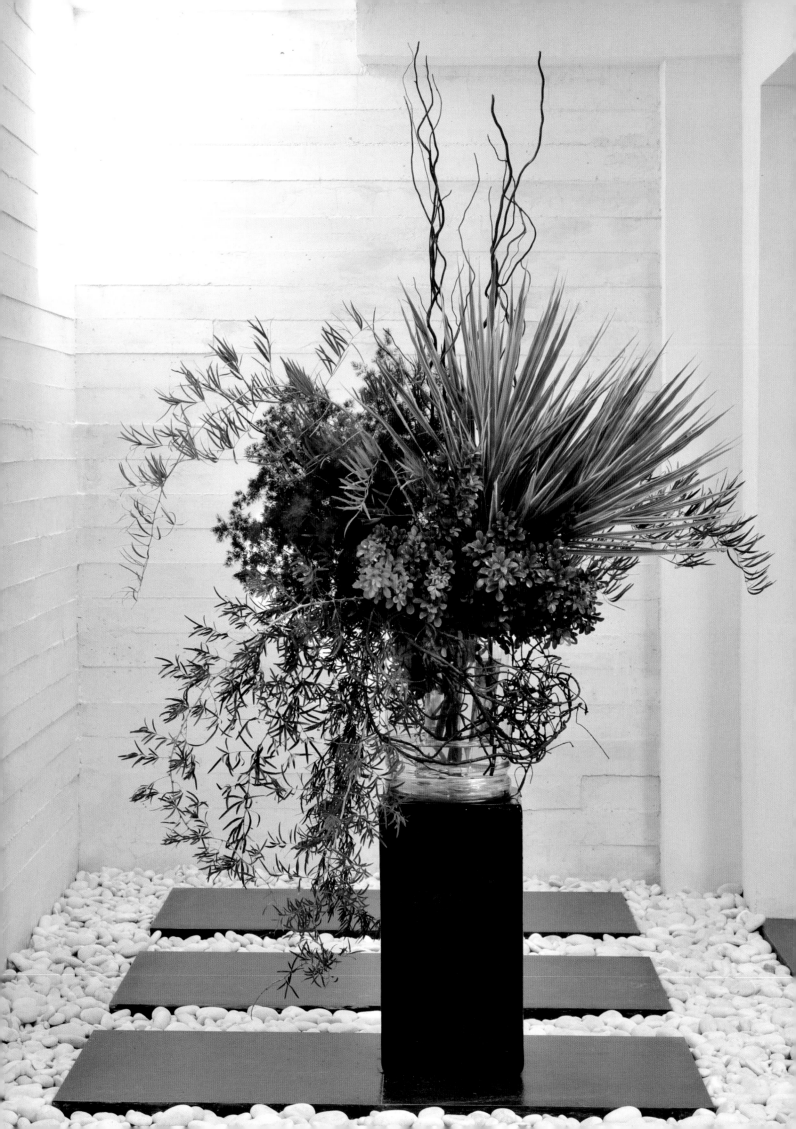

a *serene* lightness

THIS SERENE HOME is situated in Asia's once-largest subdivision, where row upon row of cookie-cutter houses reflect a typical 1970s mass residential building style. It was here that Tanya Lara, a lifestyle columnist, and edgy architect Jason Buensalido turned against the tide of history. Instead of going "out of the box", they went "into the box". The result? A house that has no windows so that one need never look out on predictable 1970s suburbia. This is a truly modern home that requires neither light nor air from the outside. An ice-cool whiteness pervades it, imbuing it with a Zen-like feeling of serenity.

Architect Buensalido explains his "into the box" design concept. "As the outer walls have no windows, the ceiling incorporates glass windows—to the sky and the light. When it rains, the water drops create interesting patterns projected by the shafts in the open interior space."

At the front door, a dramatic interplay of black and white greets visitors. Here, behind a clear glass sheet, designer and stylist Leo Almeria has installed a huge vase of flowers on a black gallery plinth. This glass assumes the role of "spirit wall," a feng shui device. It also prevents visitors from walking straight into it!

For Tanya's black and white rooms, Leo recommended the use of fresh foliage and flowers as decoration. Natural leaves in cool greens, chartreuse and tart limes make excellent base lines for the modernist environment. "You can use wild shrubbery, cogon grass—which is used for making native brooms—and dried branches for floral volume and height. They don't cost much, and they lend a very contemporary ikebana feel."

The ceiling hides an array of cubistic recessed lighting, with warm energy-saving lights. On the black and white interior treatment, every detail stands out like a painter's brushstroke on a white canvas. A black Philippe Starck chair provides a bold contrast to a long white couch, a Ray and Charles Eames chair and a side table by Eileen Grey.

A wall of open shelves contains carefully selected finds. Against black and white, cheery colored gerberas beam brightly. In a corner between stark white cube pillars, a pristine white Moroso chair flanked by a tall vase containing curious looking yellow lantern blossoms adds coolness.

The dining table is by Izamu Noguchi, paired with Panton chairs. Leo once again uses chartreuse mums on individual napkins lavishly knotted with "prosperity rings." He points out that mums can be substituted with other fresh items, such as a strawberry, a pear, or any organic curiosity—anything that can add color and textural surprise.

Tanya travels a lot for lifestyle assignments. Time permitting, she tries to bring back a "trophy" that ends up in an honored spot on her open shelves. But the oft-quoted maxim, "less is more," is an unspoken rule, especially with her signature pieces, such as a curious ottoman that looks like corks bunched together, by Kenneth Cobunpue, whose pieces often end up in the homes of screen royalty in Beverly Hills.

Think out of the box? Into the box is more like it, and the effect is refreshing and outstanding. Fresh flowers definitely harmonize the drama of black and white—and also do a lot to soften the cubistic cuts and edges.

LEFT A grand welcoming installation created by stylist Leo Almeria comprises a tactile burst of scarlet foliage from the rainbow tricolor tree and native cinamomo foliage mounted on a handsome black marble plinth. Contorted willow camouflages the round glass container.

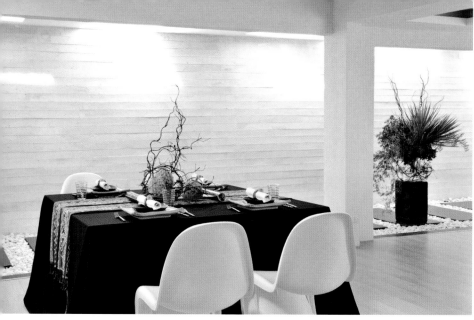

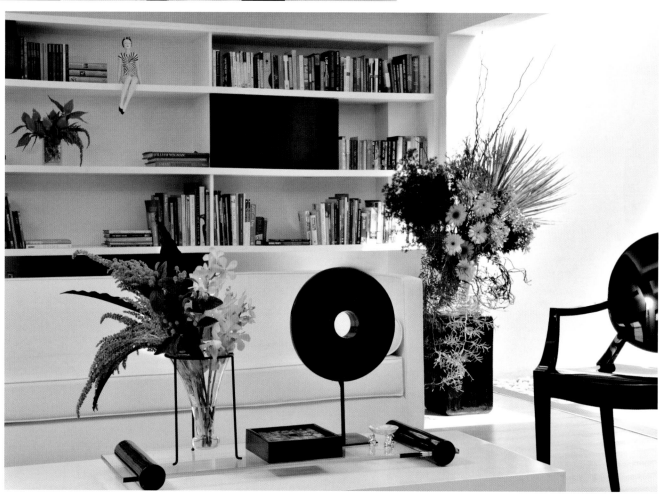

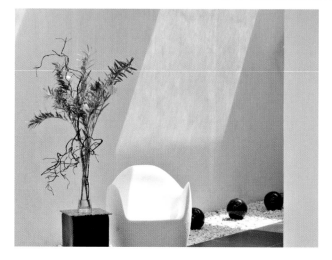

LEFT In Tanya Lara's innovative windowless home, sunlight from glass ceiling window panes bathes the Izamu Noguchi dining table and Panton chairs.

RIGHT Long beans wrap green Malaysian button mum balls amidst contorted willow branches on the glass centerpiece. More long beans form prosperity rings for the table napkins and the nests below the stacked stoneware plates designed by Leo Almeria.

ABOVE The modern white sofa and a black Philippe Starck armchair are warmed by big, bright arrangements of mokara orchids and amaranthus, multicolored gerberas and tricolor foliage.
OPPOSITE BELOW Almeria-designed stoneware plates and square inlaid trays are accompanied by bright gerberas and chrysanthemums in this cheerful breakfast setting.

RIGHT A starkly modern white Moroso chair is paired with a stately ikebana installation of butterfly flowers, green lantern pods and twisted twigs.

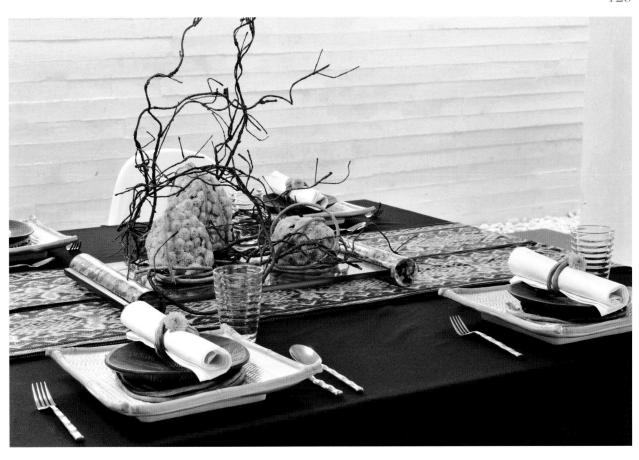

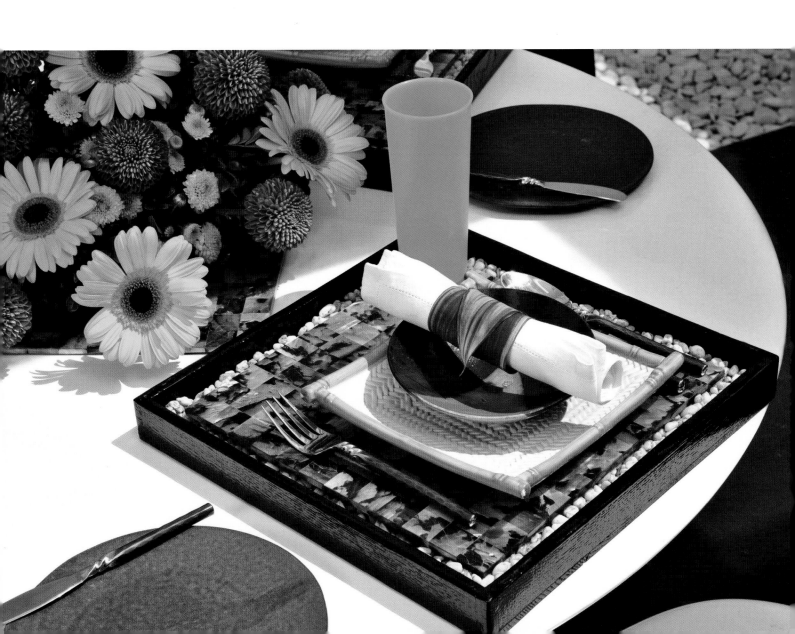

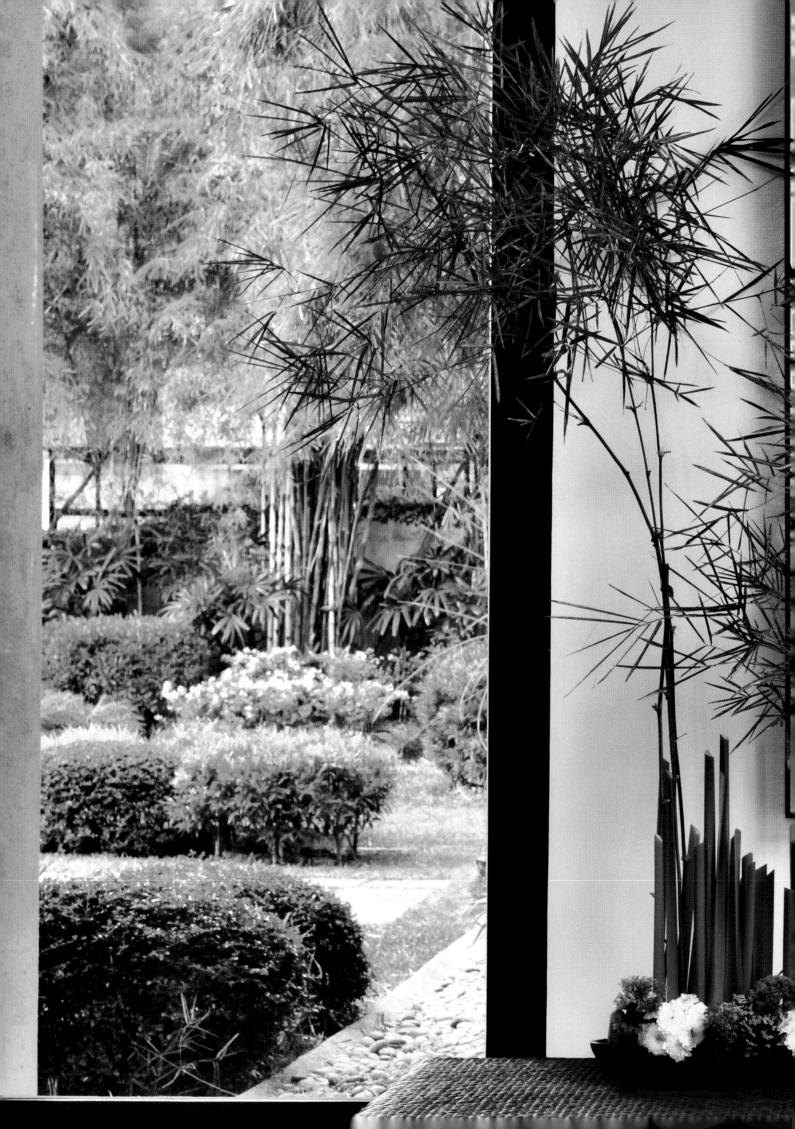

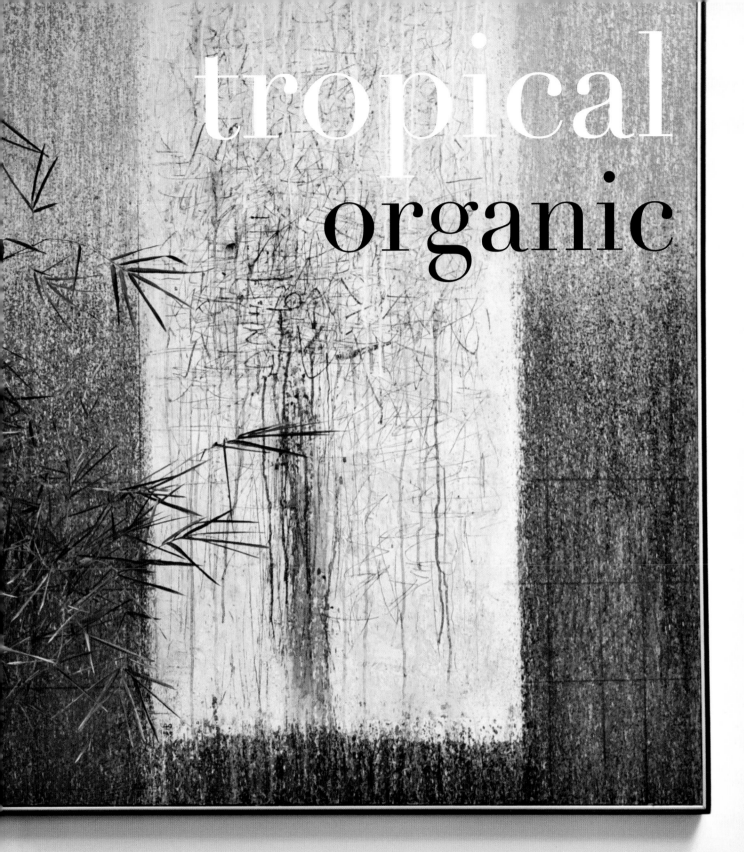

tropical
organic

FELICIANO HOUSE

Florist Pico Soriano   *Flowers* The Flower Farm

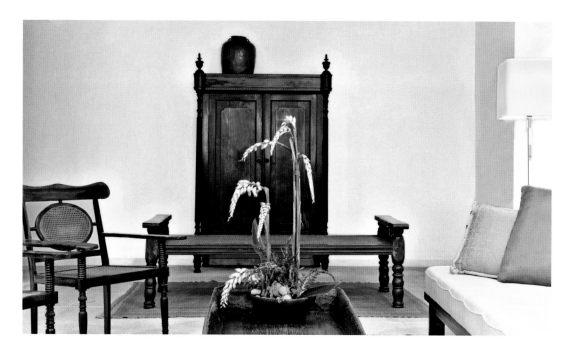

LEFT Minimal traditional Filipino furniture allows for the subtle spirit of Sogetsu ikebana. Pink shell ginger stalks rise from a base of stones and lime balls, here shown against a classic hardwood *aparador* or cabinet.
PREVIOUS SPREAD At the entry, a large ethereal work by Chinese minimalist Lao Lianben is complemented by a modern Sogetsu ikebana arrangement of splayed bamboo branches, a jagged row of chopped reed stalks and white chrysanthemums nestled among variegated papyrus greens in a narrow wooden bowl.

A LONG WHITE FENCE lined by bamboos borders this corner Ayala Alabang property. Within, calm water features outline an L-shaped house and a peaceful aura fills the air. The two-story residence, once an enclosed 1990s bungalow, has been transformed, turned around, opened up and styled by Manila's popular tropical-organic designers, Budji Layug and Royal Pineda. A separate glassed-in pavilion now serves as a venue for casual entertaining while viewing the expansive garden and large swimming pool.

Owner Roberta Lopez Feliciano simply loves being at home: "It's now so nice to stay home and enjoy the fresh air, and do my yoga while waiting for the kids!" When she is not out playing sport or managing three yoga studios, she is at home savoring the clean lines and organically furnished spaces of her home. "I've always liked minimal furnishings. I don't like much fuss and I don't collect many things."

Our guest floral stylist, Pico Soriano, approached the peaceful abode armed with a selective palette of flowers from The Flower Farm in Tagaytay. With one glance at the modern-minimalist interiors of the house, he decided to go thoroughly spare and Asian: "I opted for the Sogetsu ikebana style for the contemporary look and the Zen feel it exudes."

Pico started in the dining alcove with its modern elements—a hanging lightbox lined with fine tree twigs and sliding glass doors with pull-down blinds reminiscent of Japanese *shoji* screens. He set the table with Japanese-style dishware—large soup bowls and ceramic teacups on woven placemats. On a wooden tray, he assembled a low-slung centerpiece of giant red anthurium blossoms anchored by flat gray stones from the garden.

On the buffet, Pico created an artful Sogetsu arrangement using pink banana flower stalks anchored by palm leaves, orange gingers and garden stones. The floral sculpture echoes the hues of an abstract on the wall behind by Fernando Zobel.

Pico then created a second floral sculpture called "Green Lantern Pond." On a flat wooden tray, he wove palm leaves into a mat-like base, and there anchored green lanterns on spindly stems. The hairy green balls, new plantings from The Flower Farm, are here transformed into fine Zen sculptures. The Sogetsu arrangements made the most impact when displayed next to Roberta's modern paintings, such as the ash gray work by Lao Lianben or the bright blue modernist painting by Fernando Modesto.

Pico says of the clean, modern interior: "Minimalist doesn't mean bare and stark. Let fresh flowers—arranged in Sogetsu ikebana-inspired forms—amplify the silent drama and inner spirit of your home."

RIGHT Roberta's home mixes Filipino modern art and Japanese floral arts. A blue modernist painting by Fernando Modesto resonates with Pico's Sogetsu installation of lime green lanterns on spindly stems anchored by woven palm fronds and river stones.

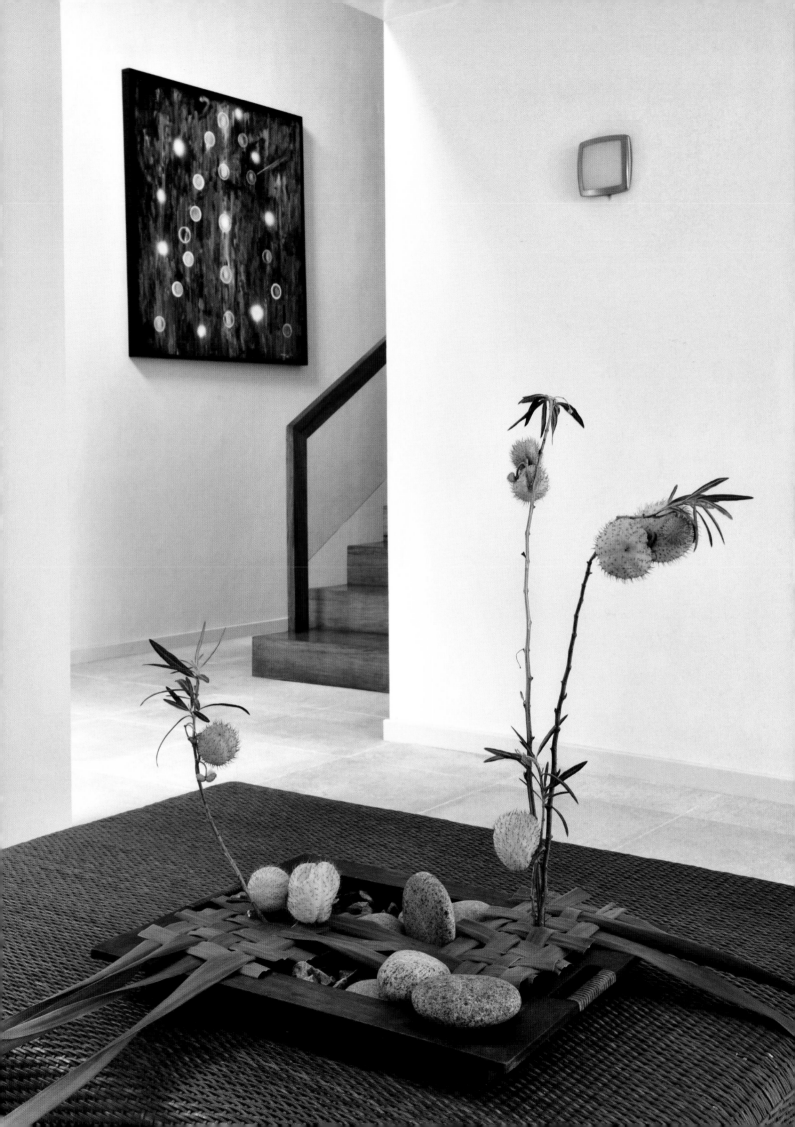

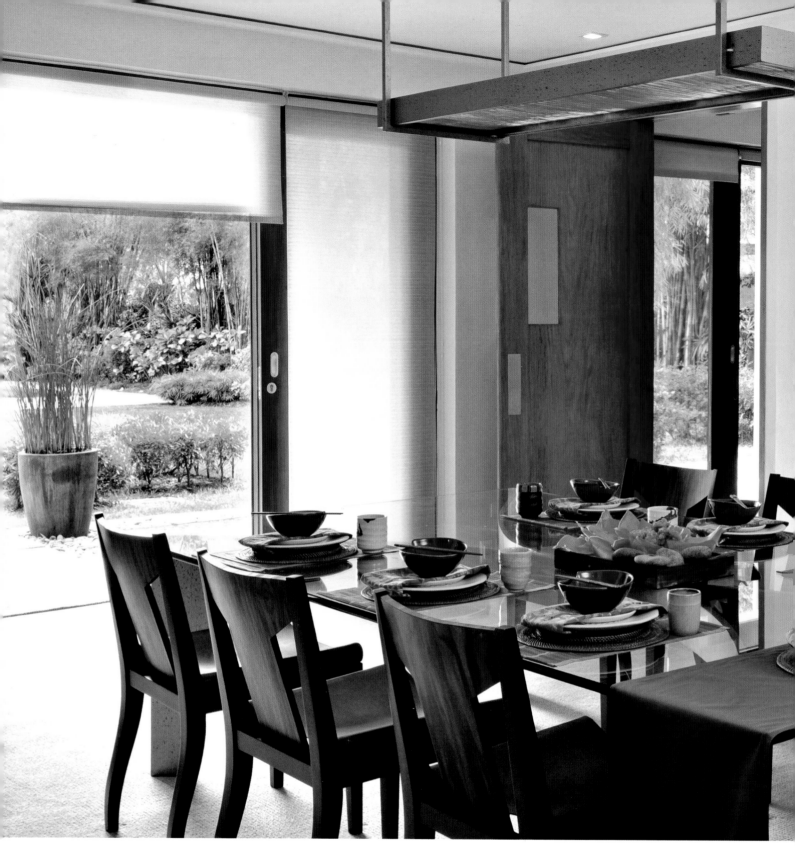

ABOVE The subtle hues of an abstract painting by Fernando Zobel form a wonderful backdrop to Pico Soriano's sideboard Sogetsu installation of flowering pink banana stalks anchored by looped palm leaves, stones and orange gingers.

RIGHT The modern Japanese table setting, created around a low-slung centerpiece of red anthurium petals arranged in the shape of a lotus blossom, harmonizes wonderfully with the woven placemats, red floral napkins and ceramic bowls and teacups.

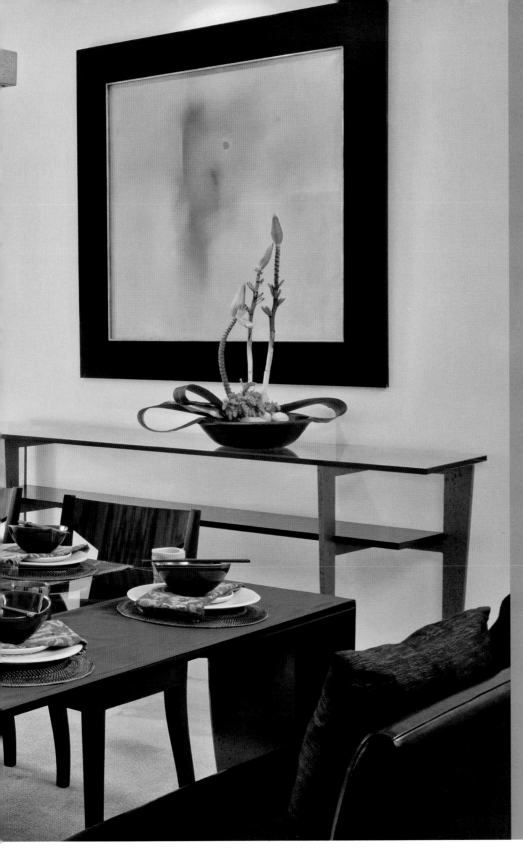

"Minimalist doesn't mean bare and stark," says floral artist Pico Soriano. "Let fresh flowers—arranged in Sogetsu ikebana-inspired forms—amplify the silent drama and inner spirit of your home."

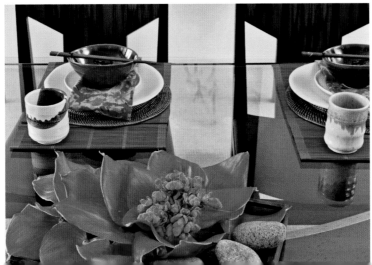

tropical organic

classical concept

A VINTAGE PENTHOUSE *Florist* Pico Soriano *Flowers* Rustan's Flower Shop

THE DIPLOMAT'S RESIDENCE lies a quick ride up a private lift to a penthouse on the 23rd floor of a condominium soaring high over Makati. The elegant residence, filled with the owners' vintage Filipino art collection, is a stately "other world." It is virtually wallpapered with a treasure trove of heirloom Philippine paintings by highly acclaimed artists, among them Hidalgo, Juan Luna, Amorsolo and Ben Cab.

The owners' architect, designer and trusted family friend, Jonathan Matti, laid out the high-rise condo residence and installed the treasury of paintings. It exudes the traditional ambience of an ancestral home, yet allows for modern functions to blend seamlessly into the magnificent décor.

The scarlet dining room, set amid classic drapery, is the crowning jewel. The owners of the penthouse use it for intimate dinner parties of ten or twelve. Here, a 19th-century French bronze chandelier casts a glow on the gold and red motifs on the stunning Limoges plateware, Saint Louis stemware and Daubain ivory-handled silverware.

To complement the splendor of the table settings on the giant hardwood table, guest florist from San Francisco, Pico Soriano, opted to use ultra-classic roses and hydrangeas. Glorious red and orange roses interspersed with pink hydrangeas are bountifully and carefully composed into graceful domes in stunning silver bowls. Pico delivers by harmonizing

with—not competing against—the surrounding interior. He says: "I did a contemporary dome-shaped interpretation of the Flemish style of the 15th to 17th centuries to echo the classic period art pieces and heirlooms in this ornate dining room."

Pico counterbalances the olden aura of the classic decor by "contemporizing" his arrangements. He manipulates scale, styling his flowers into oversized or diminutive arrangements according to the space. He also uses a monochromatic color palette to keep his floralscapes from detracting from the colorful details and timeless heritage of the paintings.

In the ultra-genteel living room, he installs more classic flowers—blue, lavender and white hydrangeas and white roses. "The large floral arrangement, again in the Flemish style, mixes tropical white anthuriums with hydrangeas, roses and clustered carnations, giving it a peony-like appearance. Clustered white pom-poms are used to mimic snowball flowers. This is a perfect classic complement to the extensive art collection and the lavish furnishings in the penthouse, serving to pull the objects and colors in the room together."

Only in the adjacent library does Pico go for an ultra-modern treatment against the dark woods, books and rustic earthenware. "I filled the jars with a Biedemeier (concentric rings of flowers) arrangement, in layers of de-spadixed anthuriums centered with a cluster of red roses."

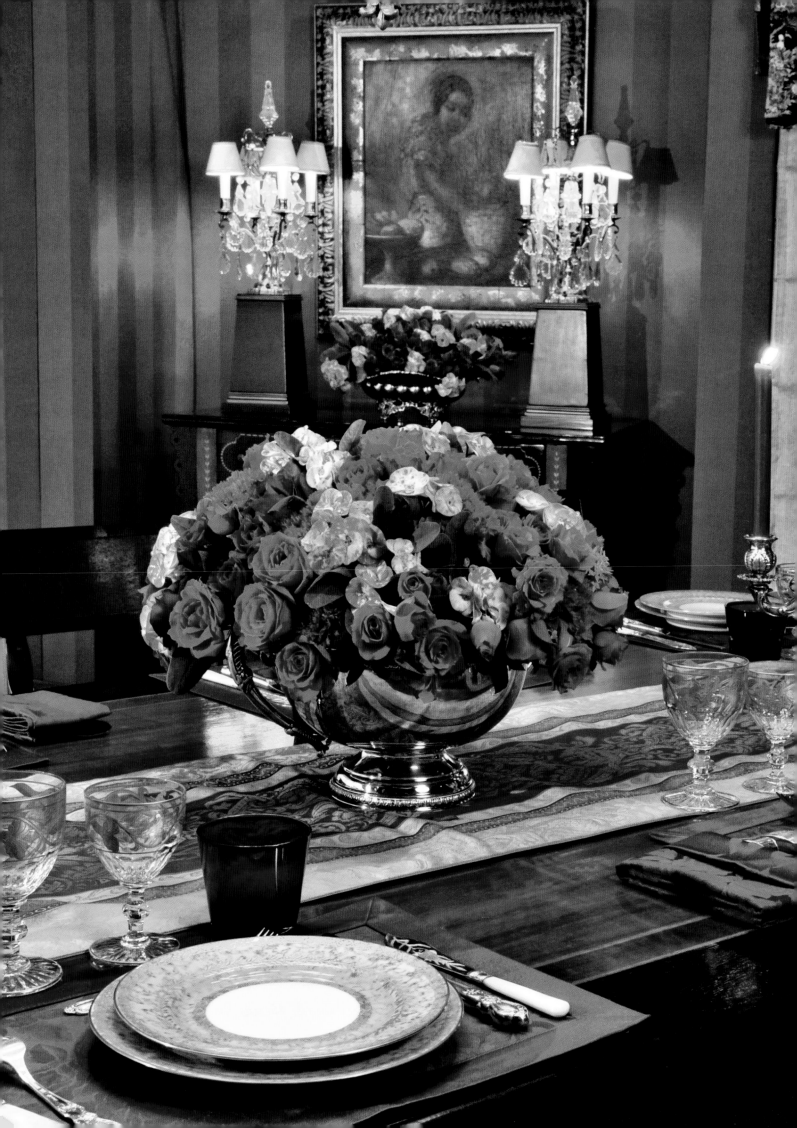

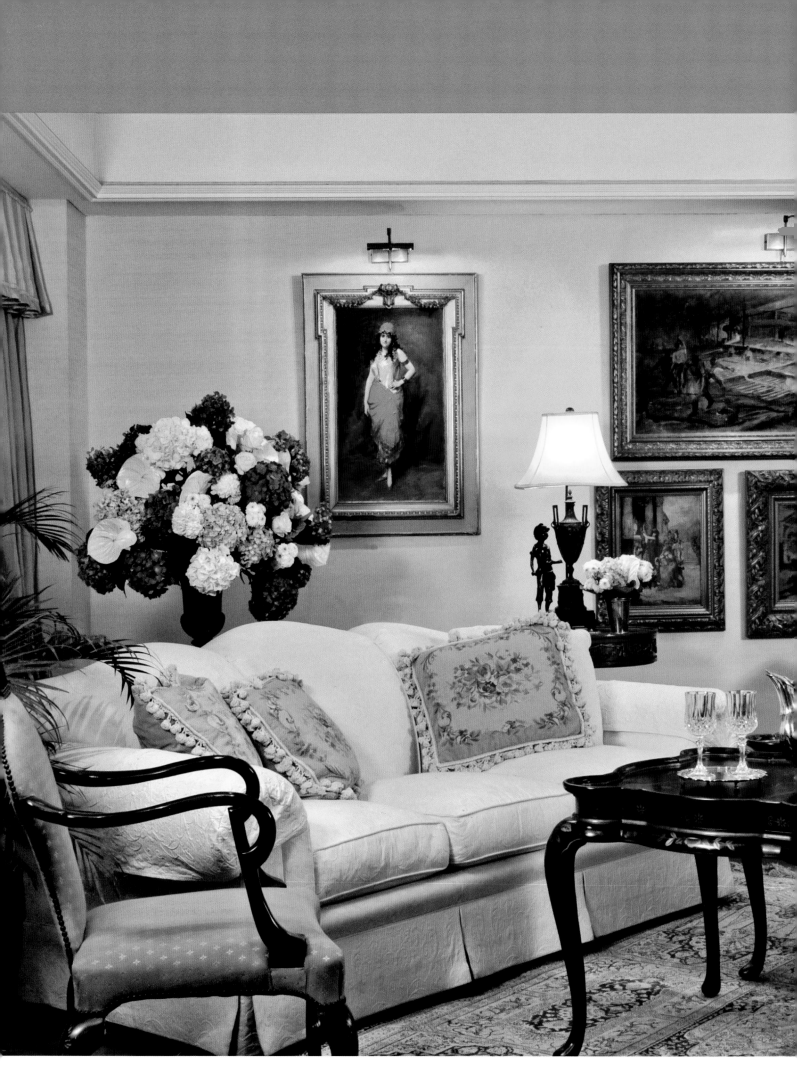

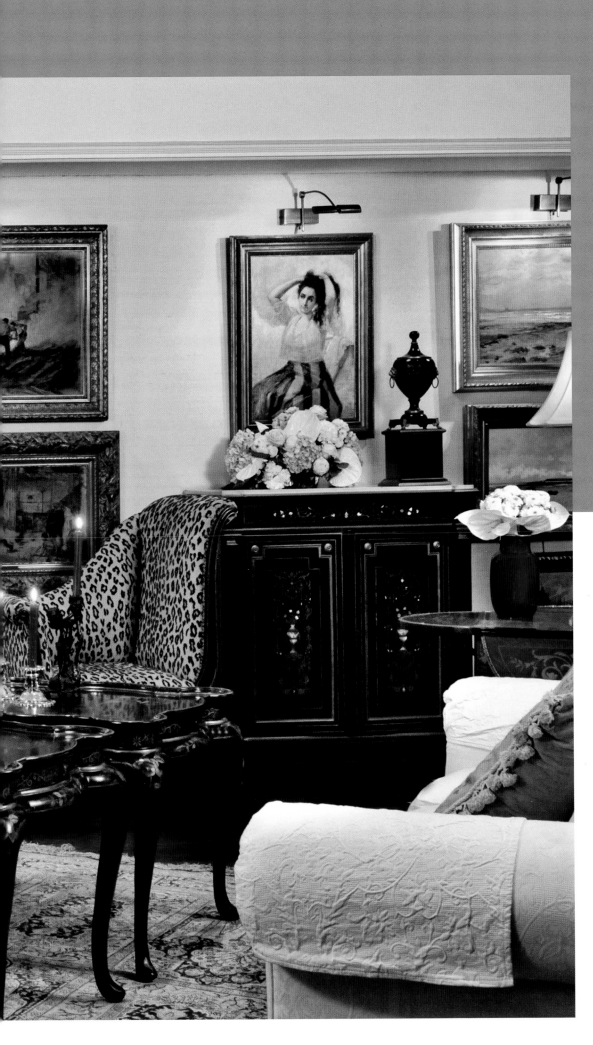

"Clustered white pom-poms are used to mimic snowball flowers. This is a perfect classic comple-ment to the extensive art collection and the lavish furnish-ings," says Pico Soriano.

LEFT A majestic mass of white purple and mauve hydrangea heads, white anthuriums and snowball flowers becomes a focal point in a room filled with Filipino classic art.

PREVIOUS SPREAD An exquisite silver bowl holds a luxuriant eye-level mass of red roses and hydrangeas that complement the rich reds and golds of the dining room décor and table setting.

classical concept

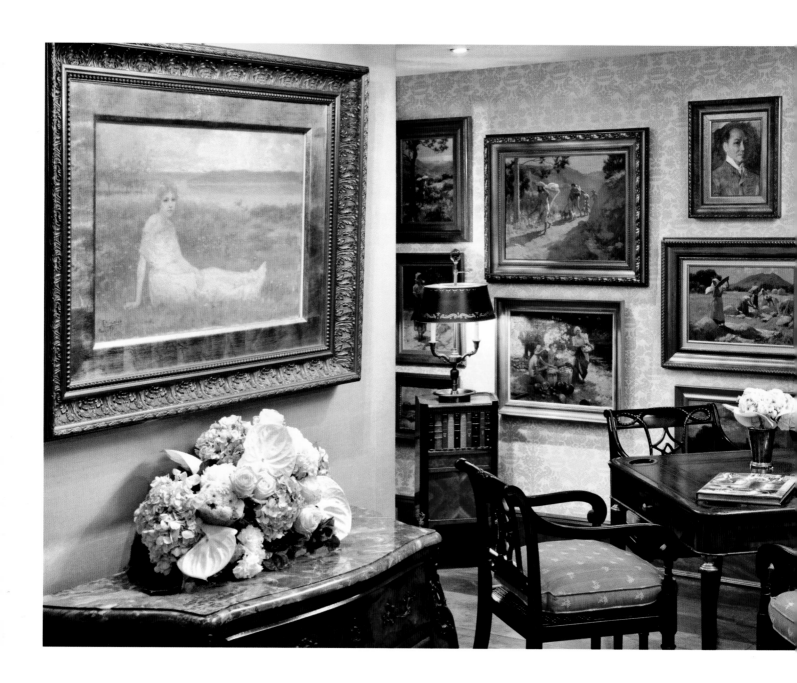

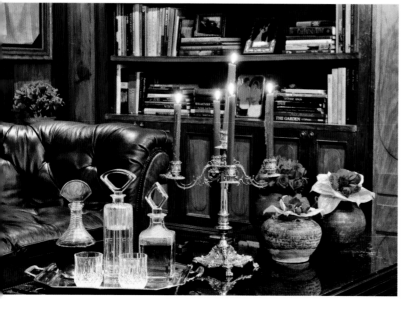

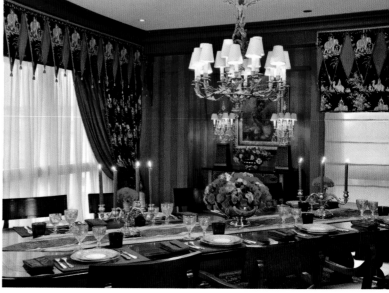

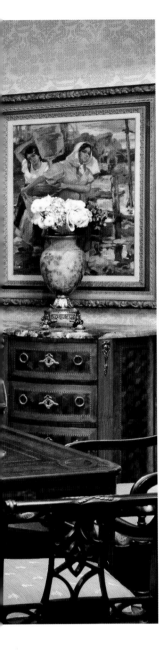

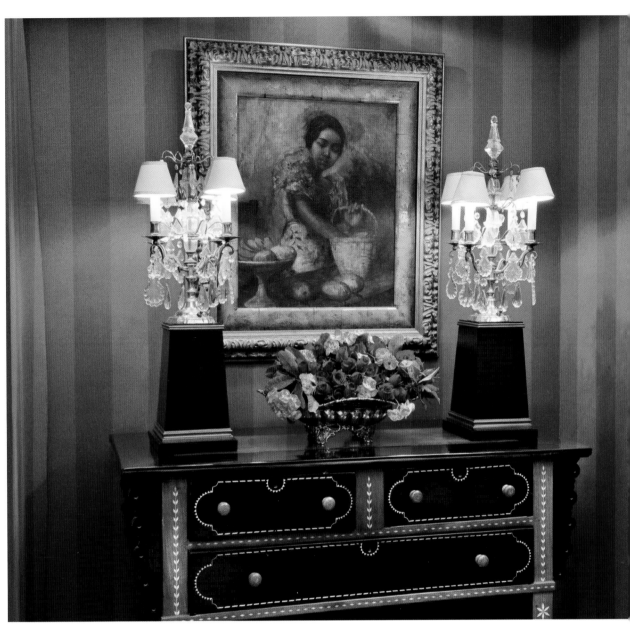

ABOVE A low arrangement of red blooms bursting out of a silver bowl is in complete harmony with the richness of the drop crystals on the mounted lamps, and adds to the color and vitality of the dining room décor.

ABOVE LEFT The muted hues of classic white hydrangeas, anthuriums and roses pull together a trove of dazzling period paintings surrounding a gaming table set on the diagonal.

LEFT The diagonal positioning of the dining table reflects the contemporizing strategy of interior designer Jonathan Matti. Vedic-patterned drapes add oriental opulence.

FAR LEFT Candelabra throw light on pink anthuriums cradling red gerberas in pre-Columbian pottery in the library-cum-study.

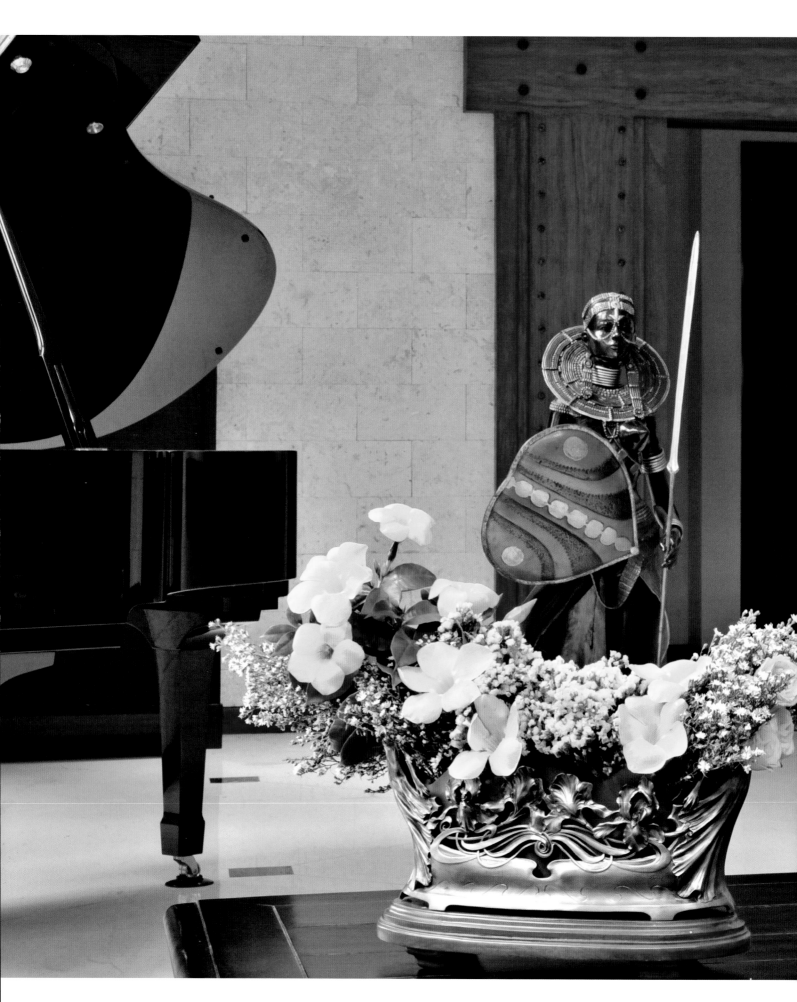

elements of surprise

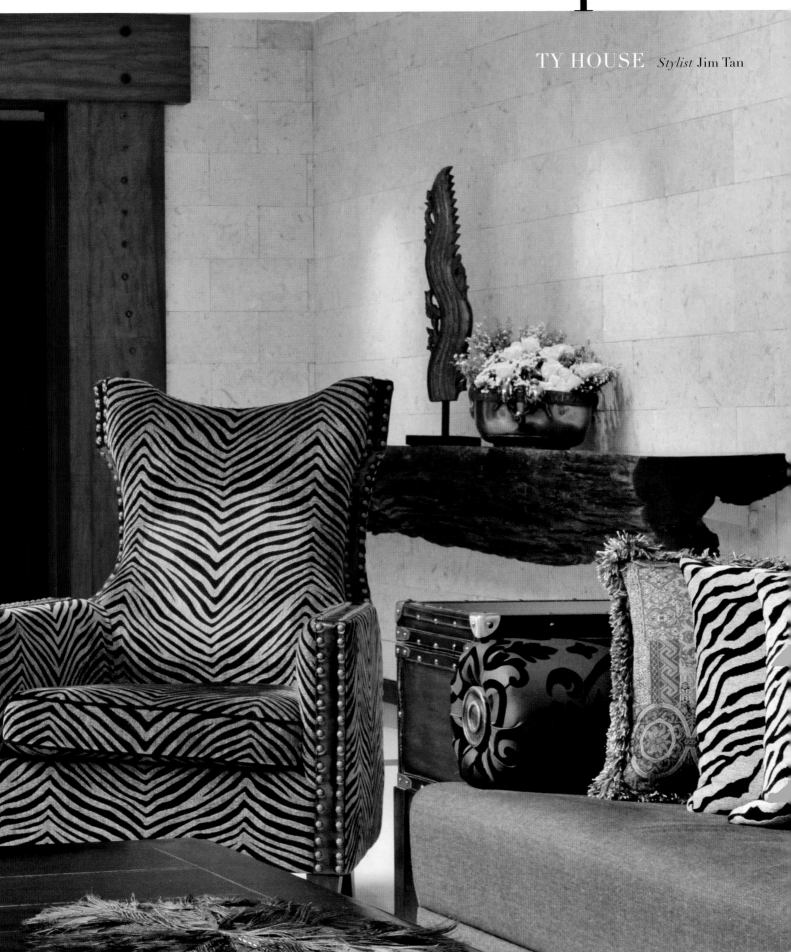

TY HOUSE *Stylist* Jim Tan

THE THREE-LEVEL HOME of Wendell and May Ty is built on an 800 sq m lot in Green Meadows, an exclusive gated community. The palatial scale of the house, outfitted in a wide range of materials, and the eclectic décor are immediately apparent in the gleaming white Mactan coral stone surfaces that look like travertine, and an ever-changing collection of *objets d'art*.

Visitors to the house are greeted at the front door by a Gothic-inspired bishop's chair designed by Jim Tan. Off the foyer, the cathedral-ceiling living room holds a grand piano, a modern L-shaped seating area and a cantilevered log wall console that supports the family's welcoming Buddha. The unique marble flooring of the adjacent *lanai* features a boldly graphic basketweave pattern created from three different kinds of marble from India and Italy.

Jim Tan, the family's design consult-ant and stylist, encourages the own-ers with his own individualistic flair, advising: "Be bold, don't be afraid to break the rules. Trust your instincts. You may surprise yourself." On the coffee table, he arranges a still life with uncommon flowers—tiny passion fruit blossoms set beside two silver figures of exotic birds.

The Tys' Chinese-Filipino roots are evident in the round dining table for twelve, where Jim Tan explains his floral design. "I like making the commonplace look uncommon." He creates an overscaled floral "nest" on the central rotating Lazy Susan using concentric circles of purple and

yellow statice flowers, along with their stalks, topped by a low vase of yellow roses. The vibrant colors of the flowers are echoed in the china—a modern departure from the usual all-white or gilt-edged service.

The home owners, who run various retail enterprises, are inveterate collectors of unusual art objects. "There's a creative challenge with each purchase," May Ty says. How about an African tribal figure by the grand piano? Or Bernie Sason's modern chairs by the Lladro porce-lain dancers? The eclectic collecting goes on. "But we edit, edit and edit," reassures husband Wendell.

RIGHT A raised wooden "boat" on a gold-embroidered Indian silk cloth is the focus of this midday spread. A red Murano flask surrounded by a culinary installation of mushrooms and quail eggs, and a tray of dump-lings ringed by purple statice, make for eclectic food presenta-tion. Celadon plates and gold flatware complete the enticing scene.
PREVIOUS SPREAD In contrast to the baby grand piano, handsome narra wood portal and golden stone walls, a pewter Art Deco vessel cradles humble alamanda flowers, yellow statice and white baby's breath.

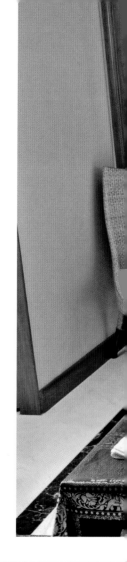

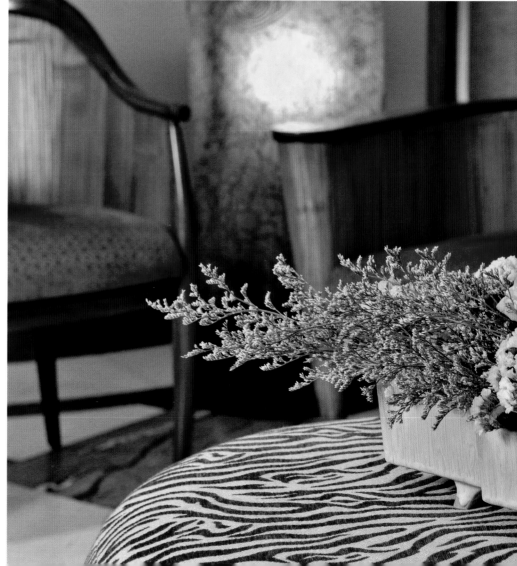

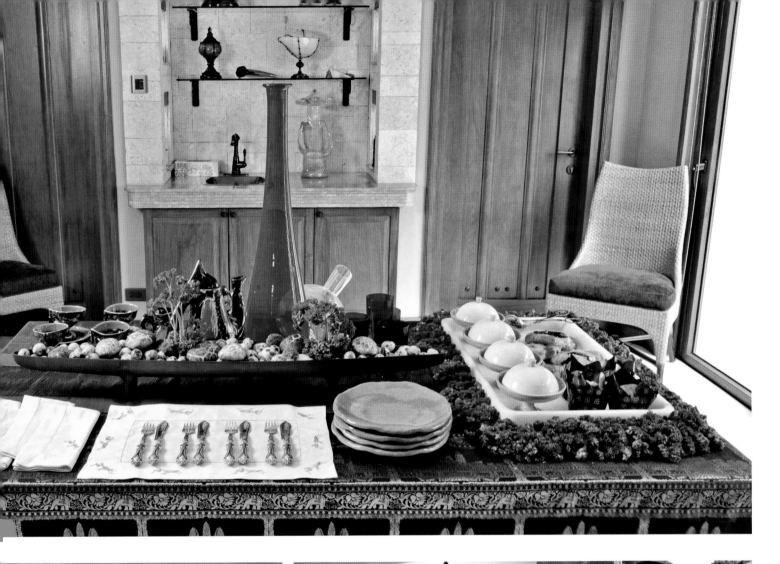

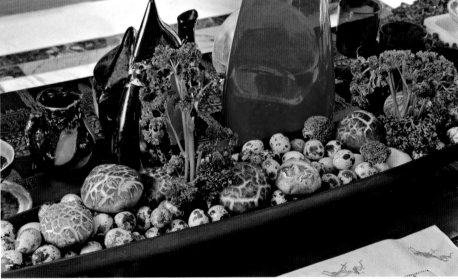

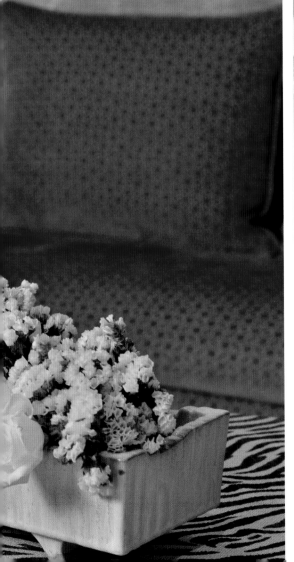

ABOVE A miniature "forest" installation of parsley "trees" standing among mushroom "boulders" and a "pebbled pathway" of quails eggs is a novel table presentation.

LEFT A simple composition of blue and yellow statice and a pair of yellow roses counterpoises the opulent animal hide fabrics and modern Bernie Sason furniture.

elements of surprise

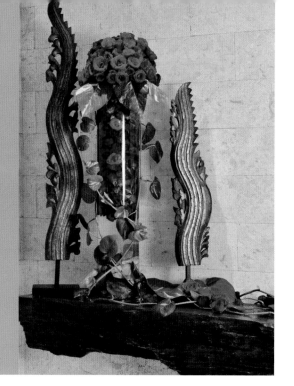

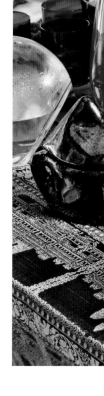

"I like making the commonplace look uncommon," interior decorator and stylist Jim Tan says of his floral arrangements.

LEFT Red roses plunged below the waterline in a translucent tubular vase, others suspended at the rim by money plant leaves, reveal another dimension in floral originality.

RIGHT An exquisite handmade chocolate brown and rose coffee set, a treasured find from Paris, complements the colors and creativity of the adjacent forest-in-boat culinary installation.

FAR RIGHT Under watchful eyes, passion flowers gleam in shot glasses near the champagne service. The aquamarine flutes are from Rustan's.

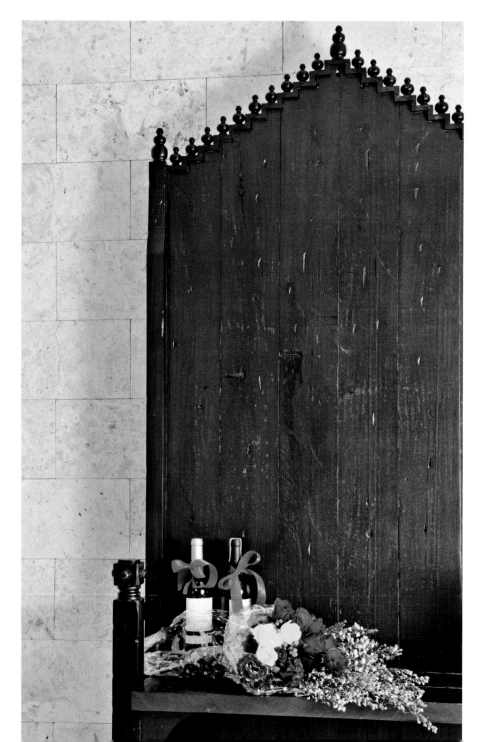

LEFT A bishop's chair designed by Jim Tan dominates the foyer.

RIGHT An exotic mix of woods in the dining room furniture is matched by an innovative floral centerpiece. In contrast to its usual role, the rotating Lazy Susan in the center of the table plays host to a layered rotunda of yellow and purple statice resting on a base of statice twigs. The central focus is a cerise bowl filled with apricot yellow roses. Colorful plate- and glassware echo the dominant tones of the flowers.

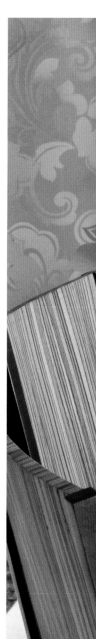

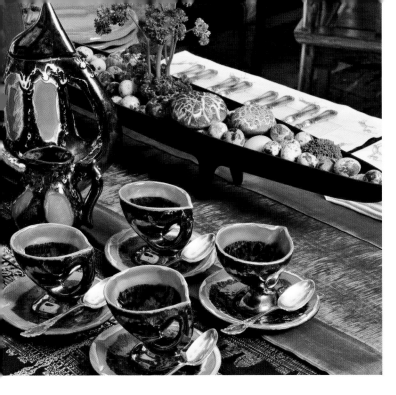

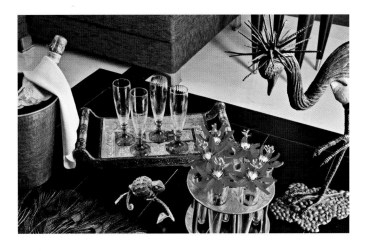

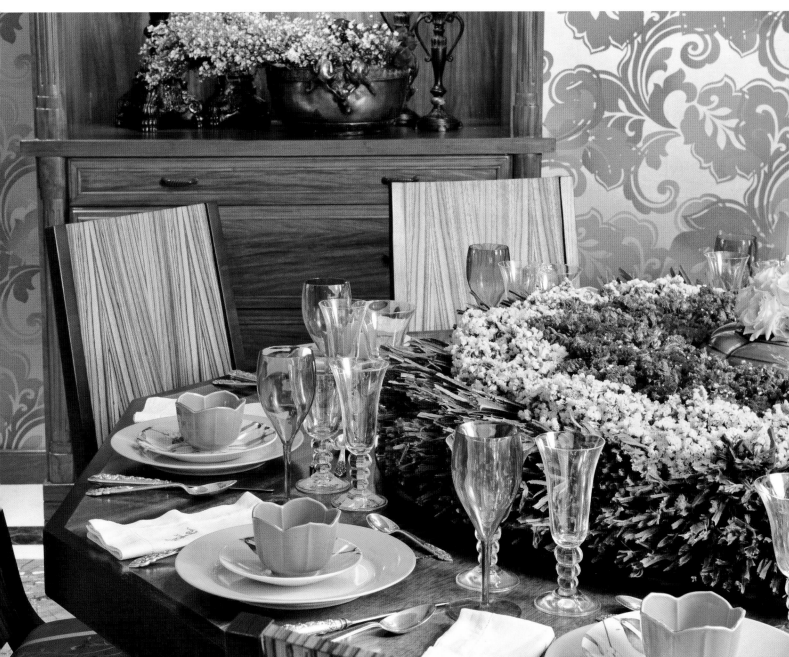

elements of surprise

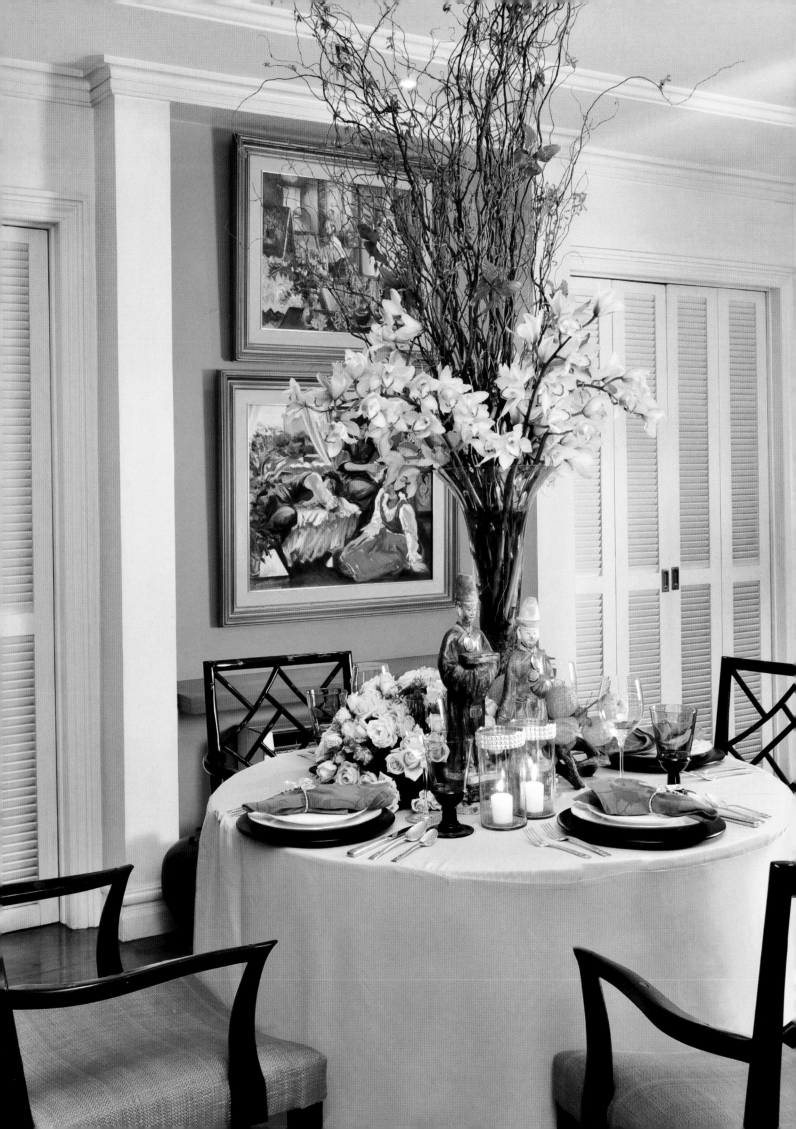

COJUANGCO HOUSE

Florist Nathaniel Aranda

opulent flair

THE FAMILY RESIDENCE of Lizette Banzon Cojuangco, located on a 800 sq m site in Manila, is rich with Filipino-Chinese art heritage. The bungalow features a gracious entertaining layout by Europhile architect Ramon Antonio, comprising an entry foyer, enclosed dining room and high-ceilinged *sala* for élite social groupings. Hostess Lizette explains her French-chinoiserie theme: "It was inspired by my collection of Chinese crafted furnishings, Filipino modern paintings and French Art Nouveau artifacts."

Classic paintings and sculptures by the finest artists and craftsmen drive the cultured spirit of the residence. When home owner Lizette offered florist Nathaniel Aranda full reign with her extensive collection of European glassware, Chinese ceramics, French silver vases and antique Philippine furniture pieces, he was inspired to embark on a stunning floral odyssey. "I decided to give my work the fullest flourish and the grandest opulence. Nothing was going to be plain!"

Nathaniel galvanized all his floral passions to express his creativity in three settings for entertaining in the French-Chinese interior. The main event unrolled in the dining room, with its wildly opulent "floral chandelier." What had started as Lizette's suggestion to install greenery on the top of the chandelier metamorphosed into Nathaniel's extravagant floral array. Masses of yellow mums hug the contours of the multi-armed lamp, forming a bright yellow "cloud" overhead. Contorted branches, vines and red orchids radiate toward the ceiling, while big globes of gerberas and a thick crystal shower of glass baubles cascade down. "I just allowed Nathaniel to express his passion and he literally went over the top!" smiles Lizette. The dinner setting was most admired by Indian friends who raved, "It's our favorite style for big celebrations and wedding parties!"

Lizette prefers her "classic romantic" setting, comprising a small round table dressed with powder green linens and Chinese Chippendale chairs, the arms inlaid with tiny butterflies. At the center, a tall flute of vines soars toward the ceiling, clustered—again, extravagantly—with pink cymbidiums, sweet akito roses and asparagus ferns. The butterfly table displays two Chinese Tang figurines standing alongside pale green lantern balls.

Overlooking the garden, Nathaniel designed a "modern Valentine's" tablescape. Knowing that hostess Lizette does *not* favor the usual dark red roses, he designed his own version of "big bold roses": deep purple and red variegated cordyline leaves were hand-rolled into floral cylinders—each "rose" needed 50–100 leaves—and took three days to assemble.

Taking inspiration from the collection of French Art Nouveau and Philippine modern art, Nathaniel Aranda has created international romance on an opulent floral scale!

LEFT For intimate dining, Lizette chose two jade-hued Tang figures flanked by pale green lantern globes to interplay with Nathaniel's towering canopy of textured willows and pink cymbidiums and a table arrangement of pink roses.

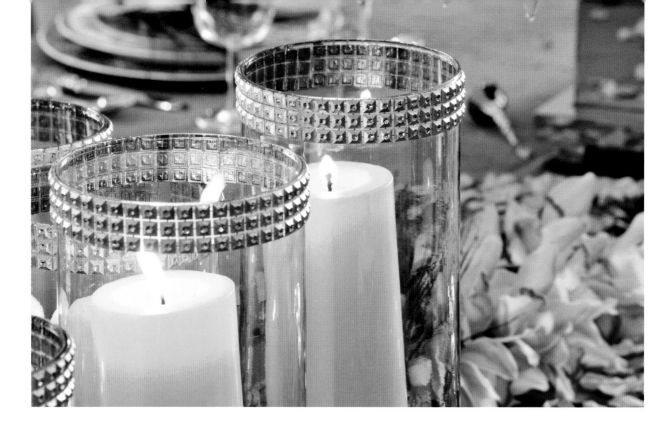

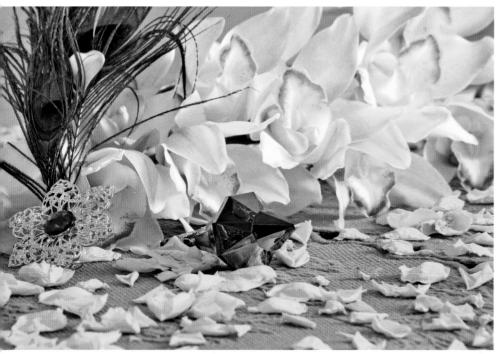

ABOVE Silver-studded glass candleholders, one of Lizette's sensational mall finds, are grouped here for maximum effect.

LEFT Fuschia-rimmed pink cymbidiums join jeweled clasps and peacock feathers on the table setting.

RIGHT A mass of jungle branches and vines and red orchids radiate above a chandelier entwined with yellow mums. A shower of baubles and chrysanthemum globes cascades down to greet the table.

BOTTOM LEFT Up close in a mirrored square vase, a mixture of tillandsias, purple-rimmed echeveria succulents from Sagada, bromeliads and red spider mums form a well-deserved conversation piece.

BOTTOM A jewel clasp and a peacock feather rest on a white linen table napkin on stacked floral-patterned English bone china.

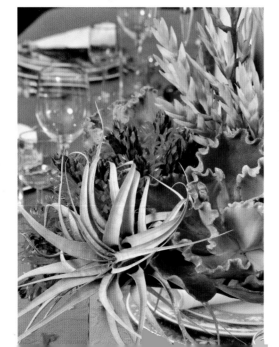

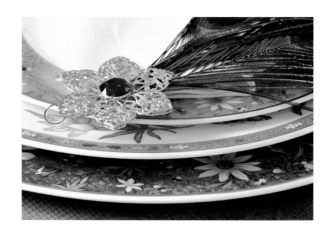

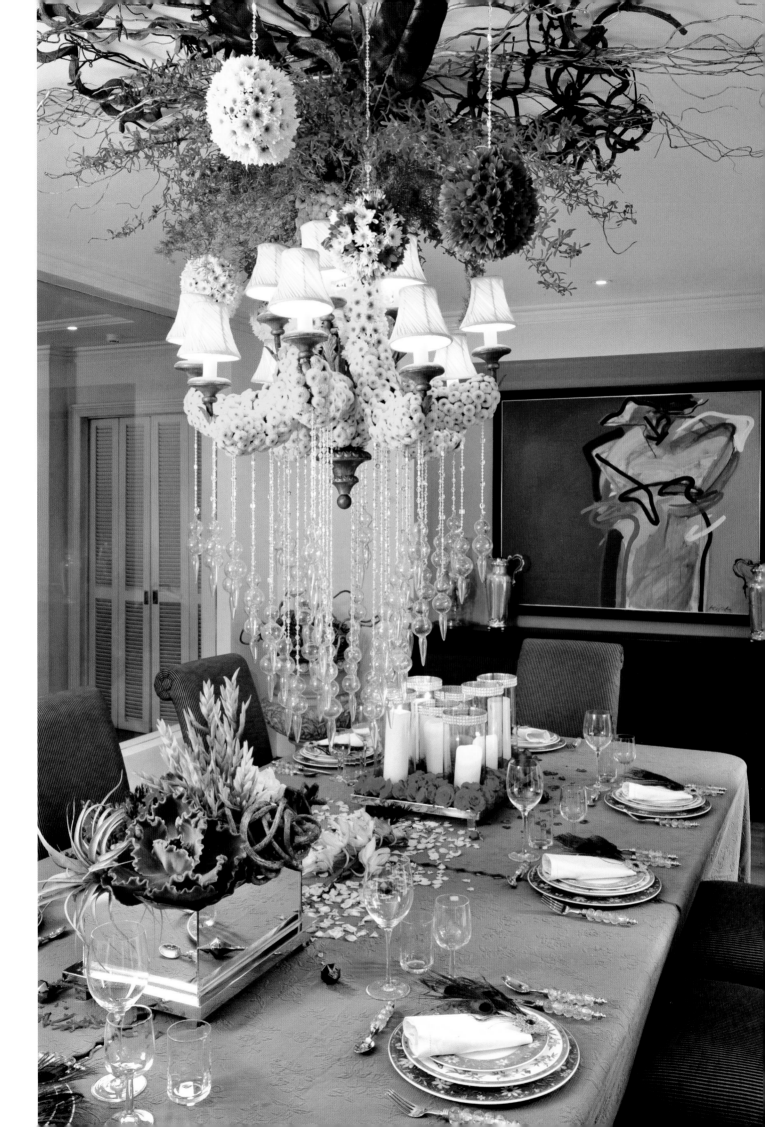

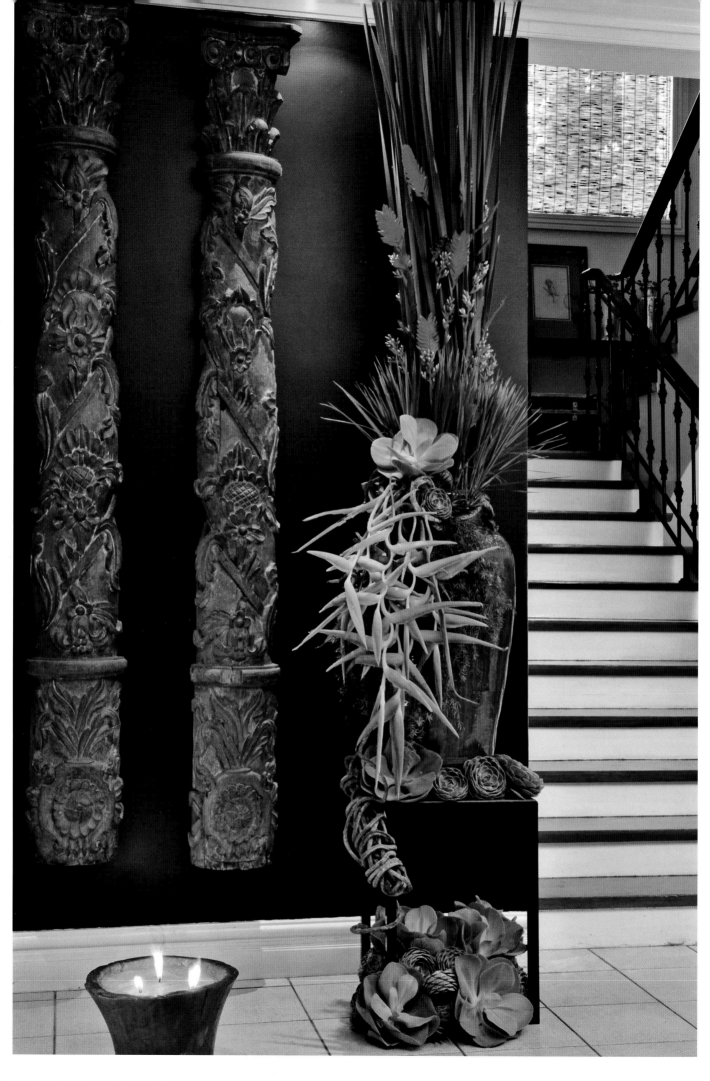

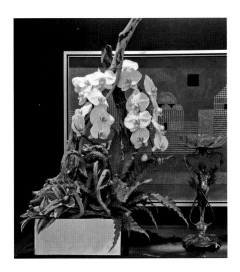

LEFT A red linear Arturo Luz masterpiece counterposes a free-flowing arrangement of white phalaenopsis orchids, jungle foliage and twisted branches.
OPPOSITE High foyer drama is expressed in two intricately carved church pillars from Bohol floating against a black wall. An ancient urn holds a floral burst of ceiling-high reeds, red bromeliads, dracena tricolor, green sexy pink heliconias, dried vines and echeveria succulents.

BELOW A master-crafted altar table backed by another Bohol church masterpiece holds cast bronze horses and a white bowl of gorgeous white roses wrapped by an aloe vera leaf, with a lime heliconia accent on top.

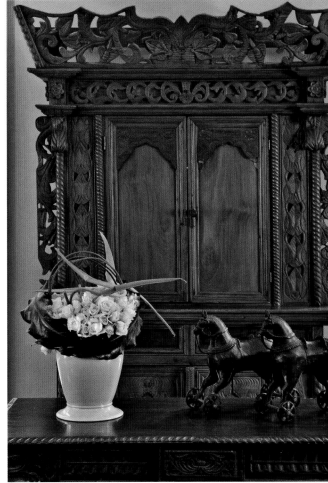

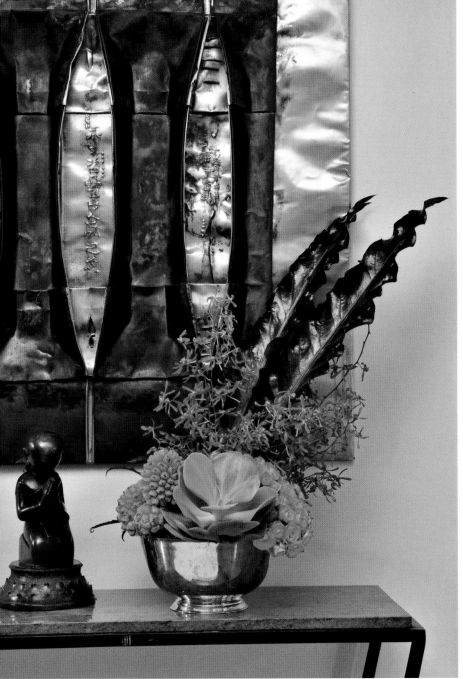

LEFT Shiny Renaissance leaves mirror the modern metallic leaf-like art. Below, a prayerful monk bows to a rose succulent flanked by fire red orchids, orange red pandanus fruit and orange roses.
BELOW Resting on a classic pillar in the foyer, dried jungle vines create a nest for celadon-hued echeveria succulents.

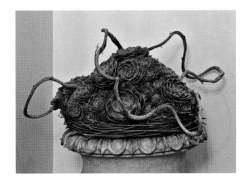

opulent flair

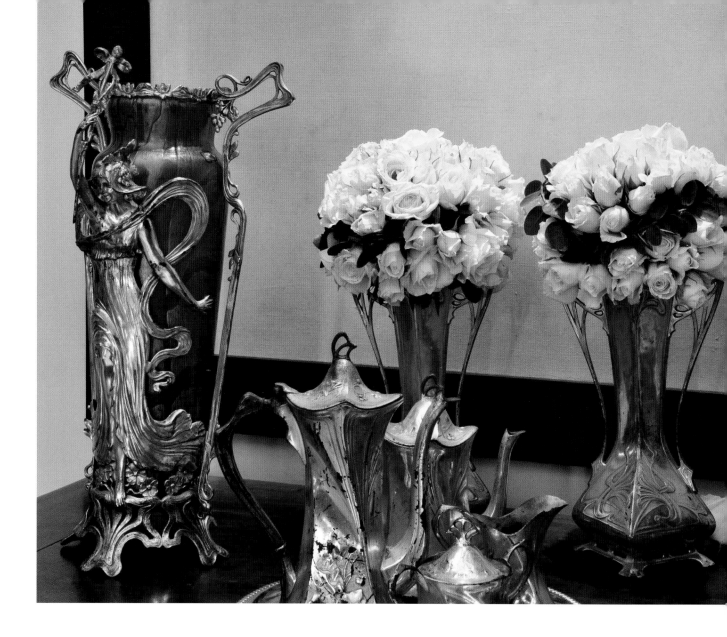

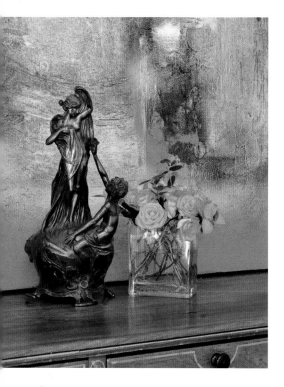

ABOVE Two Parisian Art Nouveau vases and a coffee service were spectacular finds in the family storage, where they were discovered wrapped in old newspapers. Only white roses, Nathaniel says, are worthy of showing off the fine pieces.

LEFT More Art Nouveau treasures—a flirtatious Eros courting Dawn. Pink and orange roses harmonize with the orange and gold-leafed canvas.

RIGHT A stately Art Nouveau urn matches the profile of the glass storm lamp funnel filled with a spray of pink cymbidiums.

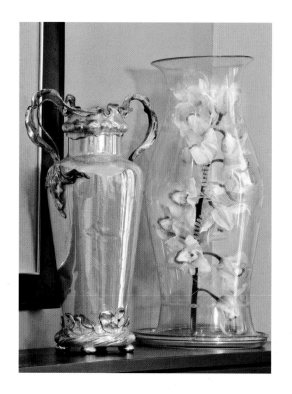

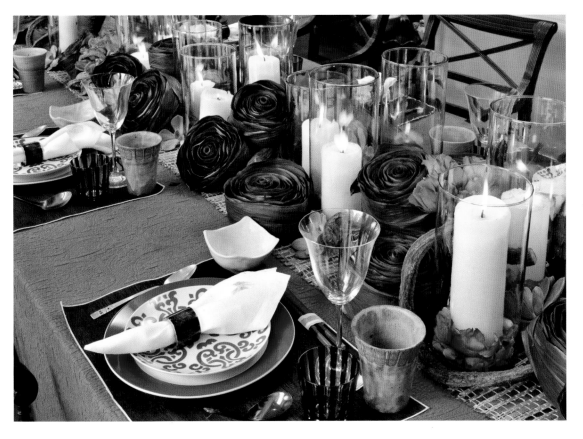

LEFT A fabulous "first" from Nathaniel—cordyline leaf roses—specially made at Lizette's request as a respite from red roses. Moroccan-patterned china on a red tablecloth are highlighted by glass-funneled white candles.
BELOW Nathaniel and his crew spent three days making these masterpieces, painstakingly rolling 50–100 leaves for each rose. The fuschia roses are a fitting accent on this *merienda cena* (late noon to early dinner) dining table setting.

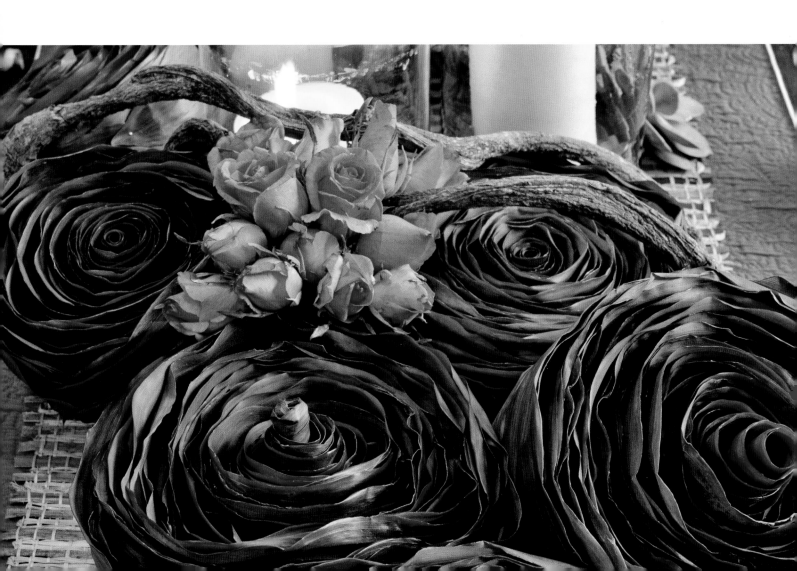

classic treasures enhanced by monochromatic *blooms*

ANTONIO HOUSE

SOUGHT-AFTER MODERNIST architect Ramon Antonio has a gracious home that is not out to make a structural statement. Located in Dasmarinas Village in the heart of Metro Manila, it exhibits an air of practical ease. More importantly, it serves as a pleasing canvas in which to showcase his impeccable sense of style as well as his passion for art and antiques and the treasures inherited from his late father, the National Artist-architect Pablo S. Antonio.

Understandably, Ramon cannot help but move within the tenets of architecture. You can see form and structure immediately, not only in the physical form of his house, the arrangement of his furniture, paintings and artifacts and the design of his garden, but also in his choice of monochromatic flower arrangements that complement but do not overpower the objects in his home.

The enclosed dining room is contemporary and chic despite its beveled glass walls and doors. A sense of Old World opulence is conveyed by the ornate gilt-edged mirror,

antique crystal chandelier from Paris, gold-rimmed Waterford plateware, Lalique glassware and MalMaison Christofle cutlery. Golden yellow spider chrysanthemums, purchased from the public flower market known as Dangwa, are arranged simply in ornate cut crystal Baccarat bud vases

The muted tones of the walls, floor and furniture fabric in the living room form a perfect "gallery" for displaying Ramon's Philippine paintings and furniture, and his Thai Andaman, Cambodian Bayon and Chinese artifacts—included among them beautifully carved chests and inlaid mother-of-pearl stools, seated Buddha images, wooden architectural eaves boards and mounted elephant tusks. Tabletops display gleaming period silver and a host of smaller carefully selected Asian artifacts.

Adding color and drama in the muted "gallery" is the humble banana flower. Masses of crimson blooms in silver and porcelain containers make a fiery contrast to the more permanent treasures on display.

RIGHT Golden yellow spider chrysanthemums springing from a grouping of cut crystal Baccarat bud vases clustered below an antique crystal chandelier from Paris are the perfect complement to the exclusive wares on the table.

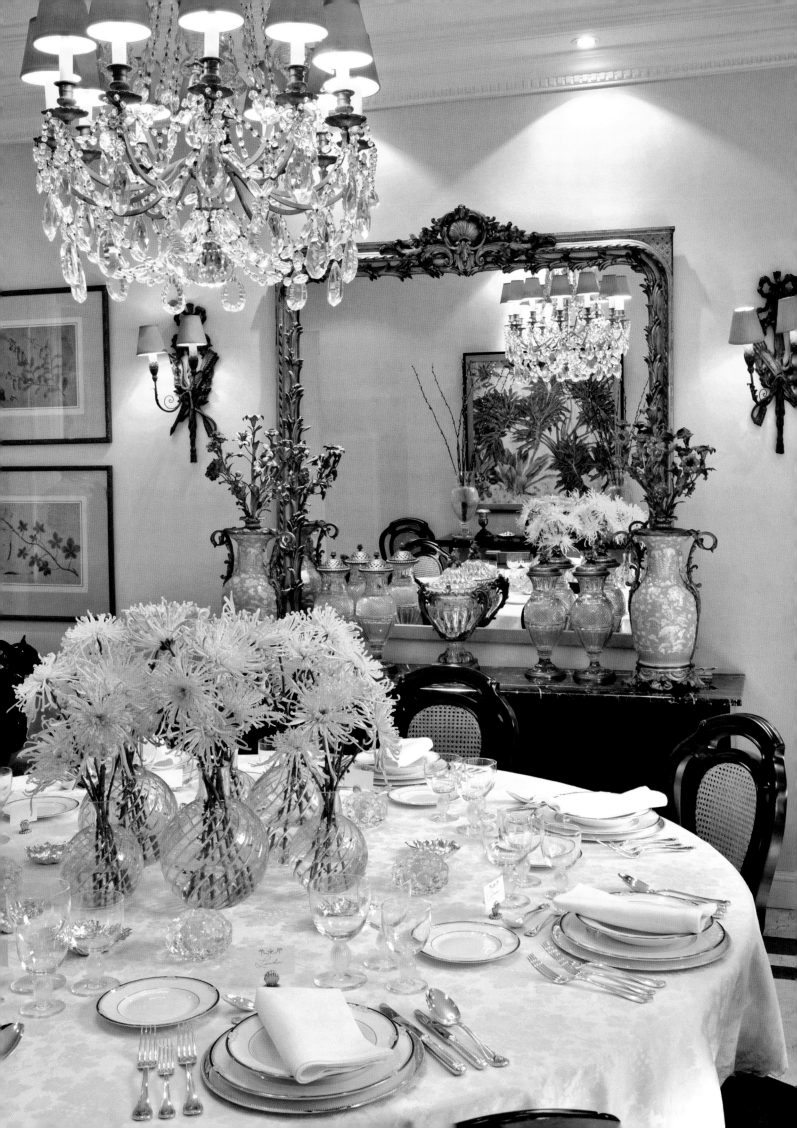

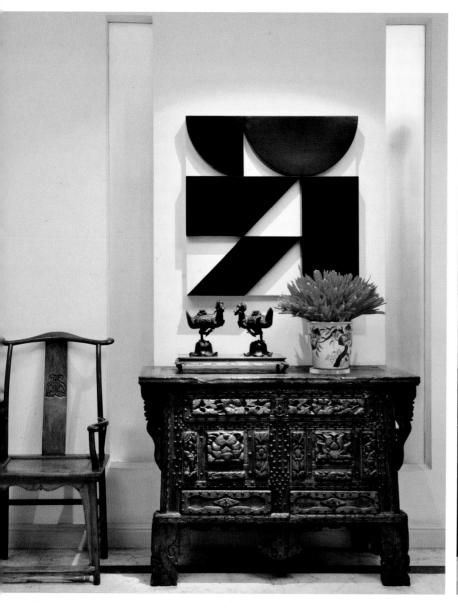

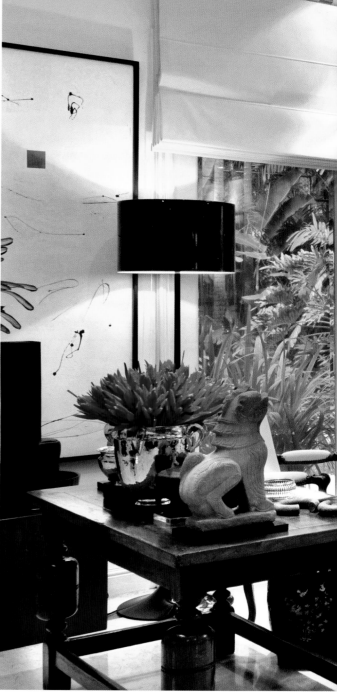

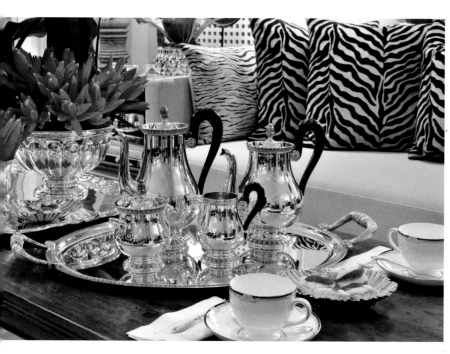

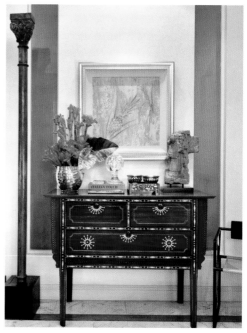

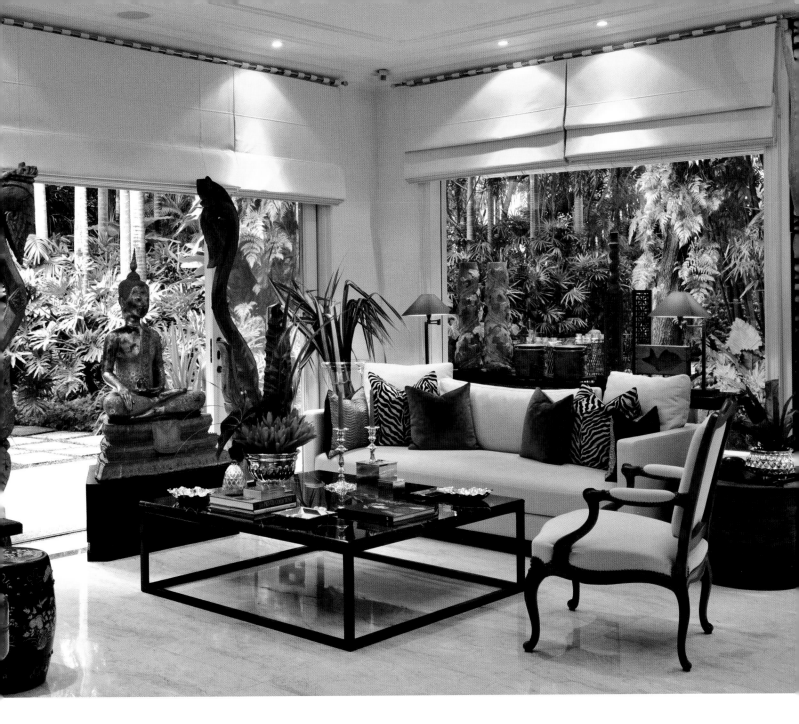

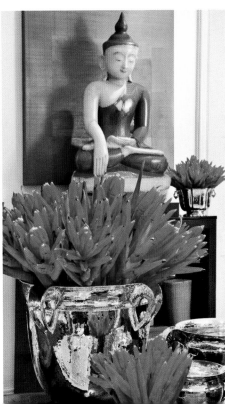

TOP LEFT The vivid blooms of the humble ornamental banana offset the bold black and white artwork by National Artist Arturo Luz hanging above a deeply carved antique table from China.

LEFT A fine bone-inlaid altar table from Batangas and a muted vegetal painting by Emmanuel Cordova are unified by the banana blossom and torch ginger arrangement and the tall Thai temple standard.

FAR LEFT Gleaming silver, red flowers and animal prints on a white linen sofa epitomize Ramon Antonio's classic-contemporary design style.

ABOVE An exquisite seated Buddha framed by a pair of wooden eave brackets from a Thai temple is the centerpiece of the *sala* that looks out to Ramon's tropical garden. Silver bowls of banana flowers add splashes of color to the muted living room scheme.

LEFT A red-lacquered alabaster Shan Buddha is honored by three banana flower offerings in gleaming silver bowls.

classic treasures enhanced by monochromatic blooms

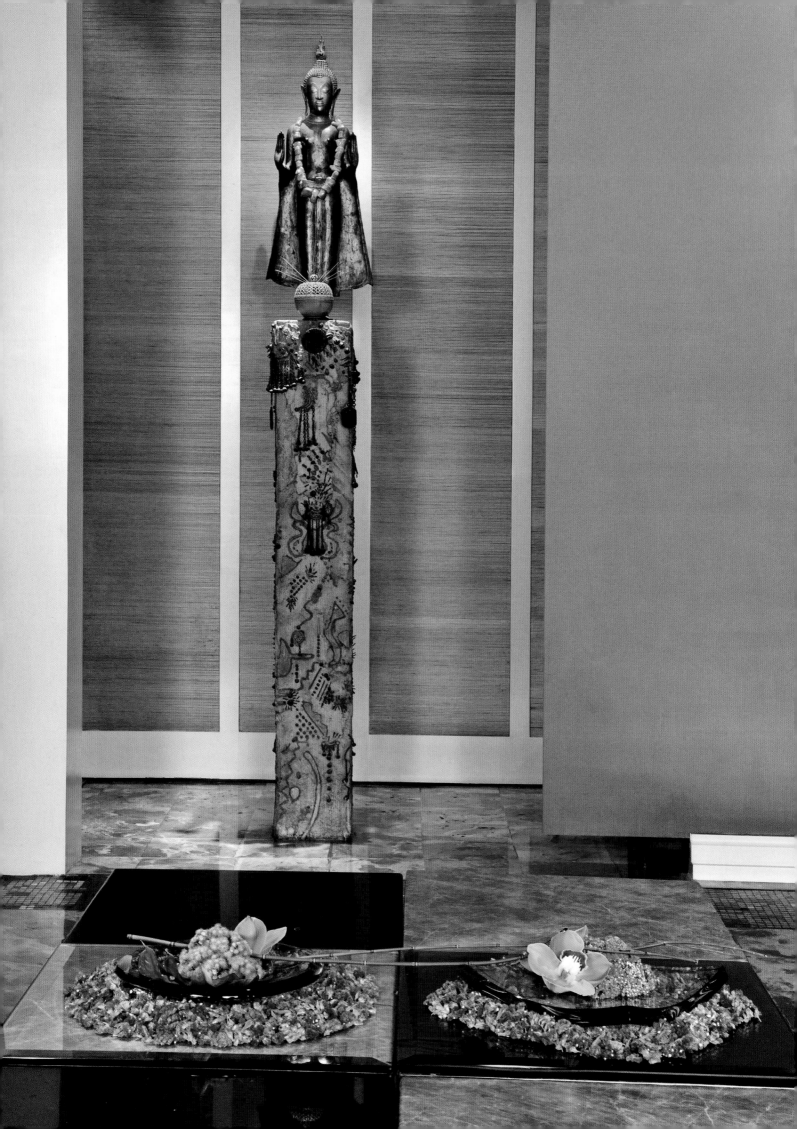

floral fantasies
weave their romantic spell

VIJANDRE-TOLEDO THEATER

FROM THE ENTRY GATE, the house, a modest 1960s split-level in Makati, welcomes visitors with a tranquil pond and a lone monk seemingly walking among the lotuses. This serene overture does not prepare the visitor for the delights ahead—a theater set of astonishing design brimming with creativity, imagination and stunning exotica.

The home owners are business partners Chito Vijandre and Ricky Toledo, a creative duo who own FIRMA and AC+632, two boutiques carrying exquisite lifestyle products. They have decorated their home to resemble a mythical collaboration of three of their favorite style legends—Dali, Versace and Saint Laurent.

The spacious reception hall contains a black and grey rectangular seat-cum-low table decorated with a twin floral arrangement of cymbidium orchids, statice and anthuriums connected by horsetail stalks. A tall Song dynasty jar balances a spray of yellow orchids—the popular "dancing ladies"—pointing the way to the main *sala* through a narrow glass door.

Inside, an alcove sofa strewn with cushions and throws in a myriad of patterns and embroidery styles sets the scene for the rest of the house. A wall of English snake prints by Albertus Seba hangs at the back of the alcove above an exuberant floral installation of wild berries and purple hydrangeas and clashing red and orange snap dragons.

Another astonishing setting is the Bedouin fantasy room, replete with large carpets and low seating, inviting guests to lounge. A blue and white Ming jar bursts with a sumptuous arrangement of carnations, lilies, eucalyptus and roses.

The home owners proudly do their own floral décor. "We try to look for flowers and foliage with unusual shapes, colors and textures," says designer Chito, who enjoys the hunt as much as the final arranging. "Blending contrasting elements like tubular grass stalks with curly cockscomb flowers or delicate snap dragons with clusters of rainforest berries.... Tension is desirable." Partner Ricky adds, "But you also have to harmonize the proportions, colors and textures. Then it's a joy to behold."

Their biggest joy and *coup de gras* is the gilt-mirrored dining room where a turquoise-feathered stuffed peacock makes an extraordinary still life amid the tablescape. Lush bouquets of lavender hydrangeas and two-toned cabbage roses, masses of silver *objets d'art*, a Venetian glass chandelier embellished with asparagus vines, Baccarat champagne flutes and crystal candleholders add to the profusion.

So what is their advice on styling one's home? Don't be locked into a single theme. Your home is your theater. Display your exotic possessions. "Start by rearranging a room and break some rules. Mad is not bad!" says designer Chito with a grin.

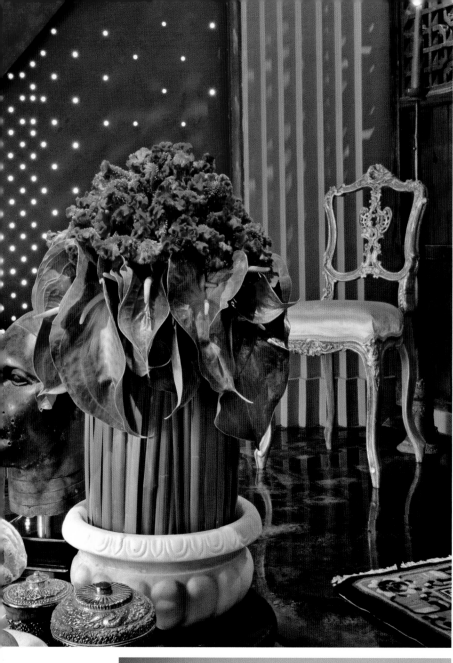

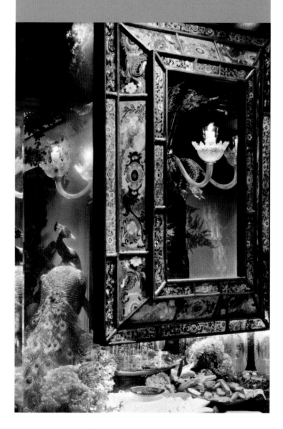

LEFT Red-throated anthuriums tied below the heads, crowned by red cockscombs and installed on a column of pandan leaves, provide a theatrical element.
RIGHT A stuffed peacock dominates the resplendent gold-leafed dining room amidst a Parisian chandelier, a lavish table arrangement of hydrangeas, cabbage roses, white mums and green berries, and gleaming tableware.
BELOW A Peruvian frame on a mirrored wall reflects a playful vignette of the lavish spread.
BELOW LEFT Tiny "dancing ladies" bundled by reeds resting on a tall Song dynasty jar point the way to the drawing room door.
PREVIOUS SPREAD A gilded Thai deity stands sentinel on a towering plinth over two glass plates bearing cymbidium orchids and anthuriums, ringed by violet statice flowers and linked by horsetail stalks.

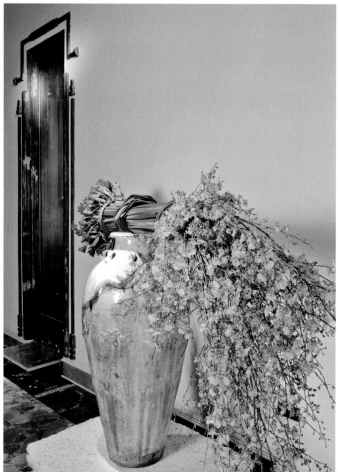

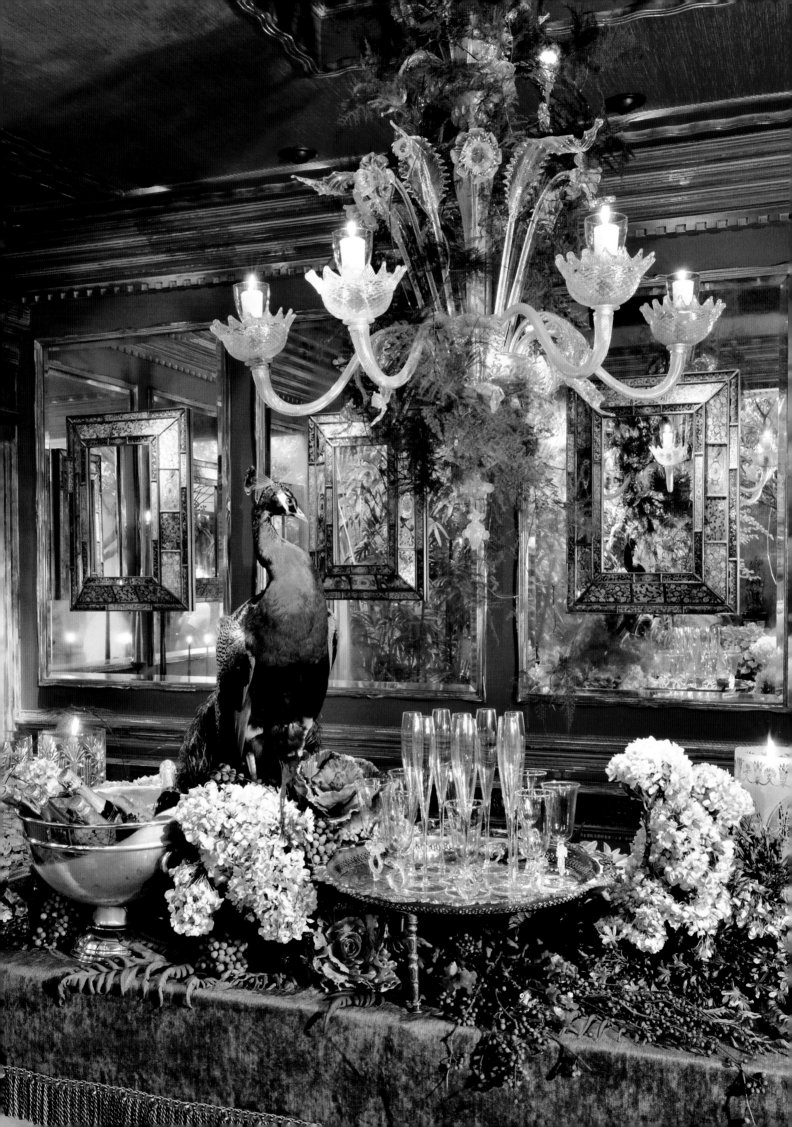

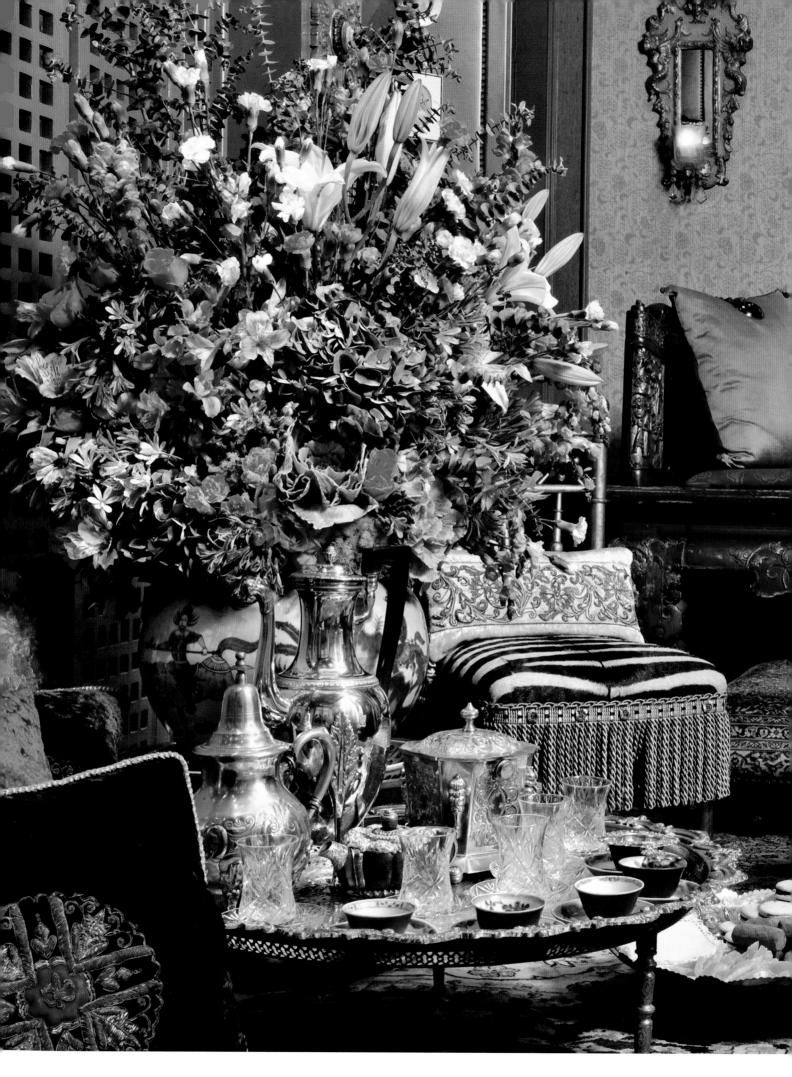

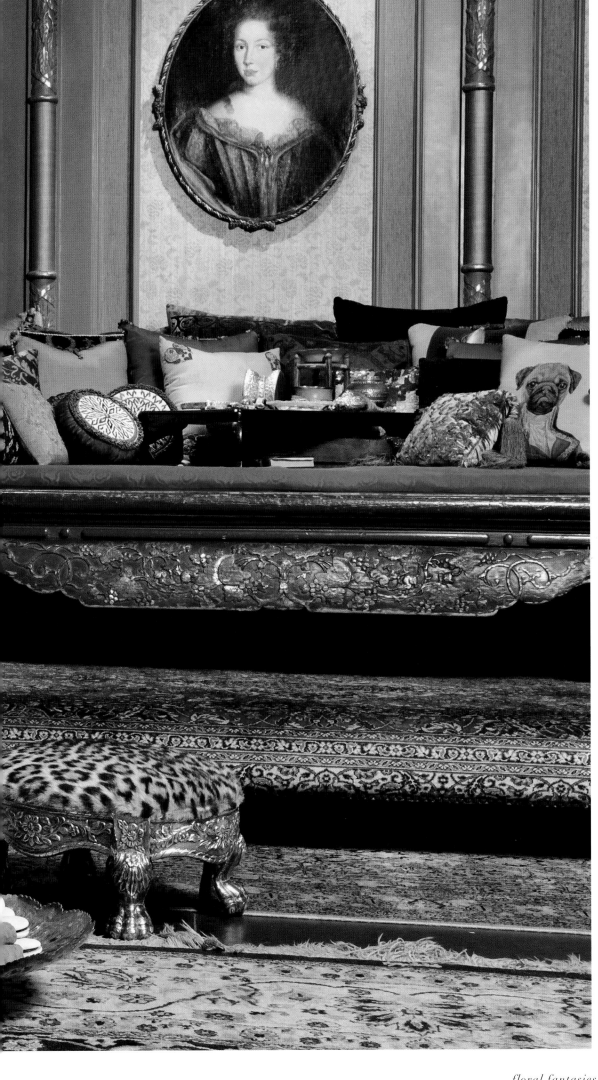

A glorious burst of carnations, Casablanca lilies, hydrangeas, agapanthus and roses spell unbridled floral decadence in the Bedouin fantasy room, complementing the rich furnishings and decorative items.

floral fantasies weave their romantic spell

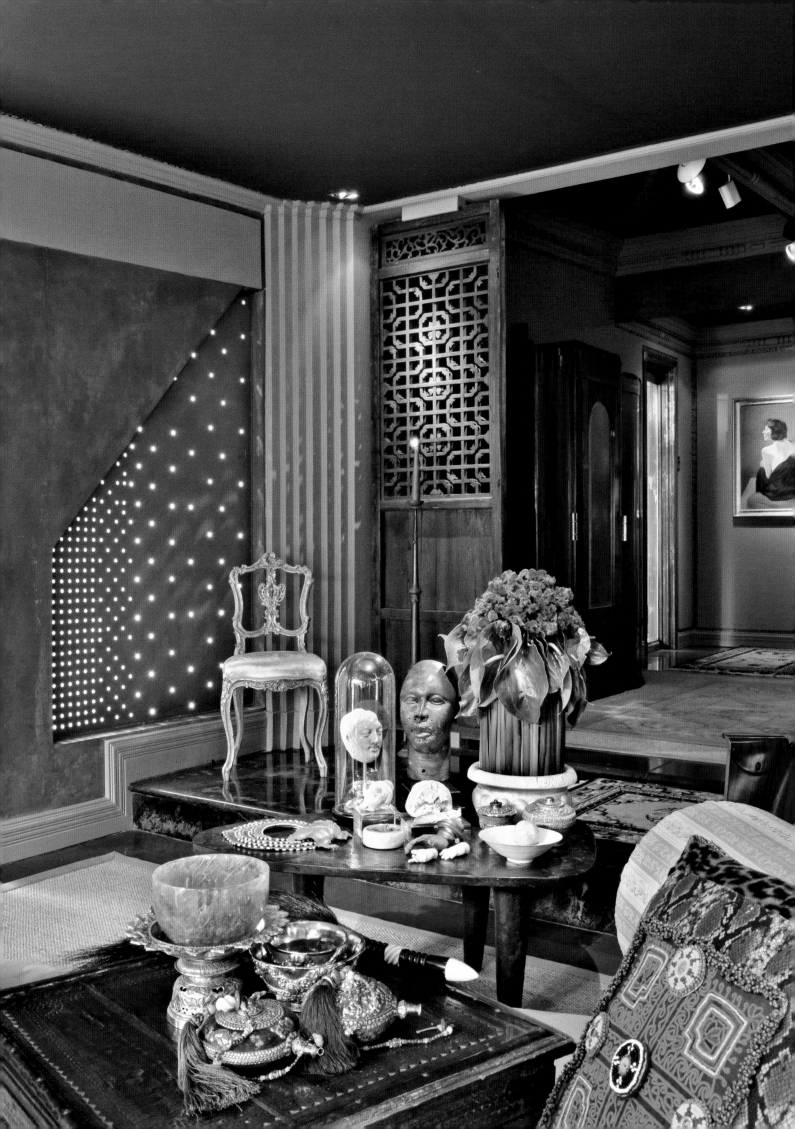

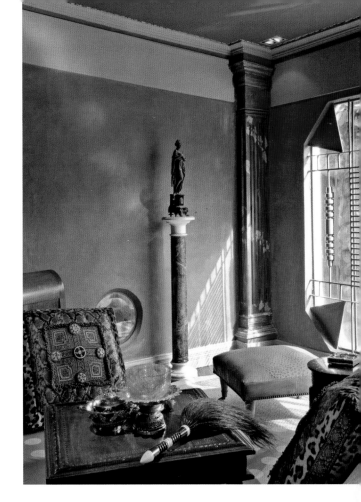

OPPOSITE A purple ceiling pulls together an array of rare finds—a Chinese wall panel, beaded fabrics over animal prints, ivory bangles and silver flasks, an alabaster bowl, marble and bronzed heads—and a stunning floral creation.

LEFT A two-level arrangement of hydrangeas, snap dragons and berries is a welcoming touch in the reception alcove.

RIGHT Textured walls, a pillared plinth, a Venetian statue and other exotica glow warmly in a stream of afternoon sun.

BELOW An alcove flanked by gold-leafed pilasters frames a wall of English snake prints by Albertus Seba. A French medallion chair is restyled with a needlepoint portrait.

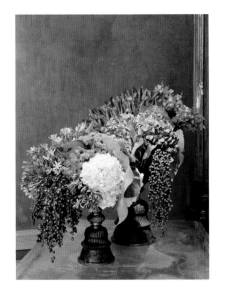

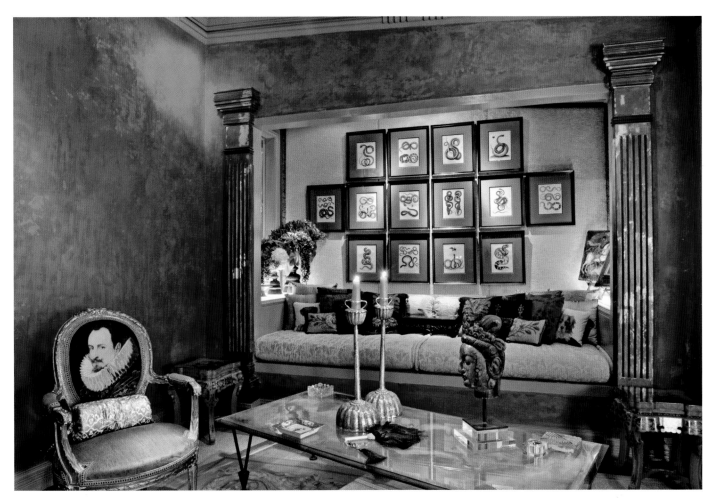

floral fantasies weave their romantic spell

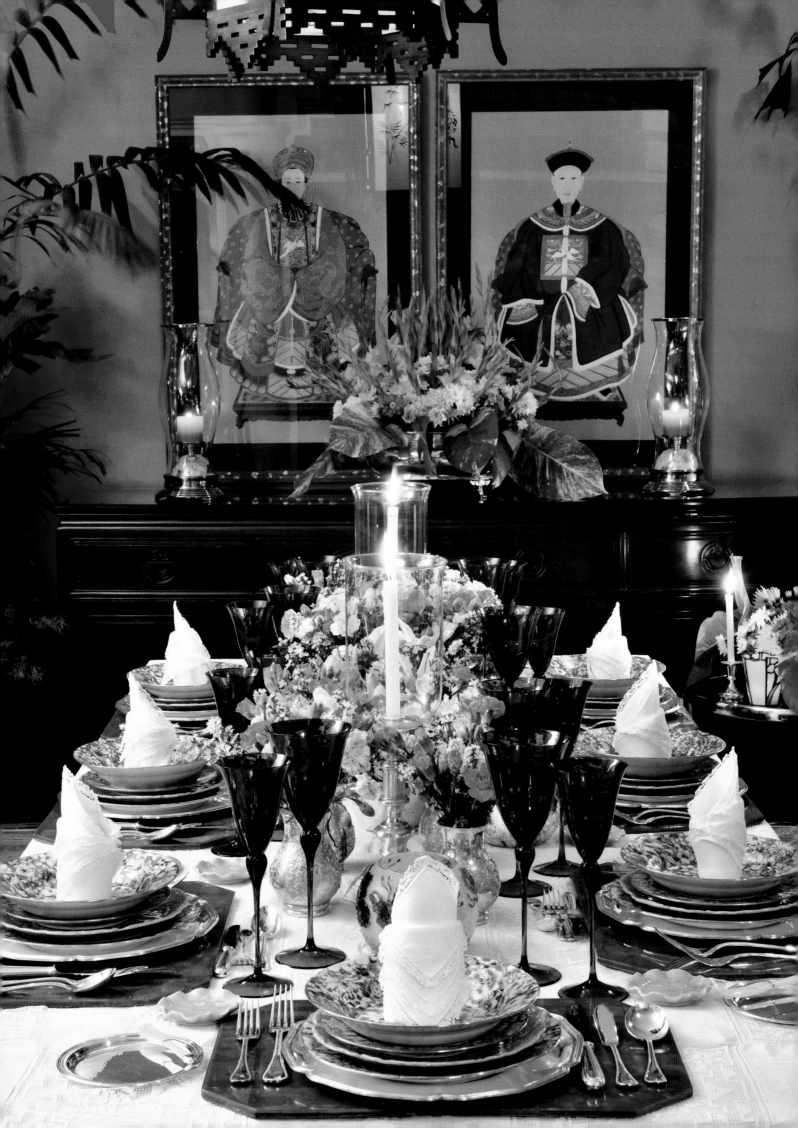

the *constant* gardener

HAPPY GARDEN HOME

THE HOUSE is a two-story structure in Paranaque, south of Manila, glowing in cobalt blue and surrounded by a glorious garden crammed with flowering and foliage plants. The owner of this gracious home declares: "Just call me a lady of the garden! But I didn't do all of this with a magic wand! My faithful gardener and my household team helped me pull it off!"

Inside the residence, a wealth of beautiful and exotic objects are proudly displayed—Chinese ancestral portraits, Muslim swords and daggers from the southern sultanate tribes, a Katmandu *tangka*, and much more—along with elegant Christofle silver and classic plates from England. "The dining ware comes mostly from my late mother, but some is also from my husband's European family."

The star attractions are not only the floral arrangements the lady of the garden has prepared throughout the house, but also the live plants she lives with every day. Her home is a *constant* garden—with flowers arrayed in giant pots and standing vases, even printed on the upholstery fabrics!

Flowers accent the formal living room, a cosy setting of Oriental artifacts beneath a black Coromandel screen. The scene-stealer is a cascade of clerodendrum (bleeding heart) with purple and white blossoms. On an armoire between two gilded monks is an arrangement of trumpet-shaped hollyhocks.

In the Mandarin red dining room, set with stacks of "Thousand Flowers" patterned plates on Limoges chargers, two palms with staghorn ferns tied to their stalks flank the buffet console. Mixed flower arrangements in a series of matching vases run the length of the table.

On the *lanai* table, surrounded by stacked plateware, is a striking arrangement—a pedestal of pineapples supporting a burst of heliconias, pink gladioli, white chrysanthemums and palm fronds.

The den displays the hostess's charming collection of bamboo birdcages, draped with Ylang-ylang blossoms plucked from the garden. The lady of the garden smilingly says, "Your own garden is the best source of ideas for decorating with flowers—naturally!"

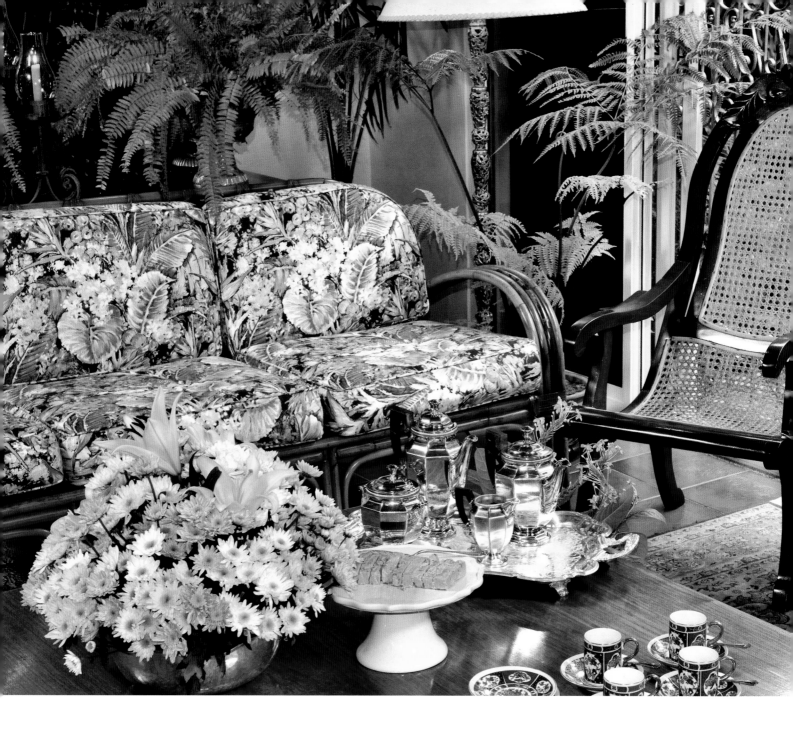

ABOVE A low bowl of yellow, white and purple daisies crowned by yellow stargazers and white roses is a harmonious complement to the floral furnishing fabric on the rattan couch.

PREVIOUS SPREAD The Mandarin red walls and black lacquered consoles in the dining room form a dramatic backdrop to a multi-vase floral "runway" of red and white carnations, stargazers, statice and white asters set between "Thousand Flowers" patterned china and cobalt blue stemware.

RIGHT Fresh green palm fronds and delicate pink gladioli springing from a base of red, pink and white chrysanthemums enhance a row of framed architectural prints of old Manila.

CENTER RIGHT Cobalt blue stemware becomes the color relief for dazzling vases filled with red carnations and white asters.

FAR RIGHT A central bank of white Casablanca lilies above a mass of spongy red cockscombs and red carnations forms part of the floral "runway" on the dining table.

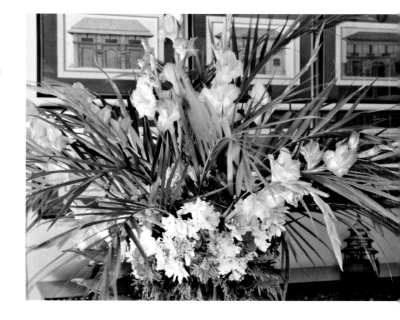

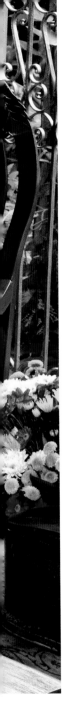

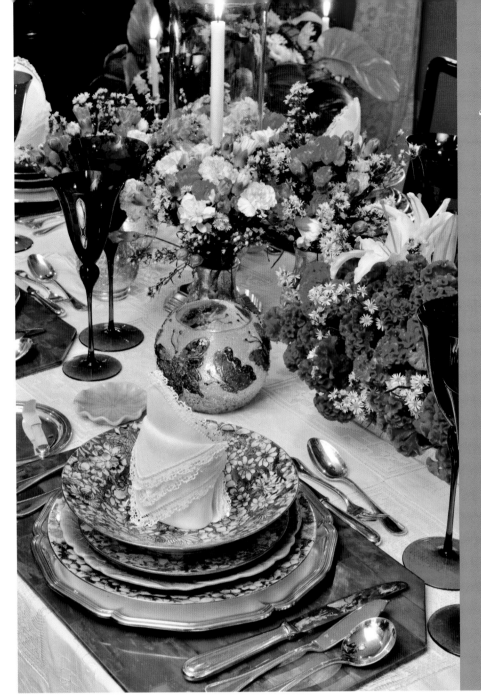

"My heirloom pieces plus my husband's truly create an East–West fusion. My garden constantly supplies what I basically need."

LEFT A "Thousand Flowers" patterned plates set the tone for a veritable table garden of cockscombs, Casablanca lilies, carnations and statice. Cobalt blue stemware is a masterful choice among all the florals.

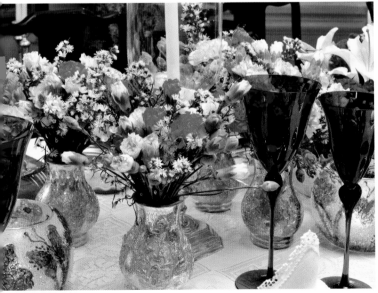

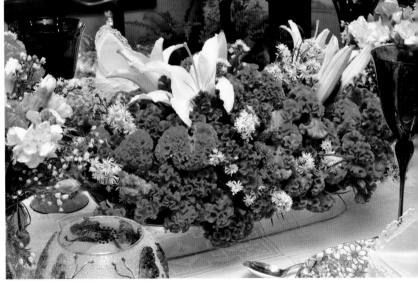

the constant gardener

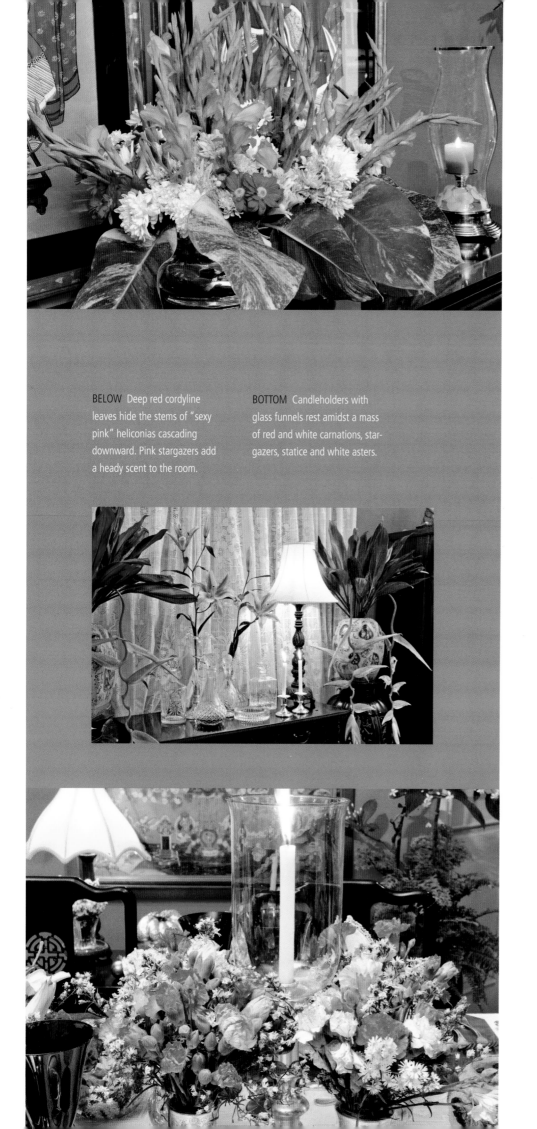

BELOW Deep red cordyline leaves hide the stems of "sexy pink" heliconias cascading downward. Pink stargazers add a heady scent to the room.

BOTTOM Candleholders with glass funnels rest amidst a mass of red and white carnations, stargazers, statice and white asters.

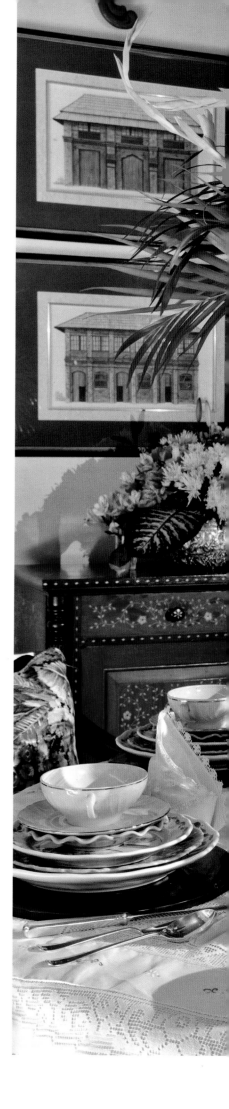

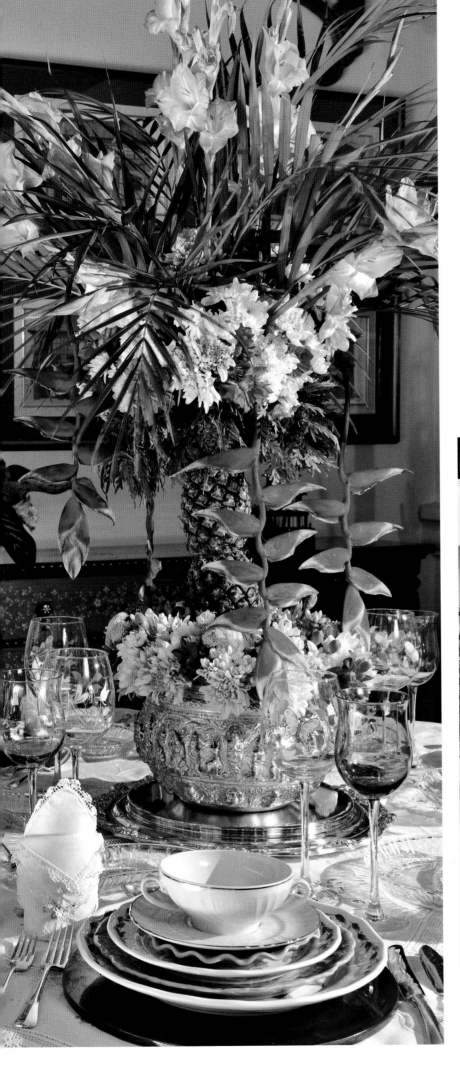

OPPOSITE TOP Pink gladioli interspersed with Malaysian mums and chrysanthemums positioned on huge philodendron leaves mirror the colors of the Chinese prints in the background.
LEFT Stacked pineapples, vivid drooping heliconias and a flourish of pink gladioli, red-toned chrysanthemums and palm leaves makes for high drama in the center of a luncheon setting.
BELOW Tricolor leaves hide the base stems of "sexy pink" heliconias drooping over rare ivory pipes.

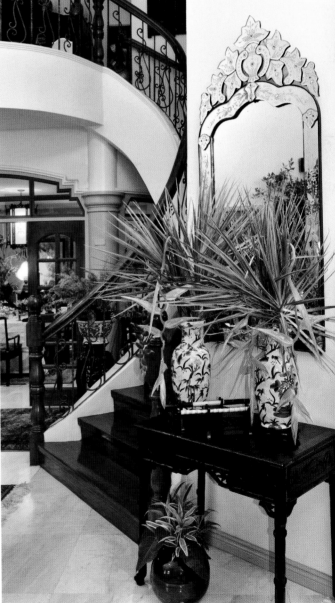

the constant gardener

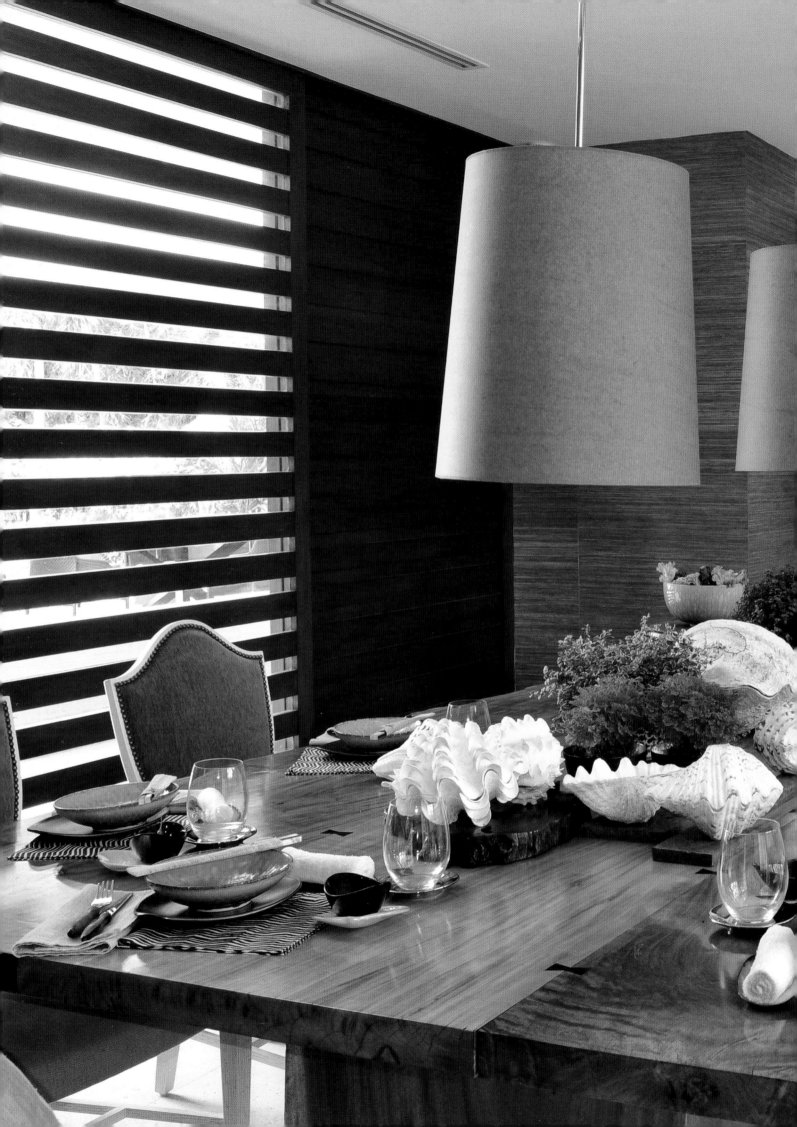

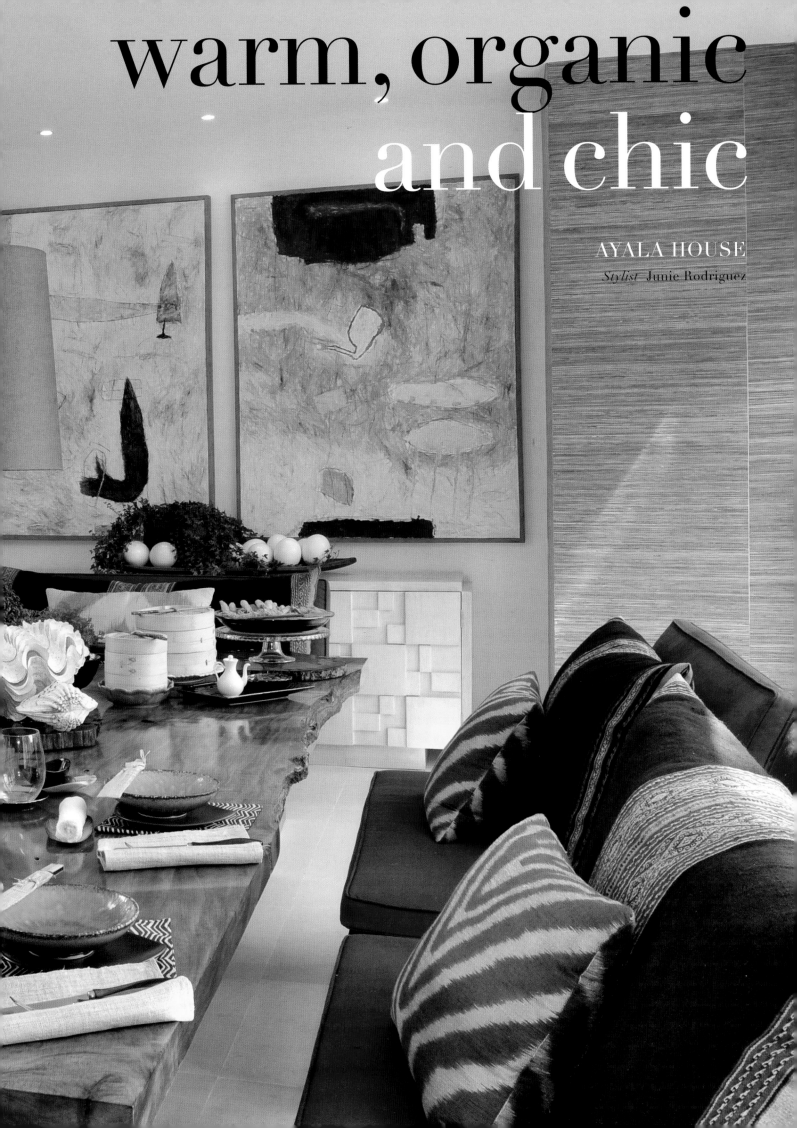

warm, organic and chic

AYALA HOUSE

Stylist Junie Rodriguez

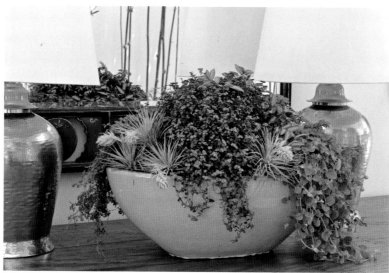

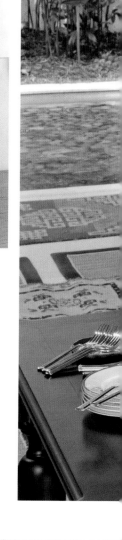

INA AND FRED AYALA have settled down "for now" after several high-flying years in the financial centers of Hong Kong and New York. Back on Philippine shores, they have chosen to be grounded stylishly in Makati, where they have also opted to escape the high-rise residences that have marked their global career trail.

Their fine new home in Dasmarinas Village, designed by modernist Anna Marie Sy, one of Manila's avant-garde architects (along with the likes of Ed Calma, Andy Locsin, Joey Yupangco and Jorge Yulo), is both gracious and spacious. Spread over 1000 sq m, the rambling two-story house comprises separate pavilions built around a large central water feature that is both swimming pool and reflection element.

The colorful interiors were styled by environmental designer Junie Rodriguez, who responded to the client's brief: "Ina really likes warm and comfortable interiors with touches of ethnic bohemian chic!"

Ina elaborated: "I wanted both space and depth, thus I asked to have my glassed-in living room look out onto the garden and pool…. Our dining room on the opposite side has the same view."

On the floral décor, she says, "My interior decorator Junie, like me, loves quiet, organic arrangements rather than blooms bursting out of vases." The Ayala home thus features fine-leafed plants and grasses composed within ceramic pots among giant shells, styled by Junie with help from gardener friend Rico Sison.

The glassed-in *sala* pavilion close to the front entry, built separately from the open-air *lanai*, is the hostess's informal entertainment area, where she displays her taste for a warm and relaxed ambience. Ina says, "I'm an ethnic fabric hoarder. Look at that ottoman—which is also a jumping pad for my boys. It's covered with a lady's embroidered skirt from Rajasthan. And here, my prized Peruvian weaves work so well with my time-worn Chinese rugs."

Interior stylist Junie Rodriguez pulled together an ethnic-organic dining table. "The huge molave block, which comprises three slabs fitted together with bow-tie wedges, dominates the dining room. Because Ina favors a lounge-like feel in her home, the table seating mixes single chairs and banquettes for two. The back cushions are covered in Ina's prized Peruvian fabrics."

A painter herself, Ina Ayala chose the Impressionist art for the walls. The main canvas over the dinner table is by Bernard Pacquing. As an equestrienne who rides daily, she has all the design elements and styles in her home well reigned in.

ABOVE The organic floral theme is illustrated by this ceramic bowl of afro grass, creeping charlie and spiky pink-bloomed tillandsias.
PREVIOUS SPREAD The large dining table with bow-tie joints is flanked by couples' banquettes swathed in Ina's prized Peruvian weaves. Blue and white pots of creeping charlie and asparagus ferns are interspersed with bleached shells on wooden slabs.

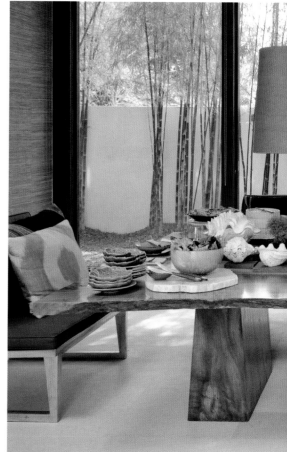

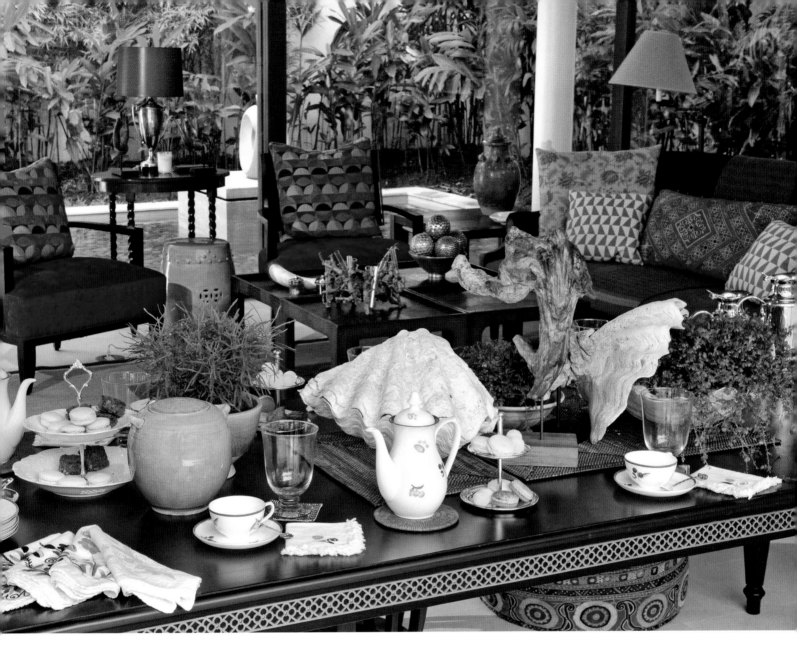

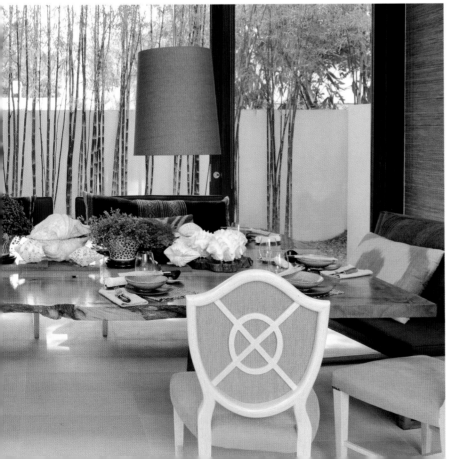

ABOVE The glassed-in pavilion near the front door is a treasure trove of handmade Rhajastani and Peruvian textiles and other "treasures" collected over the years, here displayed in eclectic disarray among a tea setting, shells and organic pot plants.
LEFT The ethnic-organic dining table, viewed from the pool through sliding slatted doors, was designed by Junie Rodrigues and made by Buddy Lagdameo. The variety of single and double seating can accommodate ten.

warm, organic and chic

latin *fusion*

GIANNA MONTINOLA, educationist and social activist, has always loved Filipiniana architecture, crafts and design. As she wanted her new home to include design elements taken from Filipino architectural traditions, her crafts-savvy designers, Dominic Galicia and Tina Periquet, built her Makati house with Art Deco multicolored glass doors adapted from the family ancestral home in Iloila, *capiz* window-style grid doors and a myriad of other touches of Filipiniana charm.

Warm, sunny and Iberian on the outside, charmingly eclectic inside, Gianna's bungalow is a multicultural fusion. Floral stylist Margarita Fores explains. "Her experience of living for years in Peru brought a bright, colorful sensibility to her taste! Her interior colors are now orange, violet, red and lime green—a fascinating blend of Peruvian highlands and tropical Philippines!"

The bright orange bungalow has spun a delightful synergy for this book. By floral fate perhaps, these two friends from childhood have collaborated to mount creative table settings of distinctive Phil-Peruvian character. Stylist Margarita visited owner Gianna twice, and discovered the charming crockery with leafy themes and folksy colors that Gianna had painted in Peru. The two then made inspired settings together.

In the large foyer area, Margarita composed an elegant Filipiniana arrangement of the country's loveliest white flowers atop a bone-inlaid table from Bulacan. Four sweet-smelling flowers—rosal, azucena (tuberoses), sampaguita and magnolia—grace the table and perfume the air. The tuberoses are tucked like tail feathers into silver and shell sculptures of Peruvian birds. Gianna's colorful plates rest upon exquisite antique *pina* or pineapple fiber placemats.

Margarita the restaurateur is most proud of her vegetal luncheon setting in the dining room. A picturesque tableau of fresh vegetables and herbs riding a wooden *sungka* game board on the console sets the scene for the table display—more gaily painted plates enclosing a central display of beaten silver boxes in the shape of vegetables and fruit, white roses and orange pandanus fruit. The predominant colors are an intense and unusual triad of violet, orange and chartreuse. "All her accessories are so inspirational!" says Margarita of Gianna's collection.

On the front doorstep, Margarita assembled a crowning work—a bulbous earthen jar from the Amazon jungle, imprinted with a woman's face, wearing a giant Andean headdress of dried calumpang fruit pods, golden shower tree pods, millionaire's cactus, cabbage succulents and Queen Anne's lace flowers.

As a florist, Margarita is constantly inspired by nature, claiming a rustic, individualist style that she calls "experimental with an edge." She says, "When I'm in the provinces, I go around always looking *up*—at the wild bushes and trees! And I bring back new branches and leaves to work with. My motto is 'It doesn't have to be expensive!'" Just experimental—with an edge.

RIGHT Art Deco glass doors adapted from Gianna Montinola's family ancestral home in Iloilo make a fine backdrop to an elegant Filipiniana table setting. Hand-painted plates by heritage hostess Gianna resting on antique *pina* mats encircle a glorious arrangement of sweet-smelling rosal, azucena, sampaguita and magnolia blooms.

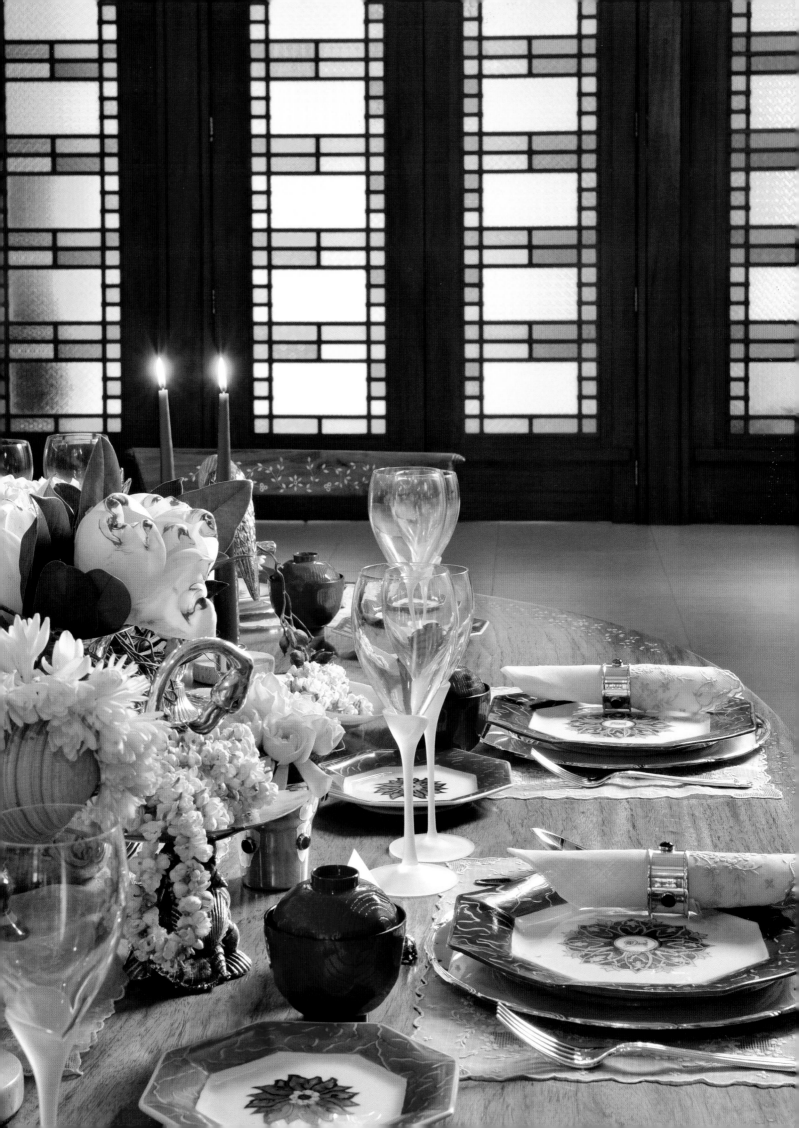

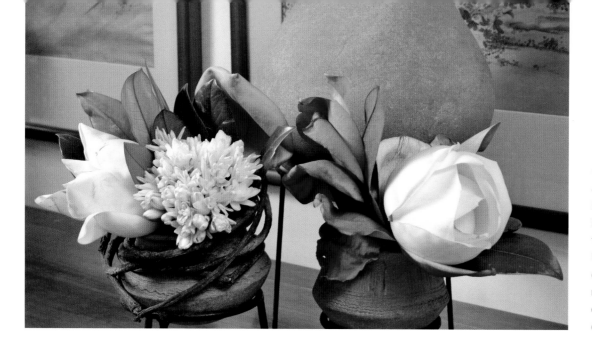

LEFT In-season giant magnolias in earthen pots grace a sideboard in the foyer.
BELOW The handsome bone-inlaid oval conference table, formerly in the Far Eastern University library in Manila, is complemented by wood grids reminiscent of *capiz* shell windows and four panel paintings of Japanese cherry blossoms.

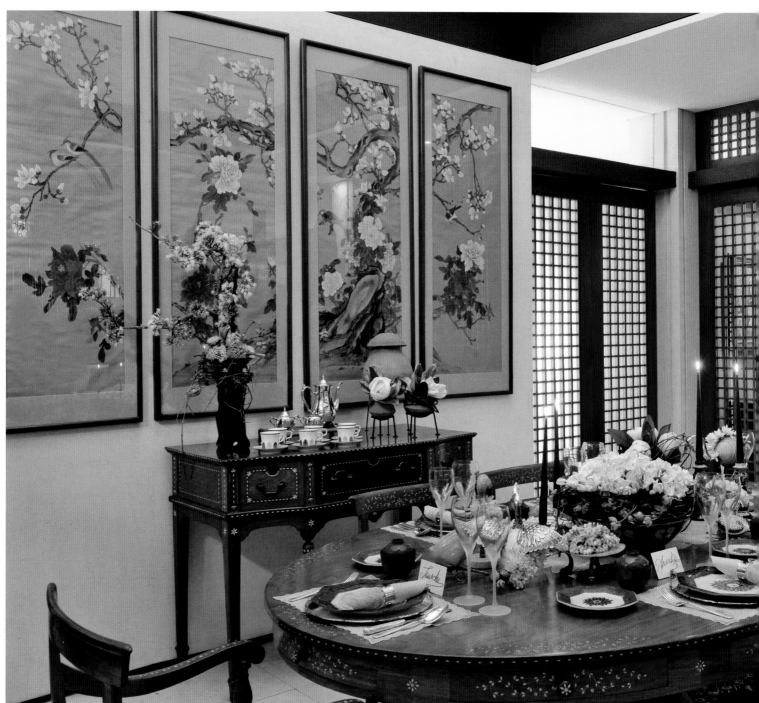

BELOW An earthen jar featuring the face of an Andean woman wears long vine tresses fashioned by Margarita and a giant headdress of dried dried calumpang fruit pods, golden shower tree pods, millionaire's cactus, cabbage succulents and Queen Anne's lace flowers.

"Gianna's experience of living for years in Peru brought a bright, colorful sensibility to her taste! Her interior colors of orange, violet, red and lime green blend the Peruvian highlands and tropical Philippines!" says florist Margarita Fores.

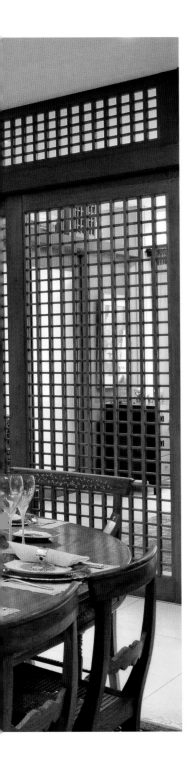

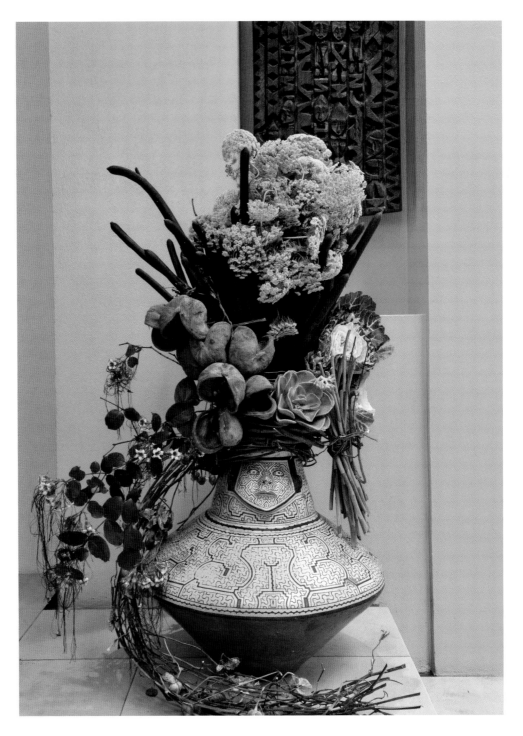

latin fusion

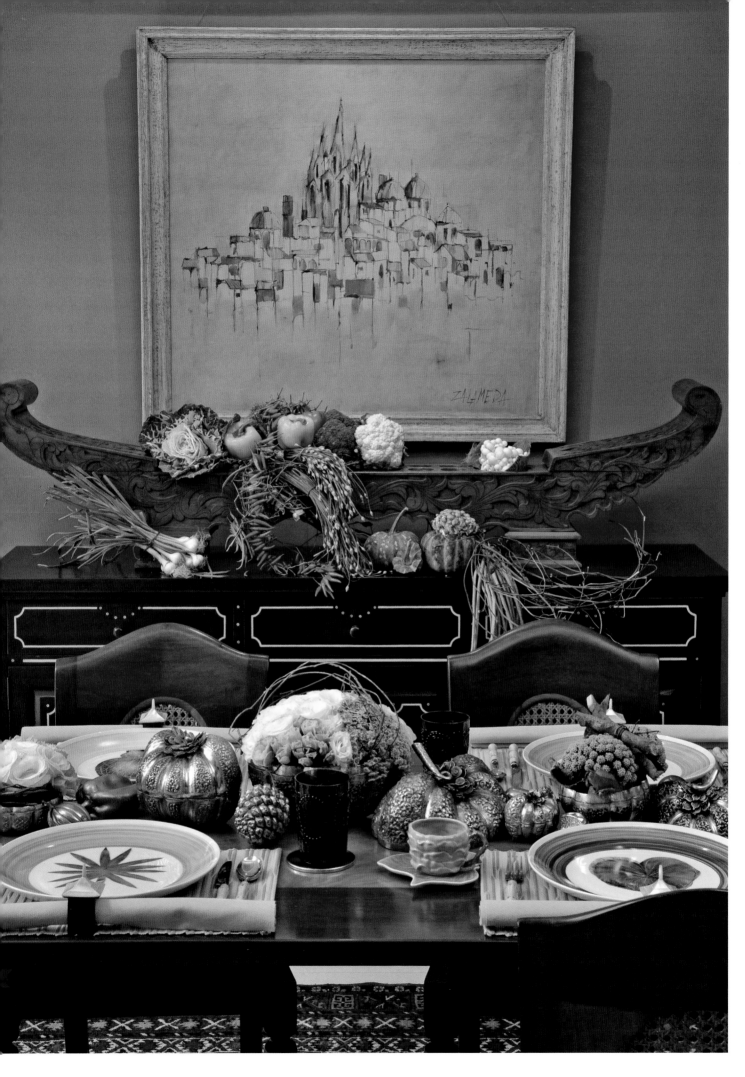

LEFT AND BELOW The stylist's vegetal luncheon table is based around the home owner's charming self-painted leaf plates. A background culinary tableau displays fresh vegetables and household herbs on a large wooden *sungka* game board.
RIGHT The table setting features Gianna's beaten silver squashes and bell peppers arranged with green wood roses and pandan flowers.

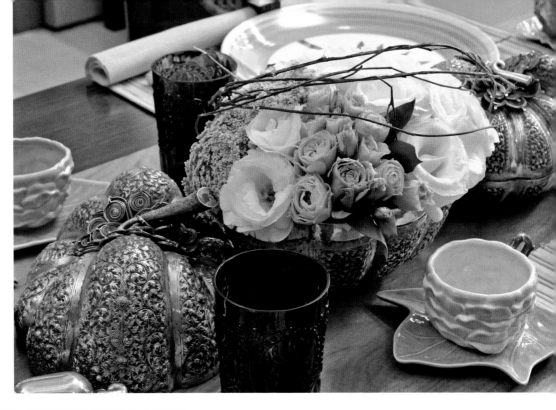

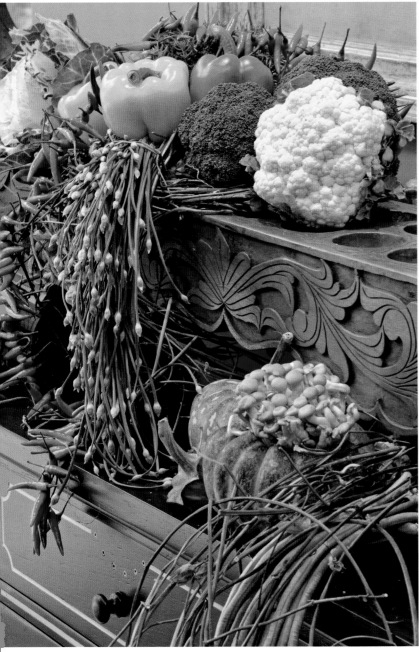

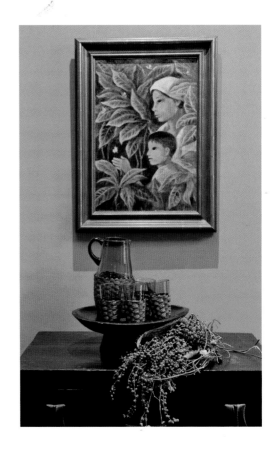

ABOVE Rustic vines and wild berries provide textural contrast to an antique pitcher and glass set on a chest. The painting on the orange wall is by Anita Magsaysay-Ho.

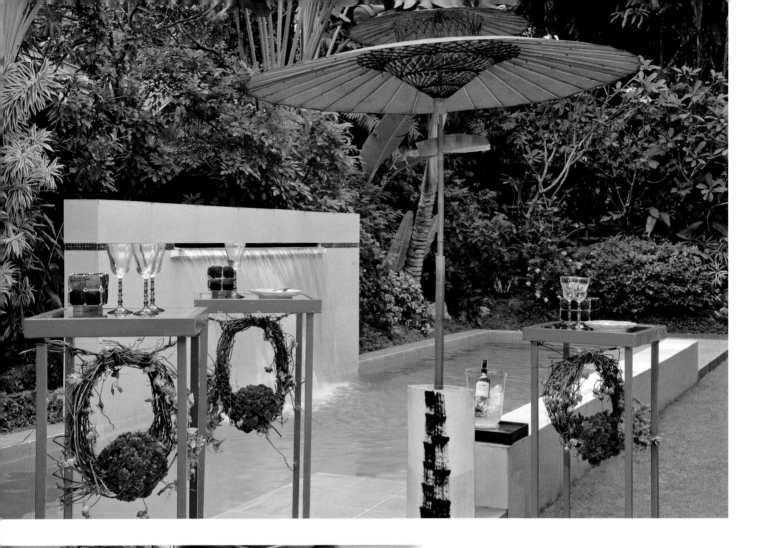

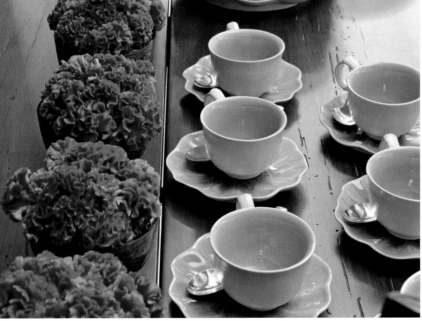

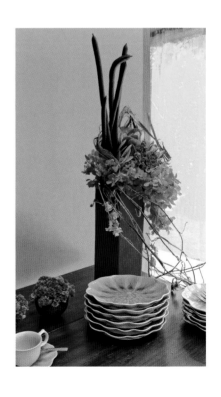

TOP Floral stylist Margarita
Fores created three red cocktail
tables for Gianna's garden. Here,
wreaths suspended under glass
carry nests of red cockscomb.
ABOVE Aqua-toned lotus teacups are lined up beside an array
of red cockscomb bouquets in
green lacquer Burmese bowls.

RIGHT Red orchid blossoms and
golden shower tree pods stand
tall in a rectangular vessel near a
stack of dainty lotus leaf plates.
OPPOSITE The Peruvian red wall
with its ornate Balinese frame is
set off by dry arrangements of
spongy cockscomb mounds in
colorful decorative boxes.

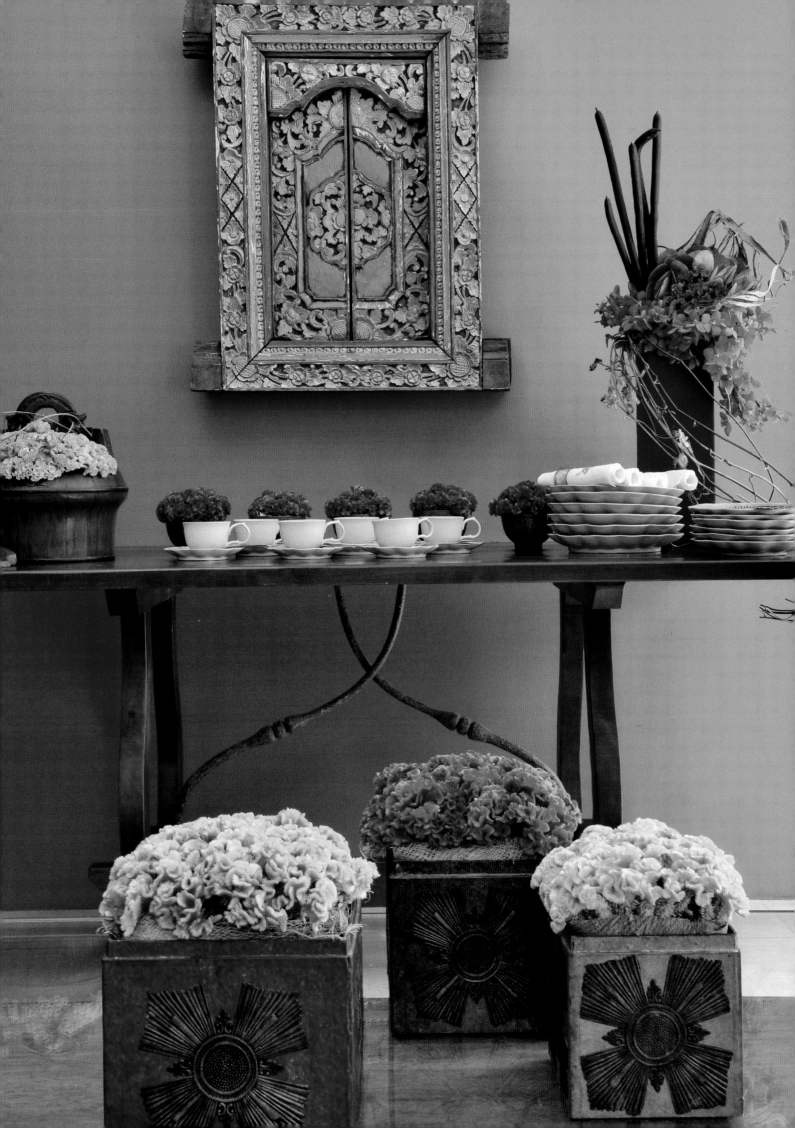

elegant *exuberance*

THIS ELEGANT TWO-STORY house is comfortably located on a 800 sq m lot in an upscale Makati village. Warmly orange and Iberian up front, the home is surrounded by a compact garden marked by tall, mature trees. A "modern-classic" residence with understated Spanish-Filipino interiors, it harbors a treasure trove of antique hardwood tables, excavated jars, rare engravings and lithographs, and vintage paintings by Amorsolo, Zobel and Dela Rosa.

The lady of the house radiates verve and creativity. She has designed fine furniture, lived a luxurious life in San Francisco and featured prominently on the social pages. To update and give a fresh look to her residence in Makati, she called on modernist architect and interior designer J. Anton Mendoza, a lover of old things but a minimalist at heart, to employ his contemporary touch to temper the heavy "period feel" of the house. She also called upon the favorite florist of the élite, Antonio Garcia of Mabolo Inc., to do her floral arrangements.

The genteel house is an ideal space in which to design a seamless interaction of flowers and exquisite *objets d'art*. "I love fresh flowers, whether we're entertaining or not!" declares the hostess of this elegant residence.

While Antonio was styling floral vignettes for the house, the hostess reflected on her exquisite collection of furniture and *objets d'art*. "That Chippendale shelf over there was from Charlotte Horsmann of Hong Kong and these French candleholders are from Gump's in San Francisco…. Ah, those were the days for great finds!"

In the updated ebony and ivory *sala*, plush white linen couches are set against a carbon black anthracite wall hung with a collection of antique engravings of old Spanish Manila. Low pin-lit tabletops of black marble display exotica such as tortoiseshell, ivory and silver artifacts and fine Chinese imperial yellow jade. Arching gracefully over the collections are groupings of white phalaenopsis orchids—as exquisite as the objects themselves.

The stylish house opens up to an L-shaped *terrazza* set for afternoon cocktails or soigné lounging. Yellow and purple dendrobium orchids decorate the cocktail buffet table. Amaranthus "rosary bead" vines, cymbidiums and broccoli heads are clustered in a huge clamshell on the molave trunk coffee table.

Inside and out, Antonio creates vignettes using small, delicate flowers—leaving the furnishings and artifacts to enjoy the attention they deserve. "Space and scale are very important," he says, as he styles his uncommon floral sets. "We imported flowers from Spain, Japan and Venezuela for this very special house."

Antonio's floral design advice for an elegant setting is to marry the finest of fresh flowers with the treasured art pieces of a collection— every day, not just for special occasions! Here, amaranthus rosary beads drip from a big silver mollusk; single cymbidium blooms beam from silver and ivory cups; the pink blossoms of cadena de amor highlight a prized Chippendale shelf, and tiny white cymbidiums offset a 17th century ivory-encrusted traveler's desk.

RIGHT Spikes of the Arabian star flower radiate from velvety mounds of boule de mousse (bun moss). Antique bone china teacups on buffalo horn plates complement the 1950s glassware from Gump's.

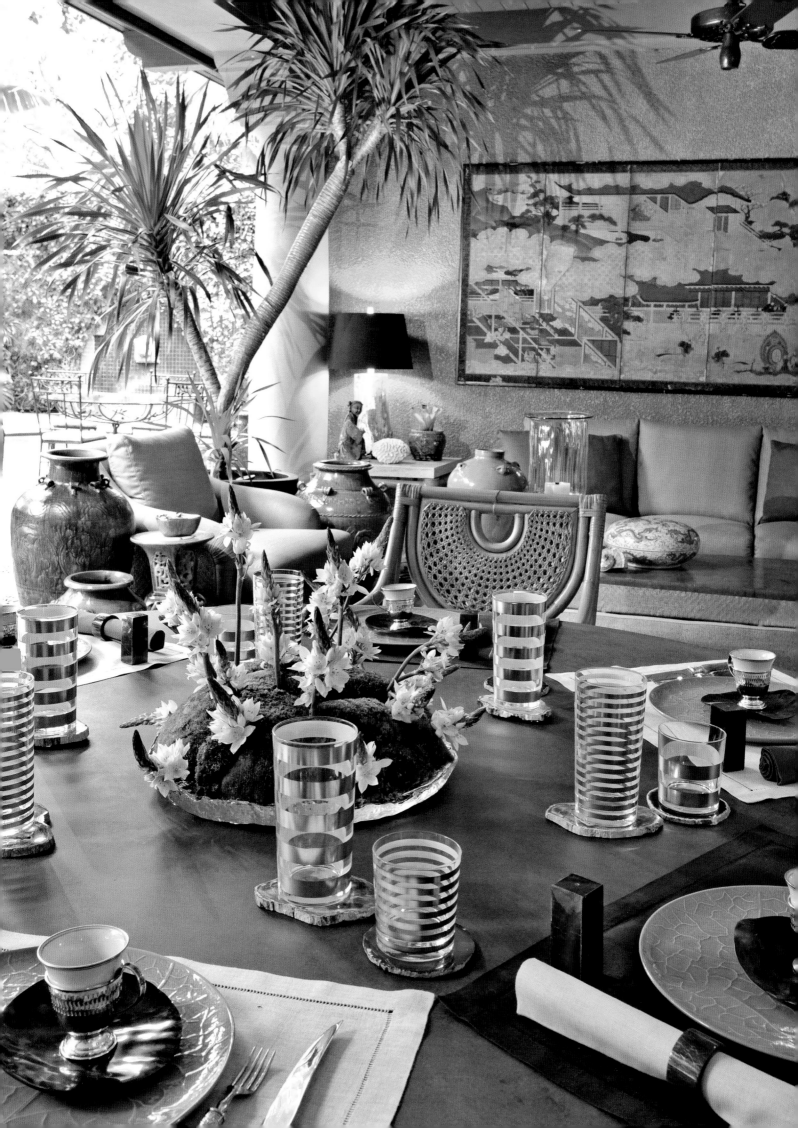

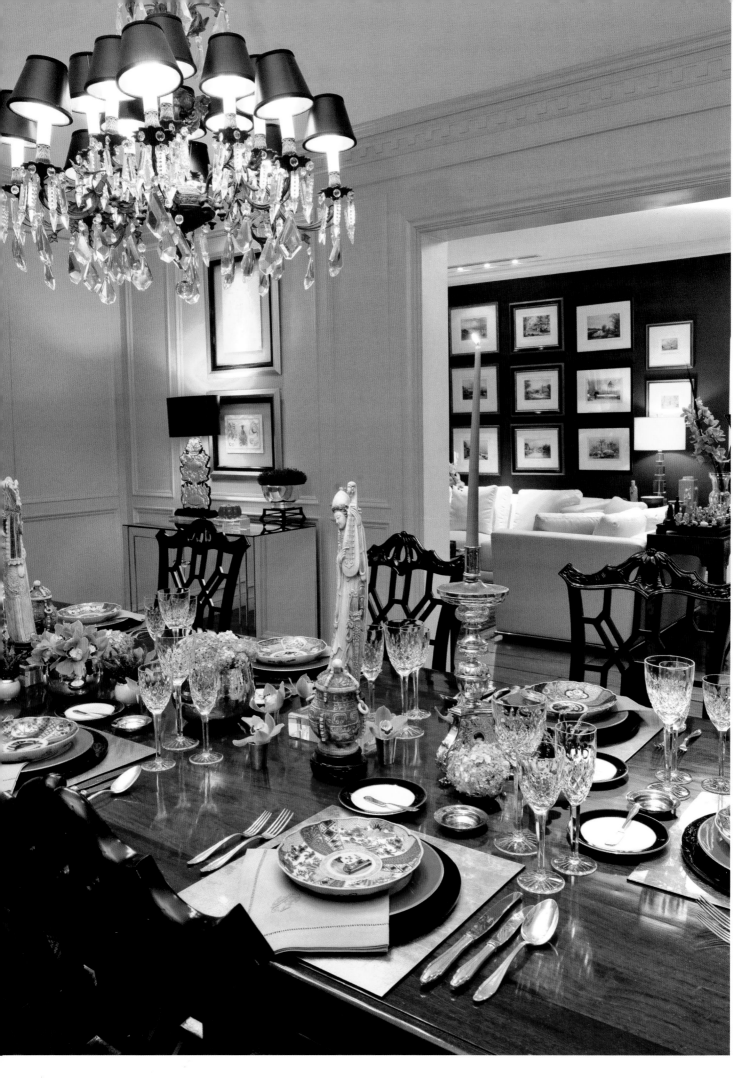

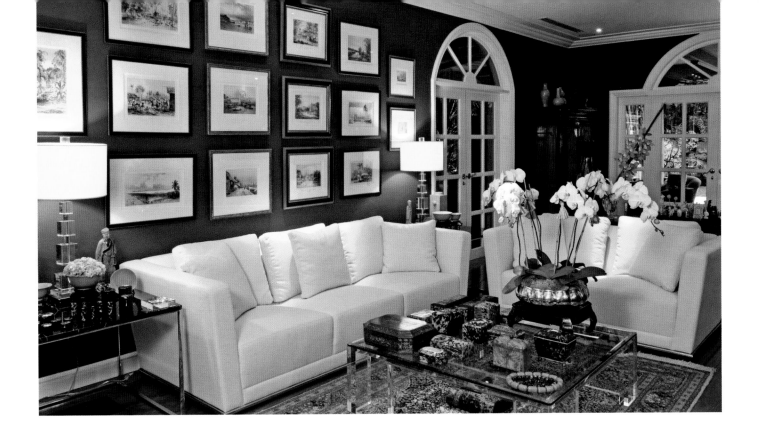

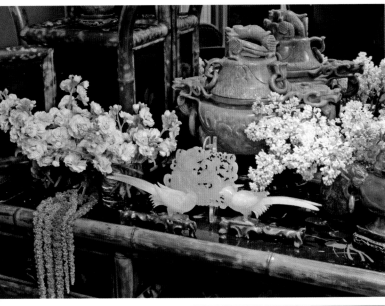

LEFT Simple vases of pink and white stocks and a garland of coral-hued amaranthus "rosary beads" spilling from a table laden with pale jade bird figures and a flawless celadon vessel show how treasured objects and fresh flowers can meet in a harmonious pairing.

ABOVE Tall white phalaenopsis orchids in an elegant silver bowl hover over the owner's fine collection of tortoiseshell boxes.

BELOW In the foyer, a trail of yellow and lime green cymbidiums cools off antique ox blood vessels on a beautiful chinoiserie cabinet.

LEFT Lime green cymbidiums in silver cups, sprigs of purple veronica in ivory bracelets and balls of white Guelder roses join oriental ivory deities, vintage Imari plates and Chippendale chairs in this elegant dining room.

RIGHT Pink cymbidiums temper the fiery opulence of tortoiseshell cabinetry and choice artifacts.

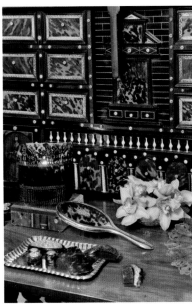

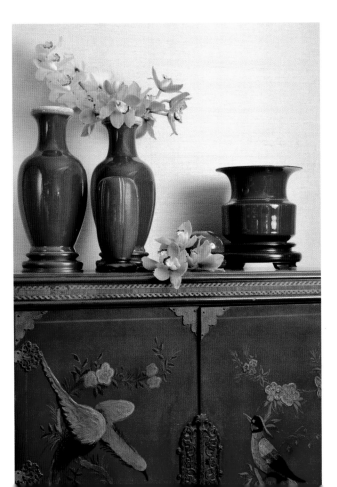

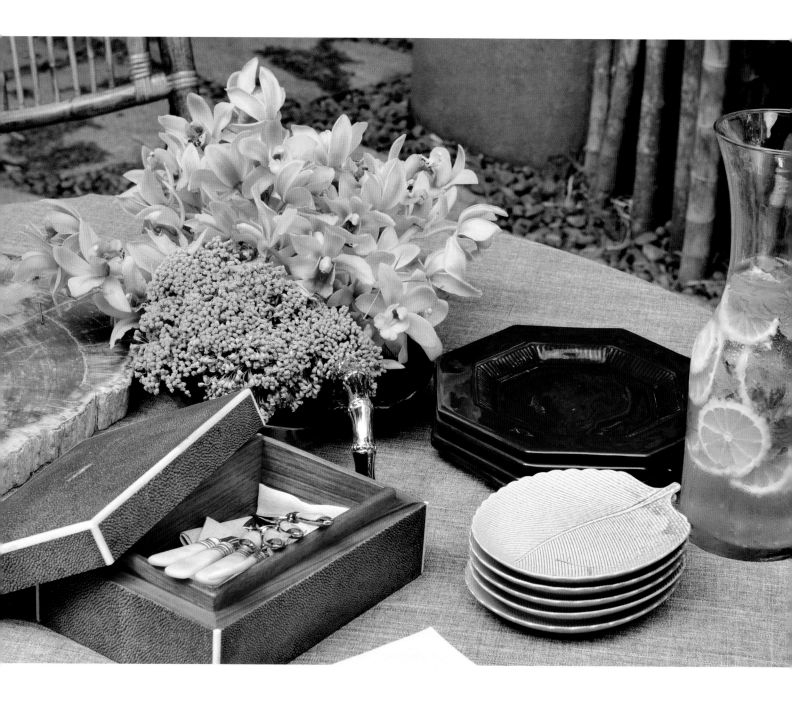

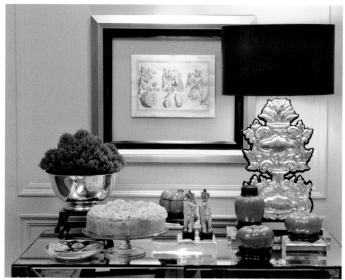

ABOVE A silver-handled buffalo horn pan makes an unusual vessel for a mass of bold yellow cymbidiums and dainty fernleaf yarrow.

LEFT Green cypress foliage in a silver bowl offsets the fiery tones of the orange cake and porcelain persimmons. A lamp with a silver altar piece base casts light on a rare print of Philippine flora.

OPPOSITE ABOVE The muted, understated floral arrangement on the *terrazza* table allows the furniture, paintings, pots and smaller treasured artifacts to take center stage.

OPPOSITE BELOW A raw linen tablecloth and yellow-hued floral arrangement bring out the rich bamboo tones of the chairs—samples from the owner's early furniture export venture.

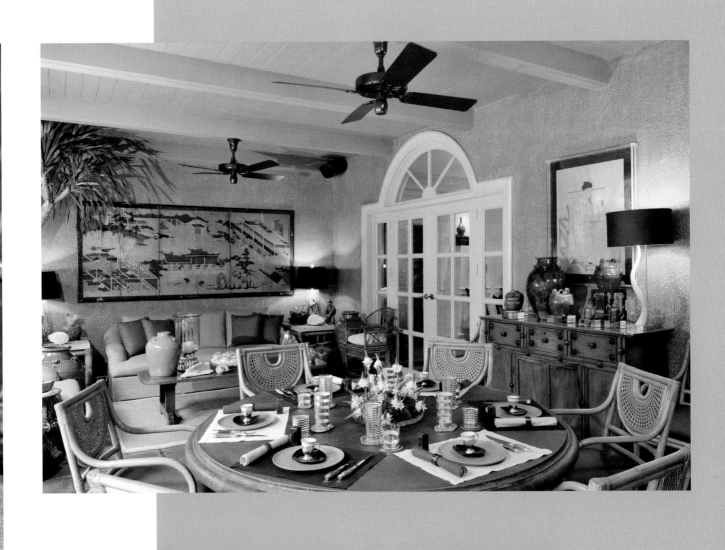
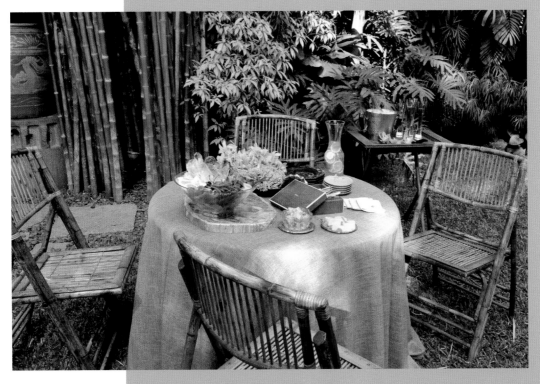

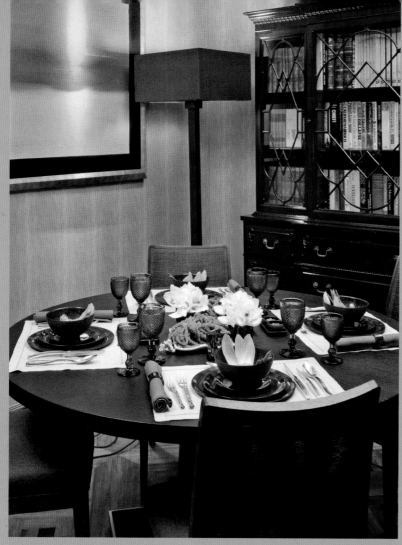

"My clients are plant and flower lovers. It's my delight to surprise them as they encourage me to bring to their homes flowers from all over our islands and the world," says florist-trader Antonio Garcia.

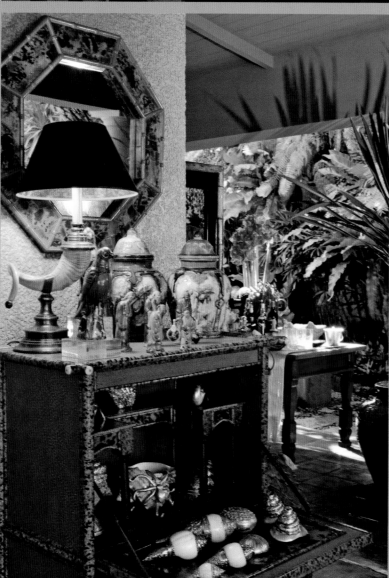

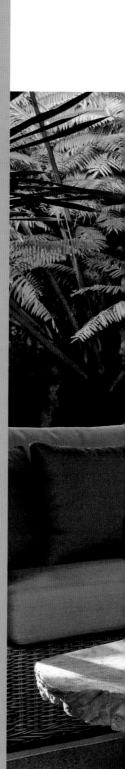

ABOVE LEFT A private library lunch calls for a centerpiece of coral "rosary bead" amaranthus and pink cymbidiums to highlight the exquisite Japanese tea plates and bowls accented with endives.
LEFT A bamboo-edged campaign chest, with the desk top open and laden with silver and ivory treasures, is one of the many fine display pieces on the L-shaped *terrazzo*. Lush garden foliage harmonizes with the greens in the porcelain on the chest.

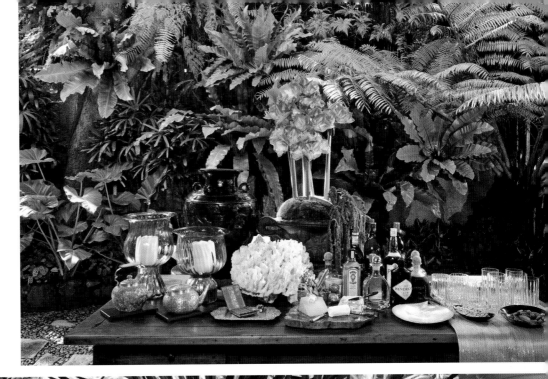

RIGHT A graphic arrangement of belladonna lilies anchored with a cascade of "rosary bead" amaranthus in a mound of boule de mousse beckons visitors to the cocktail buffet in the garden.
BELOW Broccoli heads, yellow and green cymbidiums and amaranthus beads nestle in a giant clam on the free-form molave trunk coffee table on the *terrazza*.

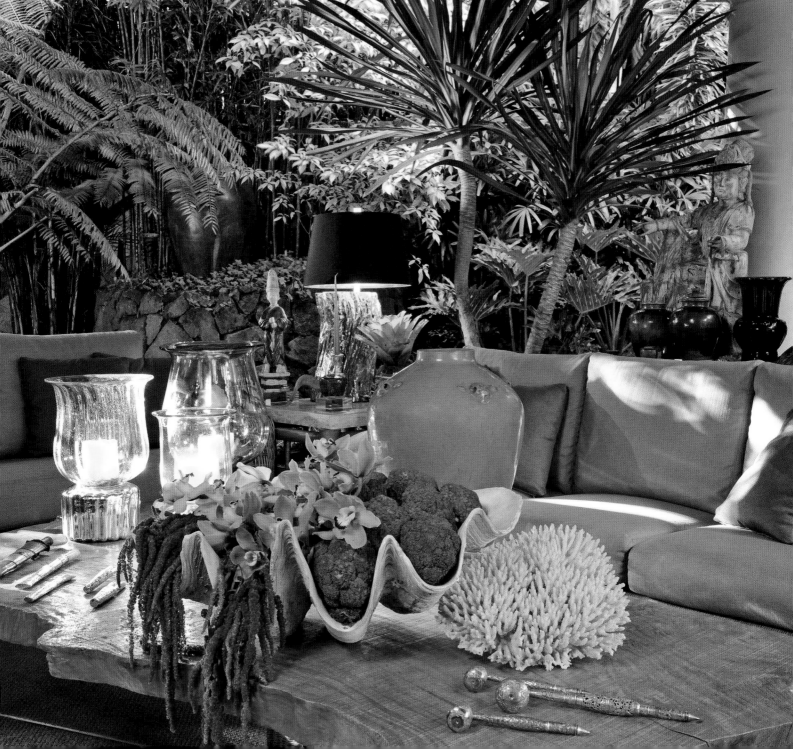

southern *belle*

ONGPIN GARDEN HOME   *Florist*   Rosabella Ongpin with Sabine Koschinger

THERE'S A NEW FLORAL DESIGNER in town. Rosabella Ongpin, better known as Belle Ongpin, has just passed her first Valentine's season as a commercial florist. She has done the annual rush for roses; done the countless sweethearts' bouquets; and survived the most hectic time of the Philippine flower trade! It must be her floral fate since her name is Rosabella (lovely rose). Indeed, she does do flowers sweetly.

Belle's home is a tall Tuscan bungalow in Alabang, south of Metro Manila. Built in 2002 by her garden-loving husband, the residence was hand-embellished by Mario Cantu, an Italian architect and art promoter from Genoa. Mario had come to help with the Ongpin residence. He stayed on for two years to explore Asia, and left behind a tapestry of *tromp l'oeil* paintings on all the walls he touched!

Belle's garden is a rambling 1200 sq m space, with clusters of ornamental plants, beds of flowers and a giant mango tree. It is both the source of flowers and the inspiration that fuels her arrangements. With the greatest of ease, she conjures up lovely bouquets and modern Sogetsu ikebana forms that most people have only seen in books. Her repertoire of styles is vast: leafy immersions in glass cylinders;

boldly beautiful compositions in rustic dishes; lush tropical arrays in standing jars; and aerial arrangements flying off the dining room chandelier all the way to the ceiling! In the evening, Belle shows off candlelit flotations in the swimming pool and rattan flower orbits lighting the way upstairs.

A particular favorite is her rustic-romantic Toscana floral log, a cluster of fuschia bougainvilleas, purple statice and blue and aqua succulents with aerial hair of Esther ferns and Queen Anne's lace flowers. The languid composite is built upon a twisted *gugu* vine and a burlap abaca wrap, sprinkled with orange everlasting flowers from Baguio and looped with silver florists' wire. The arrangement is undeniably romantic.

Belle's table stylist is linen producer Sabine Koschinger, who staged picturesque scenes of the Filipino tradition of constant dining. The spunky German decorator created an *alfresco* breakfast setting right by the neighbor's firewall (*tromp l'oeil*-painted as an Italian villa). On a marine-inspired table, she installed goldfish in a vase with a bract of vivid red heliconia. And she hand-painted dainty flowers on the linens under the mango tree. Sabine's finale tableau was a glittering dinner setting in black and gold—with faux food included!

RIGHT Stylist Sabine's colorful *alfresco* breakfast setting is placed by the firewall. Tableware comprises classic black Bavarian designs on a dotted organza tablecloth. A curvy torso vase holds a single sunflower and gerbera amid variegated croton leaves.

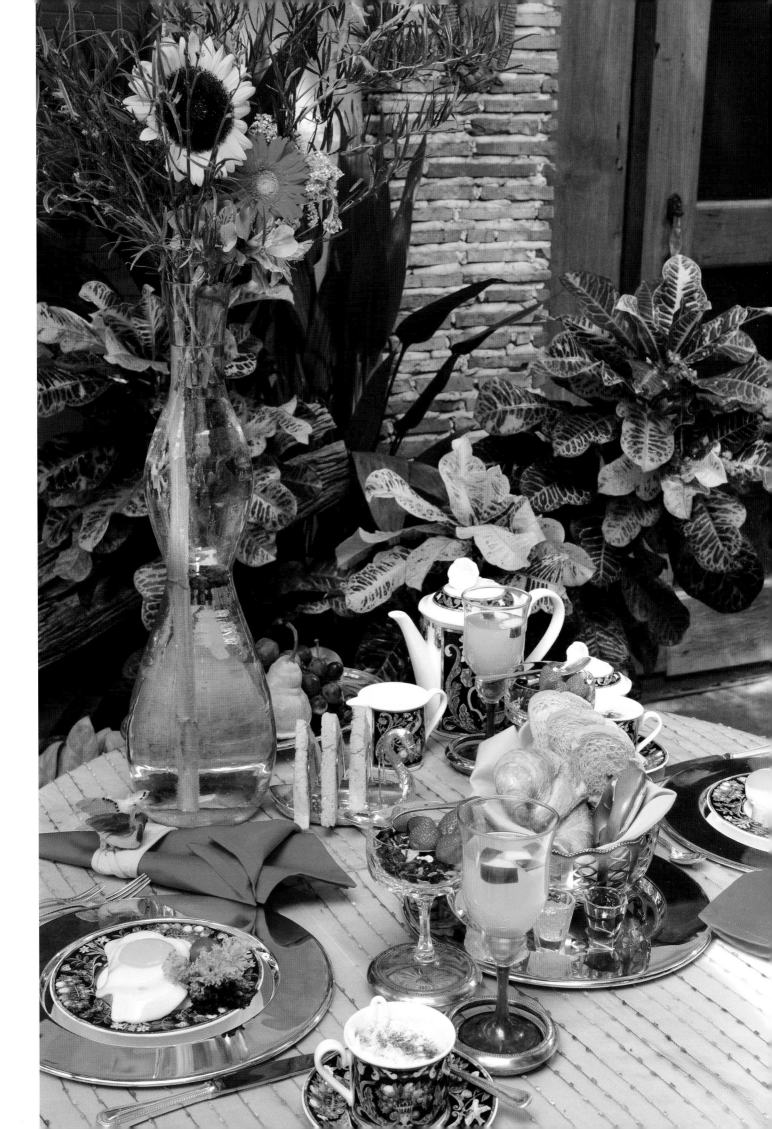

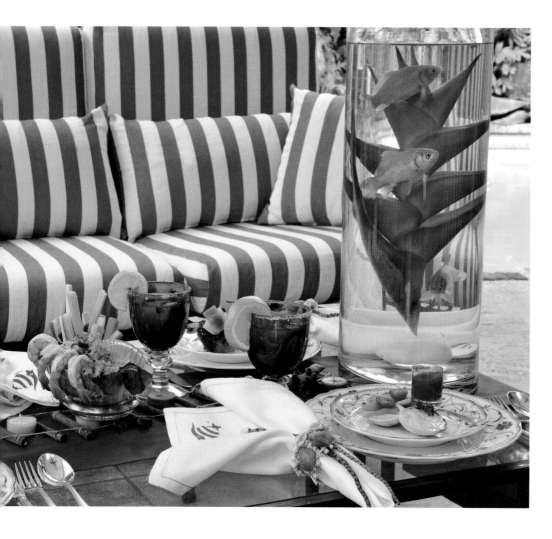

LEFT Goldfish make a dramatic and dynamic addition to a glass cylinder filled with a bold red heliconia bract anchored with a stone on this marine blue-themed luncheon table. The goldfish will, of course, be returned to their larger home after the guests have left.

BELOW Showy flowers—fuschia statice, purple vanda orchids and orange African tulips—are served in a romantic silver Art Nouveau bowl on a sideboard.

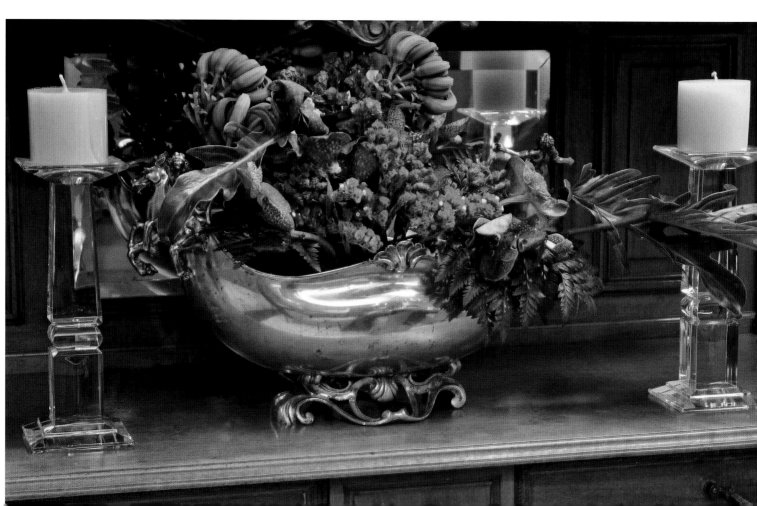

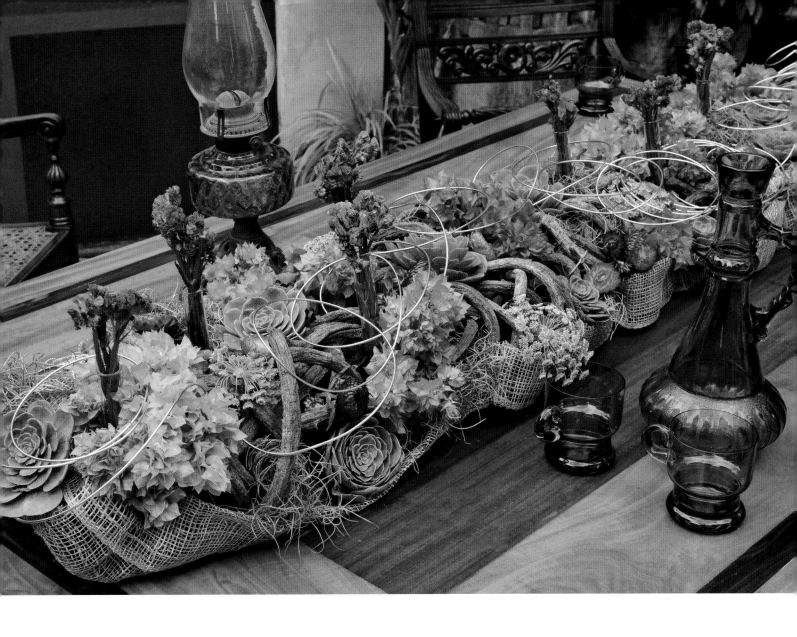

Rosabella Ongpin conjures up lovely arrangements with intuition and the greatest of ease. "I like working with cordyline leaves, crotons and gloriosas for their vibrant colors, and hydrangeas give me a natural high."

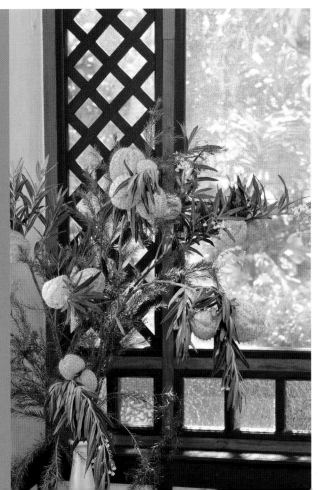

ABOVE Belle's Tuscany log is an ultra-whimsical creation containing fuschia bougainvilleas, purple statice, rose-shaped succulents, hair of Esther ferns and Queen Anne's lace arranged on a rustic burlap cloth amidst wines and twirls of silver florists' wire.
LEFT A spray of hairy balls, locally known as green lanterns, in Belle's powder room, harmonizes with the garden foliage beyond.

southern belle

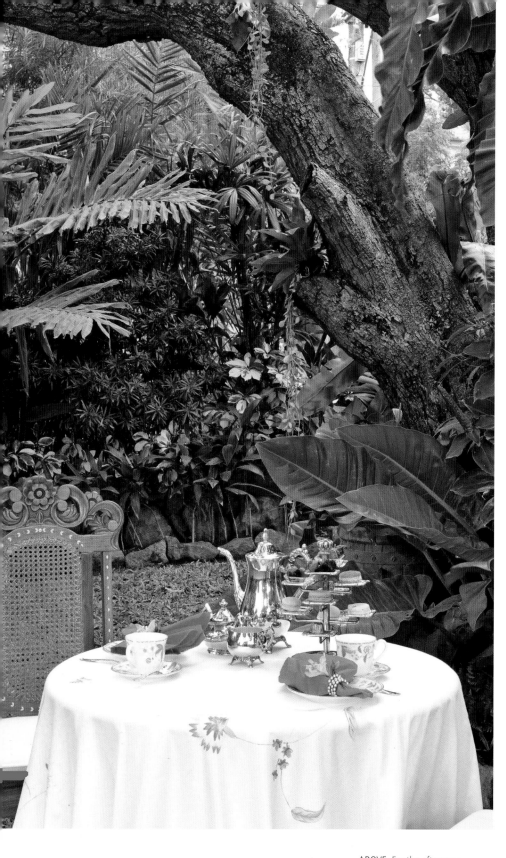

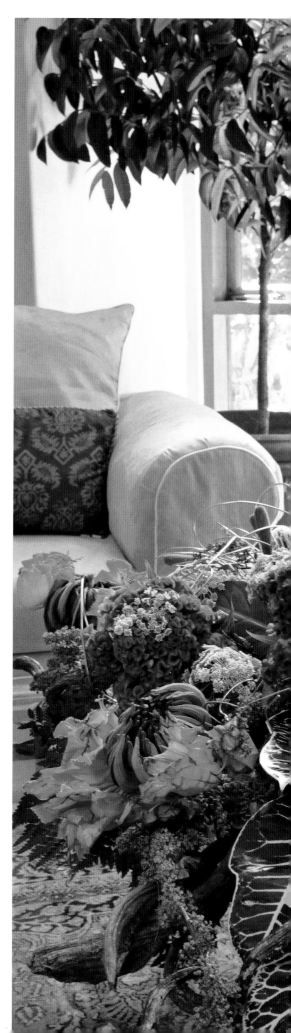

ABOVE For the afternoon *merienda* under the mango tree, Sabine hand-painted dainty flowers on the linens and served colorful cakes and macaroons on a tiered silver service.

RIGHT The airy Tuscan *sala* is a perfect setting for a ravishing display of orange African tulips, pink cockscomb and Queen Anne's lace amid luxuriant foliage, vines and florists' wire.

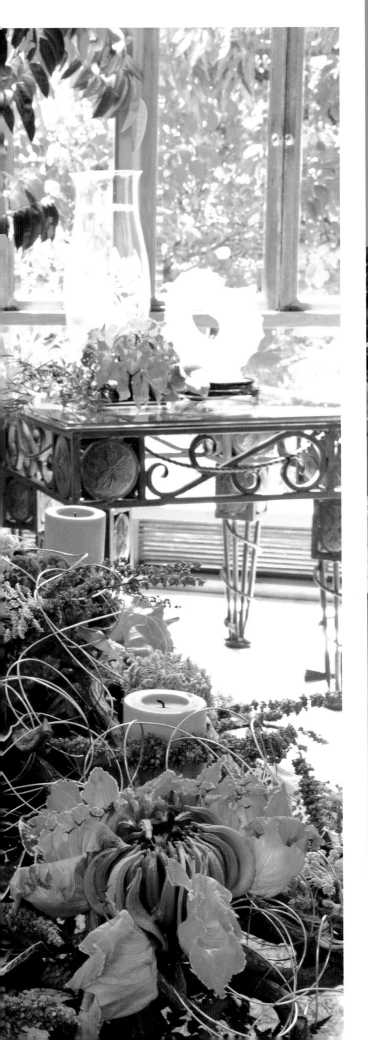

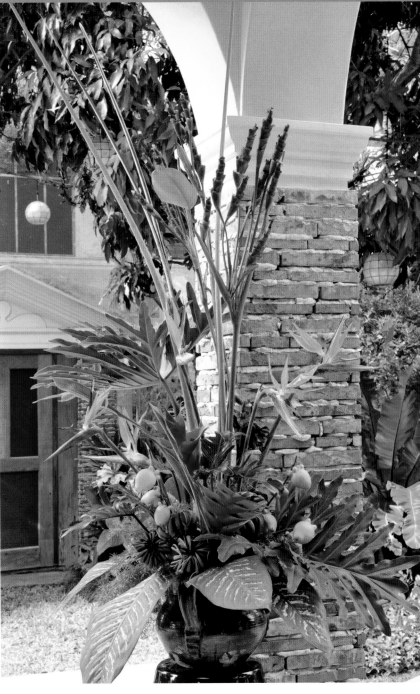

BELOW Tropical flamboyance is epitomized in this standing installation of brown gingers, red heliconias, orange and yellow birds of paradise, orange African tulips and yellow Mickey Mouse pods, supported by giant foliage.

southern belle

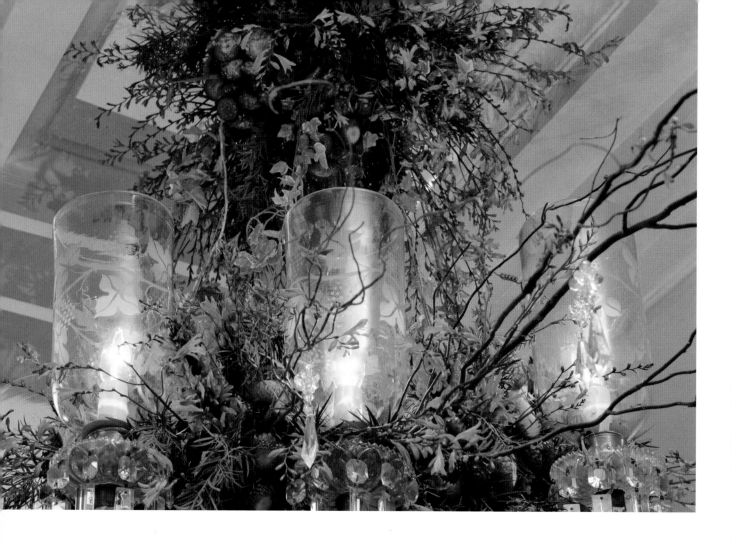

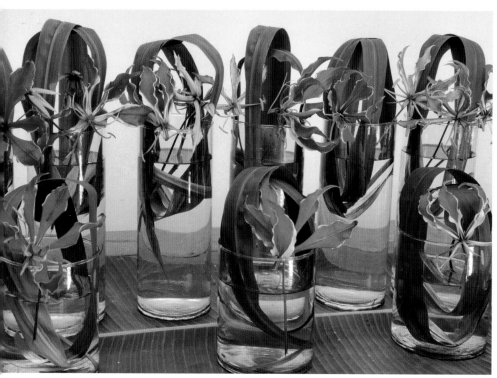

ABOVE Belle's *tour de force*—
her floral chandelier exploding
above the dining table—is a
fiery combination of firecracker
blooms, Baguio everlasting flowers, curly willow and ivy vines.
LEFT Taking inspiration from Thai
florist Sakul Intakul's betwitching
water installations, Belle places
brilliant glory lilies in two sizes of
water glasses on a banana leaf
"runner." Rolled leaves support
the blooms at the glass rims.
RIGHT Sabine's dinner tableau
is a glitzy setting in black and
gold, with red highlights from
the faux gazpacho in the bowls
and the vivid floral centerpiece.
Gilt-edged Noritake plateware
and Waterford glasses go well
with Sabine's giant candles and
diamond sprinkles.

Says Rosabella Ongpin, "I was first inspired by floral designer Richard Go in Sydney. He used twigs, vines, bark, seeds, and pods! Little did I know I would be a scavenger like him one day, when floral arrangement became my second career!"

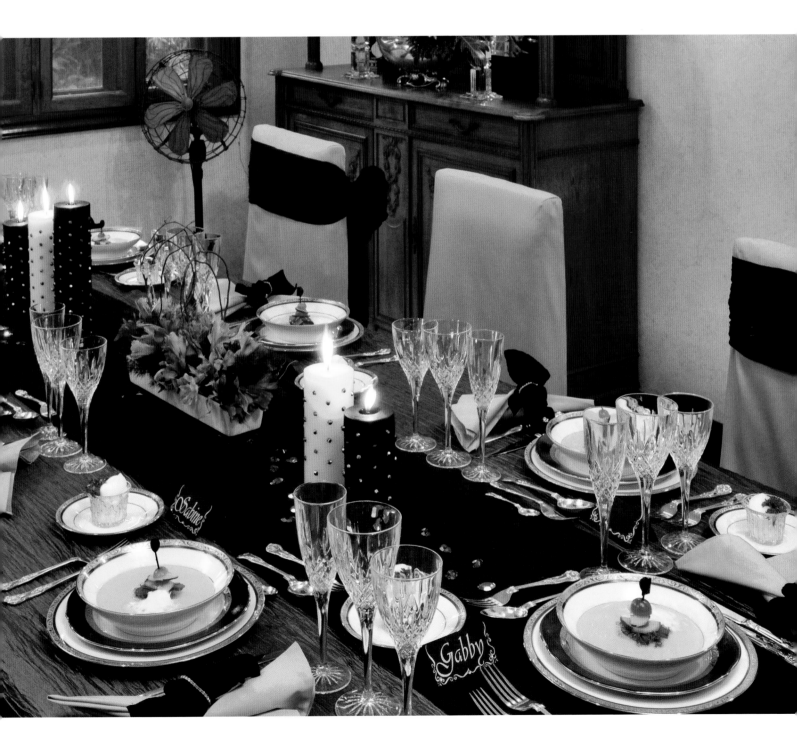

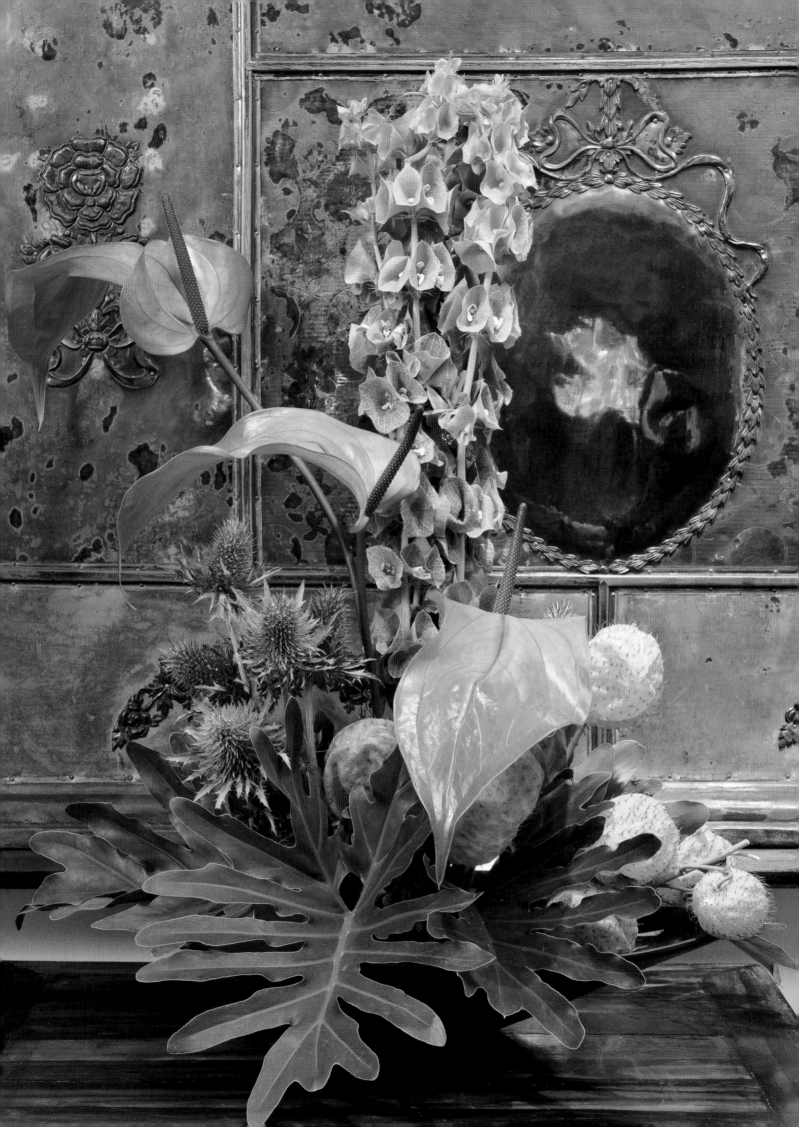

floral *hijinx*

GOPIAO FUN HOUSE *Florist* Roberto Gopiao

LANDSCAPE DESIGNER and prolific plant artist Bobby Gopiao hoards anything organic and green that can be transformed into something beautiful. Then he plays entertainer-cum-ringmaster as flowers and plants dance to his touch.

Bobby lives in a sprawling two-story 1980s home hidden behind huge double wooden gates in a noisy, dusty street in Quezon City. Inside the gates is an oasis of calm, a garden of woodland forest proportions replete with oriental elements, including a Chinese red pavilion. In a huge garden workshop in the front and back of his house, he creates awesome award-winning bonsai trees. He also collects contemporary Filipino art and nurtures young artists, helping them bloom on foreign shores. Indeed, the primordial inspiration for his floral set-up is his collection of contemporary paintings and sculptures displayed in the house among his beautiful Spanish antiques.

Bobby's Quezon City home, in contrast, is a floral fun house! In his new home extension, a steel staircase leads visitors up to a deck where all his prized bonsai are on display. A huge narra table for *alfresco* dining, hidden from view by a bank of potted bromeliads, is set with artist plates and glassware. Mint-colored tillandsias and

white and lilac paper roses spill out onto the table to form an S-shaped centerpiece.

The sitting area, set against a black pond filled with lion-head goldfish, has a high-backed chair covered with golden peat moss punctured with fire-colored torch ginger flowers. Looking down from the deck is a festive setting for a children's party. In each chair sits a smiling teddy bear—each a balloon sculpture completely dotted with yellow, chartreuse, red and ivory mums, and outfitted with kiddie knapsacks.

But the starry-eyed installation of the day is Bobby's sylvan setting in the main dining room. A nest of dry twigs on a landscape of chartreuse mums stretches across the length of the table, interspersed with sinuous green vases of cymbidiums. Perched on the fronds, over a hundred butterflies are installed in a glorious nature arrangement, a stunning tableau that stirs in the breeze.

Great good humor and elfin surprise are Bobby Gopiao's natural forte. He says: "When your home is filled with fine art you've collected for your own pleasure, then enjoy and share them more alongside an imaginative set-up that evokes feelings of joy, surprise and fantasy. Then only is your world complete."

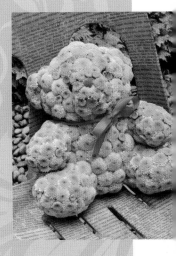

ABOVE Lime Malaysian button mums make a playful teddy bear for a child's outdoor birthday party.
OPPOSITE A silver altar base panel is a splendid backdrop for an arrangement of towering bells of Ireland above pink anthuriums, miniature pineapple-like aechmeas and green lanterns (hairy balls) resting on philodendron leaves.

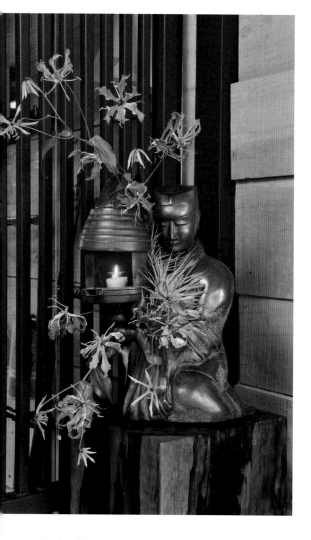

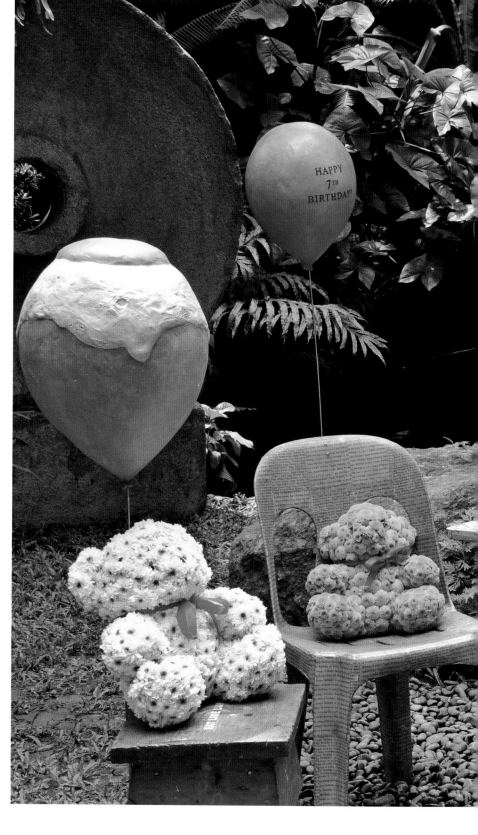

ABOVE A bronze sculpture set on on a solid pedestal of kamagong hardwood cradles a spray of pink gloriosa lilies.

RIGHT A colorful mosaic bull by local artist Plet Bolipata joins the floral quartet of teddy bears fashioned from Malaysian button mums for a child's party. The balloons and chairs are by another local artist, Pam Yan-Santos.

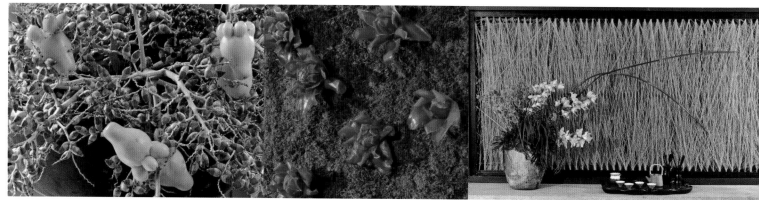

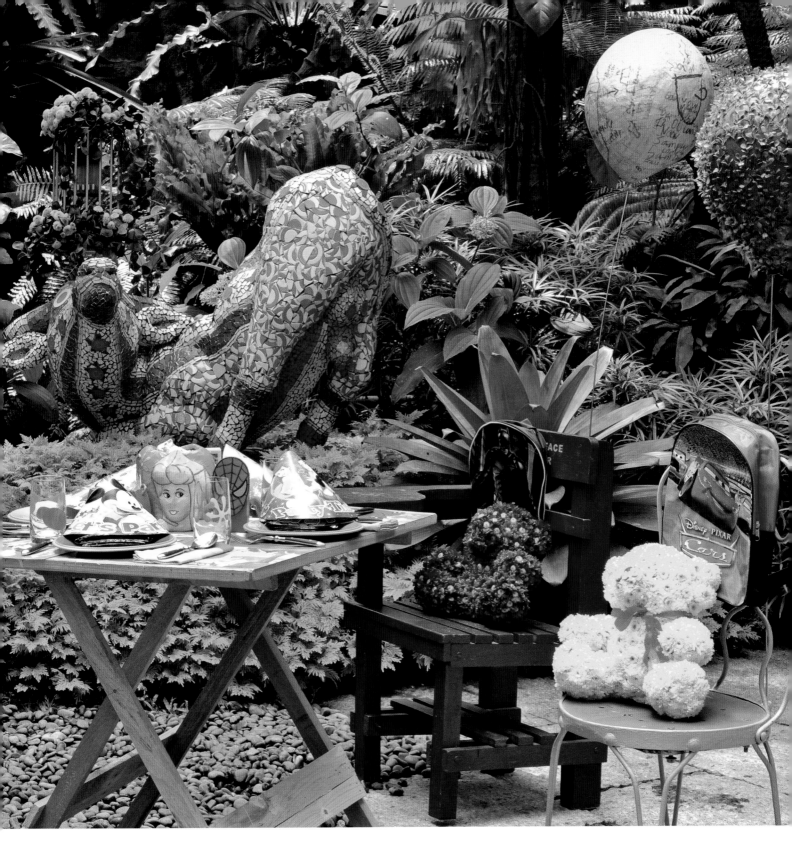

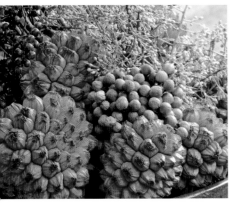

BOTTOM LEFT TO RIGHT Mickey Mouse pods with
royal palm berries; deep pink torch ginger blooms
embedded in sphagnum moss; pink cymbidiums with
bells of Ireland and philodendron leaves against a
backdrop of raw abaca string; red pandan fruit with
accents of palm berries and clusters of green berries.

floral hijinx

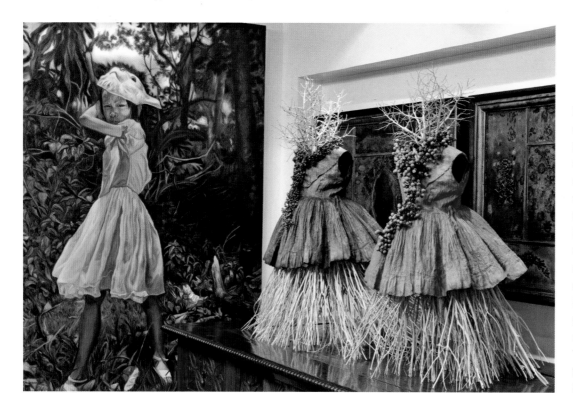

LEFT A painting of a girl with a mask by Marina Cruz is echoed by a pair of sculpted fiberglass dresses by Yasmin Sison hemmed with billowing twigs and adorned with cascading neck pieces formed of palm berries.

BELOW AND RIGHT In this sur-real forest installation, a bank of chartreuse button mums supports a twig forest of stilled butterflies. Lime cymbidiums in twisted green glass vases by Philippe Starck rear up among the dramatic still life. The white china, Art Deco print tablemats and napkins are from Rustan's.

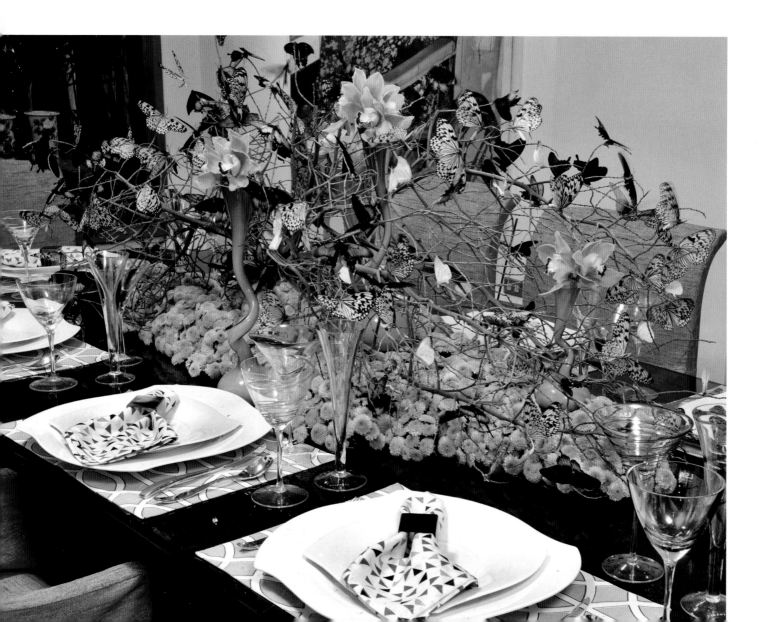

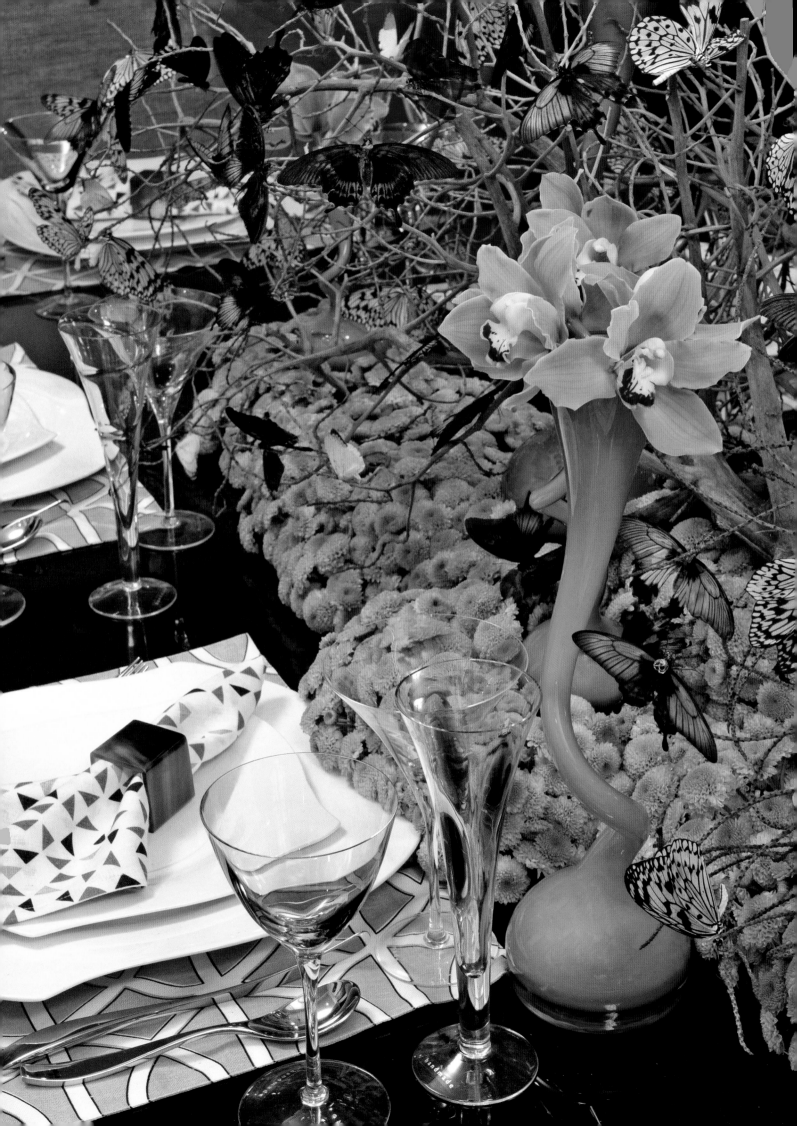

BELOW Tillandsia air plants on twisted jungle vines shade the deck with its sphagnum moss-covered table and chairs. Red accents are seen in the teaset, in the torch gingers embedded in the moss and in the cluster of Mickey Mouse plants and berries.

RIGHT A sculpted glass swirl on a black plinth frames a spray of brilliant pink gloriosa lilies.

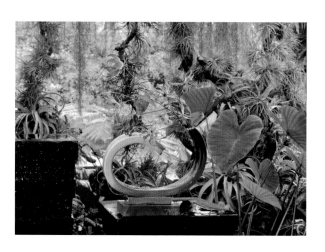

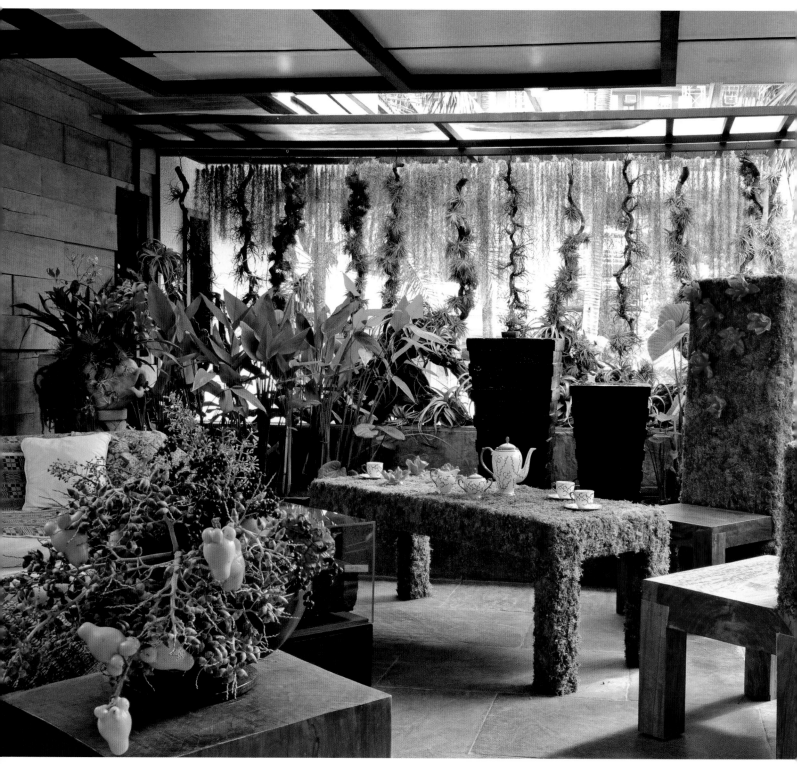

RIGHT The bole of a tree is a sturdy support for twirling palm spines and purple and lilac eustoma paper roses. BELOW A Balinese lime-stone fish sculpture is topped by a colorful clutch of red guzmania, spiky tillandsias and gloriosa lilies.

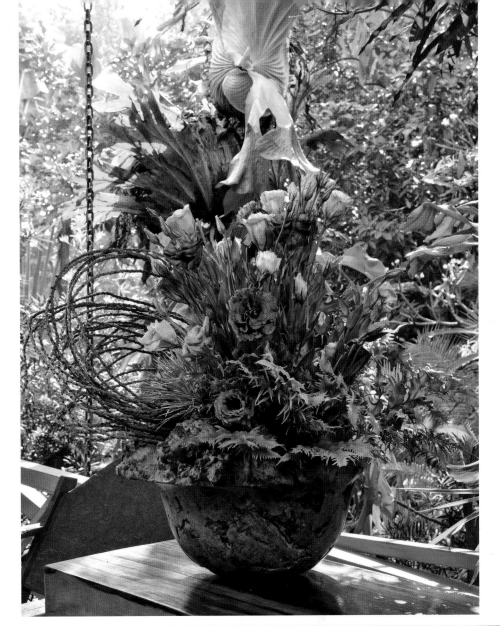

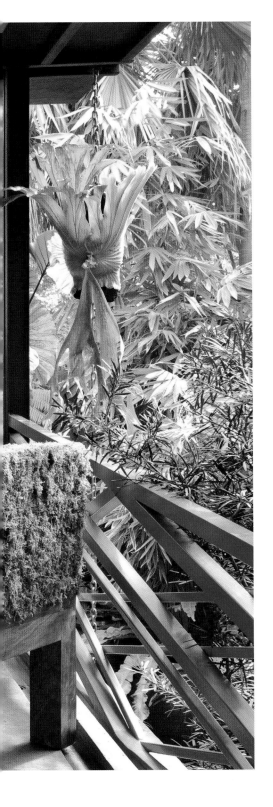

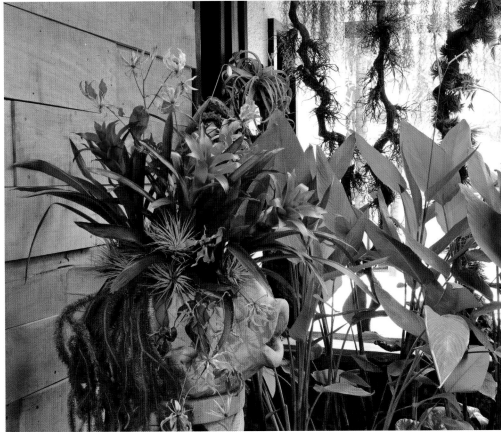

floral hijinx

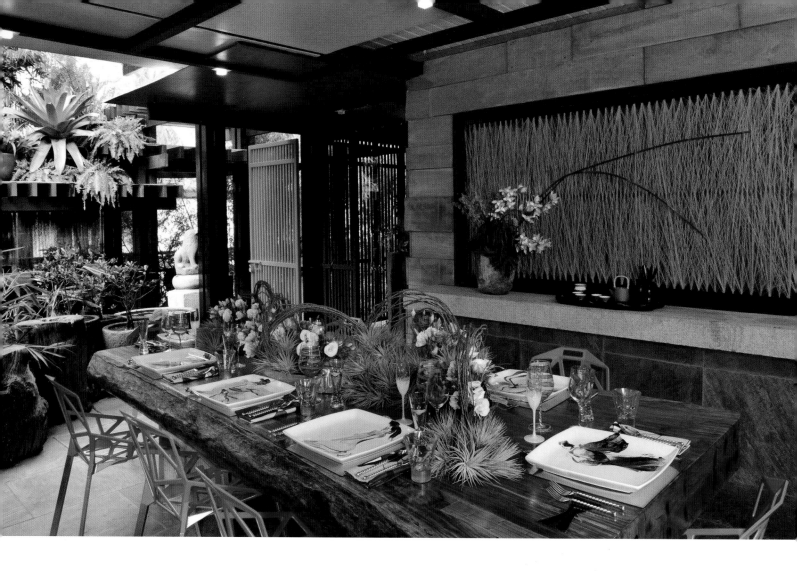

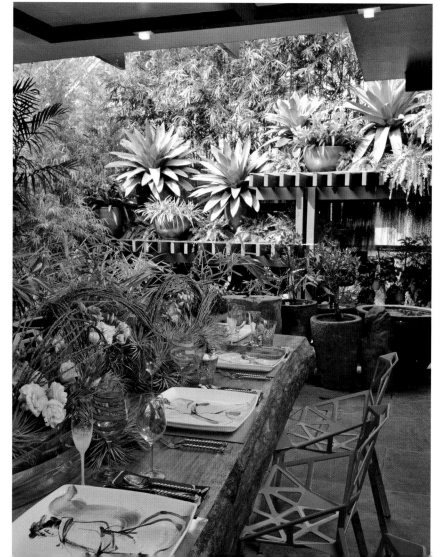

ABOVE AND LEFT Alfresco dining arround a solid narra hardwood table is afforded privacy by a high "wall" of giant rare bromeliads.
BELOW BenCab signature plates are paired with individually baked free-form frosted stemware by artist Pam Yan-Santos. Arches of palm spines shield lilac and white paper roses and spiky tillandsias air plants along the S-shaped central table arrangement.

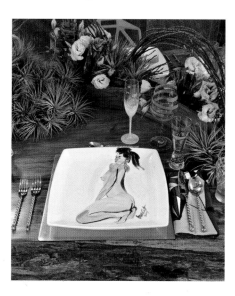

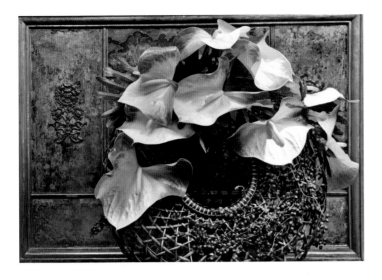

ABOVE A mass of broad-leafed green-tipped ivory anthuriums in a woven basket interwoven with berries makes an eye-catching arrangement against an old silver altar base.

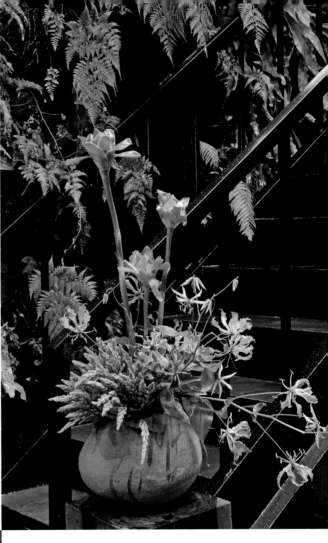

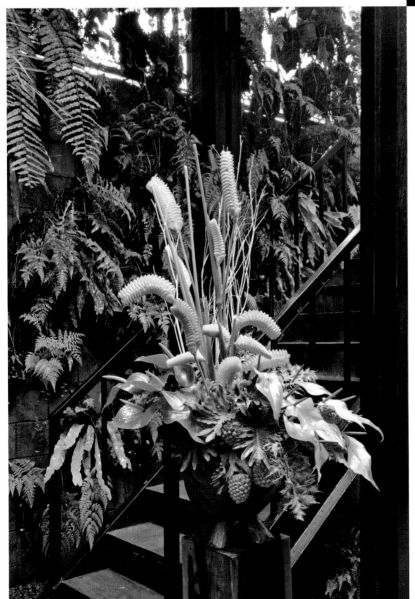

ABOVE A prized signature pottery urn by Pablo Capati is graced by torch gingers and gloriosa lilies, with dried millet accents. LEFT A profusion of tropical blooms—curious yellow rattlesnake flowers of the giant calathea, waxy red and pink anthuriums, philodendron leaves and pandanus palm fruits—stand guard at the foot of the metal stairwell leading to the deck.

floral hijinx

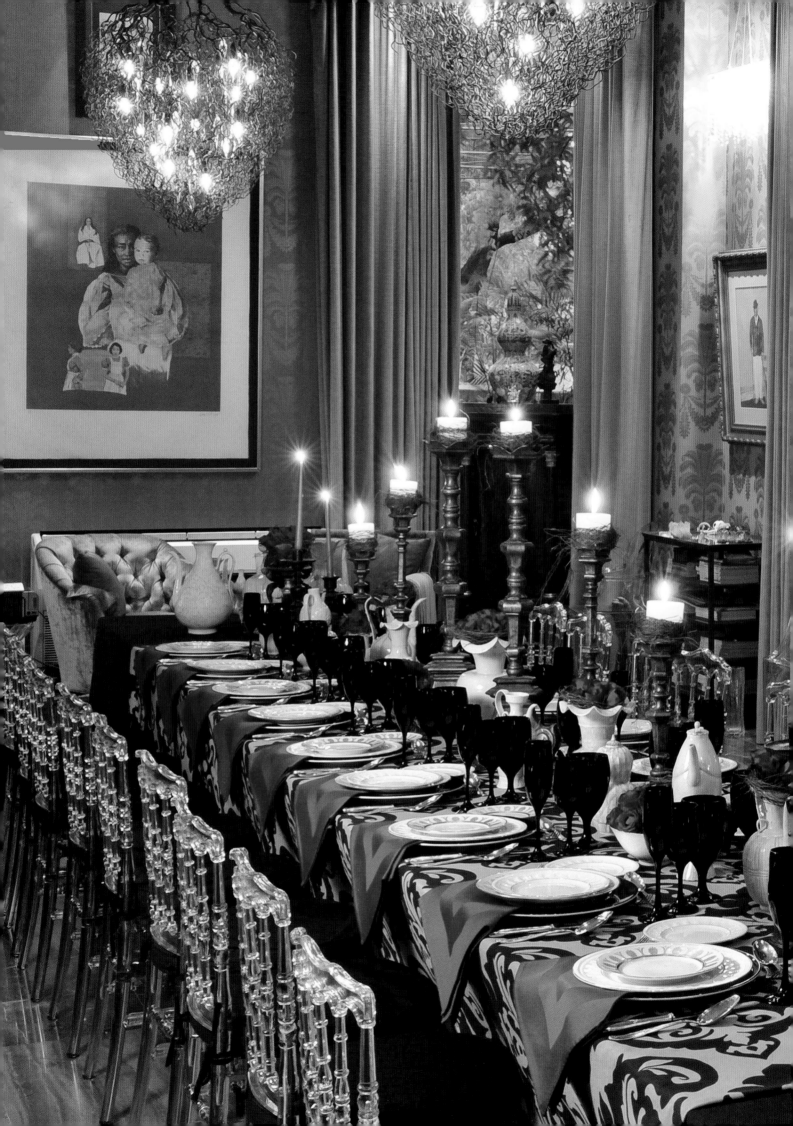

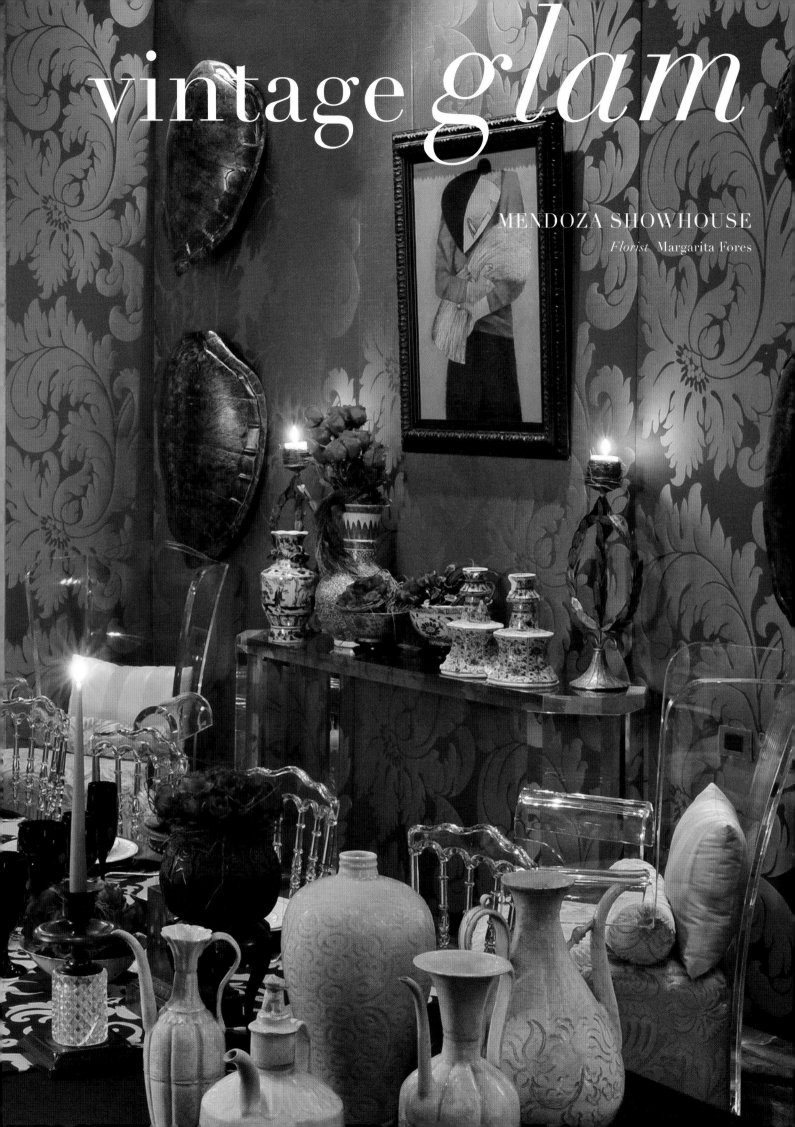

vintage *glam*

MENDOZA SHOWHOUSE

Florist Margarita Fores

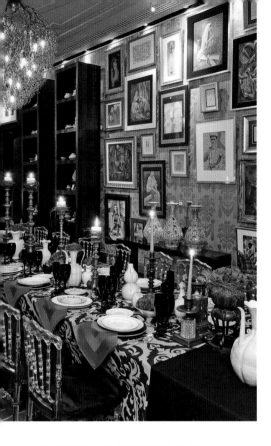

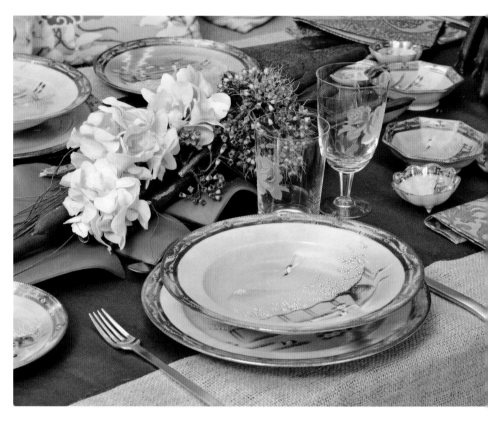

HERE IS A STYLING ACT—a creative collaboration in perfect sync—by Anton R. Mendoza, vintage-glam designer of Adora luxury shop and owner of this fabulous residence, and Margarita Fores, floral stylist of Fiori by M and creative restaurateur and friend of Anton, who is a maestro at conjuring up table settings with fanciful themes.

Anton's Dasmarinas residence is a showroom house, where he lives in uber-fashionable style and upscale comfort. The house is wrapped in blonde travertine marble and decorated with avant-garde works by visual artists and furniture designers from around the world. Anton is probably Manila's biggest collector of upscale modern European furnishings. Unusual Plexiglas chandeliers are his current passion.

Together Anton and Margarita staged an "Oriental Travelers' Soiree" on a long banquette table under the trees, enclosed by the high travertine wall just outside the house. Margarita used a fine jute tablecloth "to go with the printed beiges and browns of Chinese Kuan Yin throw pillows,"

while arts collector Anton brought out his grandfather's antique Golden Heron plates in muted shades of green. He styled the tabletop with a world traveler's exotic curios—metal binoculars and measuring tools, jade horses and tortoiseshell fans—while she installed rustic pods and wild-flowers on leather leaf plates among the curios.

In Anton's glassed-in dining room, Margarita styled her "Happy Chinese New Year" table. "I wanted to do a cheerful table setting using only the roundest and reddest of fruit!" The beveled glass table is decorated in bright living colors with celadon bowls filled with apples, oranges, mandarins and mabolo, along with violet grapes, red vanda orchids

and pink dragonfruit. Fine purple tapered candlesticks tower over the sumptuous spread.

Finally, there is the tandem team's "Gala Banquet," a dramatic ebony and ivory table setting in what Anton calls the Louis Bunuel Suite. It is a darkly elegant showcase for the owner's collection of antique white porcelain vessels and candelabra set upon the florist's vintage period tablecloth in black fleur-de-lis patterns, echoing the owner's ornate document-print walls. Blood red roses in white china ewers and bowls along the center of the table, and vividly matching napkins add color to black crystal glassware and white and gold plateware. All around there is vintage glam to feast the eyes on.

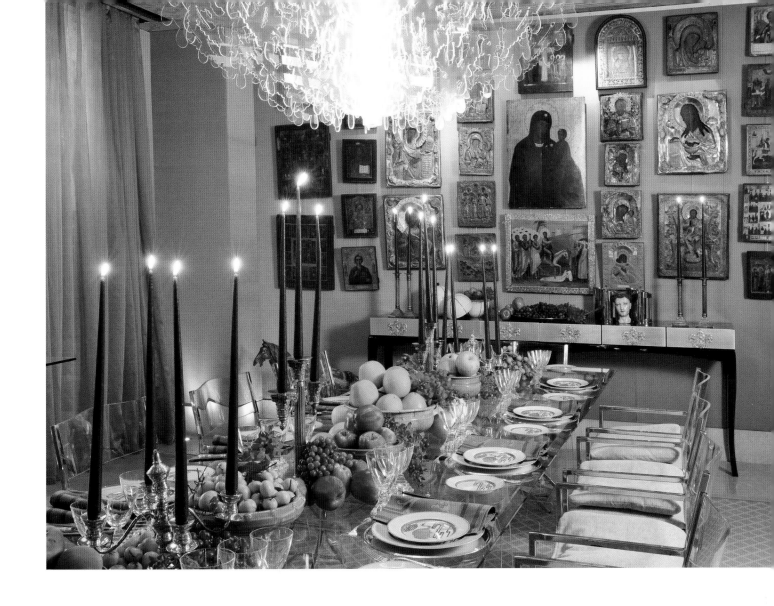

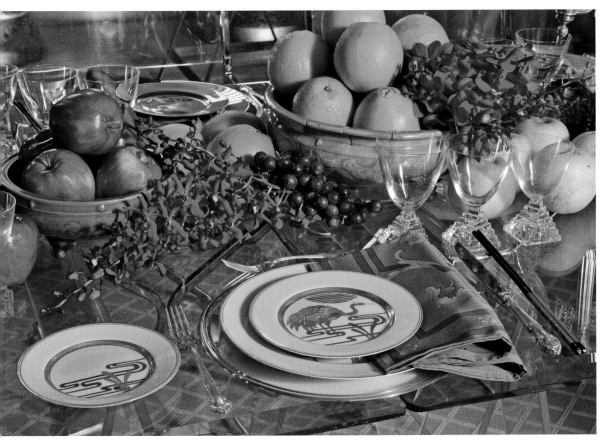

ABOVE The glassed-in dining room is florist Margarita's stage for a modern "Happy Chinese New Year" table. A fruity centerpiece of bright oranges and apples adds color to the clear glass table, Plexiglas-backed chairs and wall of religious icons.
LEFT Chinese culture is overtly expressed in the red stork plates, the apples, oranges and mandarins in celadon bowls, the scattered grapes and pears and the red vanda orchids.
PREVIOUS SPREAD The creative duo's "Gala Banquet" table in the Luis Bunuel Suite is a theatrical ebony and ivory showcase of owner Anton's black glass goblets and porcelain ewers among the candelabra and Margarita's ornate, unifying table linen.

vintage glam

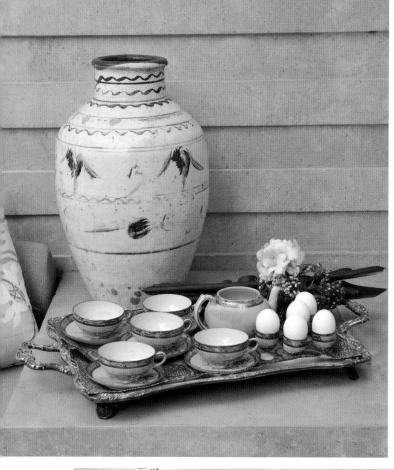

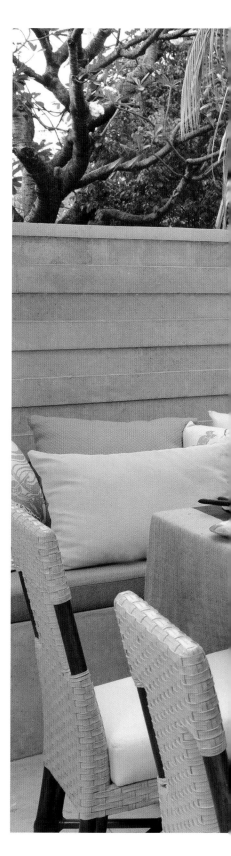

LEFT Anton's exquisite gold-rimmed Golden Heron teaset and eggcups filled with boiled eggs wait on a silver tray in a corner of the walled courtyard.

RIGHT The banquette table for the "Oriental Travelers' Soiree" is dressed with Margarita's earthy jute tablecloth and an organic centerpiece of dried golden shower tree pods and duhat tree flowers on leather leaf plates.

BELOW At the house entry, a large terracotta jar and a modern flute are filled with Margarita's signature materials—cabbage rose succulents, hairy green balls and rustic duhat vines and flowers.

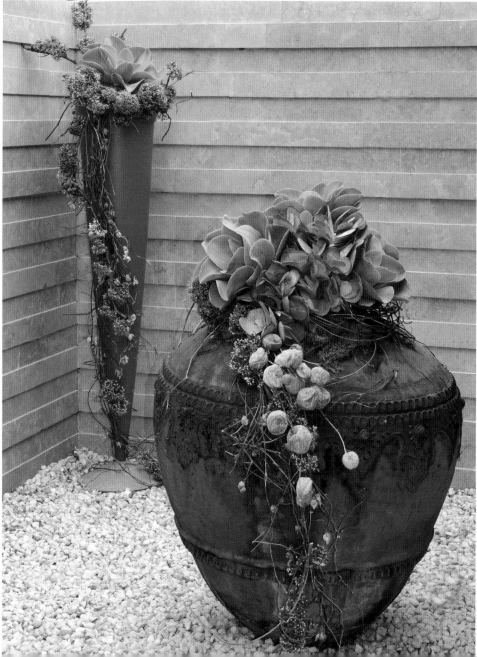

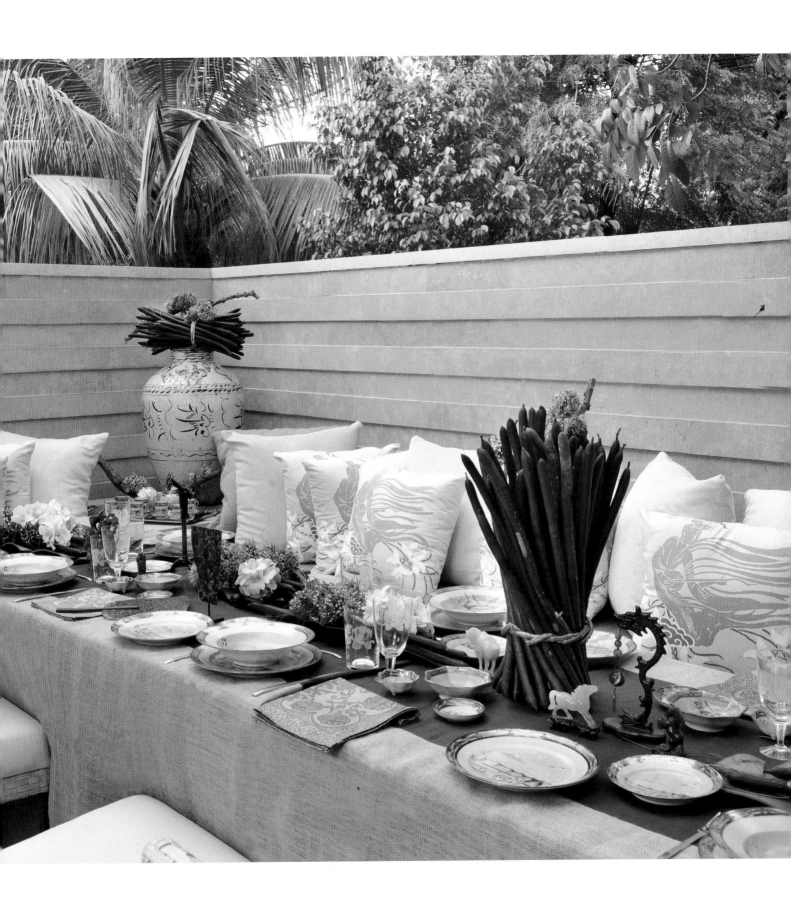

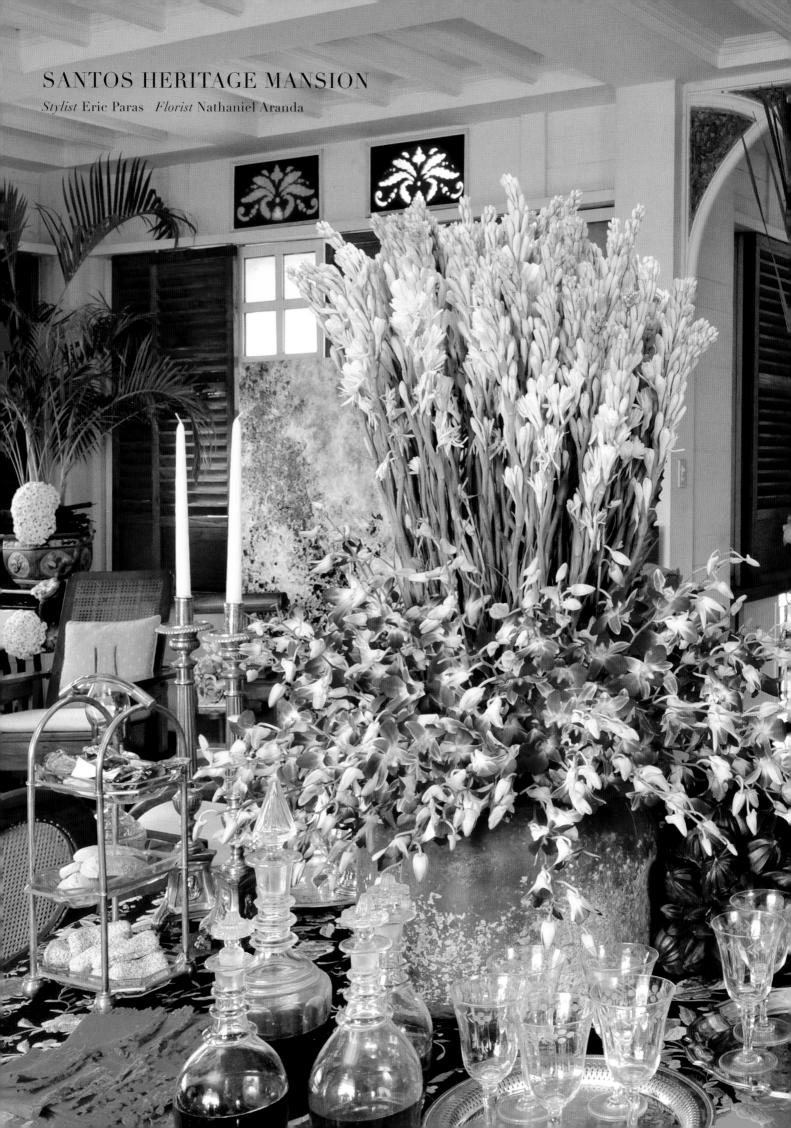

SANTOS HERITAGE MANSION

Stylist Eric Paras *Florist* Nathaniel Aranda

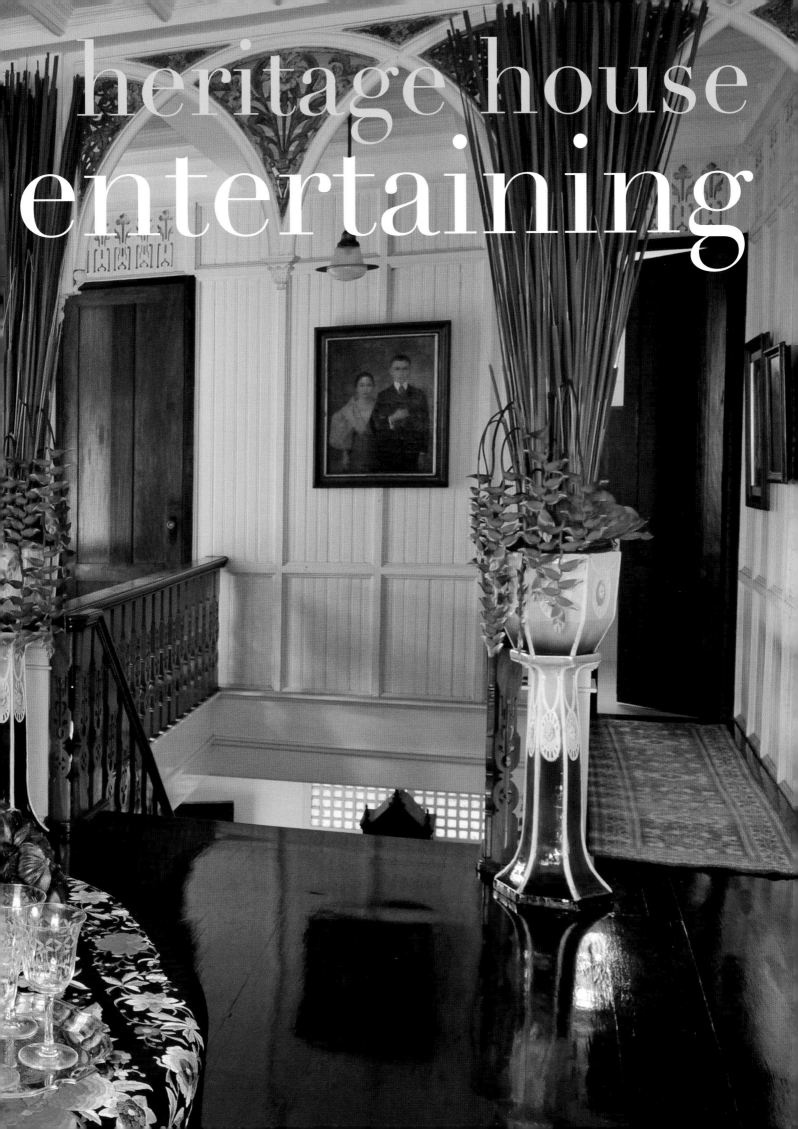

heritage house
entertaining

THE SANTOS-ANDRES FAMILY house, completed in 1917, was modest compared with other houses in the Navotas area of Manila. It was built in the Art Nouveau style at a time when Art Deco was becoming popular in the West. When floods began in the area in the 1970s and worsened each year, the home owners raised their grounds, leaving the lower floor to the waters. By the year 2000, the Santos-Andres house was ravaged and the fate of the home appeared uncertain.

Happily, three Santos heirs chose to preserve the ancestral house

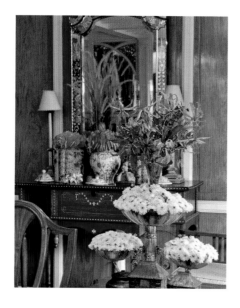

where their mother was born. Led by Mike Santos, they agreed to move the old house to higher ground. A team headed by architect Bobby Quisumbing dismantled the ancient structure piece by piece, plank by plank, and transferred it from its waterlogged ground to a new and crested location in Antipolo, Rizal, just north of Metro Manila.

Fast forward to 2011: The Santos-Andres abode is ripe with heritage, complete with heirloom furniture set in formal array and as aloof as a museum. The challenge for this book

was to style the ancestral house for a Filipino festivity, replete with the local flowers and table settings of olden times. Designer Eric Paras and florist Nathaniel Aranda teamed up for the task, deciding to transform the old house for a traditional *tertulia*—the genteel social gathering of Spanish origin, wherein family and friends entertain themselves with music and dance, poetry and art.

Eric Paras went to work with his characteristic gusto. He broke down the rigidity of the living room, moved out unnecessary pieces, brought in mid-20th century furniture from elsewhere in the house, and ordered canvas seat cushions to be sewn. A main *sala* or sitting room was created in a central area that was previously empty and forlorn.

Mike Santos's treasury of embroidered shawls (*mantones de Manila*) were draped on cane-woven sofas and over round wooden tables and hung over doorways. His antique collections of floral epergnes (Art Nouveau vases) and bookends, old hurricane lamps and quirky metal coin banks were displayed—as contemporary conversation pieces. Ornate glassware and tea accouterments served up traditional *pastillas*, cashews and *piaya* of old.

Around the piano, Eric displayed two classical sculptures by national artist Guillermo Tolentino, and brought out the family's musical instruments to embellish the traditional *tertulia* scene. The result was a relaxed and inviting musical corner suited to the ambience of the ancestral home.

For his part in this heritage tribute, florist Nathaniel Aranda focused on styling the most common flowers of the provinces in his ever-imaginative

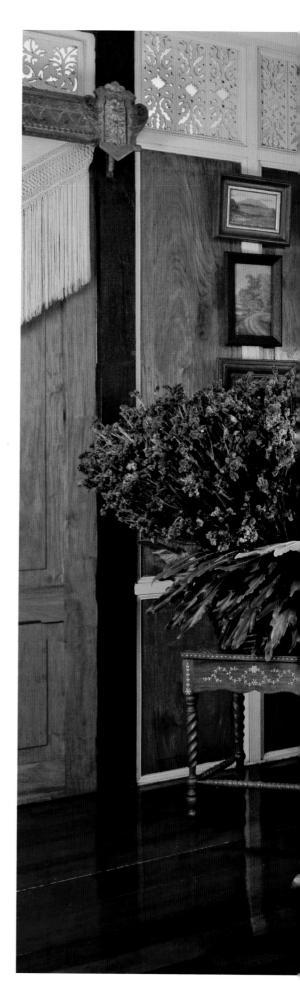

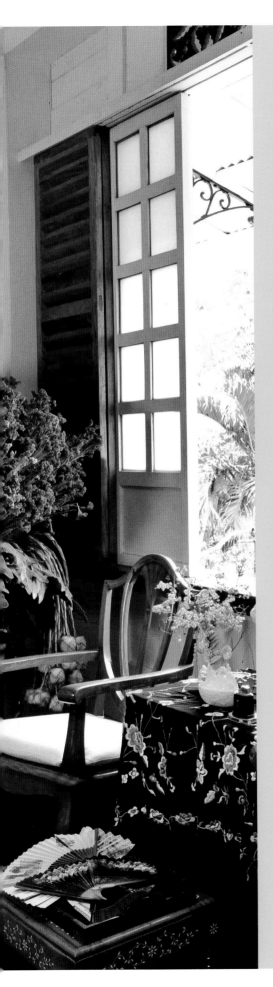

OPPOSITE Philippine floral heritage is seen in multiple views and a multitude of bouquets of white chrysanthemums in metal urns and bright red anthuriums in ceramic jars.

LEFT A billowing spray of an old favorite, purple statice, resting on a bed of philodendron leaves, with a side flourish of pandanwrapped rice balls, is a perfect complement to bone-inlaid furniture, an Art Nouveau chair, ornate ladies' fans and embroidered shawls.

BELOW In the music room, loopy vines curl out of a ceramic planter bearing large balls of white asters, the top one on a platform of dried pods, and giant cabbage succulents.

PREVIOUS SPREAD At the top of the stairs, stylists Eric Paras and Nathaniel Aranda set a festive *tertulia* buffet table laden with Philippine sweets and liqueurs arrayed around a striking centerpiece of purple dendrobiums and towering azucena (tuberoses). Soaring bulrushes with red heliconia "skirts," anchored in ceramic pedestal bowls, flank the staircase. Lovely Art Nouveau details are visible on archways and at the tops of walls and doors.

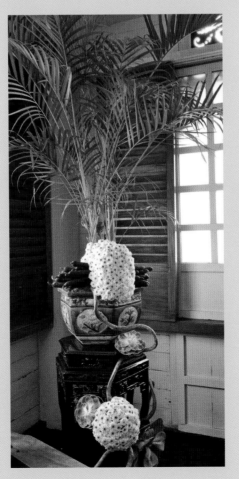

style. The main staircase was bedecked with tall arrangements of the reeds and common pods of the swamps, then draped with red heliconias.

On the central presentation table, Nathaniel installed a giant clay pot with fragrant azucena—tuberoses used in wreaths for wakes—with purple dendrobium orchids and the fruit of the nipa palm from the marshes. In the sitting area, he used red gloriosas, more nipa palm flowers and scarlet anthuriums.

Fine antique jars and vases contain arrangements of natural vines and twigs, pandanus fruit and rose pink cadena de amor, while in a corner stands a massive bouquet of purple statice above philodendron leaves and strands of palm leaf-wrapped rice balls (*puso*). Elsewhere, the florist displayed sprays of mauve Philippine sanggumay (purple rain) orchids and more ruby red gloriosas.

But the stunning star of Nathaniel's work is the heritage dining table. It is not just about flowers this time; rather, it is a stunning cornucopia of vibrant fruits of harvest—pineapples, mangoes and bananas and Paul Bunyan echeveria. Foliage ranges from the palest mauve to turquoise shades, with some pink and sky blue thrown in. There are mums and common everlasting flowers from Baguio, all clustered around baskets of eggs, garlic, onions and string beans—signaling the richness of the harvest.

Paras and Aranda visited the Santos house three times. The task of transforming an early 20th century *sala* for a Filipiniana *tertulia* in the 21st century could not have been accomplished in less time-traveling time.

heritage house entertaining

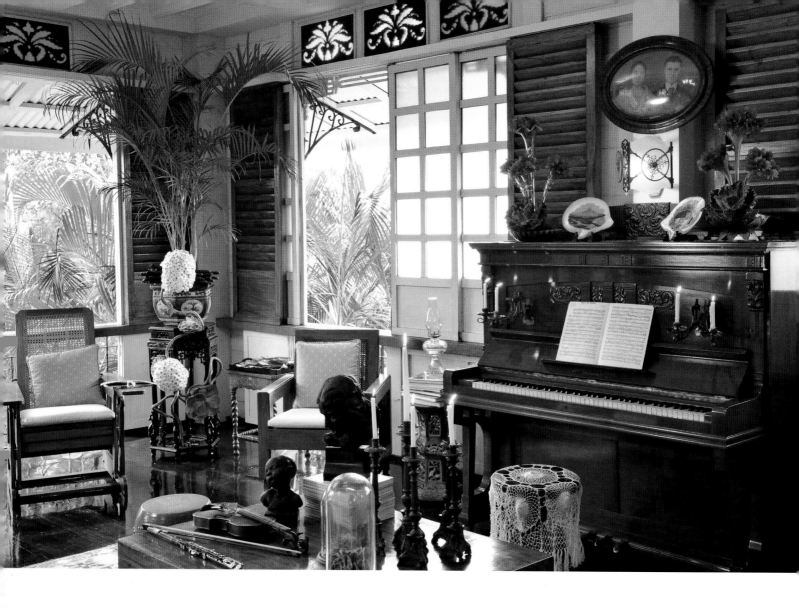

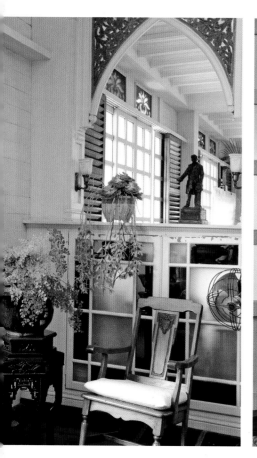

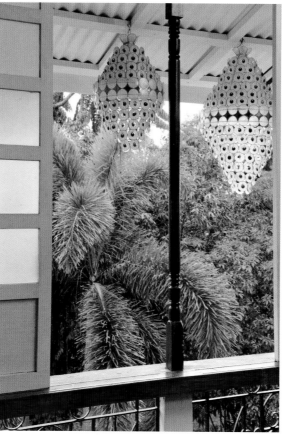

ABOVE In the music room, the old piano and violin are ready for a *tertulia*, the family's musical entertainment. As night falls, the candlesticks on the piano will cast a glow on the fiery bougainvillea blossoms inserted in Mike Santos's antique floral epergnes, anchored by large cabbage roses.

LEFT Sliding glass panel windows and grilled *ventanilla* open to a view of garden foliage from the dining room. Two fine capiz shell lanterns hang under the eaves.

FAR LEFT A quiet corner under a carved archway displays two traditional household plants—a pot of fine maidenhair fern and a cascade of purple sanggumay, the most common wild orchid of the Philippine tropics.

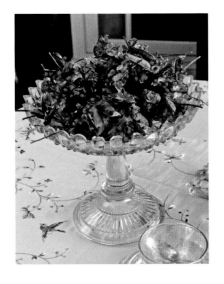

LEFT Spilling out of their dried pods, rock-hard red and black seeds from the saga seed tree, presented in an old-fashioned sweets dish on a daintily hand-embroidered tablecloth, bring back fond memories of childhood games.

RIGHT Rows of bright red anthurium heads peep over the rims of three Chinese ceramic jars on a bone-inlaid American sheraton console table, while a ceramic lass dreams below.

BELOW Fuschia bougain-villea blossoms in glass epergnes, with asters at the base, complete the romantic *tertulia* scene amidst a wonderful collection of heirloom furniture, decorative items and embroidered shawls.

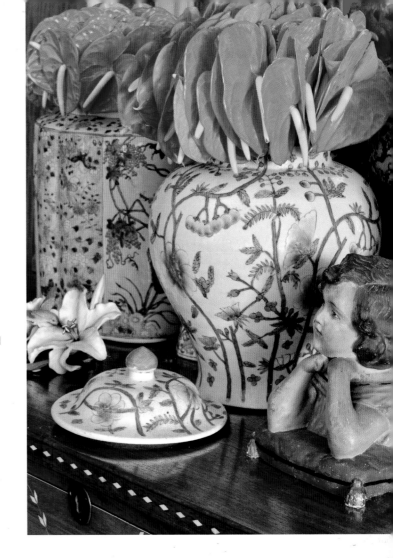

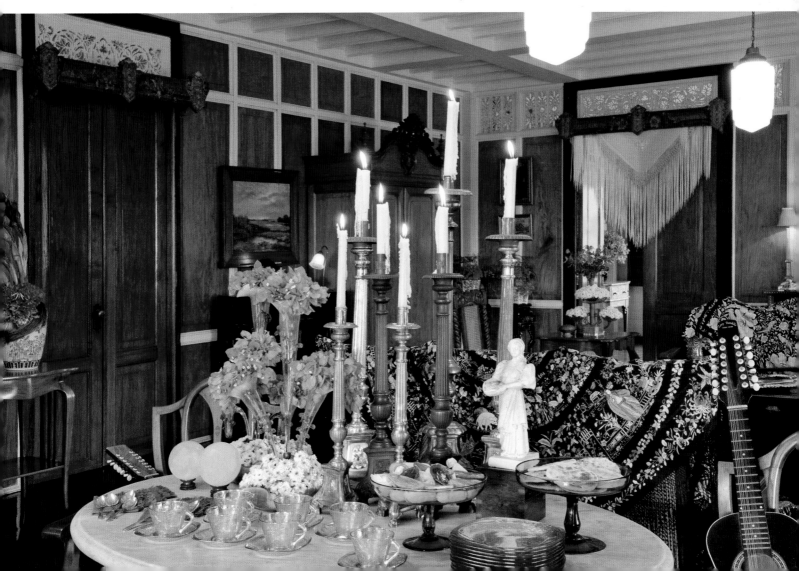

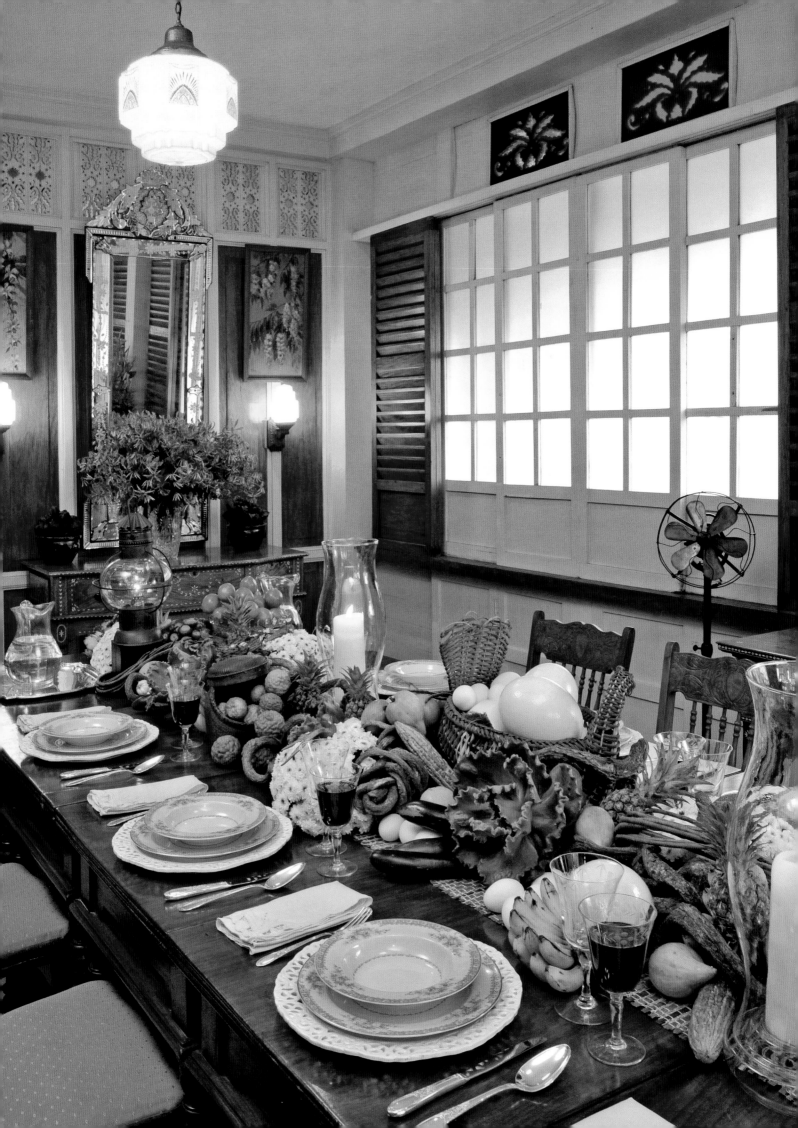

The romantic florist Nathaniel Aranda loves preparing delicious bouquets of just one type of flower ... giant bouquets looking lush and natural within an interesting vase.

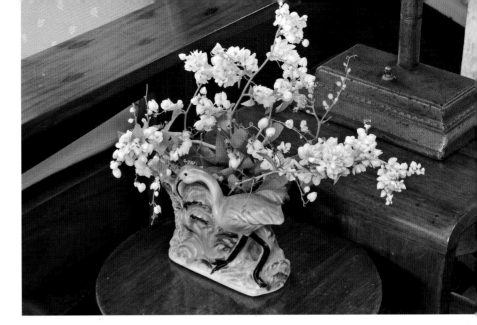

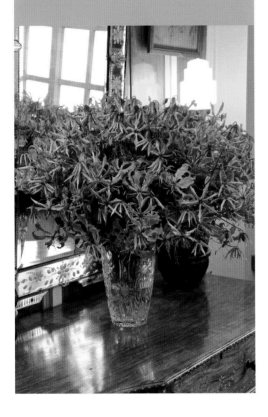

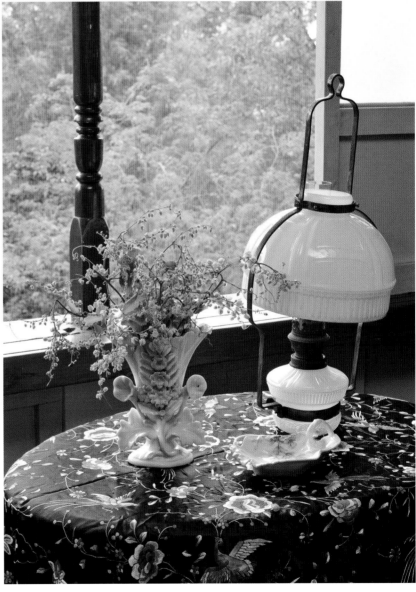

ABOVE On the Bulacan altar table turned dining console, a large bouquet of stunning gloriosas is reflected in the etched Venetian mirror behind.

LEFT The ancestral *comedor* or dining room is Nathaniel's canvas for a sumptuous array of tropical fruit and vegetables, fresh herbs and eggs (ostrich, hen and quail), arranged in baskets or laid on the woven runner among twisting vines, large echeveria succulents, balls of white asters and clusters of everlasting flowers. Glass-enclosed white candles complete this scene of tropical abundance.

ABOVE Delicate pink cadena de amor (chain of love) sprays in a classic white porcelain urn are romantically paired with a white milk-glass reading lamp and a floral dish on a black embroidered *manton de Manila* shawl.

TOP The common white cadena de amor vine springs from a colorful Art Nouveau ceramic vase decorated with a waterbird.

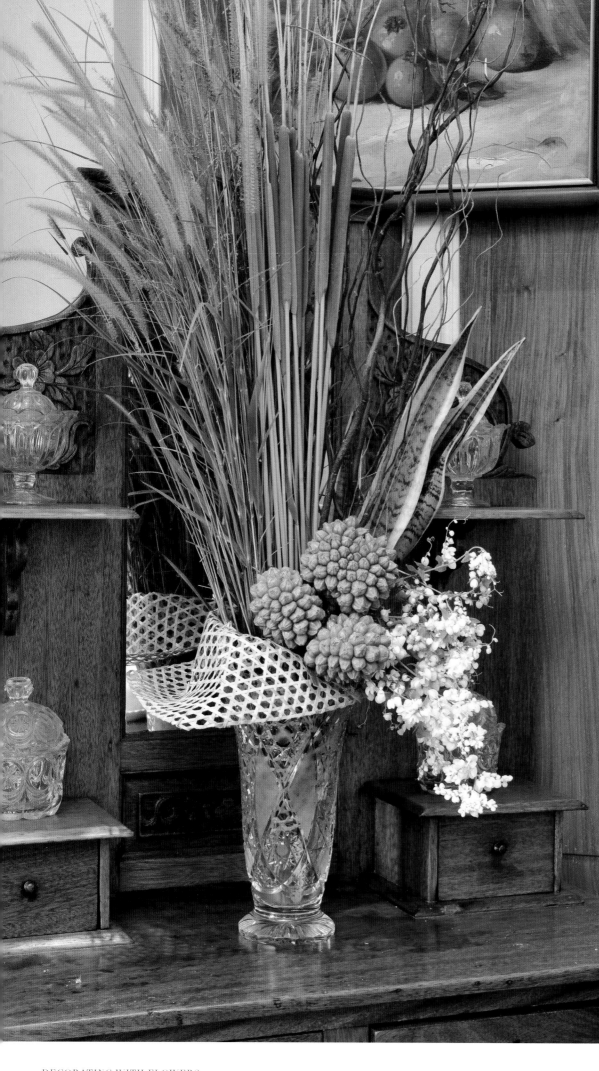

LEFT Nathaniel's eclectic arrangement of fluffy talahib field grass, stately bulrushes (cattail), curly willow and sharp mother-in-law's tongue leaves, skirted by orange pandanus fruit, white cadena de amor and a swathe of woven bamboo, makes a striking yet economical display of native flora.
RIGHT More tropical exotica grace a large Chinese porcelain jar. Dry flower stalks (provided by owner Mike Santos) mix with bright gloriosa flowers, Chinese green lace, bird's nest foliage and pink-hearted green anthuriums.

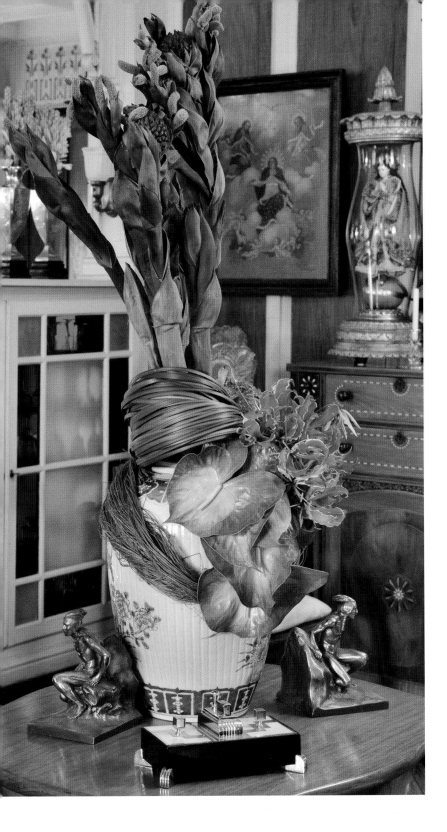

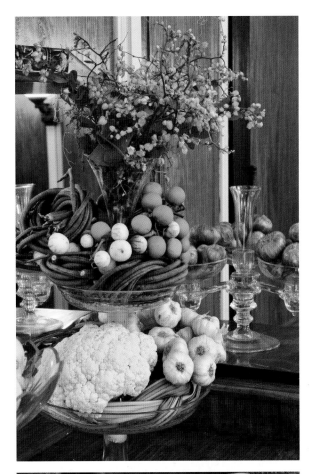

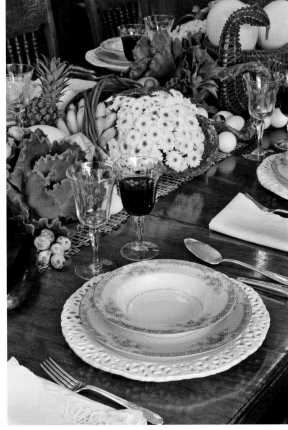

ABOVE RIGHT Another imaginative vegetal arrangement comprises a vase of pink cadena de amor standing high over tiered glass dishes filled with twisted string beans, baby eggplants, garlic pods, red onions and cauliflower.

RIGHT A section of the dining table setting showing the vintage 1950s plates and the sumptuous vegetal and floral centerpiece.

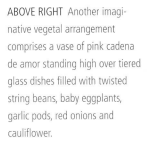

heritage house entertaining

priceless heirlooms and *modern art*

COLLECTOR'S STAGE   *Florist* Roberto Gopiao

YOU COLLECT ART AVIDLY and spectacular pieces fill your home. But how do you avoid the museum or gallery look and feel? One answer is, with fresh flowers arranged as art pieces!

Take this delightful home, a close collaboration between a young couple and their "style navigator" Roberto Gopiao, a multi-award winning bonsai aficionado.

The media shy couple recall: "We started collecting after a piece of furniture we liked turned out to be a reproduction. So we asked to see antique masterpieces. From then on, we were hooked on collecting heritage furniture, then ivory and now we have moved on to modern art! But they somehow look great mixed together!"

A linear pool with dappled koi leads visitors to the front door and the antechamber. A white Carrara marble table holds a huge glass bowl with yellow calla lilies submerged in water and feathery foxtails arching high above. A recessed shelf of whorled veneer flanks a dark wood powder room door. The shelves hold a bounty of treasures, from the ivory heads of religious statues to tribal and modern art.

A long corridor leads guests deeper into the home. A curious fiberglass sculpture of a young girl by Ronald Ventura stands out from the travertine walls.

A few steps up to yet another foyer leads to the formal living room and the grand staircase. A bishop's chair, an armoire by a Candon master, are mixed with a modernist arrangement of white anthuriums and furry achuete pods, a native reddish food dye.

In the living room, glass sculptured balls are employed to chill champagne. A huge canvas by Lao Lianben leans nonchalantly against the white walls facing a meditation garden with prized bonsai.

The dining room is spectacular, with Baccarat droplights and Philippe Starck mirrors. Striped high-backed chairs add glamour. A long canvas by National Artist Ben Cab has a base of petulant yellow roses anchored on playful pom-poms, hemmed by a waterfall of purple berries. The main table is ablaze with crystals, silver and candlelight.

Bobby Gopiao sums up the décor strategy: "Contrast pieces and sizes. Then make your florals create their fun yet spectacular counterpoint."

RIGHT A mass of lime button mums positioned around the base of stately foxtail lilies in a tall cylindrical vase makes a dramatic statement next to a hand-painted BenCab plate by National Artist Ben Cab and virginal white candlesticks.

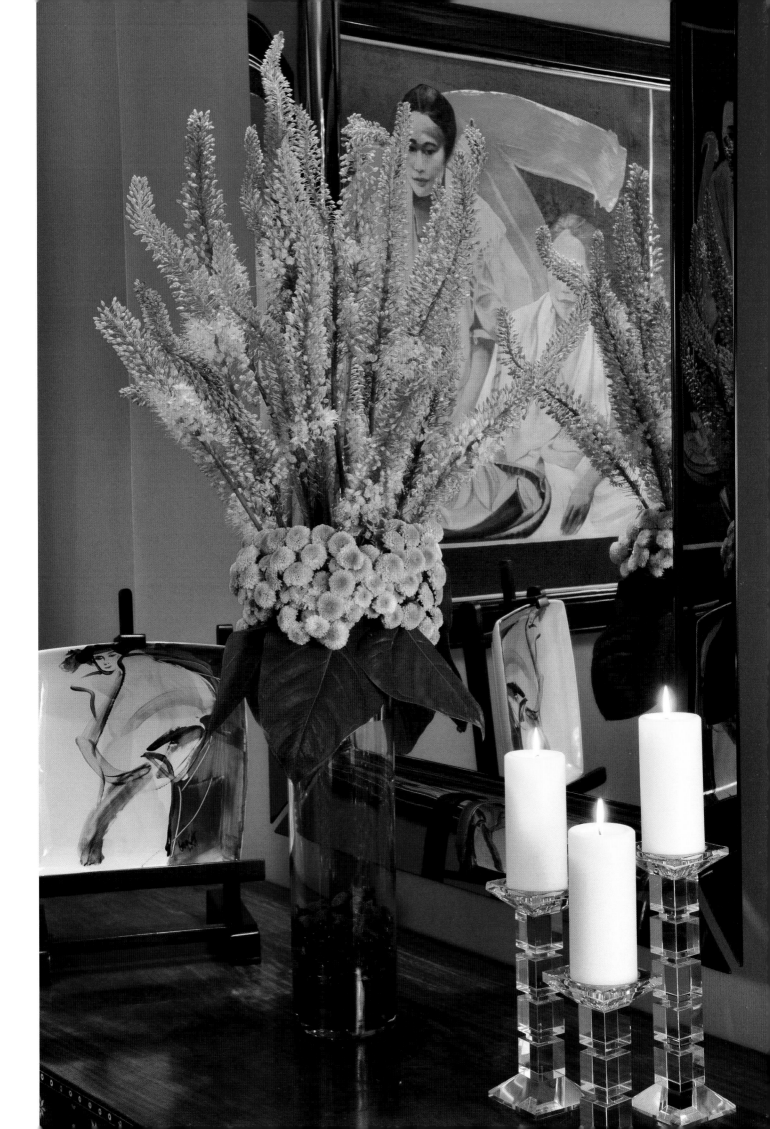

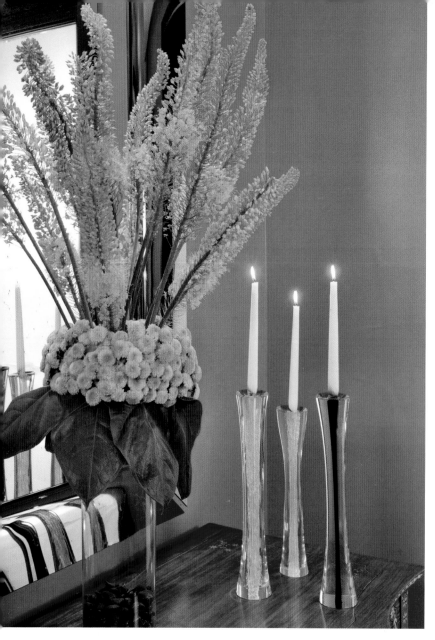

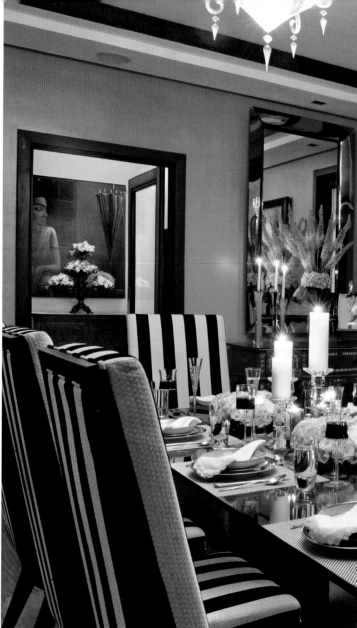

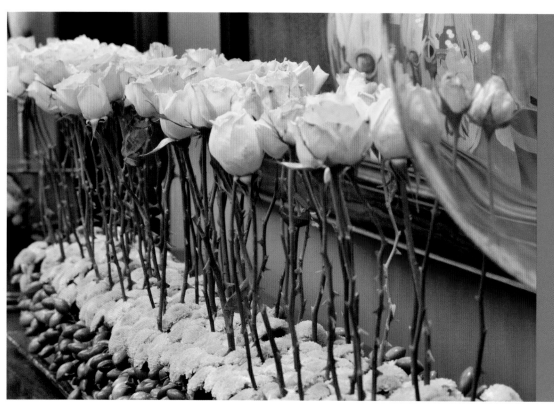

LEFT A rhythmic row of South American yellow roses appear to emerge from a bed of chartreuse mums resting on a "waterfall" of purple berries.
ABOVE LEFT Faux bubble candlesticks by Anna Torfs in delicate crystal holders provide a perfect counterpoint to a stately sideboard floral arrangement.

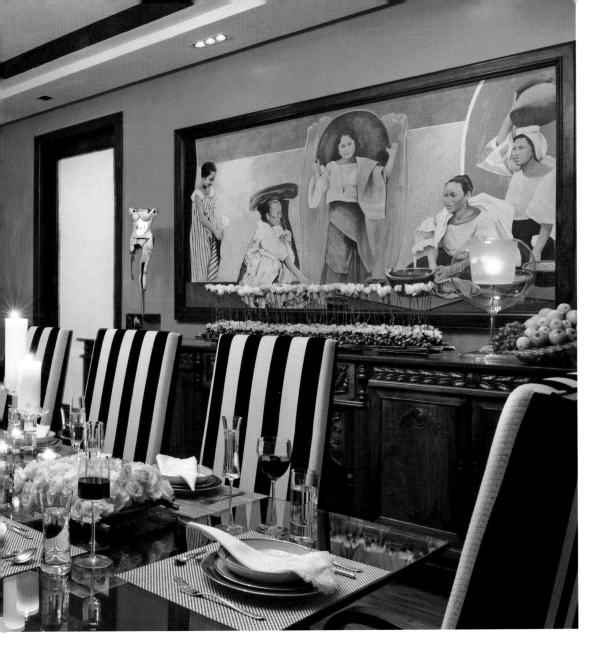

LEFT A fusion of modern and heirloom treasures, enhanced by fresh flowers transformed into pieces of modern art, sets the tone for grand modernist dining.
BELOW Low-budget arrangements of voluptuous yellow and white roses add interest and impact to a table laid with a tasteful collection of contemporary porcelain, silver and glassware.

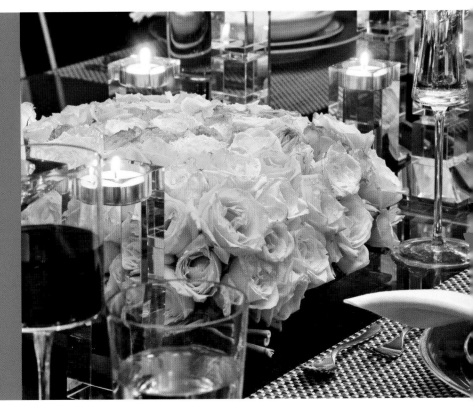

"My clients share my passion for contemporary art as well as flawless heirloom furniture and artifacts," explains Roberto Gopiao. "They can also see how fresh flowers can shake off the 'museum feel' in a home."

priceless heirlooms and modern art

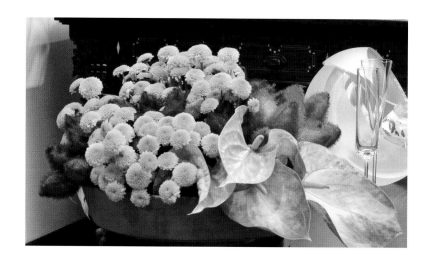

BELOW AND RIGHT A low-lying arrangement of diminutive mums, heart-shaped green anthuriums and color-contrasting red achuete pods complements rather than detracts from the modern art.

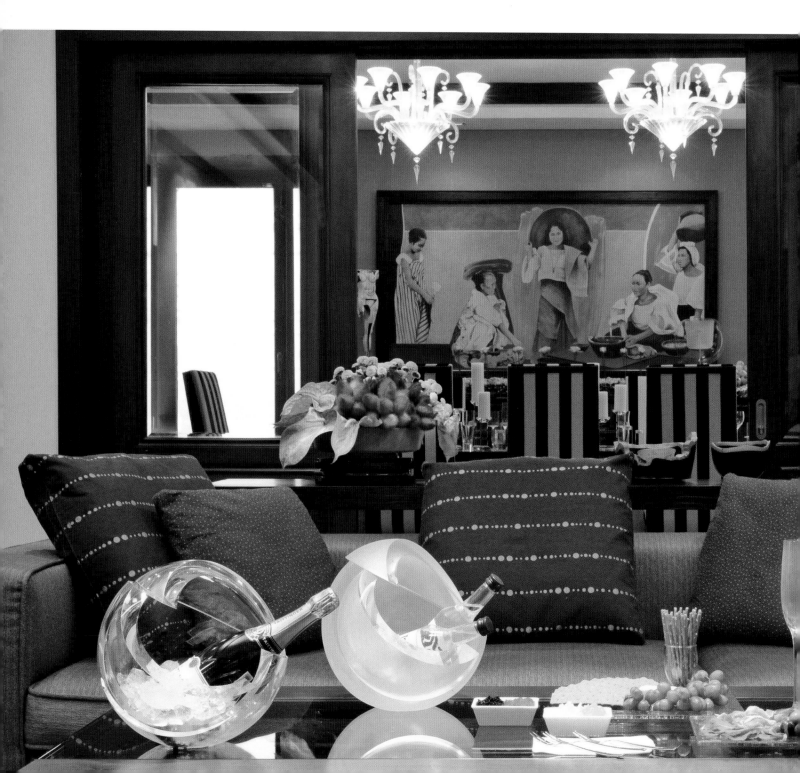

RIGHT A stunning arrangement of soaring yellow foxtails and submerged yellow calla lilies is a fitting foreground to a precious collection of ivory religious heads and pre-Christian pottery.
BELOW RIGHT Long-stemed alstroemeria balls hovering over a warm-hued composition impart color to a still life of ivory heads and a silver altar piece.

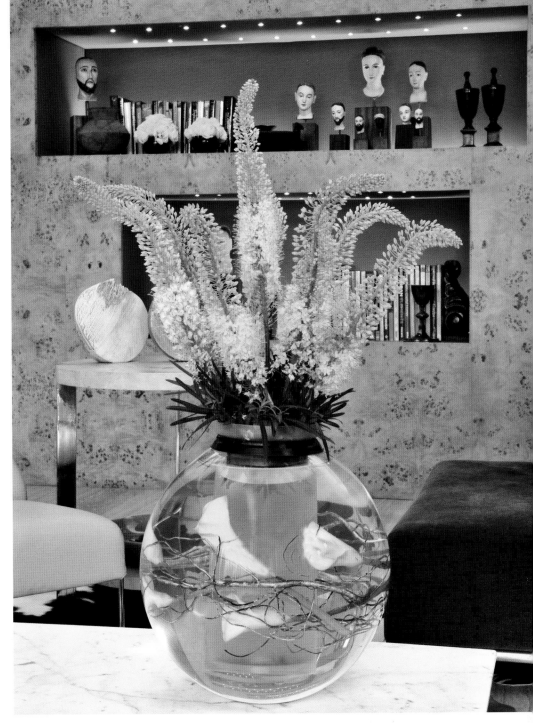

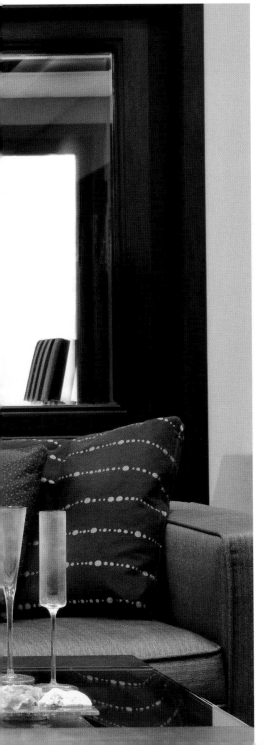

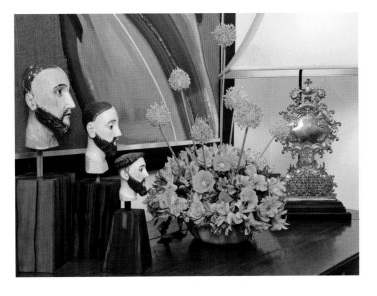

priceless heirlooms and modern art

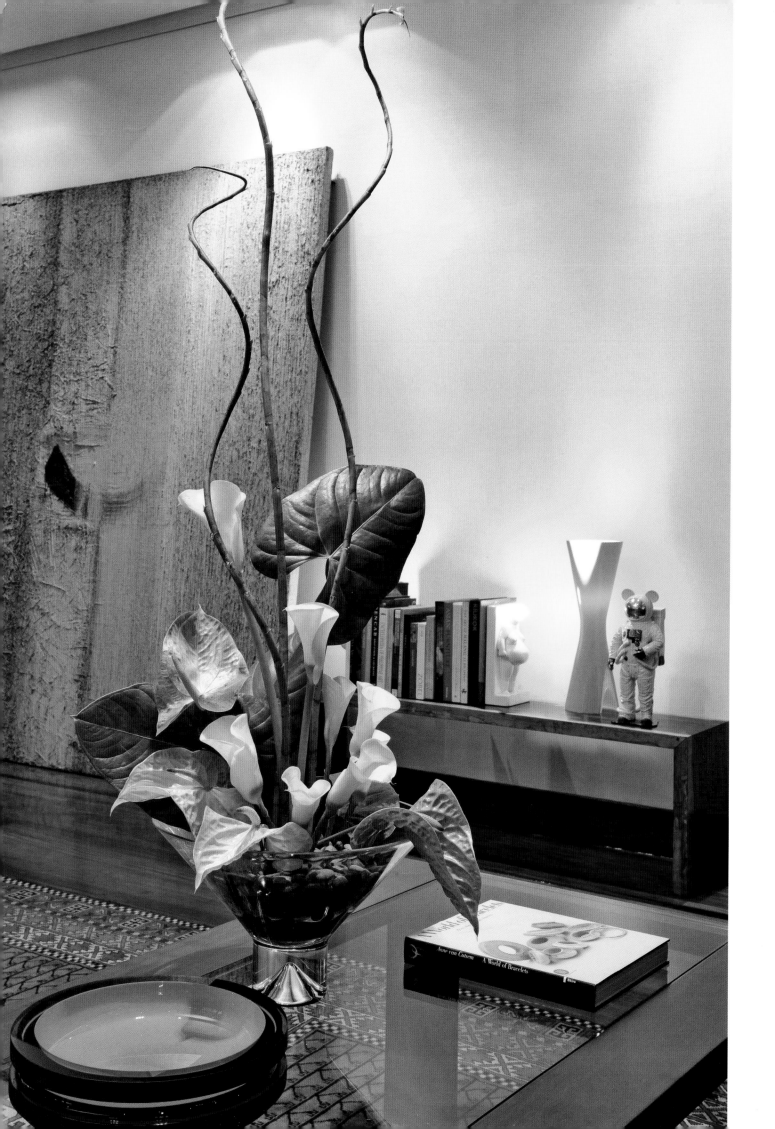

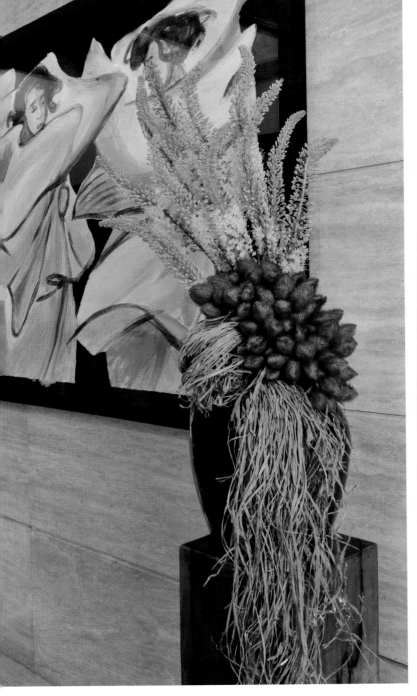

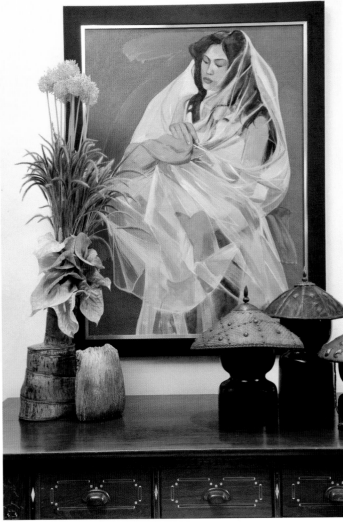

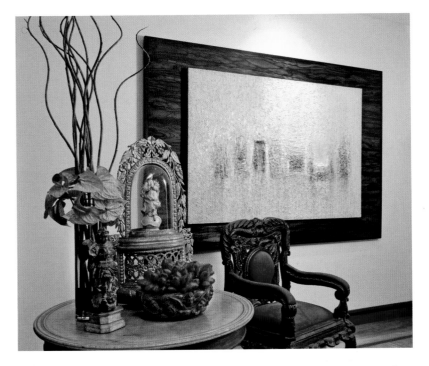

ABOVE LEFT Twirled, flowing dyed *buri* or native straw matches the tones of the brilliant achuete pods crowned by feathery foxtails.
ABOVE A simple but spectacular floral arrangement of alstroemeria, grasses and anthuriums matches the earthen palette of the furniture and artifacts.
LEFT A bishop's chair, a glass-encased ivory icon, a vase of costos stems and anthuriums and a bowl of achuete pods counter-pose a contemporary painting.
OPPOSITE Only the touch of a bonsai master could make costos stems swirl gracefully over lilies and anthuriums to complement the contemporary art in the room.

priceless heirlooms and modern art

Spirit of
Sogetsu

GONZALEZ CREATIONS

NATURE ENTERS THE HOME through ikebana. Connie Gonzalez started studying ikebana in Hong Kong during a harried time in her life. She sought to escape the madness: "I needed to preserve my sanity and relax in that fast-paced city. So I took up Sogetsu, modern ikebana, and found I was good at it." Sogetsu has been the stabilizer of her life ever since. Today, she is a leading practitioner in Manila, rated as a Level 2 teacher in Hong Kong's most esteemed atelier, under the guidance of the Sogetsu center in Tokyo.

Sogetsu spells a deep love of nature. As she explains, "One's floral arrangement shows the exposure and depth of appreciation one has for nature." Sogetsu involves gathering natural materials, processing them in your home and combining the plants at different stages of their life. "The passage of time is manifested in the changing color of the leaves."

For this book, Connie created Sogetsu works suitable for the style and scale of the Arya Showrooms in Fort Bonifacio. She placed a "Welcome" set at the entrance: "The branch installation is from a 12-year-old purple bush tree. I used oak leaf fern and white aster leaves in a standing ceramic "bamboo" culm vase made by Hadrian Mendoza."

Within a show flat, she arranged jade vine to hang like grapes over the dinner table. "Jade vine flowers are endemic to our mountain forests.... I did this to show how our exotic flowers can be used for everyday events, such as when entertaining friends."

For the lobby, she created a giant installation called "Majestic Movement." "This is made up of dried traveler's palm flowers sprayed in gold, and bird's nest fern or *dapo* leaves dried for six months in shallow water so as not to let them go too brittle. I added semi-dried light green leaves to match the subtlety of the gold, beige and brownish green shades. I bundled salmon chrysanthemums as color accents."

"I am constantly experimenting with what grows in the Philippines," Connie says. "I want to create with unconventional fresh materials found in my garden—materials not usually cultivated for the commercial florist shops. I want to achieve the angles and movements that branches from temperate lands can convey, but using what I find here."

RIGHT Exotic jade flowers, endemic to the highlands of the Philippines, form an exotic floral chandelier over a classic Chinese table setting.

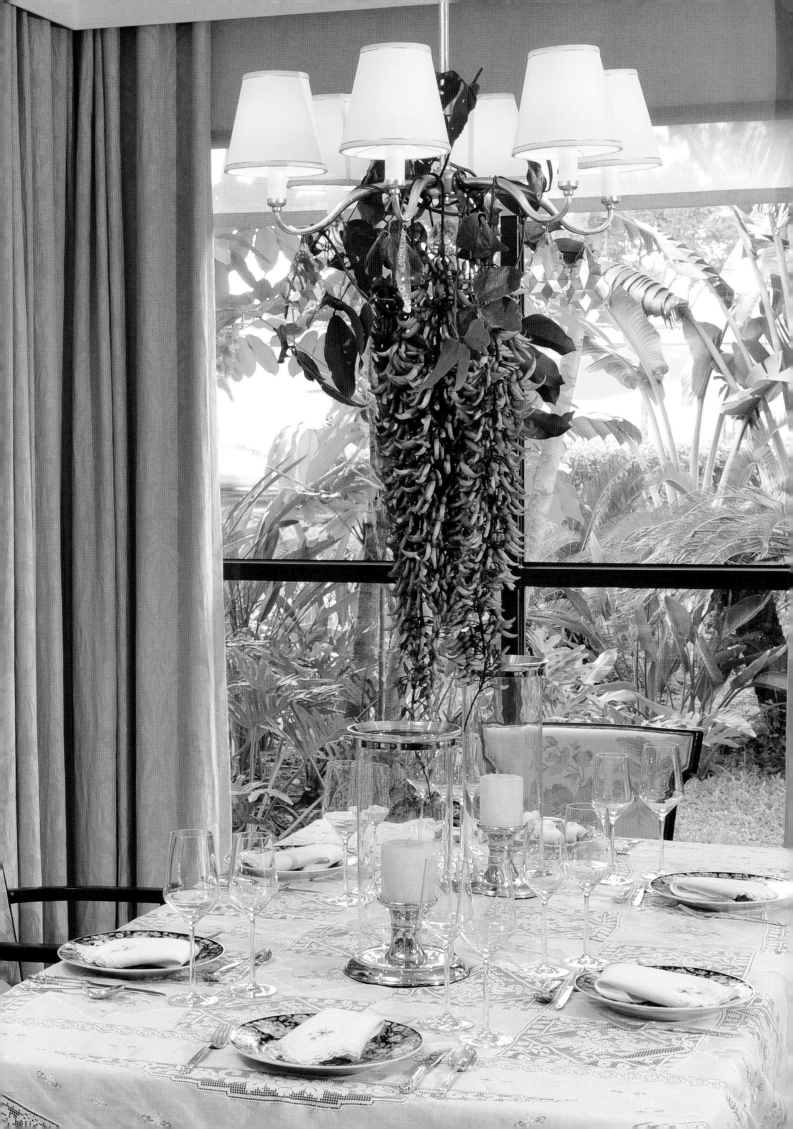

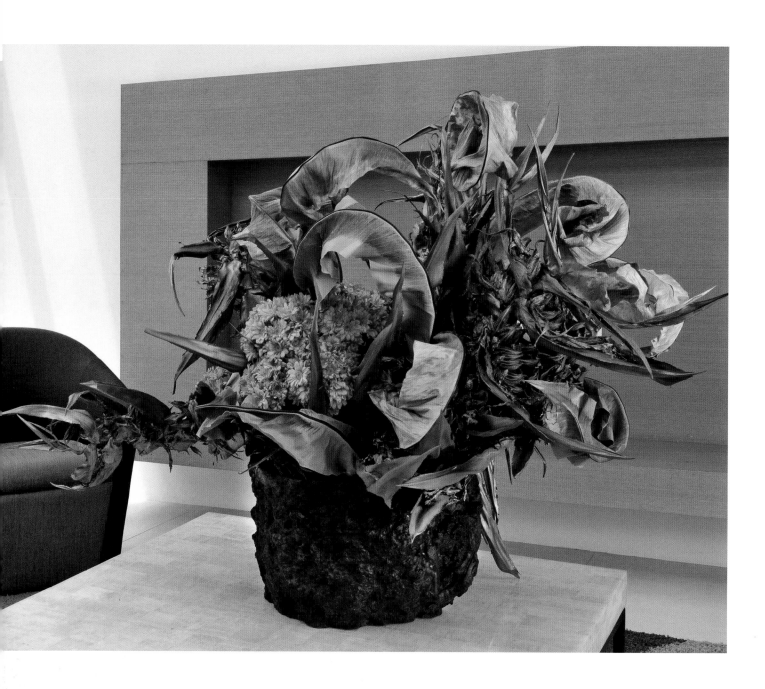

ABOVE The giant swirling installation called "Majestic Movement," created for the spacious lobby, is composed of dried traveler's palm fronds and bird's nest ferns set in a natural burlwood bole. A cluster of small salmon chrysanthemums adds subtle color to the arrangement.

RIGHT Fresh pink chrysanthemums nestle at the heart of this modern Sogetsu arrangement, amid large, semi-dried and curling foliage.

OPPOSITE The foyer statement is a purple bush branch installation dressed with oak leaf fern and white aster leaves, in a tall ceramic "bamboo" culm vase by Hadrian Mendoza.

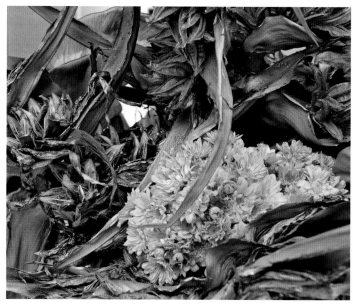

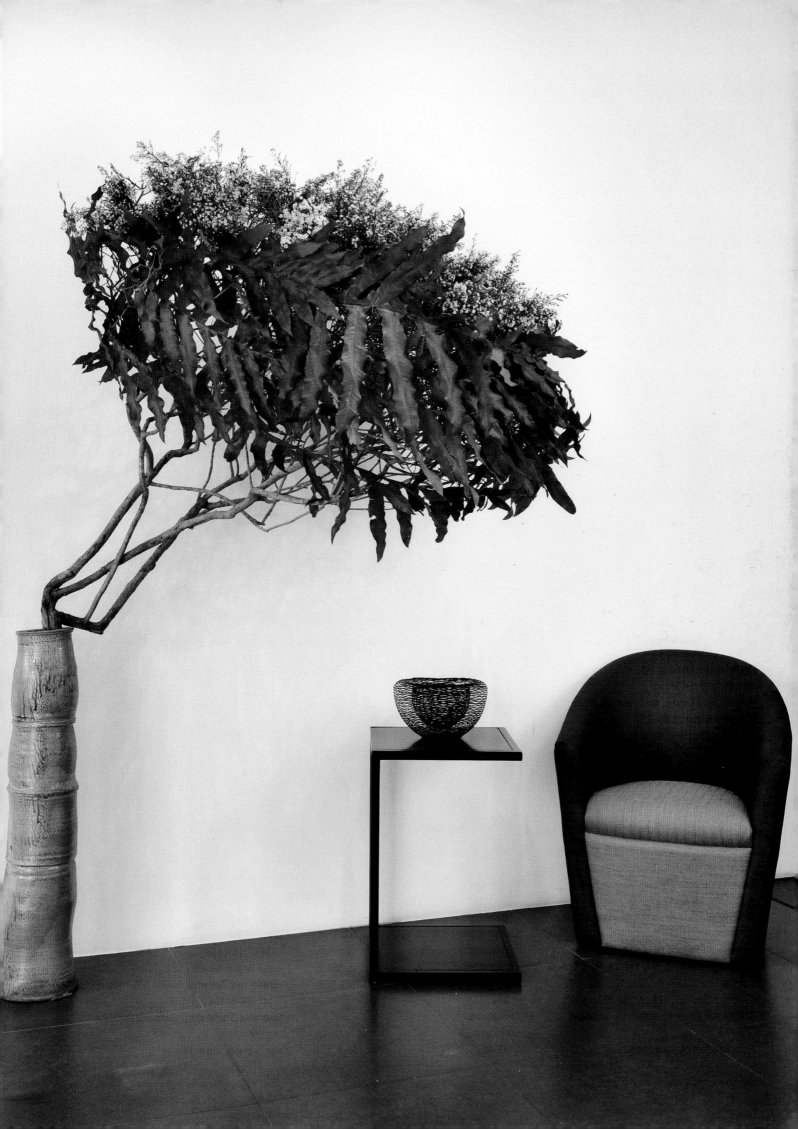

Plant Directory

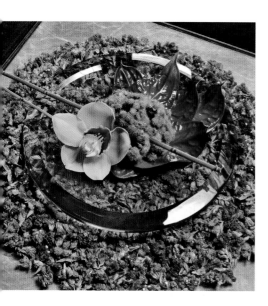

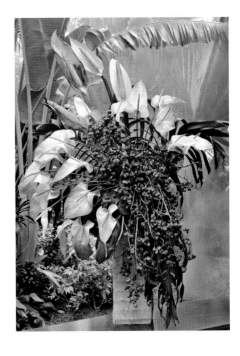

OPPOSITE TOP A green cymbidium, red anthuriums and purple cockscomb merge on a heavy crystal plate within a wreath of lavender statice flowers (page 156).

ABOVE An arc of green and ivory anthuriums, a cluster of brown berries and cordyline leaves harmonize with garden foliage (page 22).

Florist Profiles

Cynthia Almario

An interior designer by profession, Cynthia received her training in Los Angeles, California, from Dennis Reedy Design Consultants, along with designer sister Ivy, and for a decade designed spaces for an upscale Los Angeles clientele. After returning to Manila in the late 1990s, the sisters established a design company, Atelier Almario Inc., developing it into a market leader for home and corporate interiors in the California "chic" style. Ivy specializes in interior architectural forms while Cynthia directs the soft furnishings and floral accents. Cynthia started her floral career arranging flowers for weddings and other special events in Los Angeles, eventually opening a flower shop called The Ivy House in Beverly Hills. In 1997, Cynthia sold contemporary floral arrangements at the Lifestyles arcade in Rockwell's Power Plant, Makati. Her color-coordinated floral arrangements are an integral part of the photo vignettes she creates for interior design installations. She also does flowers for media pictorials, and styles party theme events for friends and special clients.

ATELIER ALMARIO
2601 Antel 2000 Corporate Building
121 Valero Street, Salcedo Village, Makati City, Metro Manila
632 8174016 / 17
www.atelieralmario.net; atelier_almario@yahoo.com.ph

Leo Almeria

Leo Almeria is a multi-award winning Filipino interior designer, product designer, photography stylist and floral stylist. A leading academic of the Philippine Institute of Interior Designers (PIID), he conducts design lectures and contributes to the popular media. He is currently doing a postgraduate degree in Cultural Heritage Studies at the University of Santo Tomas in Manila. Leo worked for many years with pioneer Filipino designer Edith Oliveros, and was an associate of Russell Emmert (USA) before forming his own design studio (LADS) in 1988. He offers professional interior design services (residential, commercial, contract and hospitality) here and abroad. Among his floral strengths is thematic styling, ranging from simple floral installations to grand events like weddings or product launches. He is also a creative designer, producing household accessories, particularly table lamps, decorative boxes, serving plates and trays. His modern items are fashioned out of sustainable local indigenous materials such as stone, seashells and coco shells. As an advocate of heritage conservation, green design and architecture, he favors free-form monochromatic floral arrangements using organic materials.

LEO ALMERIA DESIGN STUDIO
Interior Designer
41 Mark Street, Filinvest Heights, Batasan Hills, Quezon City, Metro Manila
632 4314378 / +63 917 4546816
almeriadesign@yahoo.com

Nathaniel Aranda

Purchasing Manager of the Sala group of restaurants, this graduate of accounting and commerce had been buying food supplies for ten years before he started dabbling with fresh flowers to enhance the ambience of his three stylish restaurants. In the process, he evolved a new floral design career—and a Makati floral shop called Mille Fiori. His floral style varies widely with the function and mood of a given space. His clients often request minimalist, monochromatic arrangements, a given space. His clients often request minimalist, monochromatic arrangements, which he produces with ease. Nathaniel prefers his designs to look natural and not contrived, and he likes to work with masses of one type of flower to create a dramatically different look. Nathaniel is fast earning a reputation for incorporating a cornucopia of fruits, vegetables and herbs into his work, especially to create dining table centerpieces. Arrangements with common flowers and foliage of the rural countryside is another interest, as is using recycled items not normally used in floral arrangements.

MILLE FIORI *Floral Design*
2241 Chino Roces Avenue, San Lorenzo Village, Makati City, Metro Manila
632 8466050 / +63 917 5686981
floraldesign.millefiori04@gmail.com

Anton Barretto

From childhood, Anton Barreto would rearrange the furniture and accessories in his mother's house, instinctively knowing the right combination and positioning of elements to reinvent and restyle a space. After leaving high school, he designed theater stage sets before taking courses at the Philippine School of Interior Design (PSID). In the early 2000s, Anton opened Nest in partnership with friends, a highly visible Makati shop specializing in decorative candles and accessories for stylish homes. A latent floral hobby later transitioned into a thriving professional enterprise, the Floriade Company, in 2009, with high school friend Judith Zapanta Berenguer-Testa whose mother had started a flower shop that was ready to embark on a new direction. Since then, the two highly creative friends have taken floral décor to a new level, styling theme weddings and other gala events. Going far beyond merely providing floral centerpieces and bouquets, they make an effort to source unique floral blooms and create an atmosphere that will inject a new dimension into an event. They also bring in furniture to dress up spaces and to stage and support special themes.

FLORIADE Flower Shop
Zeta2 Building, 191 Salcedo Street, Legaspi Village, Makati City, Metro Manila
623 8938862 / +63 920 9703210
www.cereocandleexchange.com
loriade_fs@yahoo.com.ph

Margarita Fores

After obtaining an economics degree from Mt Holyoke, USA, and a CPA honors degree from Assumption College Manila, Margarita Fores ventured into the food service business around 1986, and today, after more than twenty years in this line, runs ten branches for Cibo, which specializes in Italian comfort food. In 2007, and many times since then, she was given an Outstanding Woman Entrepreneur award. In addition to driving her distinctive style in food, in 2006 Margarita ventured into floral artistry. Today, her business, Fiori de M Food and Floral Scapes, is a creative source of stylized arrangements and earthy tablescapes for élite parties and special events. Margarita is recognized as probably the leading "organic" florist in Manila, based on the signature look she has so successfully established—she incorporates cacti and succulents along with natural branches and vines, weeds, twigs and other raw, found materials in her floral creations. Margarita constantly explores new ideas in food and flowers, both during her biannual trips to Europe and the USA but also during visits to the Philippine countryside, where she collects branches and leaves and other natural materials to incorporate in her work.

FIORI DI M *Food and Floralscapes*
Greenbelt 5, Ayala Center, Makati City, Metro Manila
632 7030370
fioridiM@yahoo.com

Antonio Garcia

Antonio Garcia is a freelance designer and creative consultant for projects ranging from interior design to architectural design and landscaping; his personal forte is "poetic garden spaces." After completing the basic course at the Philippine School of Interior Design, Antonio embarked on a series of art, anthropological, archeological and design research studies at the Archeological Museum of Mexico and Museo Tamayo in Mexico City. He did diverse arts-related courses, including crafts, landscaping and botanicals in California and Hawaii—setting the direction for a lifetime career in creative expression. For ten years, Antonio was the designer at Una Pacifica, an export company, doing product development of home accessories and furnishings for a Western market. Then, representing the Philippines, he embarked on a four-year UNESCO project to develop the design and manufacture of furnishings in metal using the latest laser technology. In 1996, Antonio moved toward flowers, with a vision of making flowers a lifestyle element in the daily lives of the Filipino. As the creative director of Mabolo Flower Gallery, he is responsible for innovative floral trends and lifestyle concepts for discriminating social events. On the side, he advocates the Agri Alternative of Foliage Farming, spurring a rural cooperative to grow foliage that can withstand natural disasters.

MABOLO Floral Gallery
Jannov Plaza, Ground Floor, 2295 Pasong Tamo Extension, Makati City, Metro Manila
632 8935689
info@maboloflowers.com

Roberto Gopiao

By profession, Roberto Gopiao is a versatile landscape designer with a special green thumb. His greatest expertise lies in the practice of bonsai, the Japanese art of nurturing and shaping miniature trees. He has been president of the Philippine Bonsai Society since 2003 and has won numerous prizes in international competitions. By avocation, however, Roberto's greatest passion is Filipino contemporary art. Alongside earning a BSc. in Management at the Ateneo University and academic units in Landscape Architecture at the University of the Philippines, Roberto has pursued a deep interest in the arts, building and distilling an outstanding collection of paintings. His own art form is creating unique nature installations inspired by his art collection—designing flowers and foliage to reflect or interact with manmade contemporary art and modern interiors. This special talent as a floral designer has been honed by his long exposure to Philippine arts and antiques, and to horticulture. He lives amid a lush garden environment full of tropical plants, bonsai trees and garden accessories. Today, he designs garden landscapes for housing estates or private residences, and creates visual feasts for his own artful environment.

RPG CORPORATION
168 B. Gonzales Street, Loyola Heights, Quezon City, Metro Manila
632 9209349-50
r_gopiao@yahoo.com

Rosabella Ongpin

After university, Rosabella (Belle) Landingin Ongpin worked with Cathay Pacific for seventeen years, discovering the world and flowers round the globe: "When traveling abroad, instead of visiting museums, I would go to the flower markets of different countries." Her real passion for flowers started in 1993, when she was inspired by the works of floral designer Richard Go in Sydney, who used twigs, bark, seeds, and pods of plants picked up from wherever he went. After leaving Cathay Pacific, Belle arranged flowers for her Alabang neighborhood, and did a diploma course in commercial floristry at the Institute of Philippine Floral Techniques/Instituto Mexicano Tecnico Floral. She also attended floral courses and conventions in Manila, Singapore, Malaysia and New Zealand, studied floral design

with Phil Rulloda in Los Angeles and Mark Pampling in New Zealand, and basic ikebana with Joyce Kato. In 2011, Belle opened a new shop called Flowers by Rosabella in a hotel in Alabang. From there, she caters décor for corporate functions, weddings, debuts, funerals, and residential parties.

FLOWERS BY ROSABELLA
The Bellevue Hotel
North Bridgeway, Filinvest, Alabang, Muntinlupa City, Metro Manila
632 7718181 Loc. 8010
flowersbyrosabella@yahoo.com

Eric Paras

Eric Paras, an interior design graduate from the University of the Philippines, is a creative consultant to several furniture export companies. He is also the individualist creative director of a design and furniture company called A-11 Gallery, located in a 1950s compound in Pasay City, Manila. Eric claims that his talent for styling florals comes from what Filipinos call *oido*—natural instinct. He only does flower arrangements for friends and for clients of his design projects. His personal style of floral arrangement is relaxed, not contrived. To him, the floral style is set by the flavor or look of an interior space setting and its function. He uses flowers just to enhance and perk up the spirit of the interior spaces. Because of the eclectic nature of his interiors, he likes to juxtapose the old and the new for visual balance. For him, the container or vase is as important as the flowers used. The vessel and the flowers should "marry" as one. He particularly likes to use quaint vessels sourced from rural farms and old houses. Eric has always followed Japanese architecture, gardens and ikebana, but he also gathers inspiration during travels abroad and on provincial trips. He finds it challenging to "make do," using plant materials which are endemic and adaptable to the Philippine's tropical climate. He also enjoys creating all-foliage arrangements without flowers.

A11 GALLERY SHOWROOMS
2680 F. B. Harrison Street, Pasay City, Metro Manila
632 8329972
ericparas2680@gmail.com

Pico Soriano

Filipino-American Pico Soriano went through four career changes before he "found" floristry and decided to educate himself about the subject and immerse himself in everything floral. He took a three-year floriculture program at the College of San Mateo, worked at the yearly floral conventions, and got exposed to floristry techniques not taught in school. Since earning a California certificate in floriculture and Sogetsu #1 in 1998, Pico has been styling flowers for bridal and special events. Recently, he has been winning the biggest floral competitions of the San Francisco Bay Area. His latest coup, in 2010, brought him national attention—First Place in the San Francisco Flower and Garden Show Floral Competition and, most recently, Bay Bella's "Best of the Bay Bridal," First Place in the floral category. Pico, who returned from the US for a working vacation to style flowers in five homes specially for this book, is inspired by designers such as Jeff Leatham—"His devil-may-care way is intriguing, amazing and inspirational"—and Daniel Ost, "A truly gifted artist and floral engineer.... His way is truly mind-boggling." His own favorite flowers are the unusual *baging* vine succulents, artichokes, sunflower centers and fiddlehead ferns. For modernist homes, he likes working with hardy flowers that can be pave'd, glued and worked into waterless installations and out-of-the-glass floral sculptures, while they retain their luster and color.

PICO SORIANO
Event and Bridal Floral Designer
1 Lido Circle, Redwood City, California 94065, USA
650-888-2736
www.picodesign.com; http://picosorianodesigns.blogspot.com/

Acknowledgments

The authors and the photographer would like to express their huge gratitude to a multitude of artistic people who offered us support, cooperation and coordination during the production of this book.

Gracious Friends and Homeowners

Ramon Antonio • Sylvia Araneta-Malik • Ina Ayala • Lisa Tinio Bayot • Jeffrey Co • Lizette B. Cojuangco • Roberta Lopez Feliciano • Margarita Moran Floriendo • Connie Y. Gonzales • Roberto Gopiao • Tanya Lara • Violeta Lim • Gianna Montinola • Moon Gardeners: Peter Geertz, Emily Campos, Ely Bautista • Paulino Que • Carmen Soriano Rojas • Vicente Roman Santos • Bienvenido Tantoco • Marilen Tantoco • Wendell and May Ty • Chito Vijandre and Ricky Toledo • Portofino, Vista Land • Denise Weldon • Pilar S. Zimonyi

Contributing Stylists

ROBERT BLANCAFLOR, www.robertblancaflor.com; Twitter: @RobBlancaflor; 632 6283870 / +63 917 9874954

J. ANTONIO MENDOZA Y. GONZALES, YL Bldg 3/F, #115 Herrera St, Legaspi Village, Makati City; mendozaarchitects@gmail.com 632 8159025 / +63 917 8937236

SABINE KOSCHINGER, Linens International Inc., RMT Industrial Complex, Muntinlupa, Metro Manila; linens@pldtdsl.net

JONATHAN MATTI, 41 Montepino Bldg, #138 Amorsolo St, Legaspi Village, Makati City; jonathanmatti@yahoo.com; 632 8103137 / +63 917 5262339

ANTON R. MENDOZA, 2/F Jannov Plaza Bldg, 2295 Pasong Tamo Extension, Makati City; arm@antonmendoza.com 632 8672206 / 632 8136444

ESTIEN QUIJANO, Private Atelier VXVII www.estienquijano.com; estienquijano@yahoo.com

JUNIE RODRIGUEZ cesferod@gmail.com; +63 917 5338500

JIM TAN, 41 Lincoln St, Greenhills West, San Juan City; lahars @skybroadband.com.ph 632 5841559 / 5841405 /+63 920 9100855

PONCE C. VERIDIANO, Tropic Asia Landscape Design, #3105N Lee Gardens Condo, Lee St cor. Shaw Blvd, Mandaluyong; 632 5845521 / +63 917 8810578

Floral Suppliers

FIORI di M Food and Floralscapes, Margarita A. Fores, Greenbelt 5, Ayala Center, Makati City; fioridiM@yahoo.com 632 7030370

FLORIADE Floral Shop, Anton Barretto and Judith Berenguer-Testa; Zeta2 Bldg, 191 Salcedo St, Legaspi Village, Makati City 632 8938862

FLOWERS BY ROSABELLA, Rosabella Ongpin, The Bellevue Hotel, North Bridgeway, Filinvest, Alabang, Muntinlupa City flowersbyrosabella@yahoo.com 632 7718181 Loc. 8010

MABOLO Floral Gallery, Antonio Garcia Jannov Plaza, Gd fl, 2295 Pasong Tamo Exten, Makati City; info@maboloflowers.com 632 8935689

MILLE FIORI Floral Design, Nathaniel Aranda, 2241 Chino Roces Ave., San Lorenzo Village, Makati City; www.millefiorifloraldesigns.com floraldesign.millefiori04@gmail.com 632 8466050 / +63 917 5686981

THE FLOWER FARM, Ging de los Reyes, RCI Bldg, 105 Rada St., Legaspi Village, Makati City; info@theflowerfarm.com.ph 632 8156665 / 632 8156668

THE RUSTAN'S FLOWER SHOP, Zenaida R. Tantoco, CEO, Rustan's Group of Companies www.rustans.com.ph

Furnishings and Accessories

AVELLANA ART GALLERY, Albert Avellana, 2680 FB Harrison, Pasay City avellana_gallery@yahoo.com

CLASSIC PARTY RENTALS, Sue Legget 1635 Rollins Rd #A, Burlingame, CA 94010 www.sanfrancisco.classicpartyrentals.com (650) 652-0300

FIRMA & AC 632, Chito Vijandre and Ricky Toledo, Greenbelt Malls, Ayala Center, Makati City; firma2@vasia.com

RUSTAN'S GROUP OF COMPANIES, Zenaida R. Tantoco, CEO www.rustans.com.ph

TESORO'S TREASURE HOUSE OF THINGS PHILIPPINE, Ma. Isabel Tesoro, Group CEO www. tesoros.ph; tesoros@tesoros.ph

THE PIETRO COLLECTION, La Fuerza Cmpd, 2241 Pasong Tamo, Makati City thepietrocollection@mail.com 632 3105164

TOWNES FABRICS, Elit Pacho, Arnaiz Ave, Makati City eypacho@townes.com.ph

Editorial Support and Consultants

Ponchit Ponce Enrile
Cristobal Labog
Toni Serrano Parsons
Ging de los Reyes
Loreto Sasi

Creative Support Team Manila

Karen Tanchanco Caballero
Rene Guatlo
Nicanor Lazaro
Beatrice Dy Pimentel
RS Video & Film, Set Crew and Transport
Nelia Silverio
Ricardo Jose Vasque
Cleo Mangulabnan Webb

The Tuttle Story

Most people are surprised when they learn that the world's largest publisher of books on Asia had its beginnings in the tiny American state of Vermont. The company's founder, Charles Tuttle, came from a New England family steeped in publishing, and his first love was books—especially old and rare editions.

Tuttle's father was a noted antiquarian dealer in Rutland, Vermont. Young Charles honed his knowledge of the trade working in the family bookstore, and later in the rare books section of Columbia University Library. His passion for beautiful books—old and new—never wavered through his long career as a bookseller and publisher.

After graduating from Harvard, Tuttle enlisted in the military and in 1945 was sent to Tokyo to work on General Douglas MacArthur's staff. He was tasked with helping to revive the Japanese publishing industry, which had been utterly devastated by the war. After his tour of duty was completed,

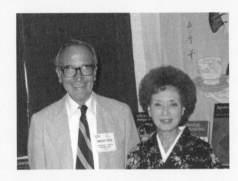

he left the military, married a talented and beautiful singer, Reiko Chiba, and in 1948 began several successful business ventures.

To his astonishment, Tuttle discovered that postwar Tokyo was actually a book-lover's paradise. He befriended dealers in the Kanda district and began supplying rare Japanese editions to American libraries. He also imported American books to sell to the thousands of GIs stationed in Japan. By 1949, Tuttle's business was thriving, and he opened Tokyo's very first English-language bookstore in the Takashimaya Department Store in Ginza, to great success. Two years later, he began publishing books to fulfill the growing interest of foreigners in all things Asian.

Though a westerner, Charles Tuttle was hugely instrumental in bringing knowledge of Japan and Asia to a world hungry for information about the East. By the time of his death in 1993, he had published over 6,000 books on Asian culture, history and

art—a legacy honored by Emperor Hirohito in 1983 with the "Order of the Sacred Treasure," the highest honor Japan bestows upon non-Japanese.

The Tuttle company today maintains an active backlist of some 1,500 titles, many of which have been continuously in print since the 1950s and 1960s—a great testament to Charles Tuttle's skill as a publisher. More than 60 years after its founding, Tuttle Publishing is as active today as at any time in its history, still inspired by Charles' core mission—to publish fine books to span the East and West and provide a greater understanding of each.

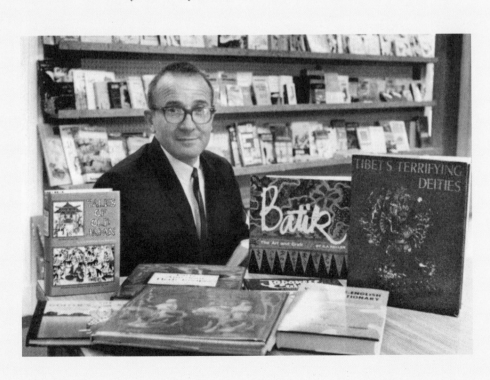

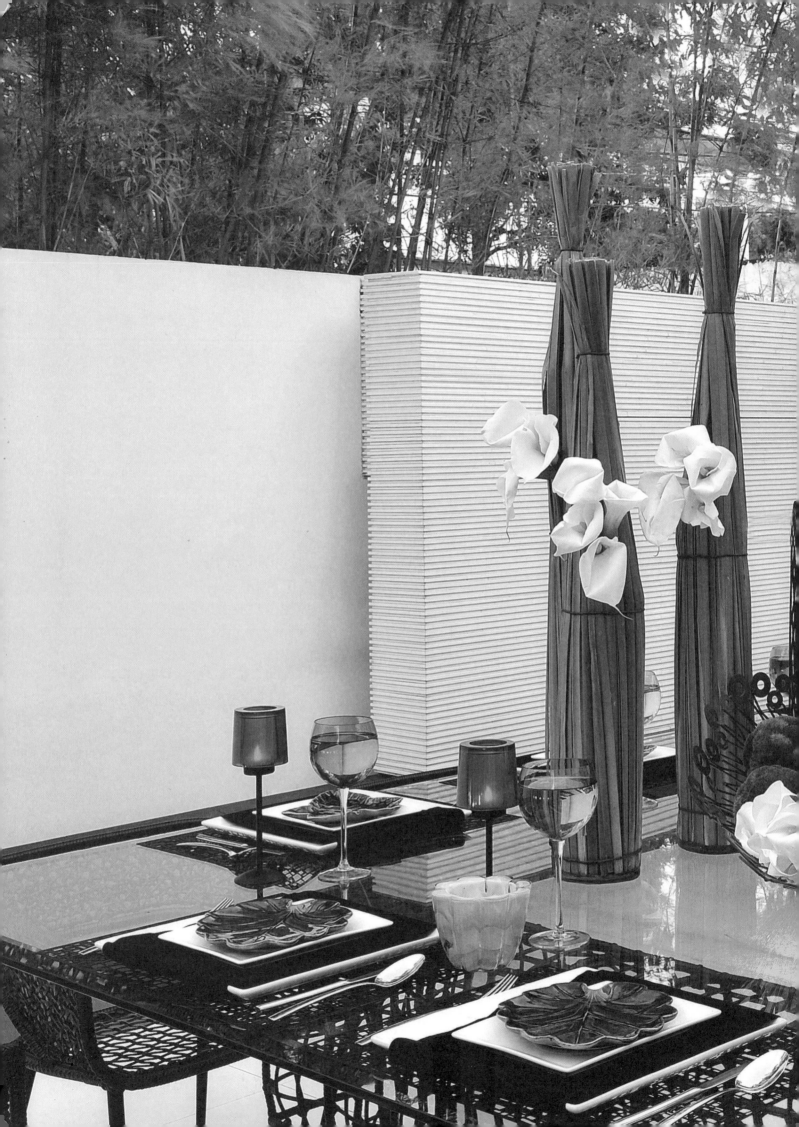